MOBILE SUIT GUNDAM SEED DESTINY

3

ART BY MASATSUGU IWASE

ORIGINAL STORY BY HAJIME YATATE AND YOSHIYUKI TOMINO

TRANSLATED AND ADAPTED BY
Ikoi Hiroe

LETTERED BY
Ryan & Reilly

D1240598

BALLANTINE BOOKS • NEW YORK

Gundam Seed Destiny, volume 3 is a work of fiction. Names, characters, places, and incidents are the products of the authors' imagination or are used fictitiously. Any resemblance to actual events, locales, or persons, living or dead, is entirely coincidental.

A Del Rey Books Trade Paperback Original

Gundam Seed Destiny, volume 3 copyright © 2006 by Hajime Yatate, Yoshiyuki Tomino, and Masatsugu Iwase. © Sotsu Agency, Sunrise, MBS.

English translation copyright © 2007 by Hajime Yatate, Yoshiyuki Tomino, and Masatsugu Iwase. © Sotsu Agency, Sunrise, MBS.

All rights reserved.

Published in the United States by Del Rey Books, an imprint of The Random House Publishing Group, a division of Random House, Inc., New York.

DEL REY is a registered trademark and the Del Rey colophon is a trademark of Random House, Inc.

Publication rights arranged through Kodansha Ltd.

First published in Japan in 2006 by Kodansha Ltd., Tokyo

ISBN 978-0-345-49276-0

Printed in the United States of America

www.delreymanga.com

9 8 7 6 5 4 3 2

Translator/Adaptor—Ikoi Hiroe
Lettering—Ryan & Reilly

A Word from the Editor

From volume 2 of Gundam SEED Destiny on, you may notice that a few names are being spelled differently than they were in volume 1 of the series.

Transliteration, or the translation of Japanese characters into the English language's roman alphabet, is a delicate art, and there is often more than one correct way to spell a name originally written in Japanese characters in our alphabet. We've chosen to change some names in the manga in order to bring our spellings in synch with the "canonical" spellings used in the *Gundam SEED Destiny* anime.

Contents

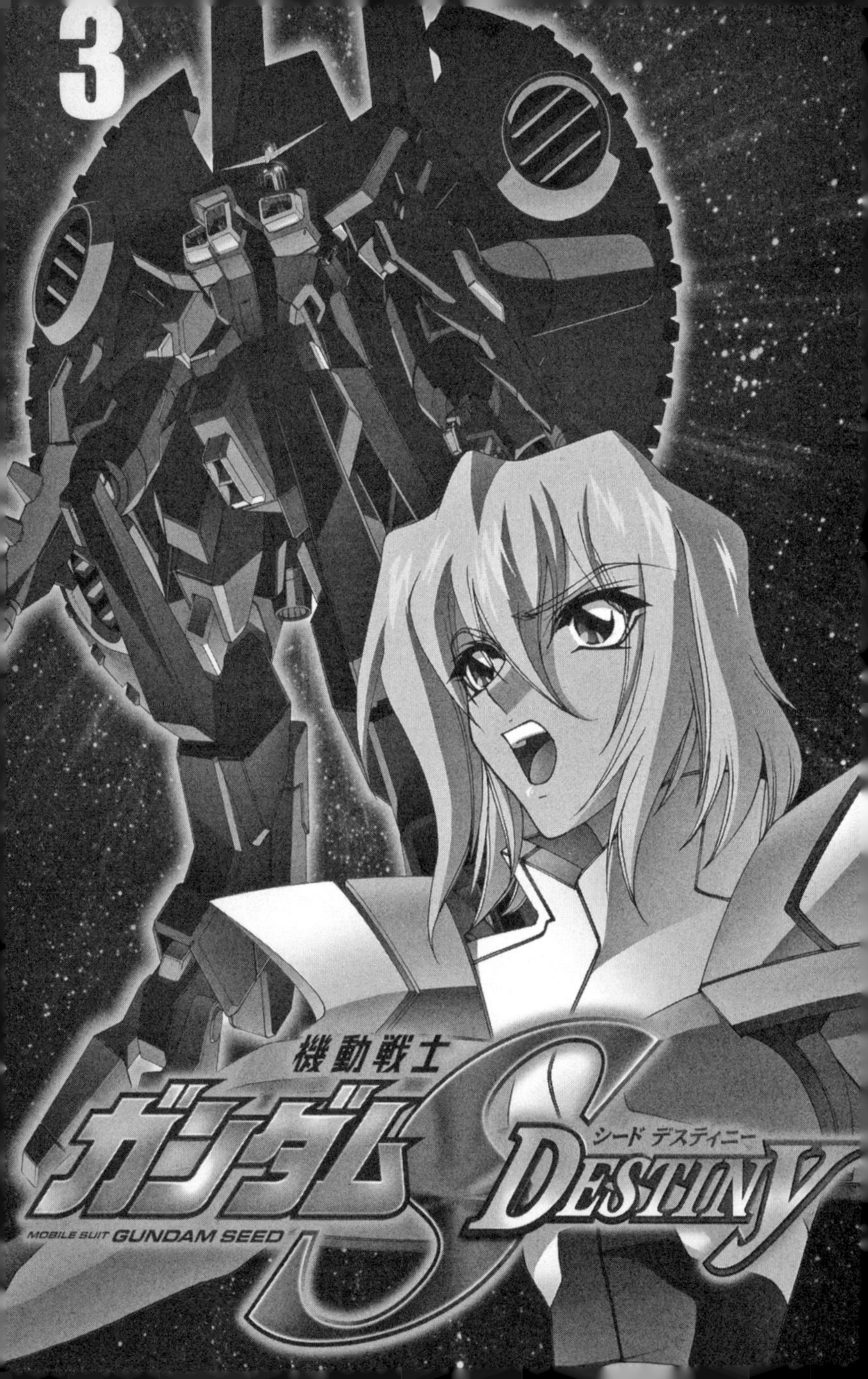
3
機動戦士
ガンダム
MOBILE SUIT GUNDAM SEED
シード デスティニー
DESTINY

OCTOBER, CE 73: AFTER JUNIUS SEVEN CRASHES INTO THE EARTH, ANOTHER WAR RAGES BETWEEN ZAFT AND THE EARTH ALLIANCE. ORB HAS JOINED FORCES WITH THE EARTH ALLIANCE NOW THAT CAGALLI IS NO LONGER PRESENT TO OVERSEE THE COUNTRY'S AFFAIRS. AS A RESULT, THEY ARE NOW AN ENEMY OF THE PLANTs. SHINN AND ATHRUN LEARN ABOUT "LOGOS," A SINISTER FORCE CONTROLLING THE WAR BEHIND THE SCENES, FROM CHAIRMAN DURANDAL AFTER A HARD BATTLE TO CAPTURE THE SUEZ CANAL.

SHINN IS DEEPLY DISTURBED BY THIS REVELATION OF A NEW ENEMY. SOON AFTER, HE SAVES A GIRL NAMED STELLA. SHINN SWEARS TO PROTECT HER FROM HARM AND RETURNS HER TO HER FRIENDS.

MINERVA WELCOMES A NEW FAITH PILOT CALLED HEINE WESTENFLUSS. WITH HIS LIGHT-HEARTED NATURE, HE FITS IN WITH THE CREW RIGHT AWAY. HOWEVER, HEINE TELLS ATHRUN ABOUT MINERVA'S ORDER TO DEPLOY TO THE BLACK SEA, WHERE THEY WILL HAVE TO FACE THE ORB IN BATTLE! ATHRUN IS DEEPLY CONFLICTED. A FIERCE BATTLE BREAKS OUT ON THE BLACK SEA, BUT THE ARRIVAL OF FREEDOM AND ARCHANGEL ON THE SCENE MAKES AN ALREADY EXPLOSIVE SITUATION MORE DIFFICULT AND LEADS TO HEINE'S DEATH.

THROUGH A CHANCE MEETING WITH MIRALLIA, ATHRUN ARRANGES A MEETING WITH CAGALLI AND KIRA AND EXPRESSES HIS DISAPPROVAL OF THEIR CONDUCT DURING BATTLE—CONDUCT THAT RESULTED IN THE DEATH OF THEIR FRIEND. HE DEMANDS THAT THEY RETURN TO ORB, BUT ATHRUN BECOMES EVEN MORE CONFUSED WHEN HE DISCOVERS THAT THE PLANTs HAVEN'T BEEN FORTHCOMING ABOUT EVERYTHING...THEY ARE TRYING TO ASSASSINATE THE REAL LACUS CLYNE!

DURING AN INVESTIGATION OF AN EARTH ALLIANCE RESEARCH FACILITY, SHINN IS ATTACKED BY A GAIA. AFTER THE FIGHT, HE DISCOVERS THAT THE PILOT IS STELLA. HE BRINGS THE INJURED STELLA BACK TO BASE FOR TREATMENT, ONLY TO DISCOVER THAT SHE IS AN EXTENDED.

MINERVA IS SET TO FACE ORB ONCE AGAIN IN BATTLE. ATHRUN AND KIRA FACE OFF IN COMBAT, AND SHINN TAKES OUT HIS ANGER ON THE EARTH ALLIANCE.

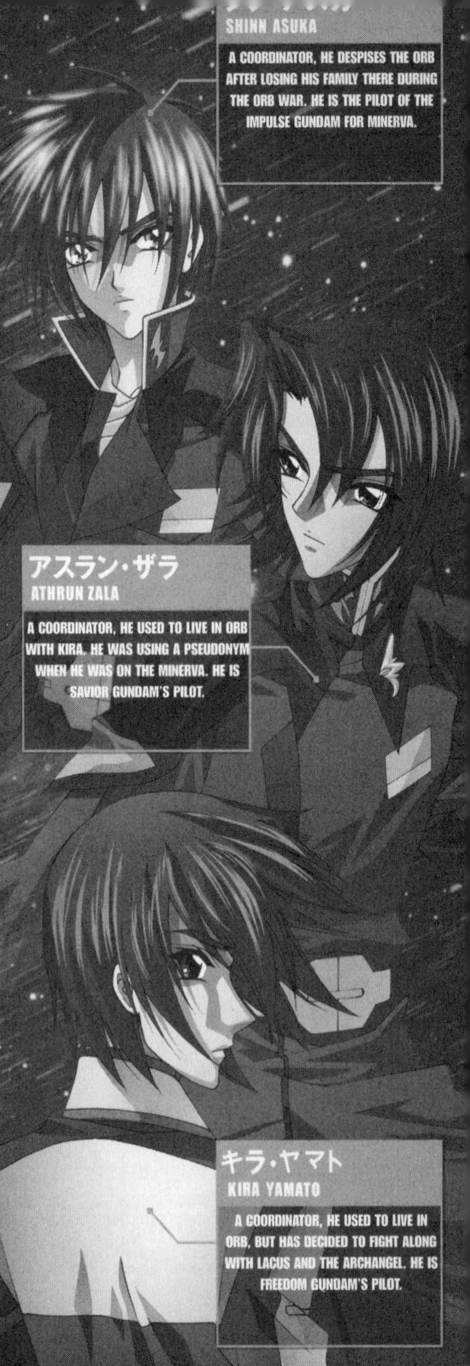

SHINN ASUKA
A COORDINATOR, HE DESPISES THE ORB AFTER LOSING HIS FAMILY THERE DURING THE ORB WAR. HE IS THE PILOT OF THE IMPULSE GUNDAM FOR MINERVA.
アスラン・ザラ
ATHRUN ZALA
A COORDINATOR, HE USED TO LIVE IN ORB WITH KIRA. HE WAS USING A PSEUDONYM WHEN HE WAS ON THE MINERVA. HE IS SAVIOR GUNDAM'S PILOT.
キラ・ヤマト
KIRA YAMATO
A COORDINATOR, HE USED TO LIVE IN ORB, BUT HAS DECIDED TO FIGHT ALONG WITH LACUS AND THE ARCHANGEL. HE IS FREEDOM GUNDAM'S PILOT.

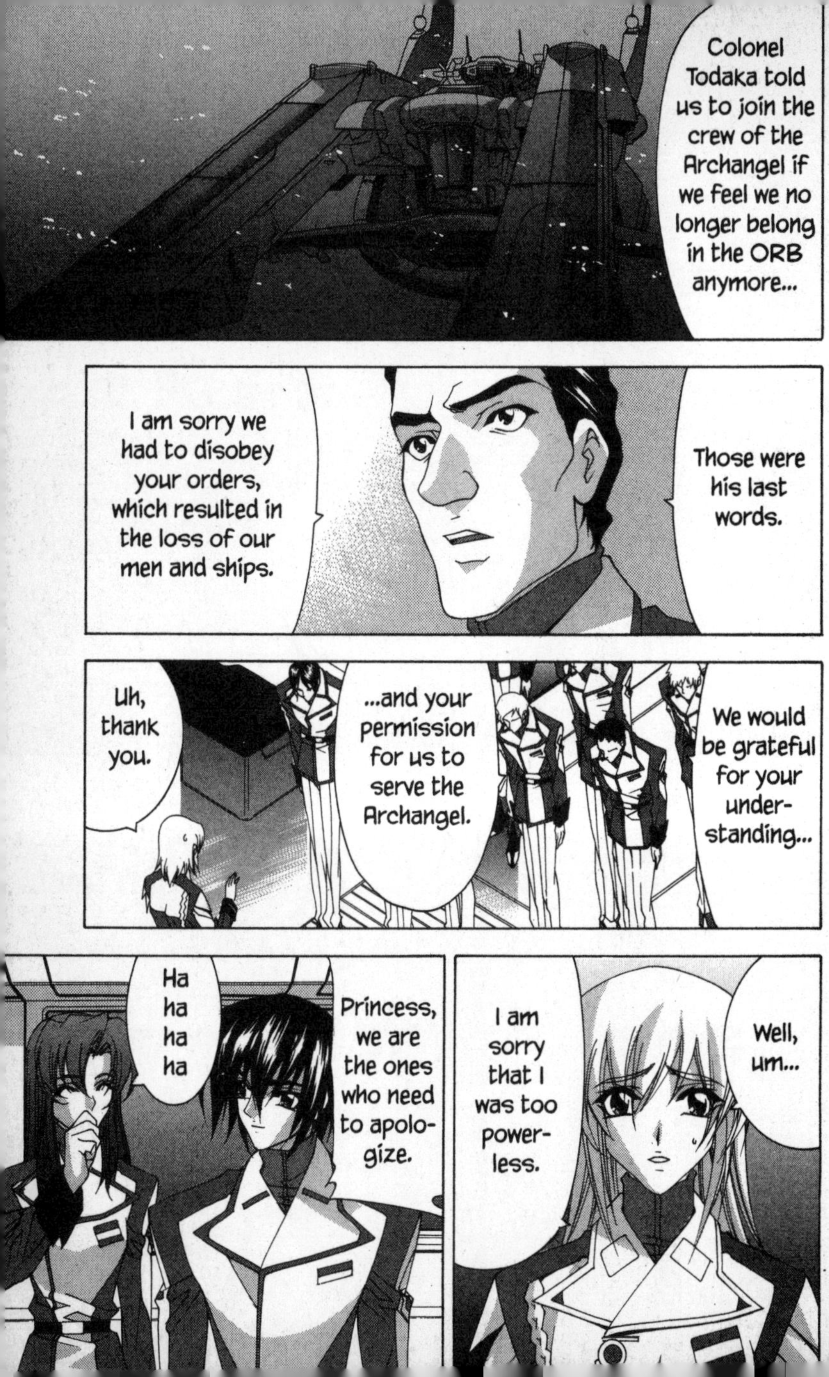
Colonel Todaka told us to join the crew of the Archangel if we feel we no longer belong in the ORB anymore...
Those were his last words.
I am sorry we had to disobey your orders, which resulted in the loss of our men and ships.
We would be grateful for your under-standing...
...and your permission for us to serve the Archangel.
Uh, thank you.
Well, um...
I am sorry that I was too power-less.
Princess, we are the ones who need to apolo-gize.
Ha ha ha ha

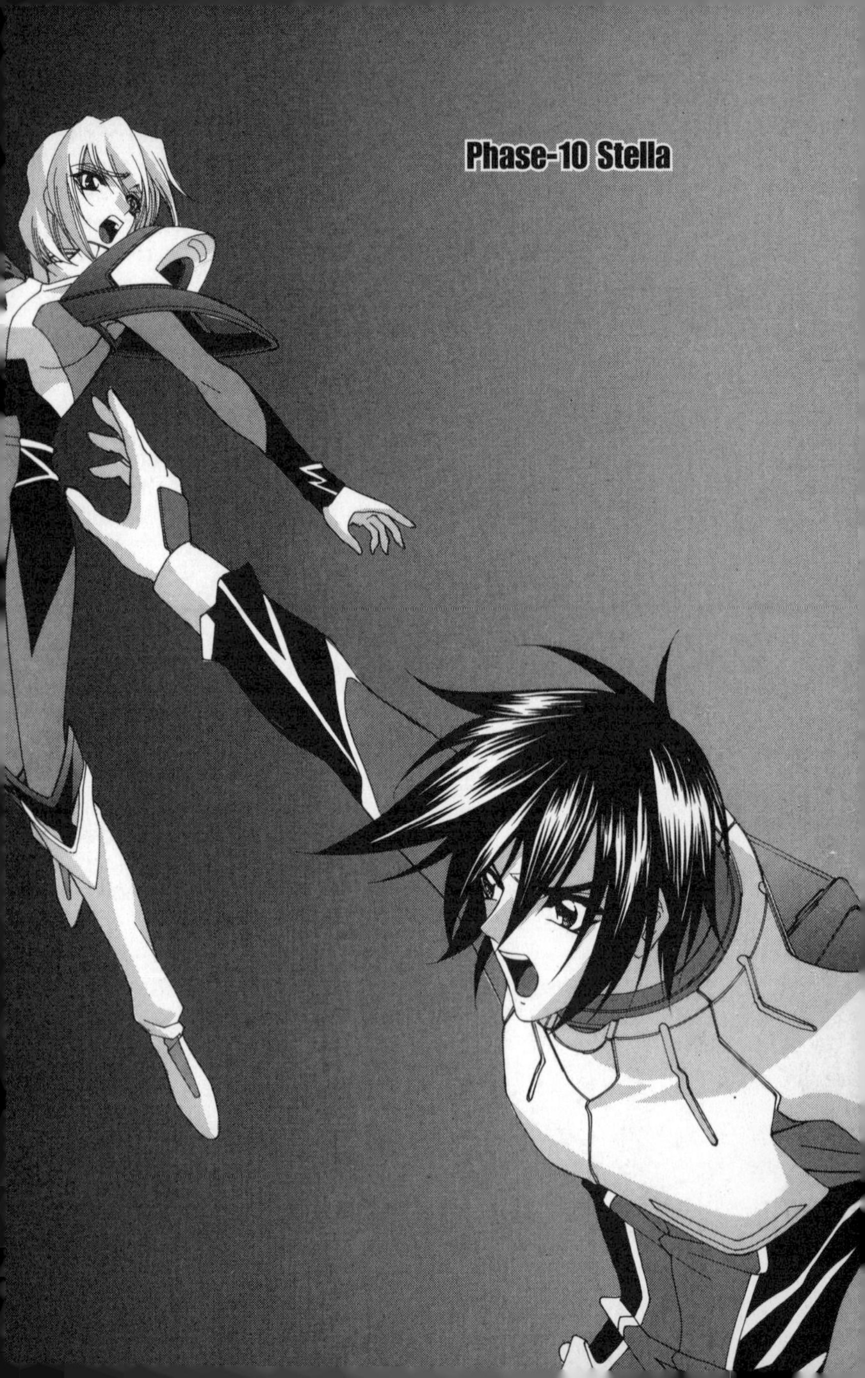
Phase-10 Stella

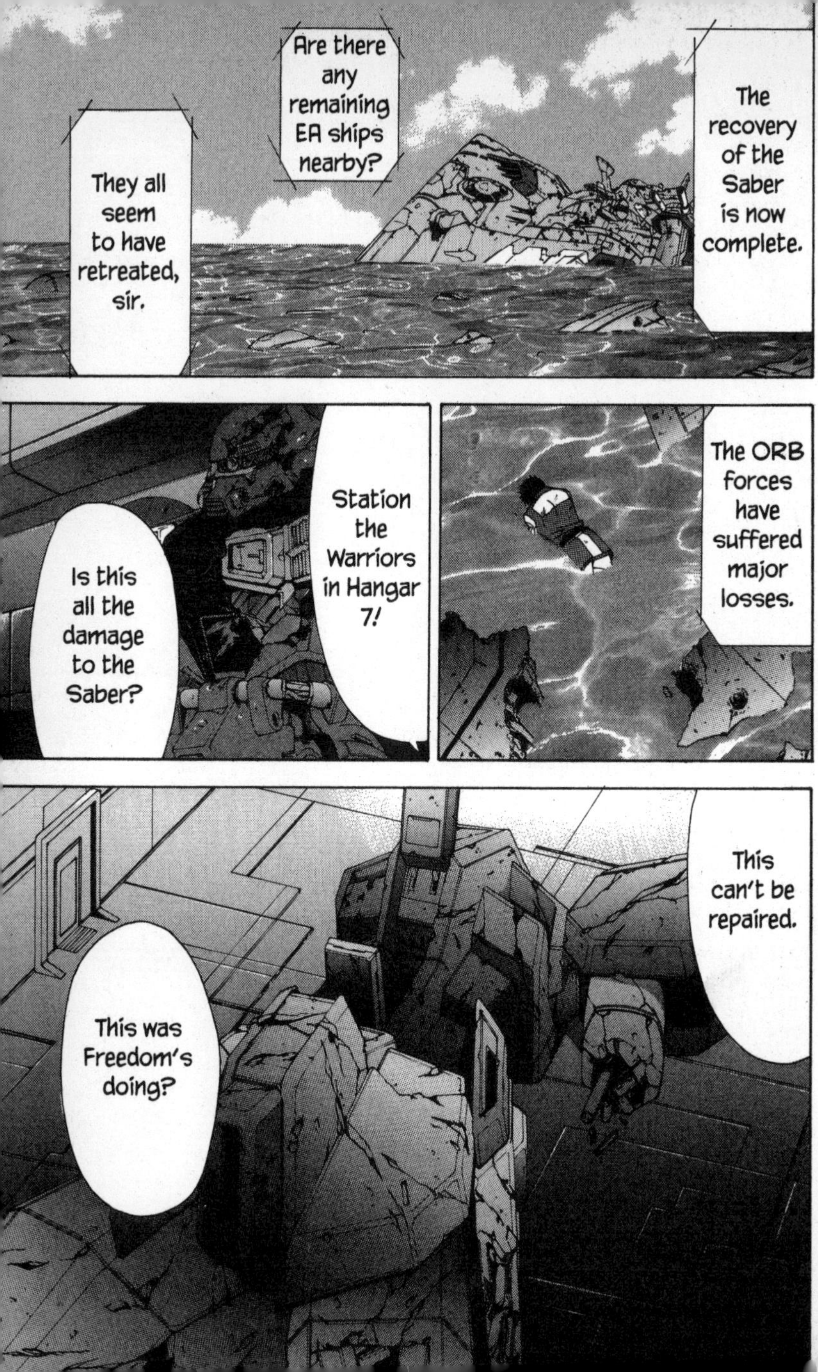
The recovery of the Saber is now complete.
Are there any remaining EA ships nearby?
They all seem to have retreated, sir.
The ORB forces have suffered major losses.
Station the Warriors in Hangar 7!
Is this all the damage to the Saber?
This can't be repaired.
This was Freedom's doing?

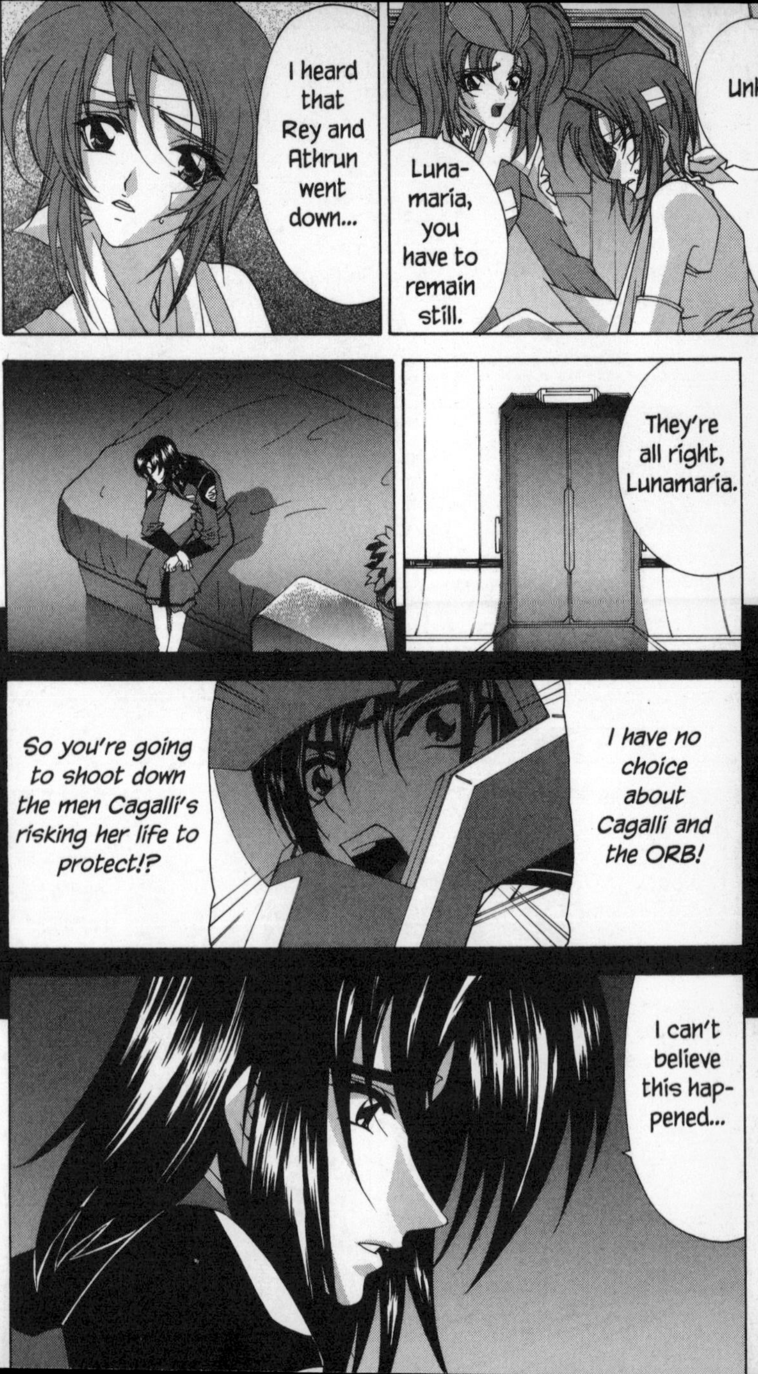
Unh...
Lunamaria, you have to remain still.
I heard that Rey and Athrun went down...
They're all right, Lunamaria.
I have no choice about Cagalli and the ORB!
So you're going to shoot down the men Cagalli's risking her life to protect!?
I can't believe this happened...

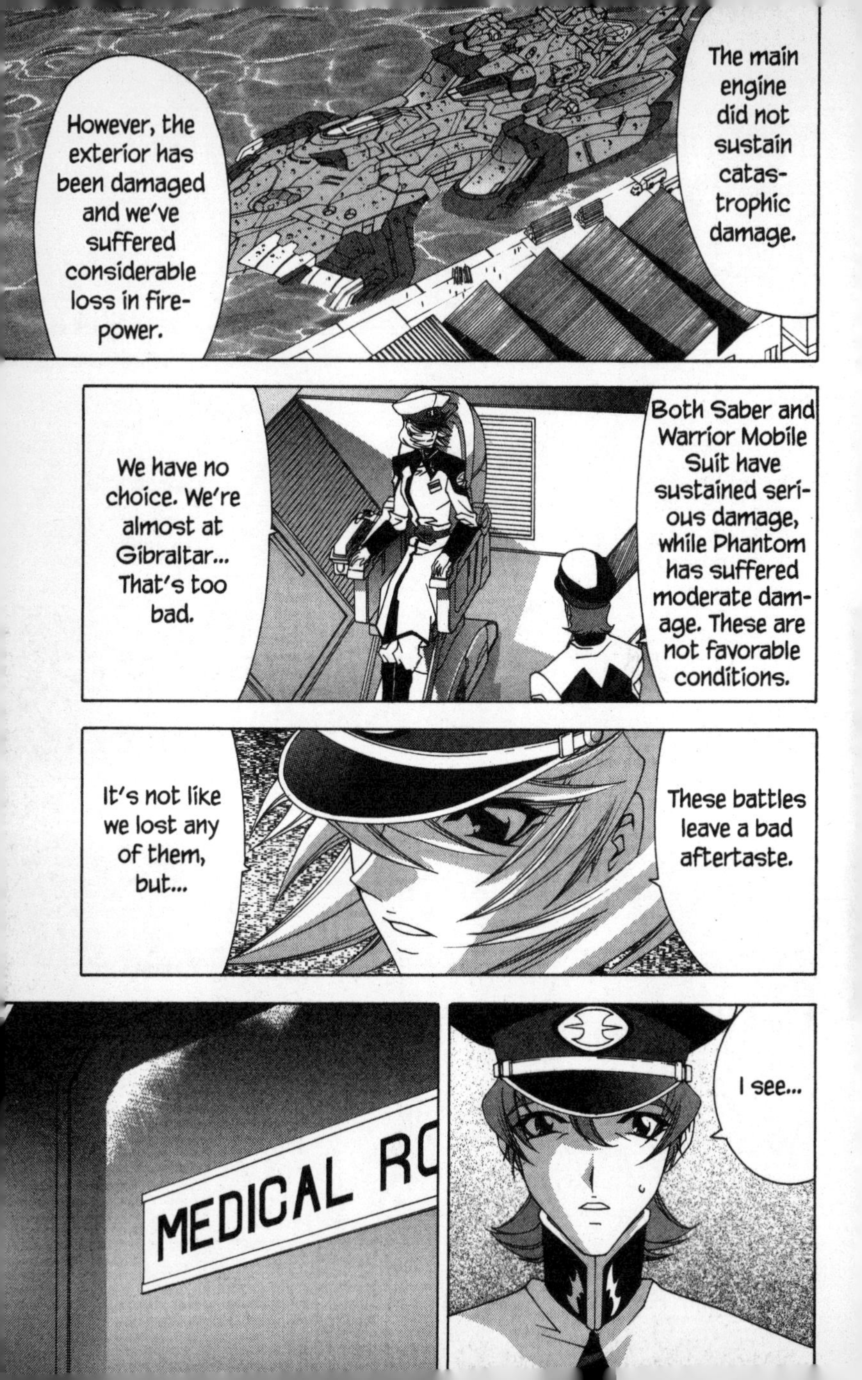
The main engine did not sustain catas-trophic damage.
However, the exterior has been damaged and we've suffered considerable loss in fire-power.
Both Saber and Warrior Mobile Suit have sustained seri-ous damage, while Phantom has suffered moderate dam-age. These are not favorable conditions.
We have no choice. We're almost at Gibraltar... That's too bad.
These battles leave a bad aftertaste.
It's not like we lost any of them, but...
I see...
MEDICAL RO

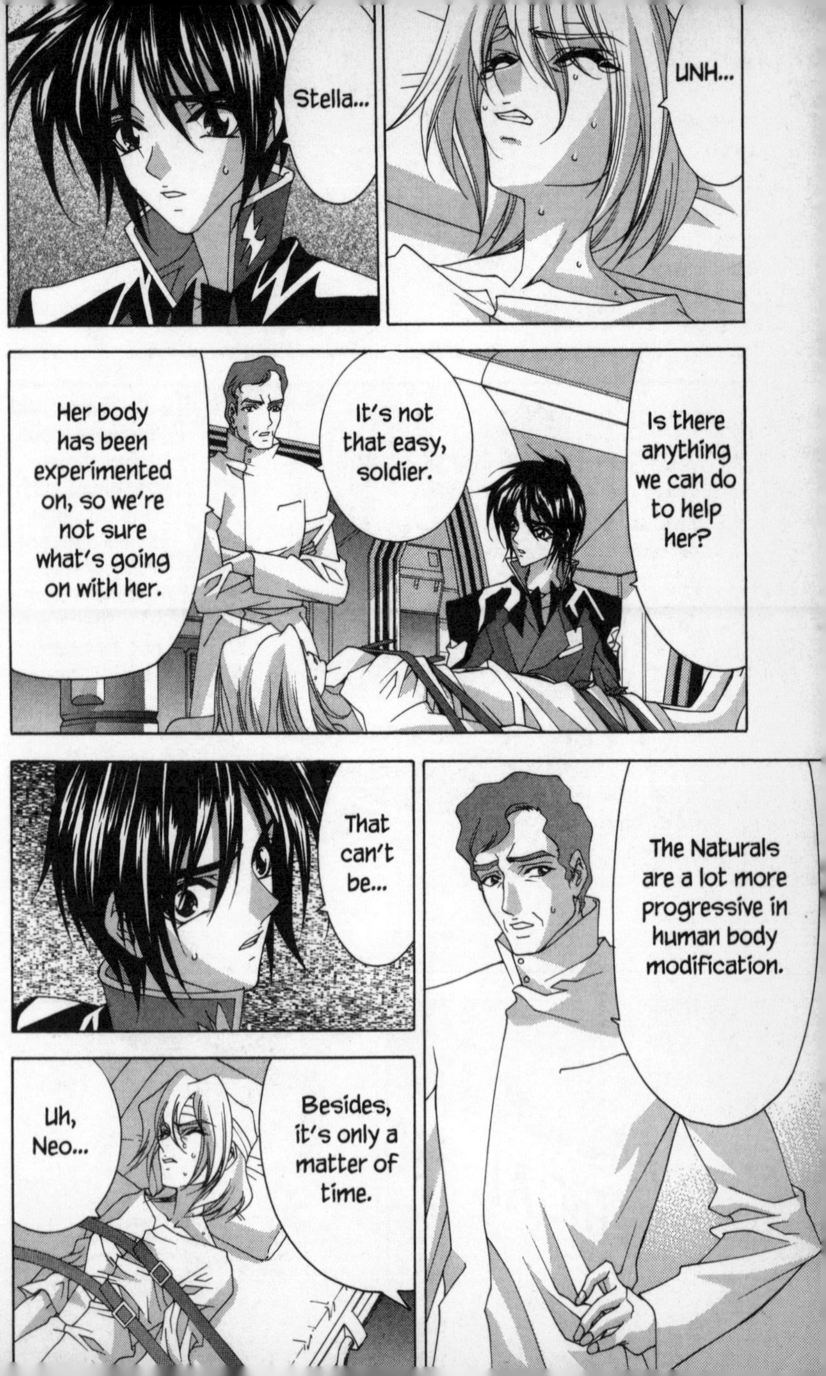
UNH...
Stella...
Is there anything we can do to help her?
It's not that easy, soldier.
Her body has been experimented on, so we're not sure what's going on with her.
The Naturals are a lot more progressive in human body modification.
That can't be...
Besides, it's only a matter of time.
Uh, Neo...

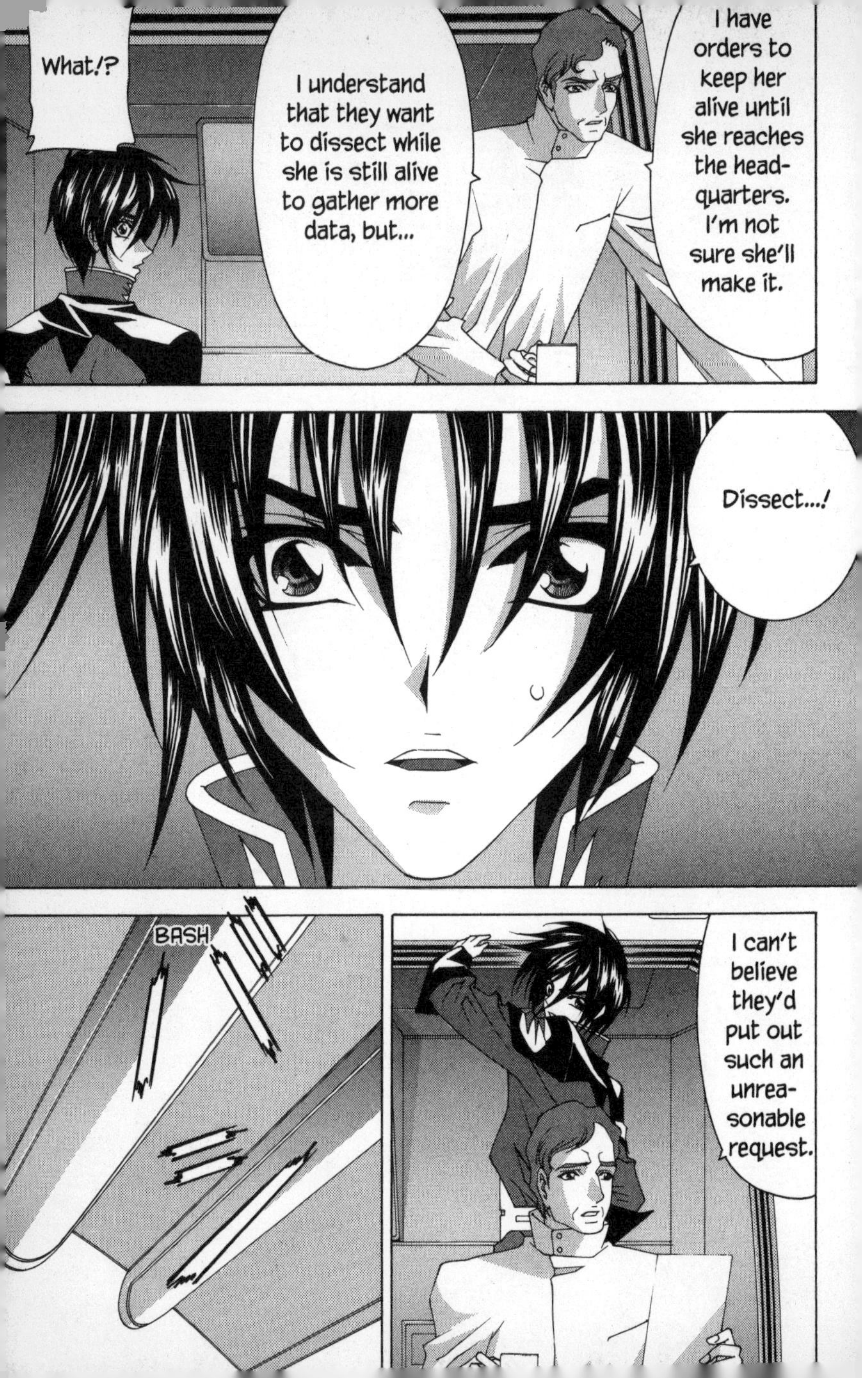
I have orders to keep her alive until she reaches the head-quarters. I'm not sure she'll make it.
I understand that they want to dissect while she is still alive to gather more data, but...
What!?
Dissect...!
I can't believe they'd put out such an unrea-sonable request.
BASH

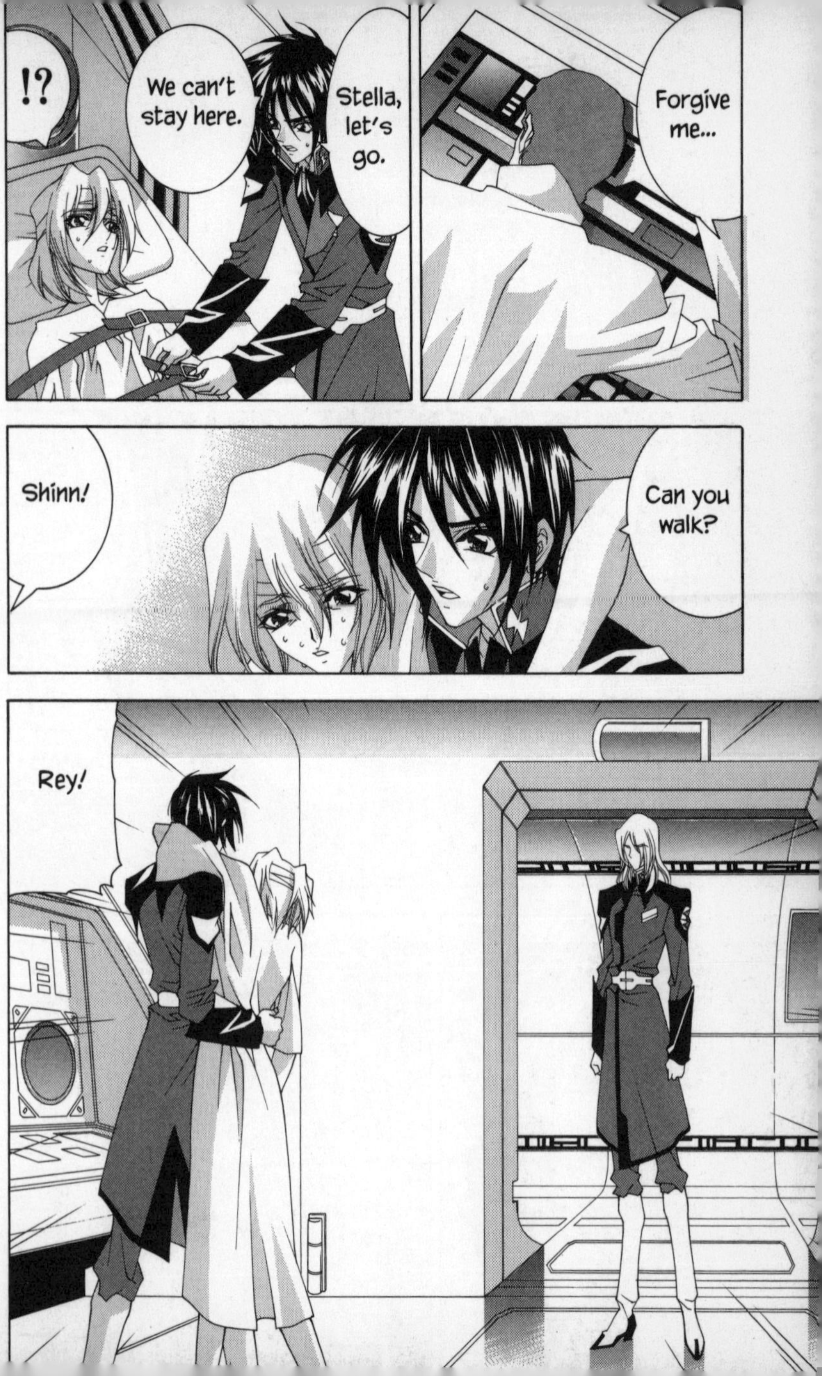
Forgive me...
Stella, let's go.
We can't stay here.
!?
Can you walk?
Shinn!
Rey!

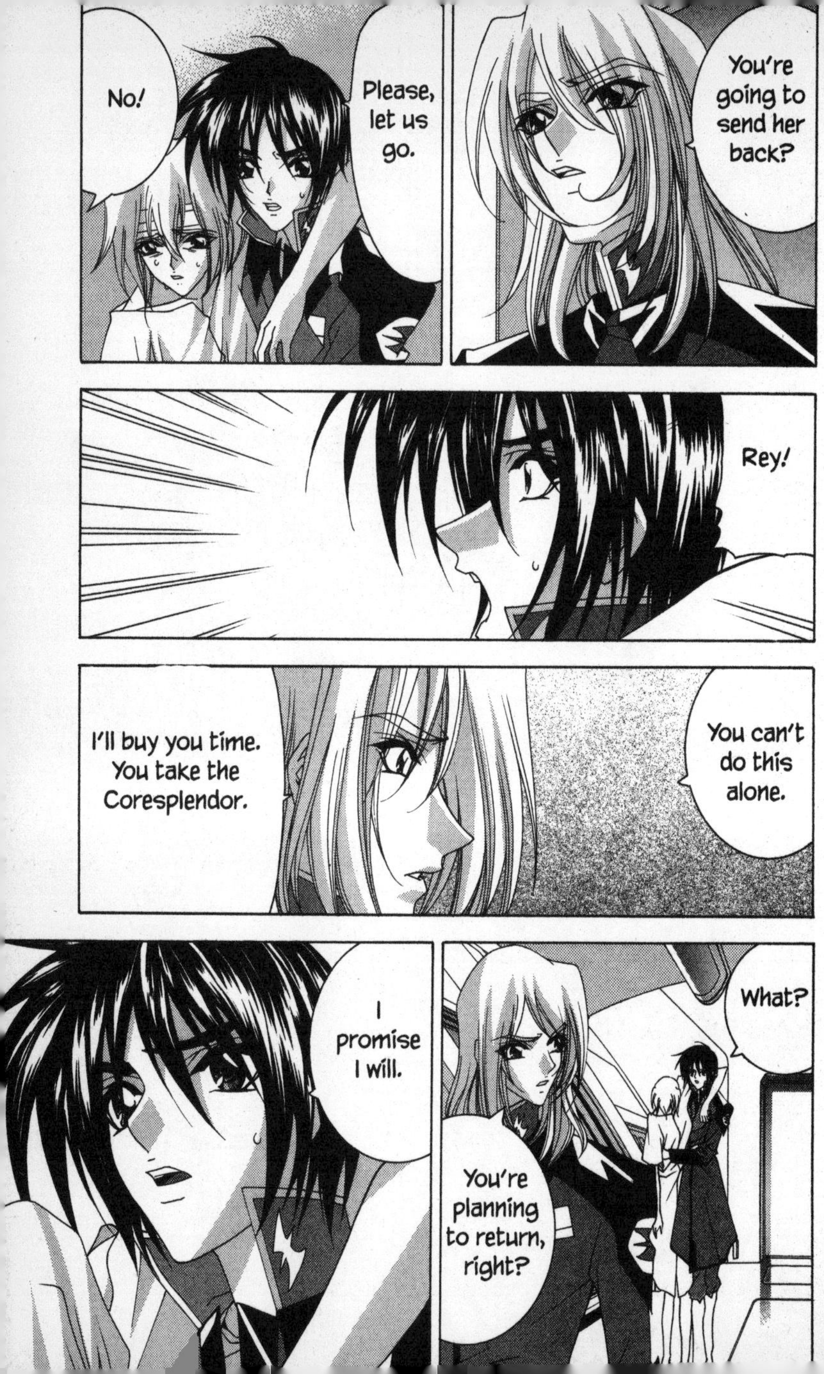
You're going to send her back?
Please, let us go.
No!
Rey!
You can't do this alone.
I'll buy you time. You take the Coresplendor.
What?
You're planning to return, right?
I promise I will.

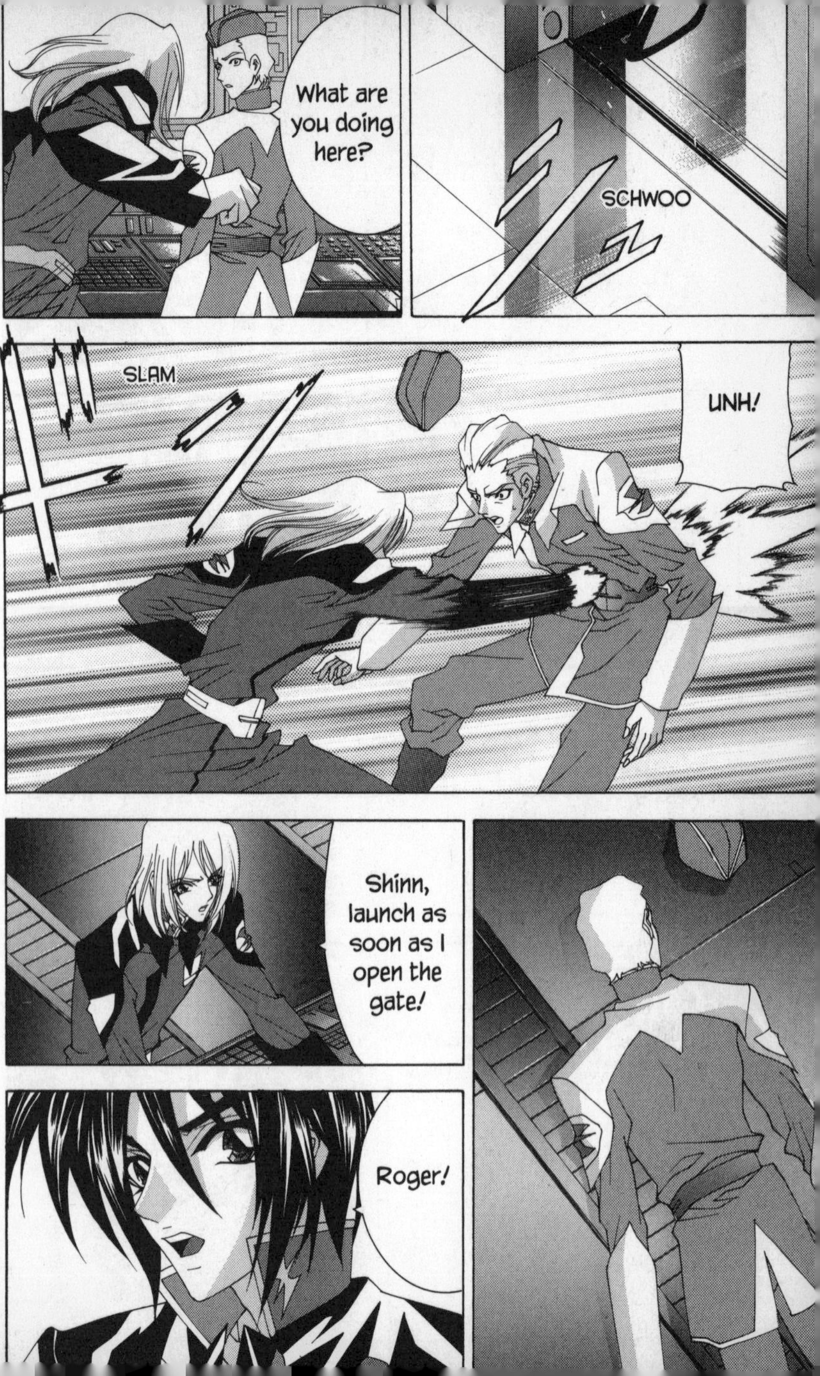
SCHWOO
What are you doing here?
UNH!
SLAM
Shinn, launch as soon as I open the gate!
Roger!

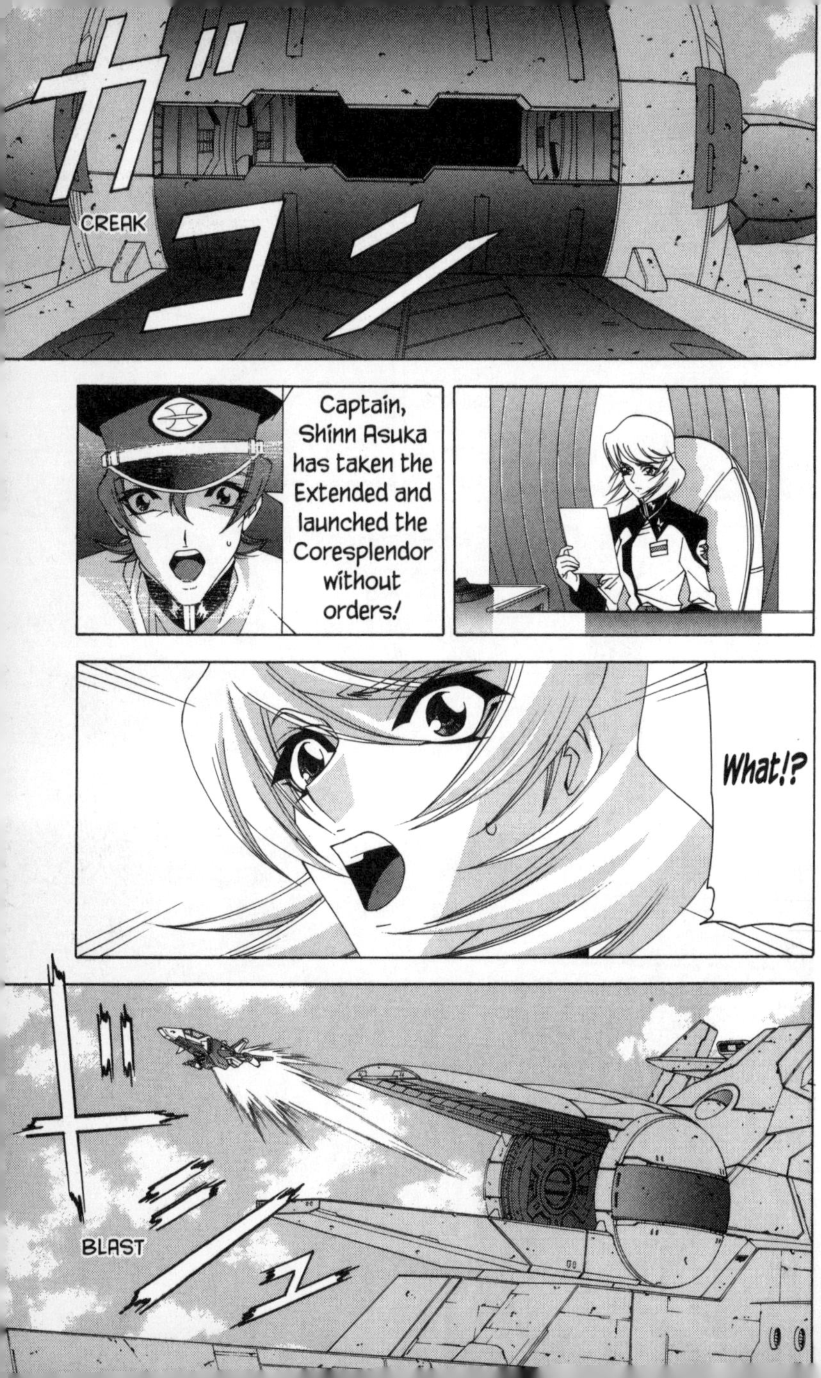
ガゴン
CREAK
Captain, Shinn Asuka has taken the Extended and launched the Coresplendor without orders!
What!?
BLAST

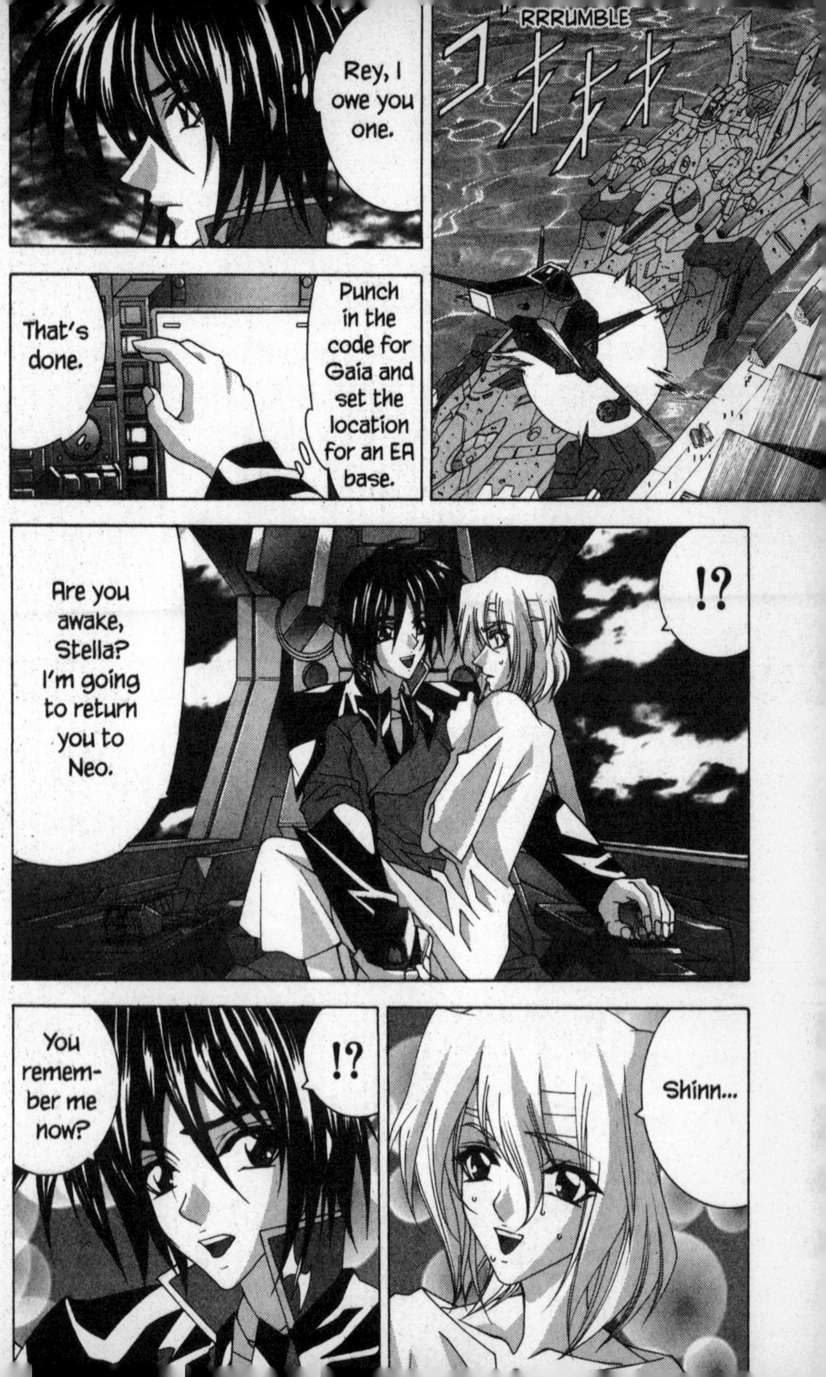
RRRUMBLE
Rey, I owe you one.
Punch in the code for Gaia and set the location for an EA base.
That's done.
Are you awake, Stella? I'm going to return you to Neo.
!?
Shinn...
!?
You remember me now?

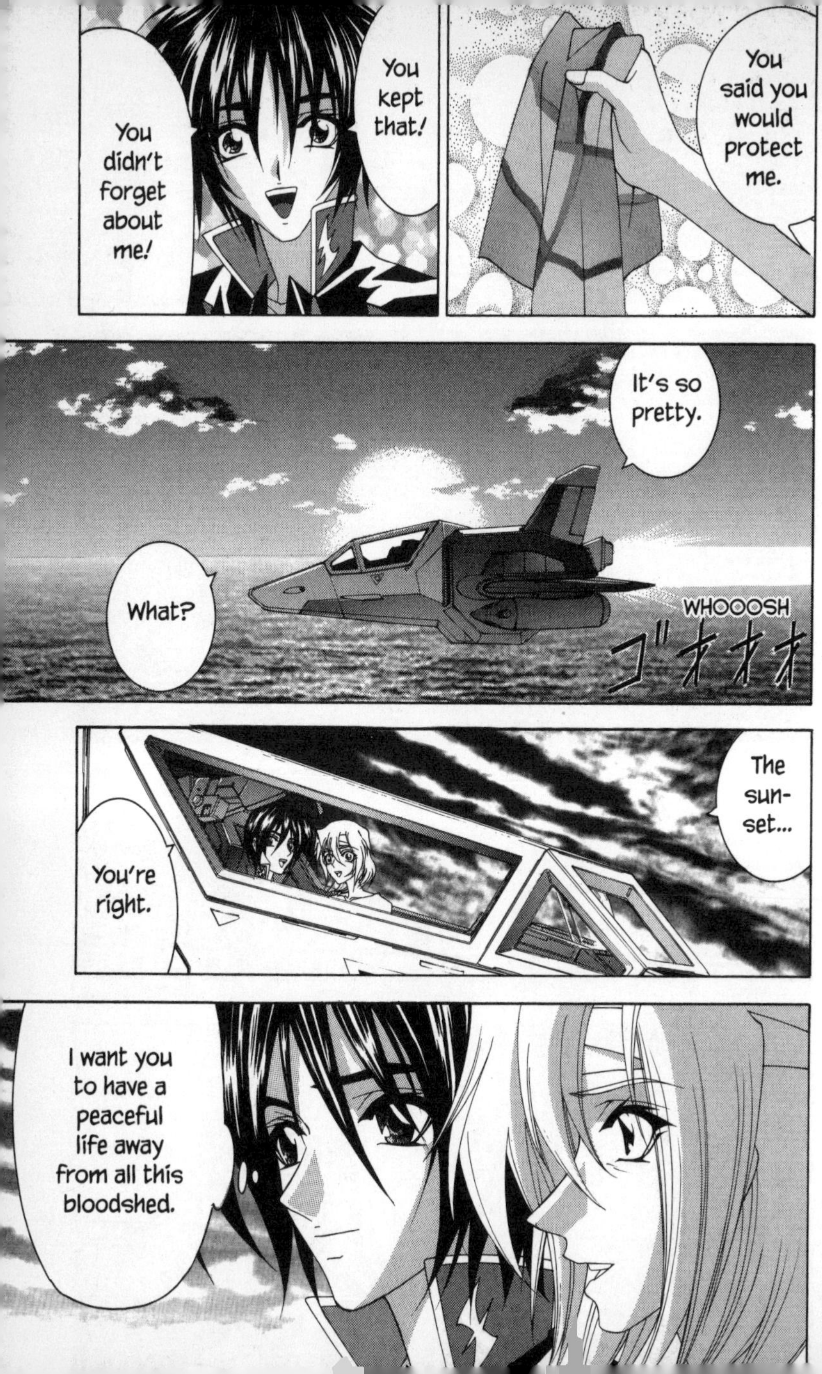
You said you would protect me.
You kept that!
You didn't forget about me!
It's so pretty.
WHOOOSH
ゴオオオ
What?
The sun-set...
You're right.
I want you to have a peaceful life away from all this bloodshed.

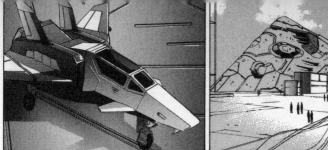

CLANG

For what?

I'm sorry.

For getting you involved.

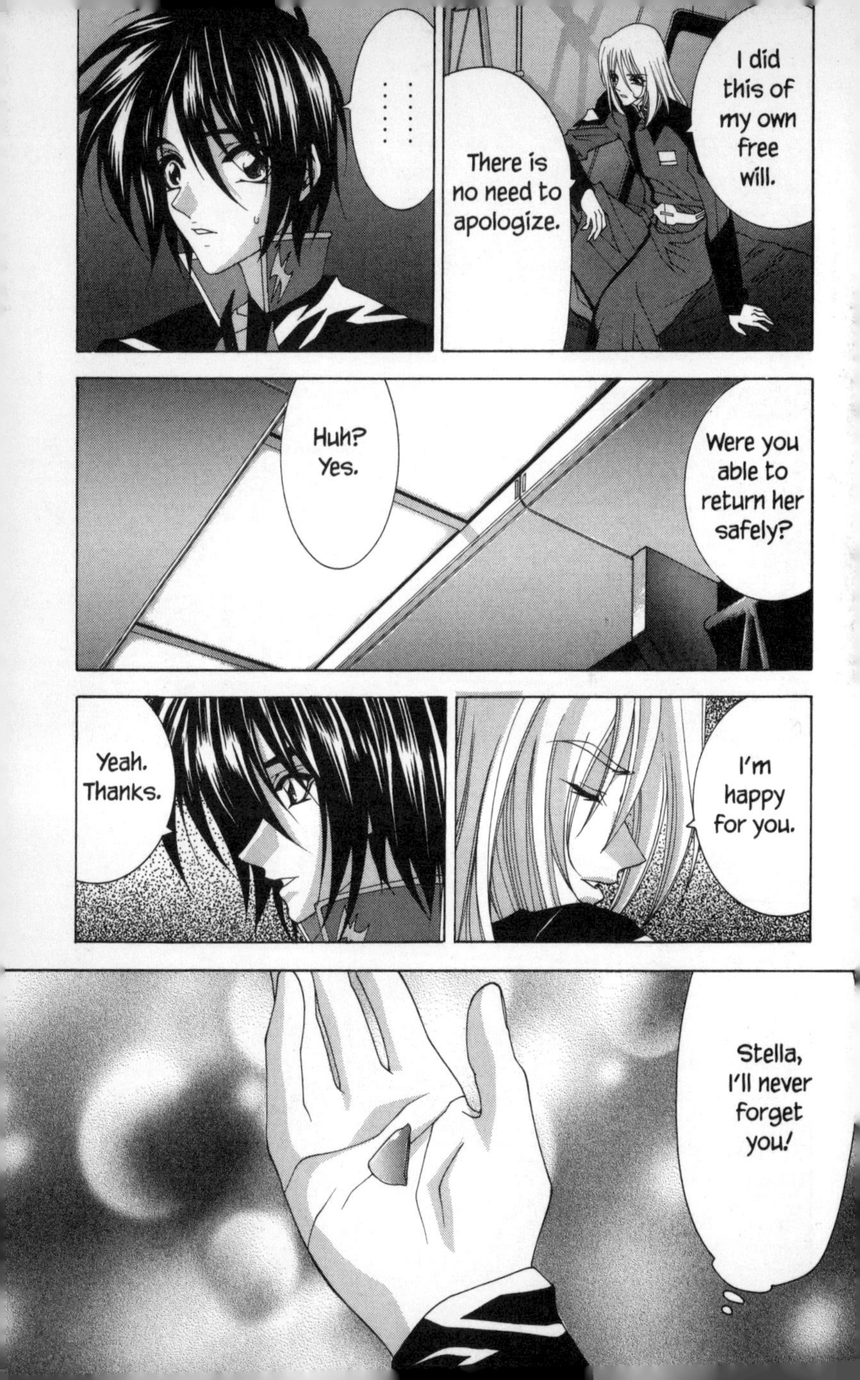
I did this of my own free will.
There is no need to apologize.
……
Were you able to return her safely?
Huh? Yes.
I'm happy for you.
Yeah. Thanks.
Stella, I'll never forget you!

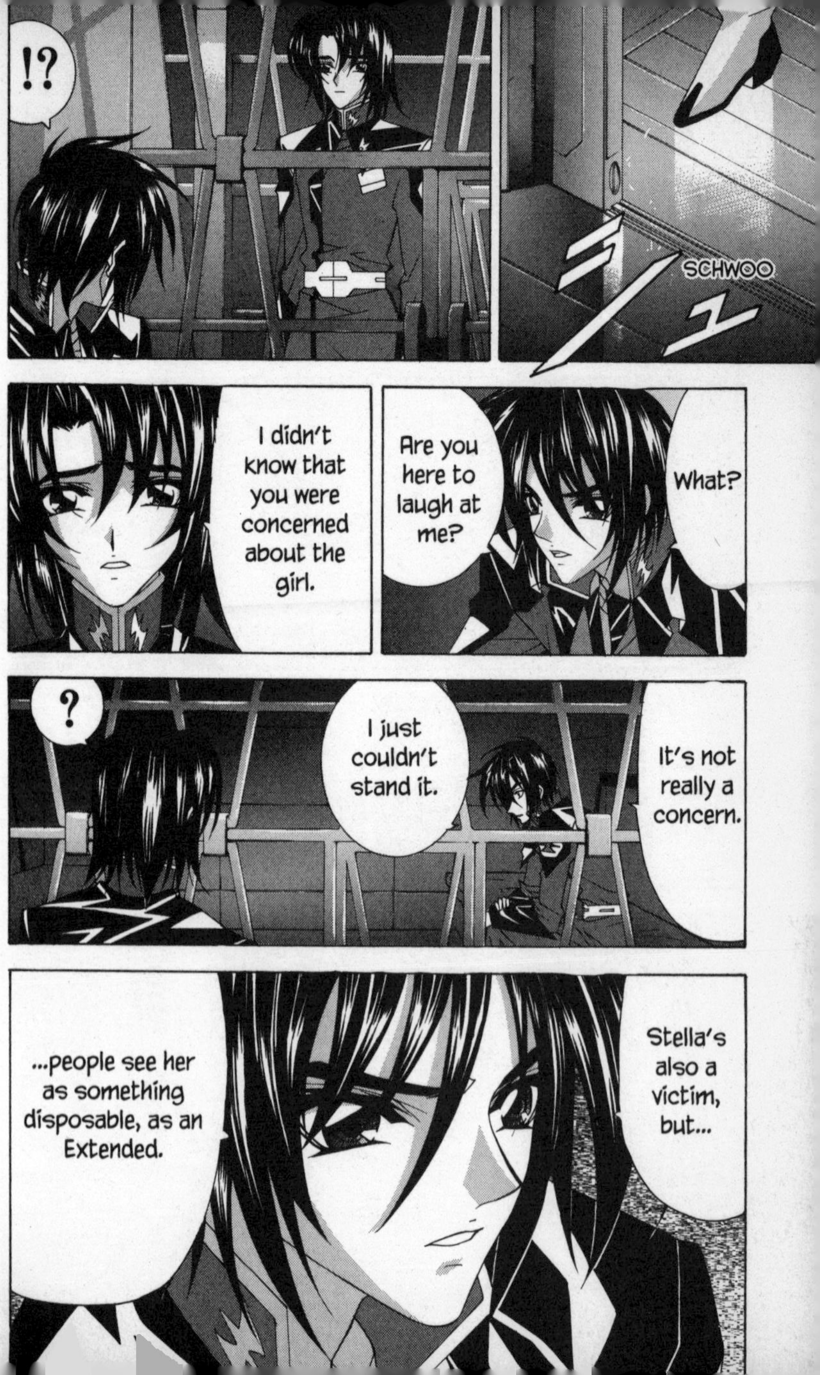
SCHWOO
!?
What?
Are you here to laugh at me?
I didn't know that you were concerned about the girl.
It's not really a concern.
I just couldn't stand it.
?
Stella's also a victim, but...
...people see her as something disposable, as an Extended.

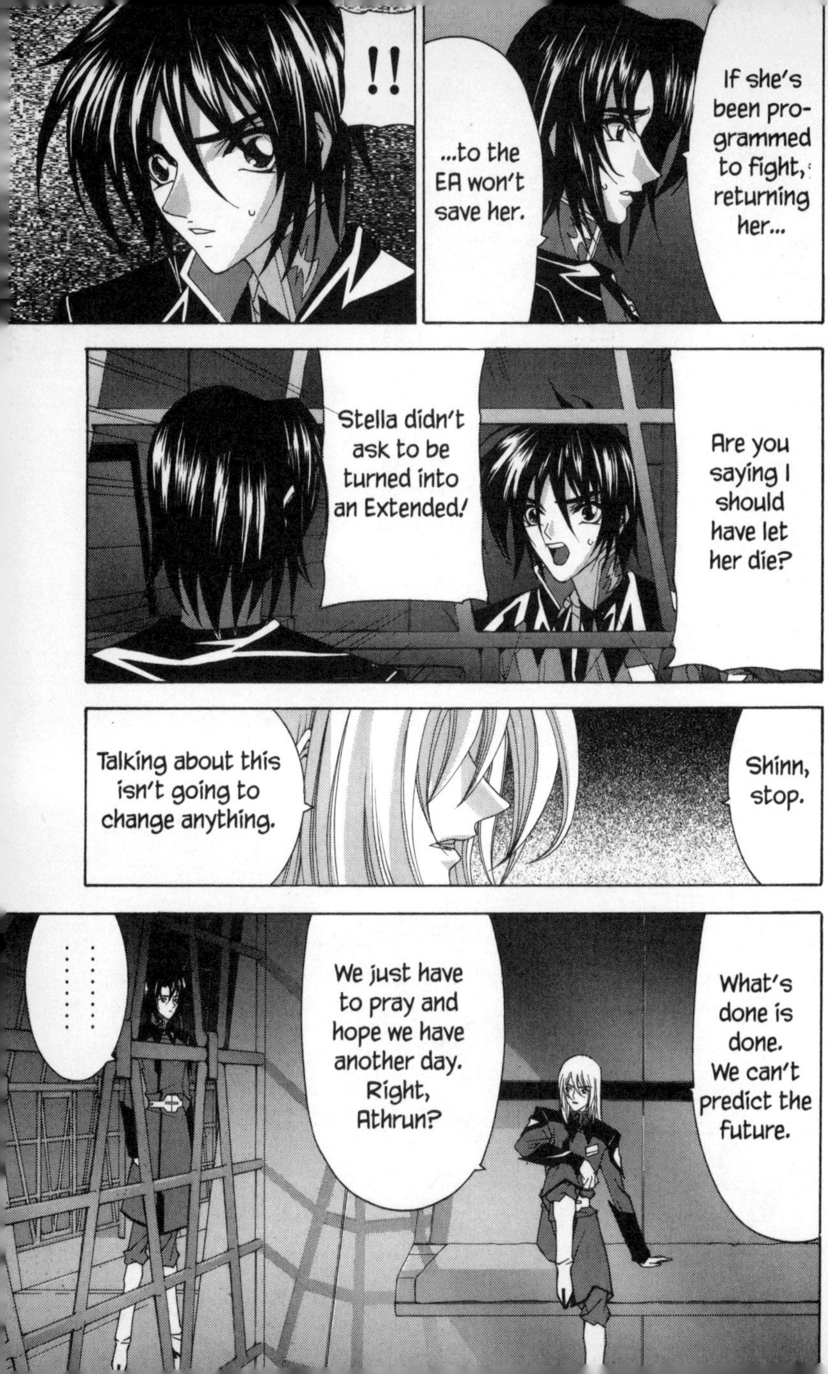
If she's been pro-grammed to fight, returning her...
...to the EA won't save her.
!!
Are you saying I should have let her die?
Stella didn't ask to be turned into an Extended!
Shinn, stop.
Talking about this isn't going to change anything.
What's done is done. We can't predict the future.
We just have to pray and hope we have another day. Right, Athrun?
......

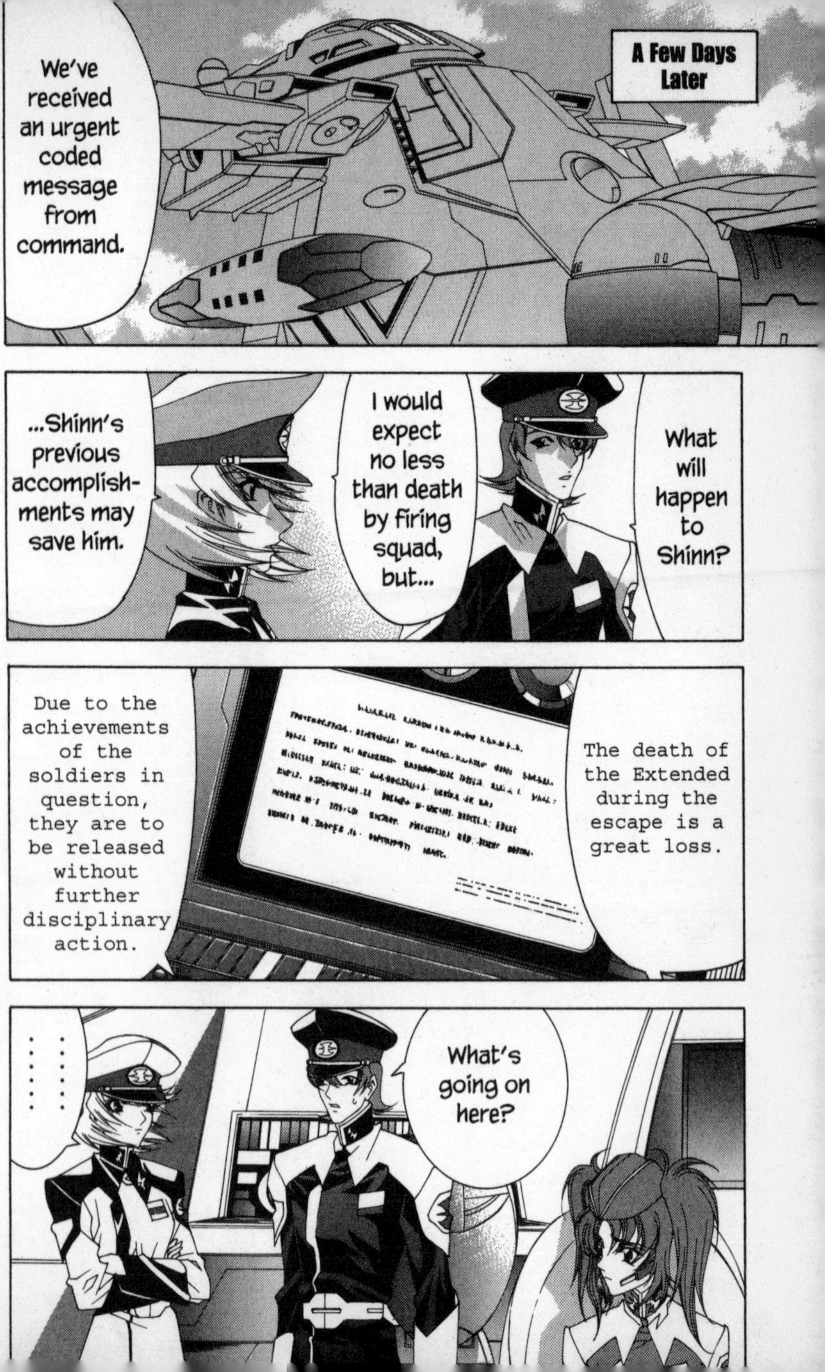
A Few Days Later
We've received an urgent coded message from command.
What will happen to Shinn?
I would expect no less than death by firing squad, but...
...Shinn's previous accomplishments may save him.
The death of the Extended during the escape is a great loss.
Due to the achievements of the soldiers in question, they are to be released without further disciplinary action.
What's going on here?
......

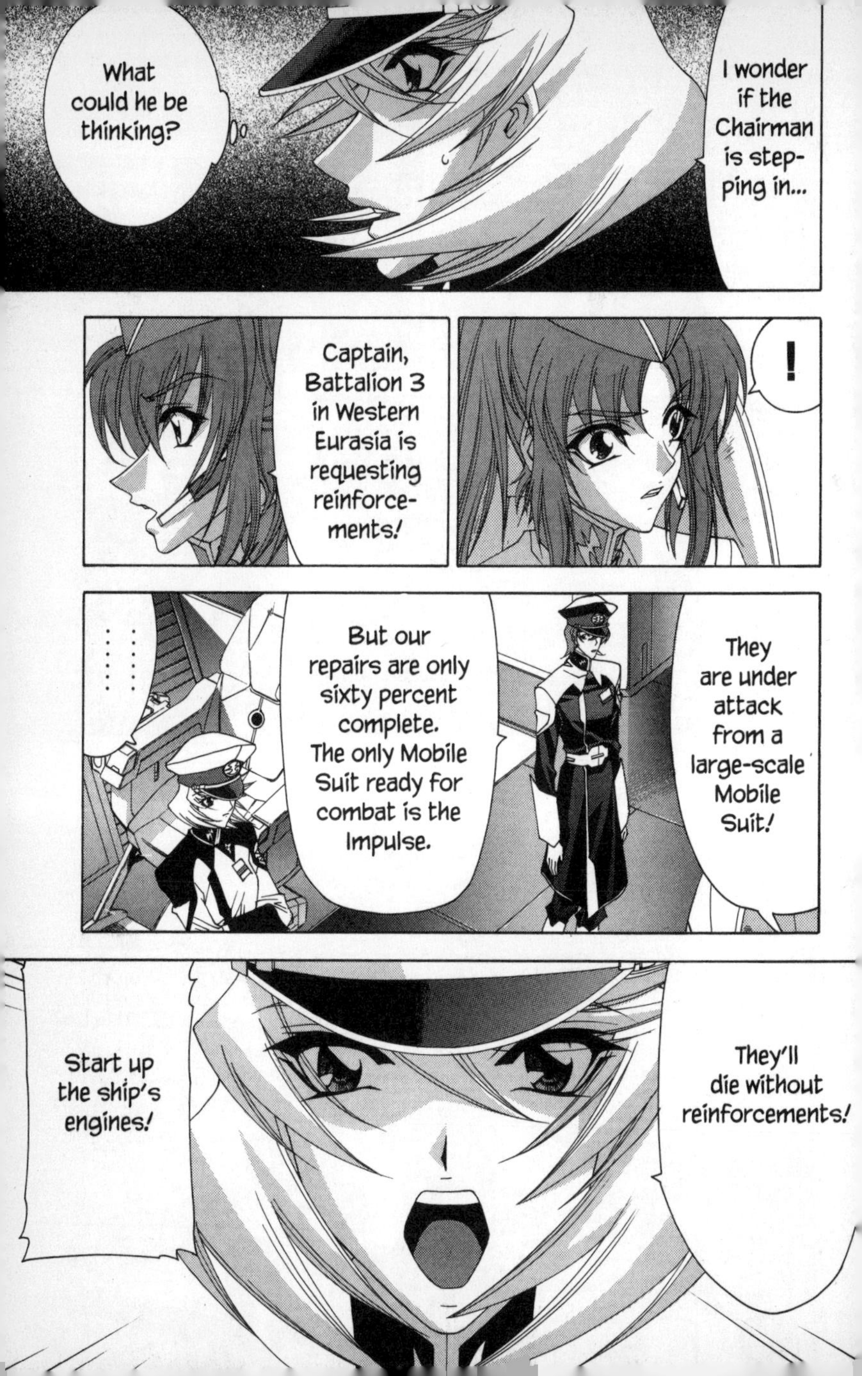
I wonder if the Chairman is step-ping in...
What could he be thinking?
!
Captain, Battalion 3 in Western Eurasia is requesting reinforce-ments!
They are under attack from a large-scale Mobile Suit!
But our repairs are only sixty percent complete. The only Mobile Suit ready for combat is the Impulse.
......
They'll die without reinforcements!
Start up the ship's engines!

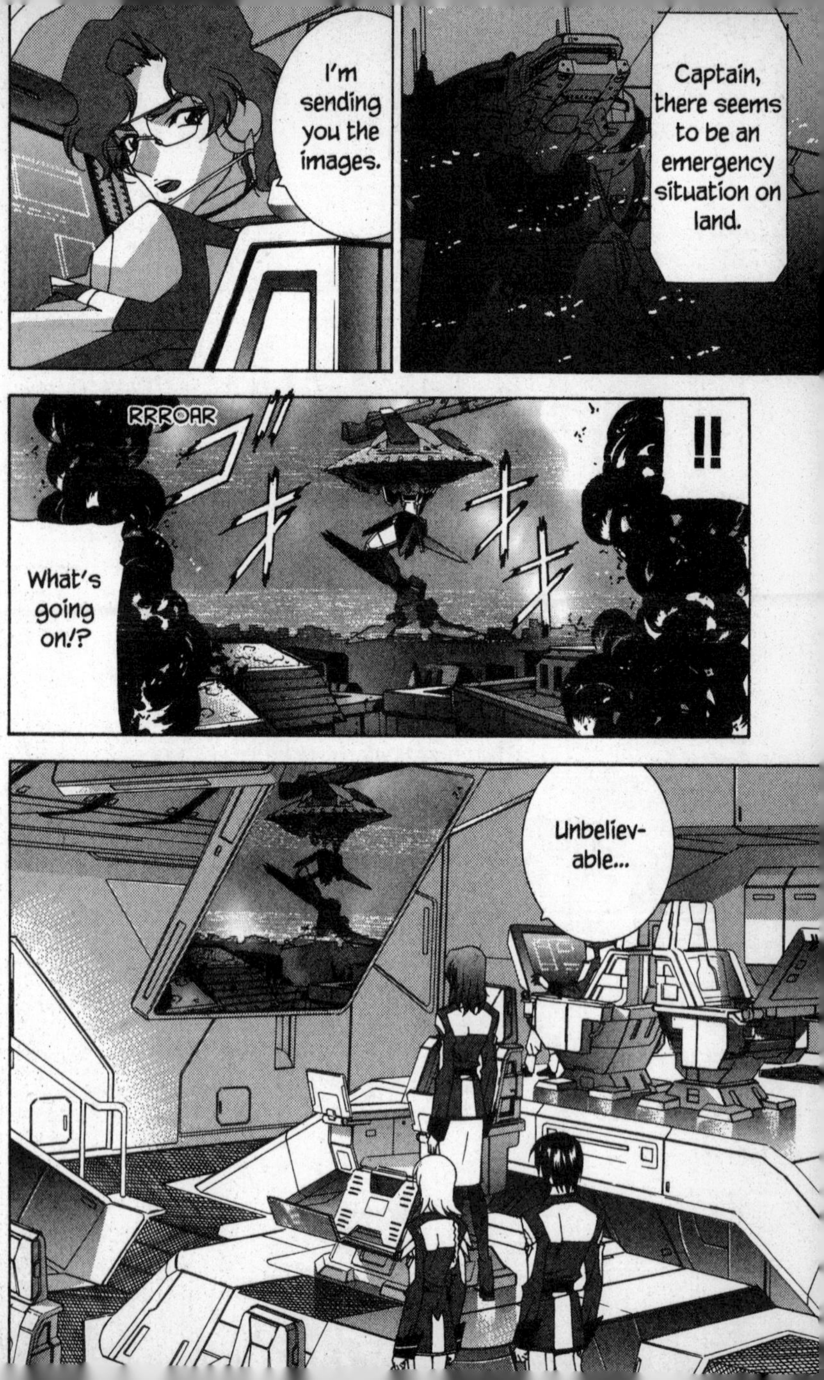
Captain, there seems to be an emergency situation on land.
I'm sending you the images.
!!
RRROAR
What's going on!?
Unbelievable...

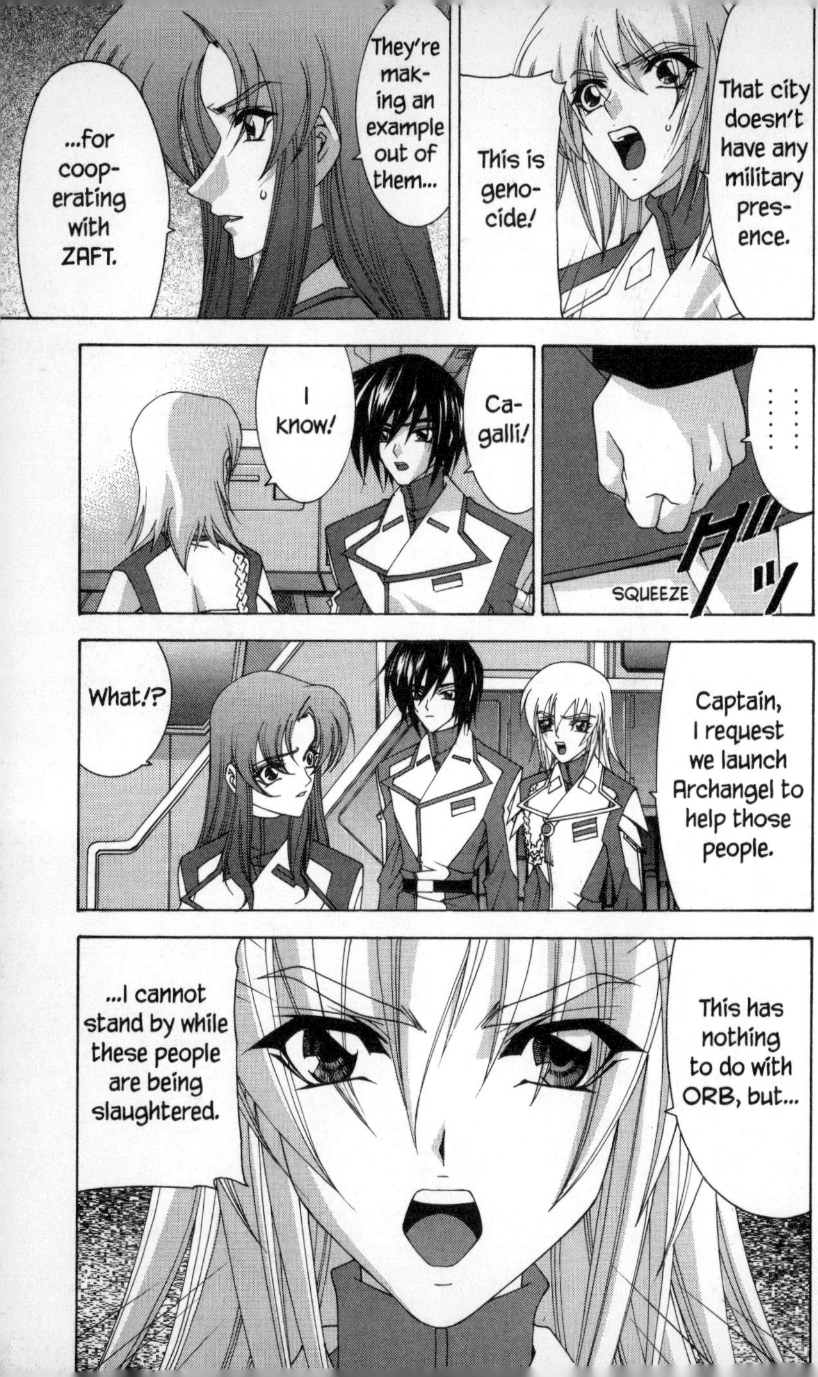

That city doesn't have any military presence.
This is genocide!
They're making an example out of them...
...for cooperating with ZAFT.
......
SQUEEZE
Cagalli!
I know!
Captain, I request we launch Archangel to help those people.
What!?
This has nothing to do with ORB, but...
...I cannot stand by while these people are being slaughtered.

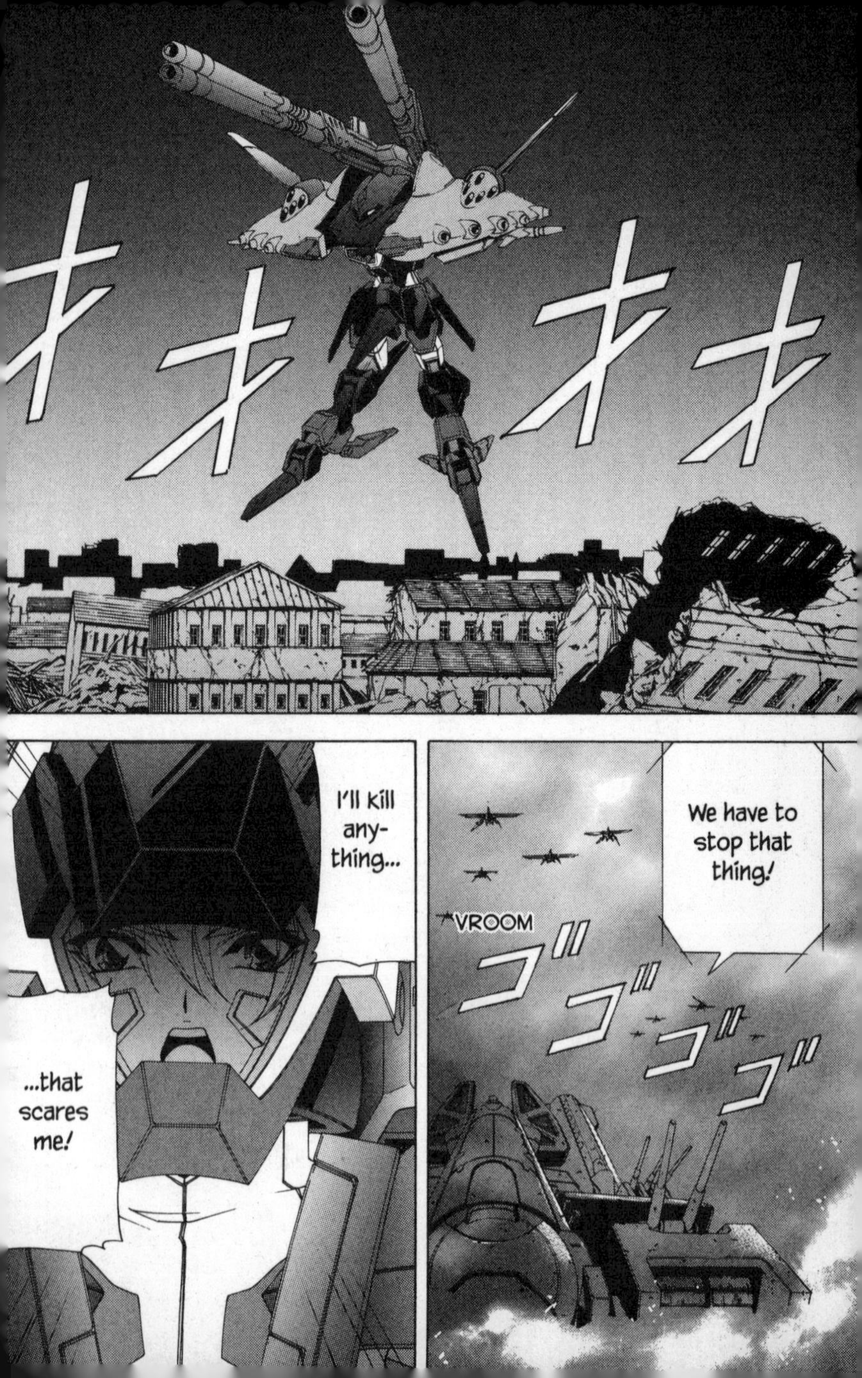
オオオオ
We have to stop that thing!
VROOM
ゴゴゴゴ
I'll kill any-thing...
...that scares me!

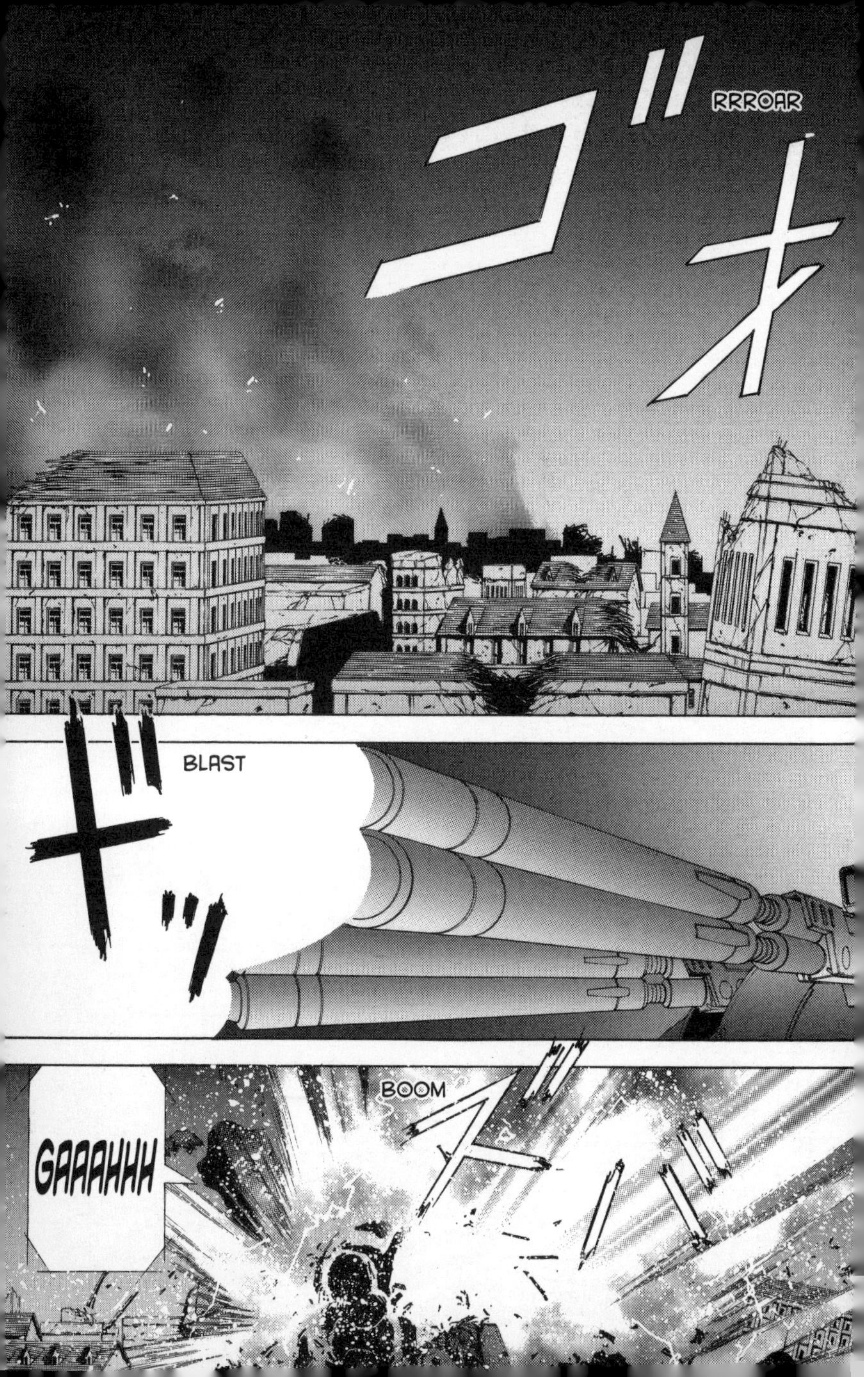
ゴオ
RRROAR
ギッ
BLAST
ズバ
BOOM
GAAAHHH

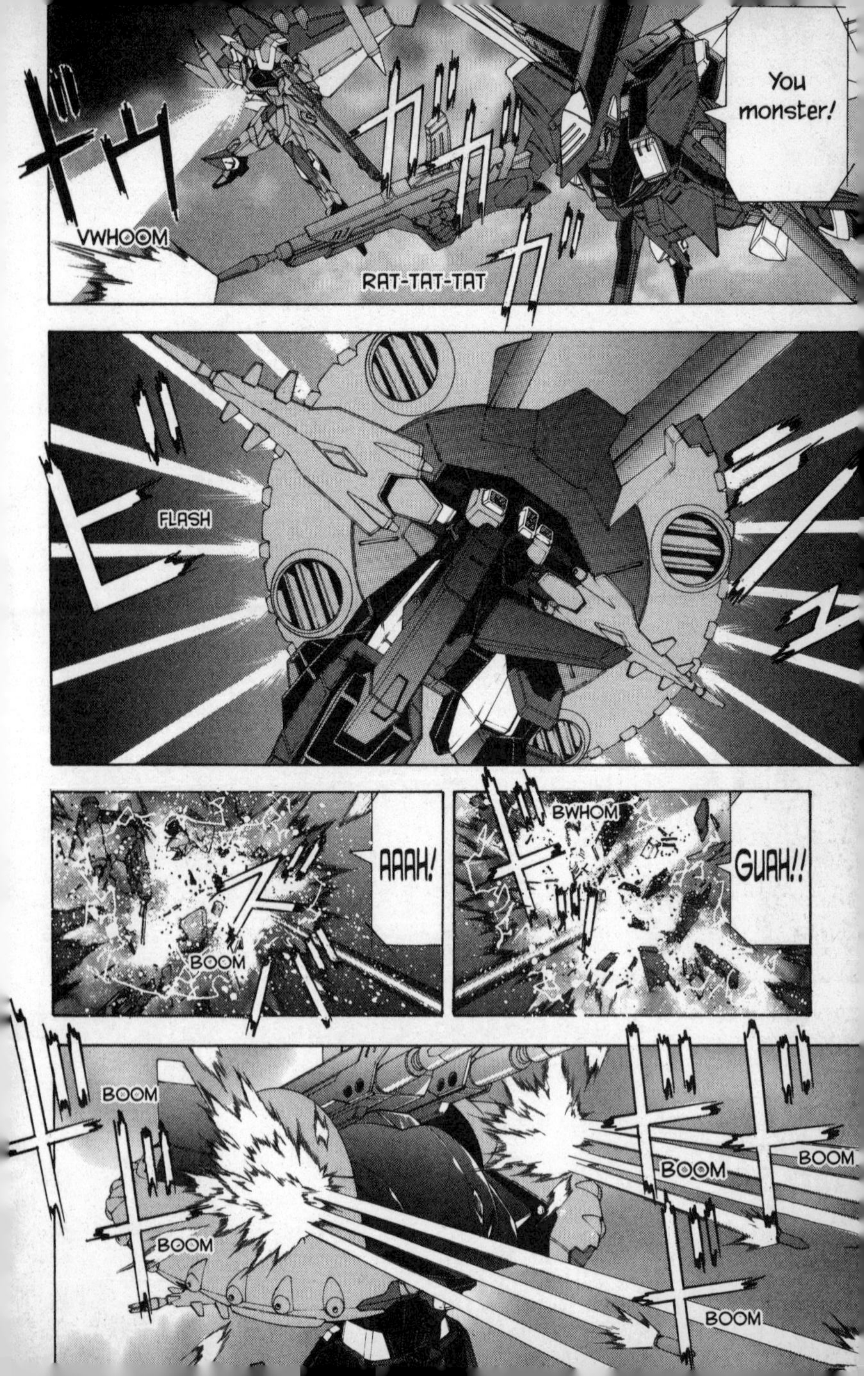
You monster!
VWHOOM
RAT-TAT-TAT
FLASH
BWHOM
GUAH!!
AAAH!
BOOM
BOOM
BOOM
BOOM
BOOM
BOOM

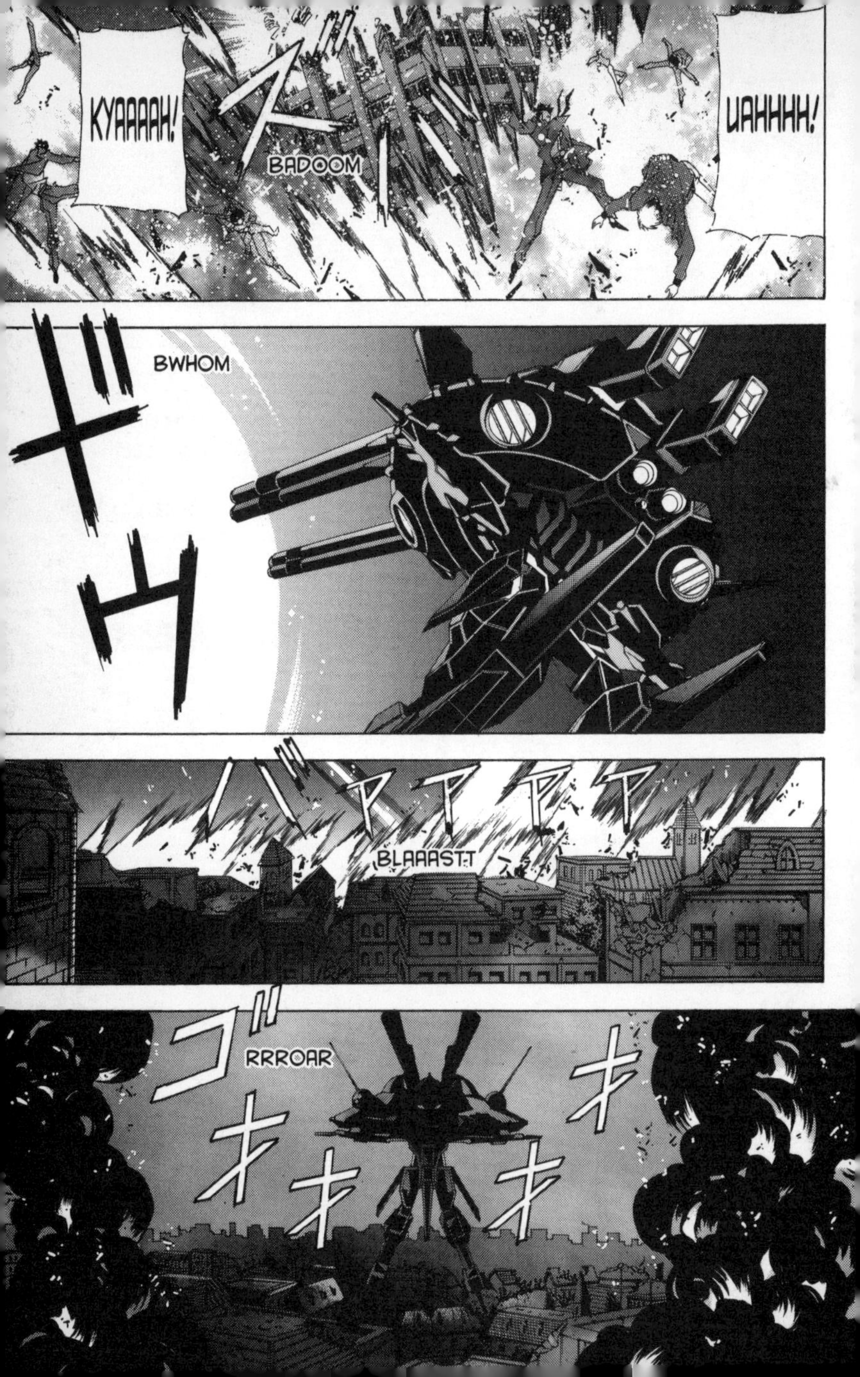
UAHHHH!
BADOOM
KYAAAAH!
BWHOM
BLAAASTT
RRROAR

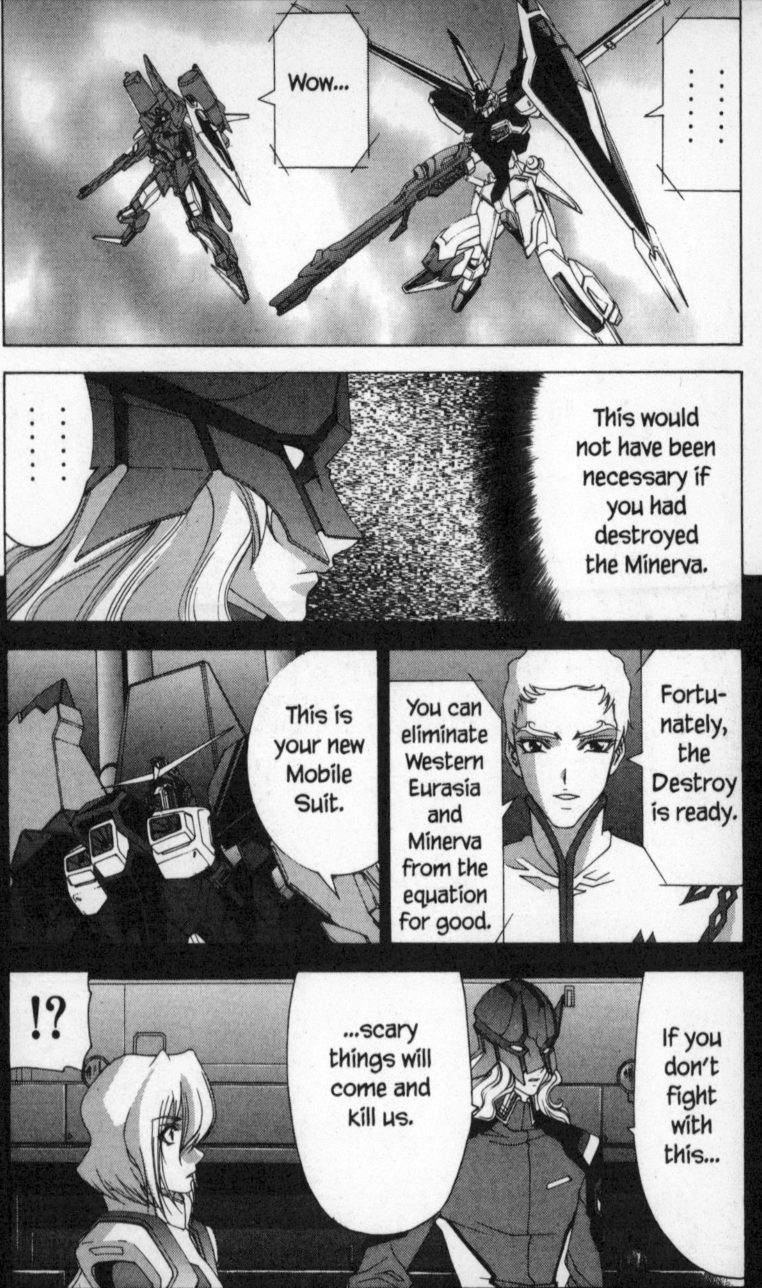
……
Wow...
This would not have been necessary if you had destroyed the Minerva.
……
Fortu-nately, the Destroy is ready.
You can eliminate Western Eurasia and Minerva from the equation for good.
This is your new Mobile Suit.
If you don't fight with this...
...scary things will come and kill us.
!?

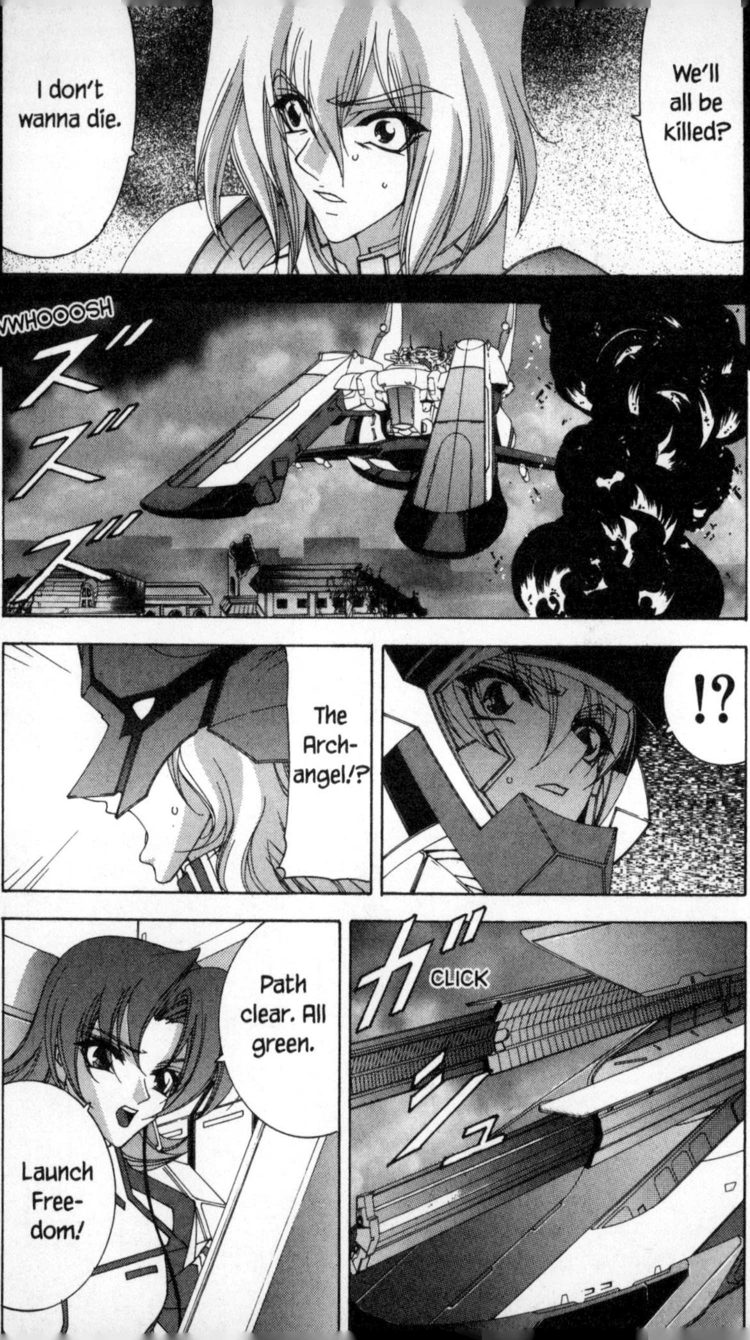
We'll all be killed?
I don't wanna die.
VWHOOOSH
!?
The Arch-angel!?
CLICK
Path clear. All green.
Launch Free-dom!

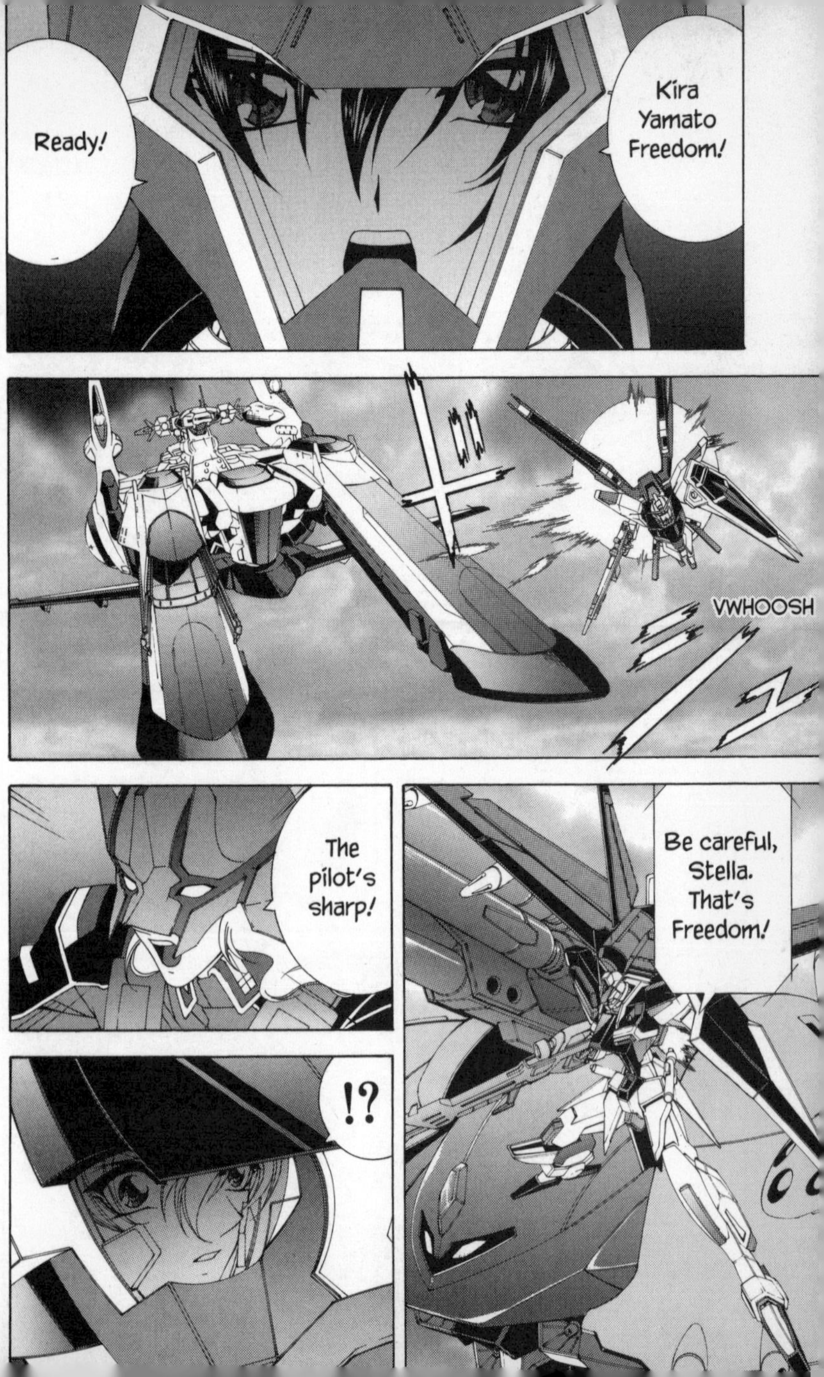
Kira Yamato Freedom!
Ready!
VWHOOSH
Be careful, Stella. That's Freedom!
The pilot's sharp!
!?

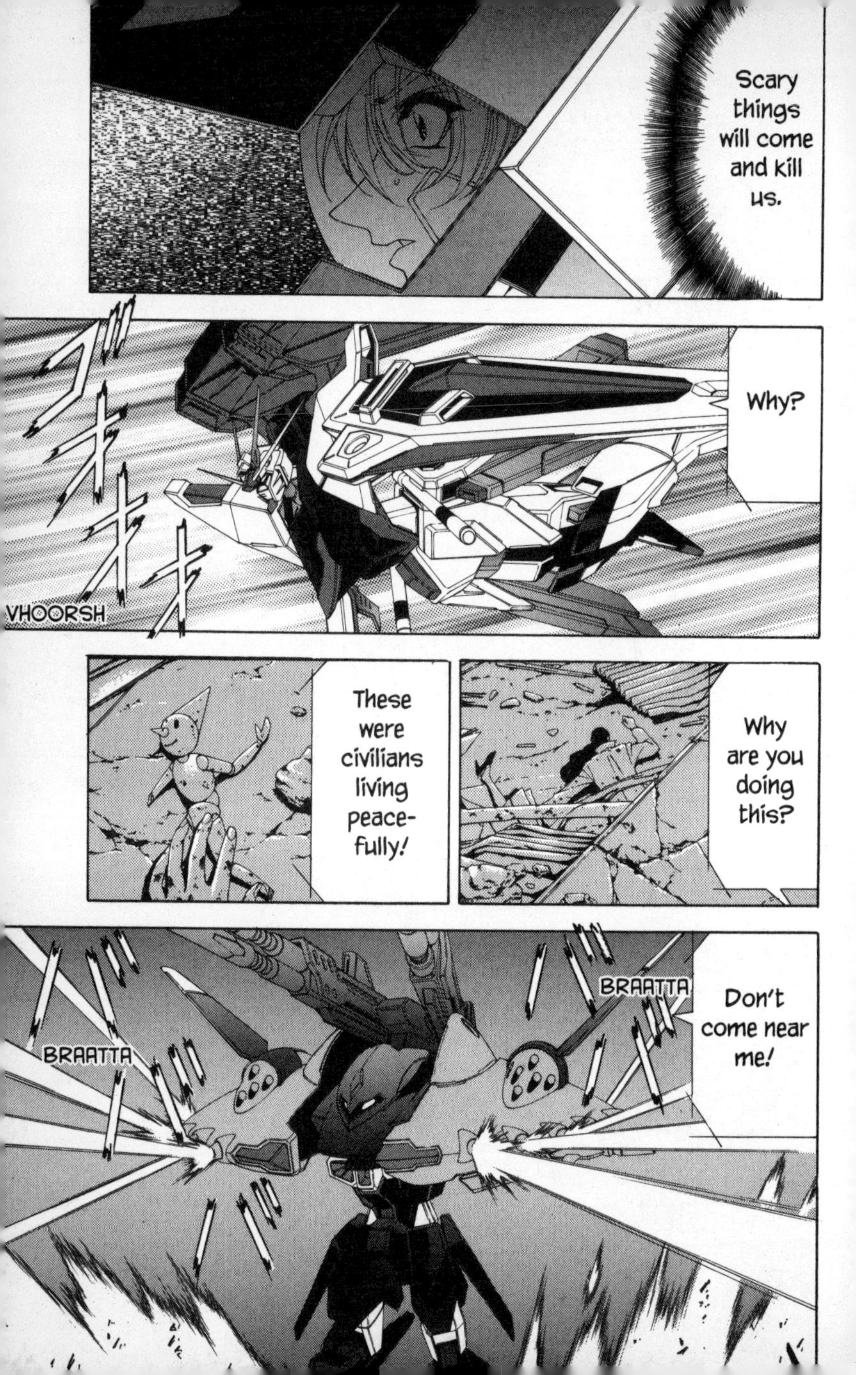
Scary things will come and kill us.
ブオオオ
VHOORSH
Why?
Why are you doing this?
These were civilians living peace-fully!
BRAATTA
Don't come near me!
BRAATTA

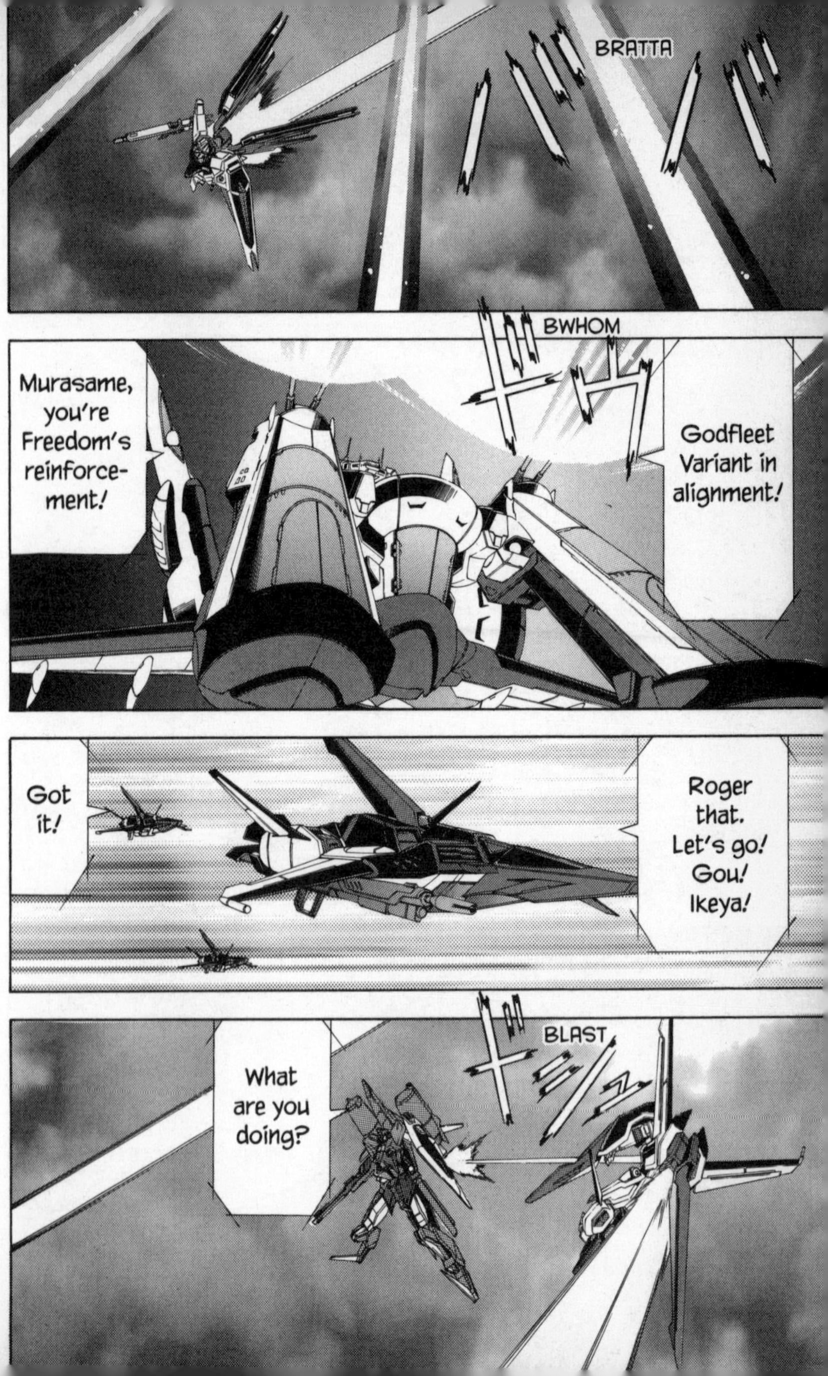
BRATTA
BWHOM
Godfleet Variant in alignment!
Murasame, you're Freedom's reinforcement!
Roger that. Let's go! Gou! Ikeya!
Got it!
BLAST
What are you doing?

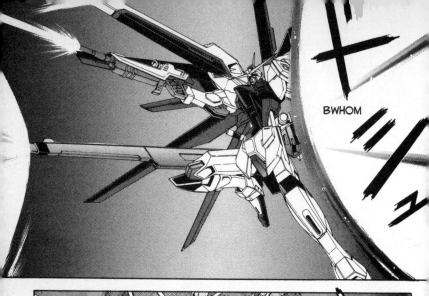

BWHOM

BSHHT

RRRUMBLE

The beam bounced right off!?

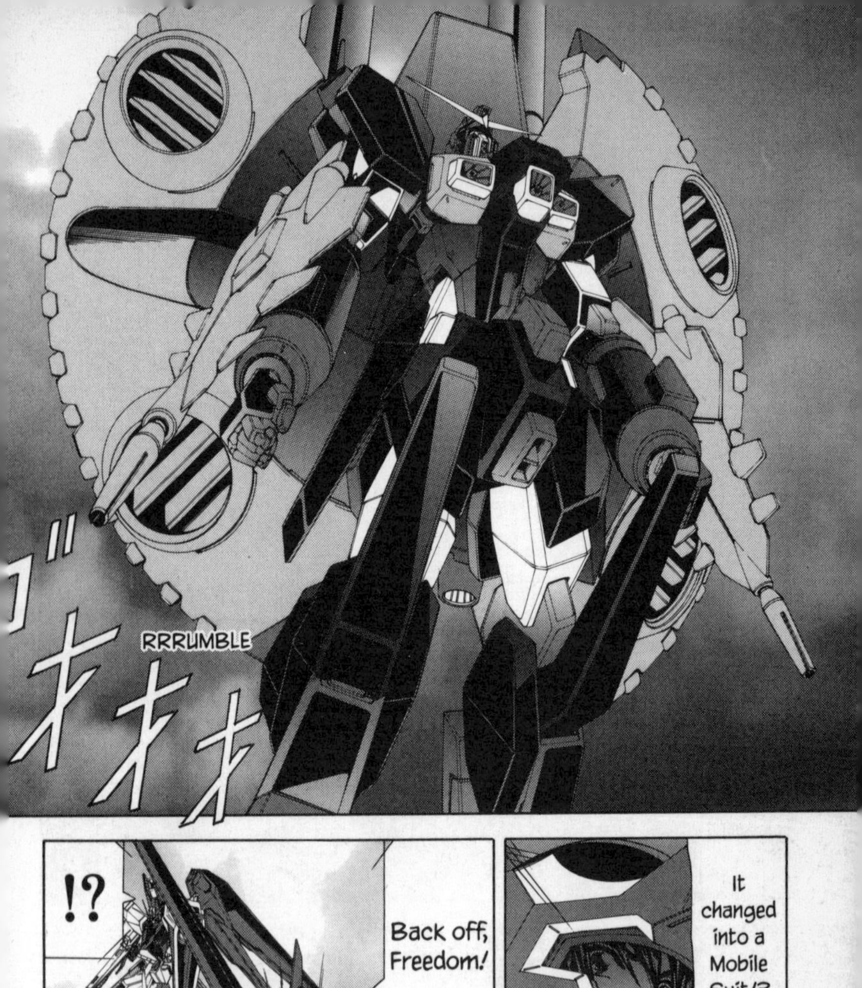
RRRUMBLE
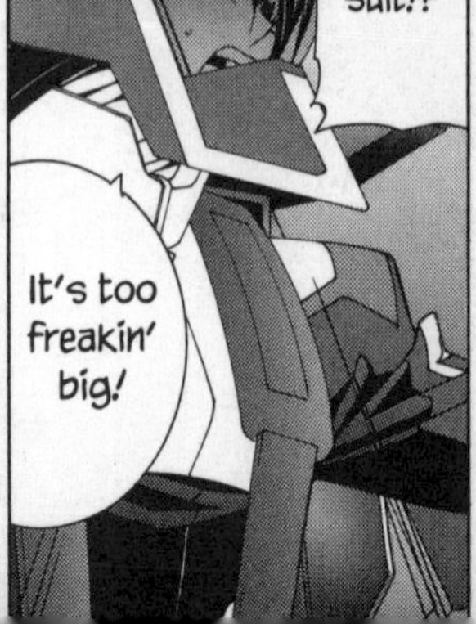
It changed into a Mobile Suit!?
It's too freakin' big!
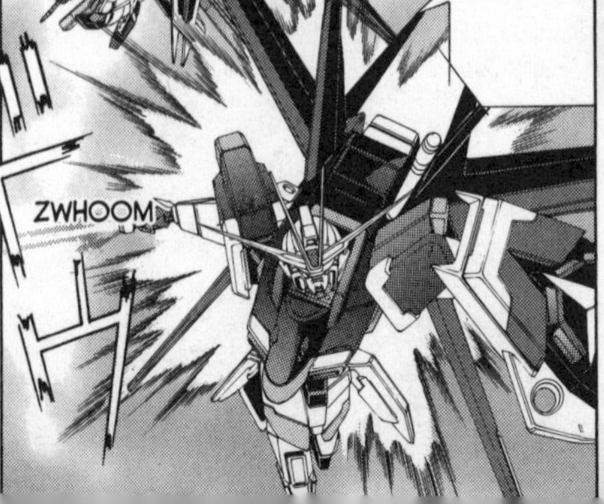
Back off, Freedom!
!?
ZWHOOM

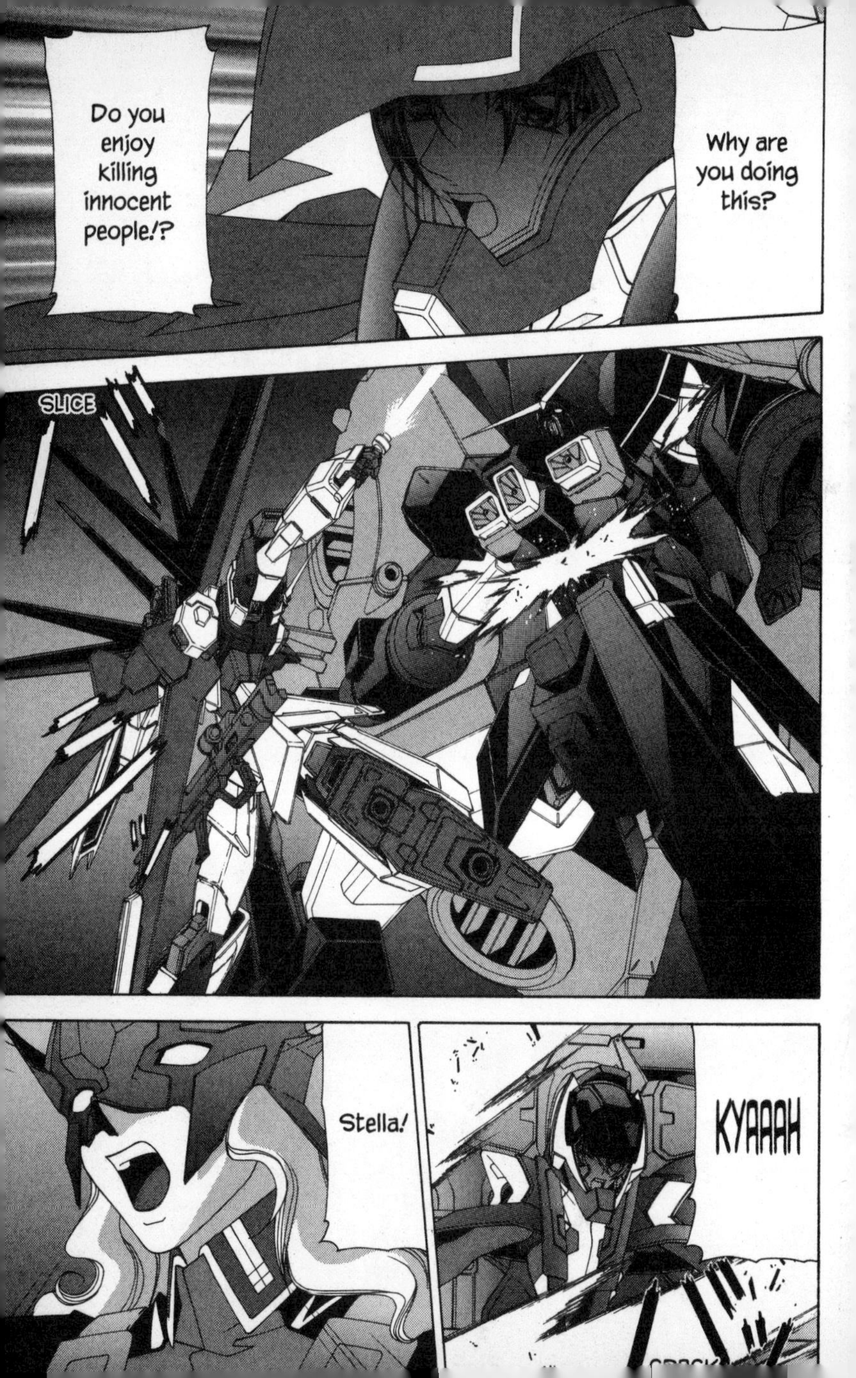
Why are you doing this?
Do you enjoy killing innocent people!?
SLICE
KYAAAH
Stella!

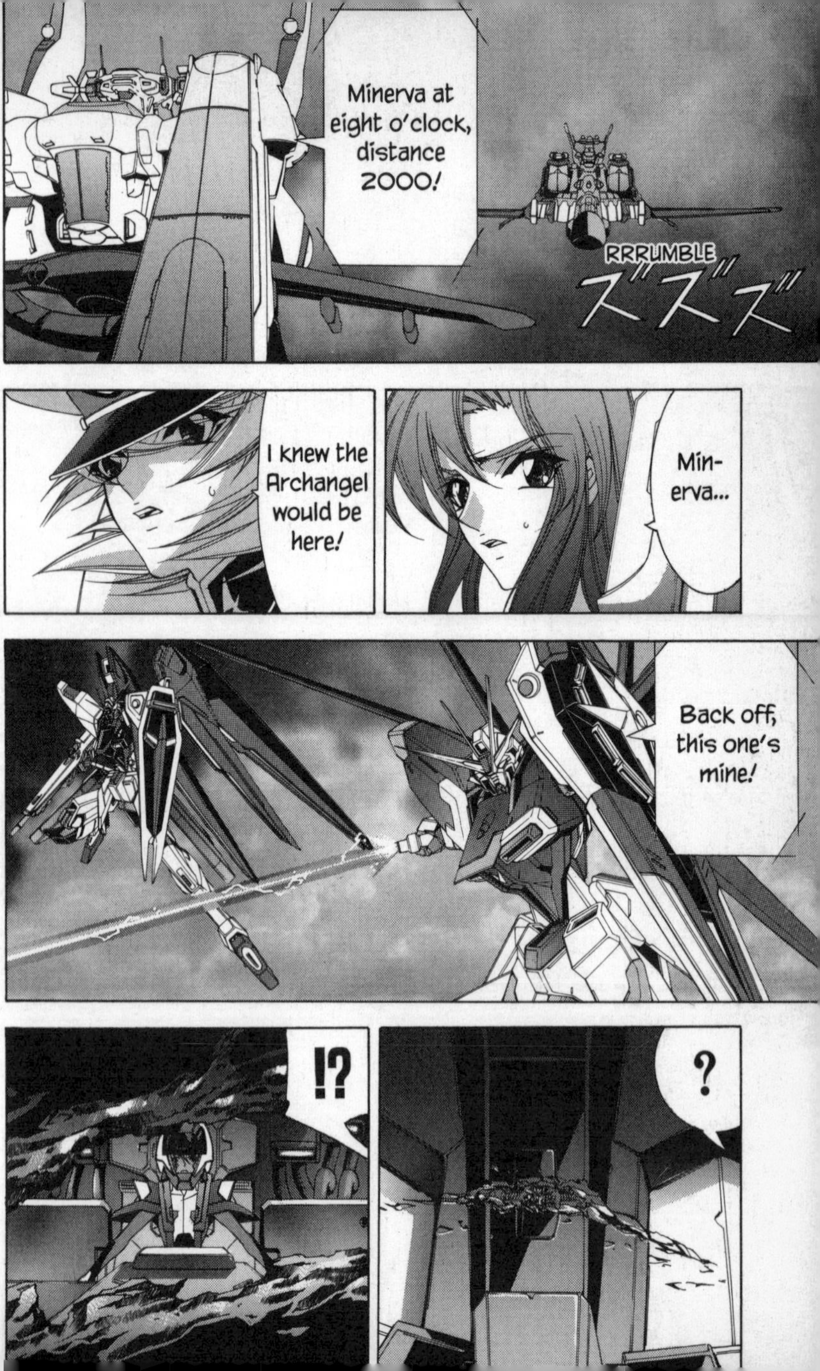
Minerva at eight o'clock, distance 2000!
RRRUMBLE
ズズズ
Min-erva...
I knew the Archangel would be here!
Back off, this one's mine!
?
!?

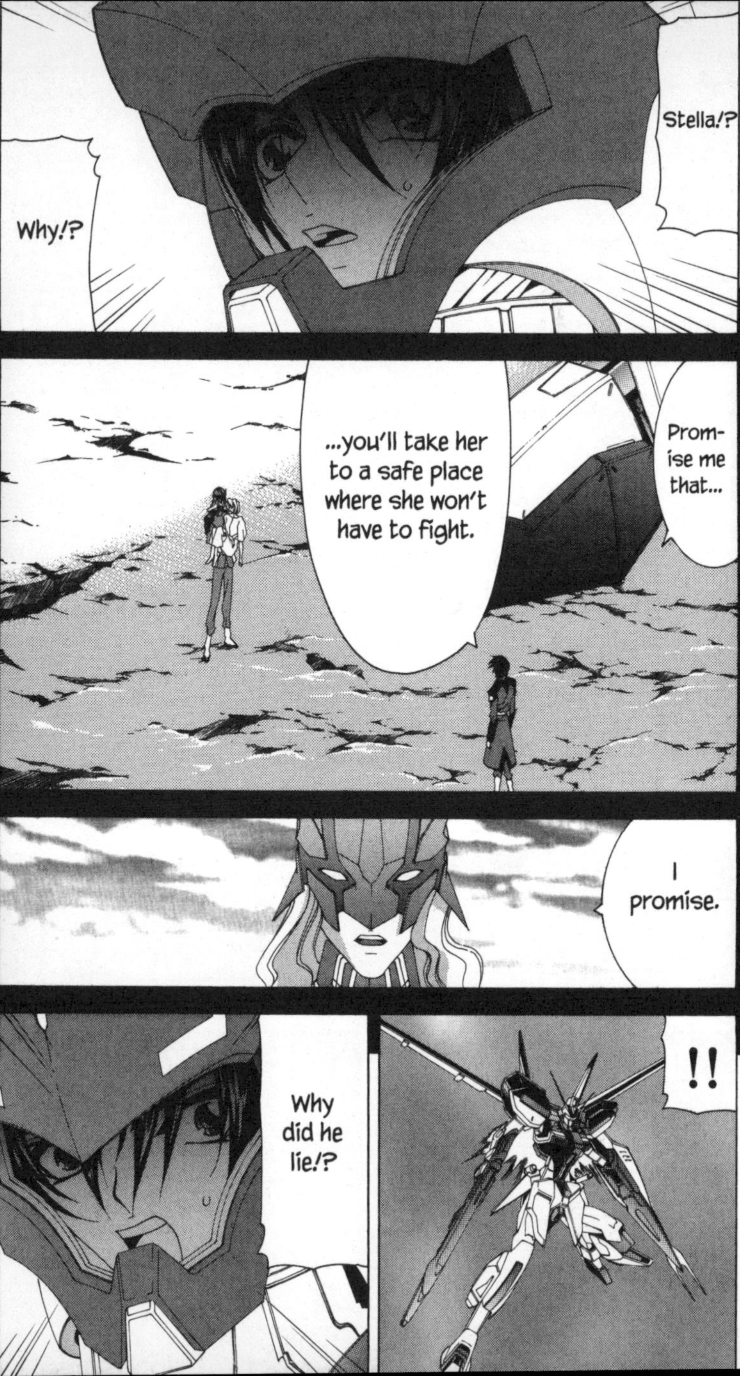
Stella!?
Why!?
Prom-ise me that...
...you'll take her to a safe place where she won't have to fight.
I promise.
!!
Why did he lie!?

Why!

LEAP

SLICE

!!

SLAMM

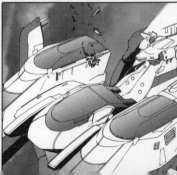

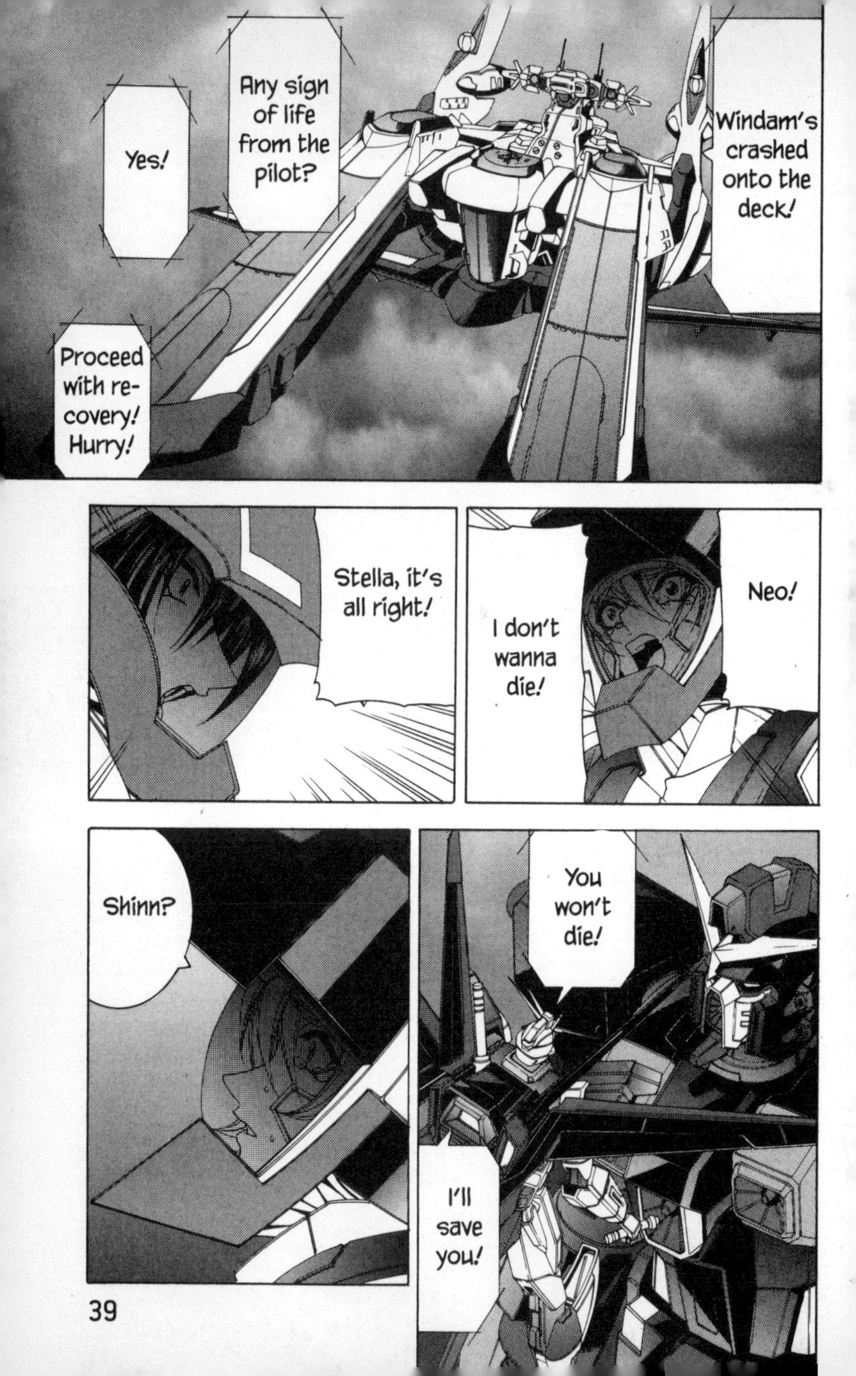

Windam's crashed onto the deck!
Any sign of life from the pilot?
Yes!
Proceed with re-covery! Hurry!
Neo!
I don't wanna die!
Stella, it's all right!
You won't die!
I'll save you!
Shinn?

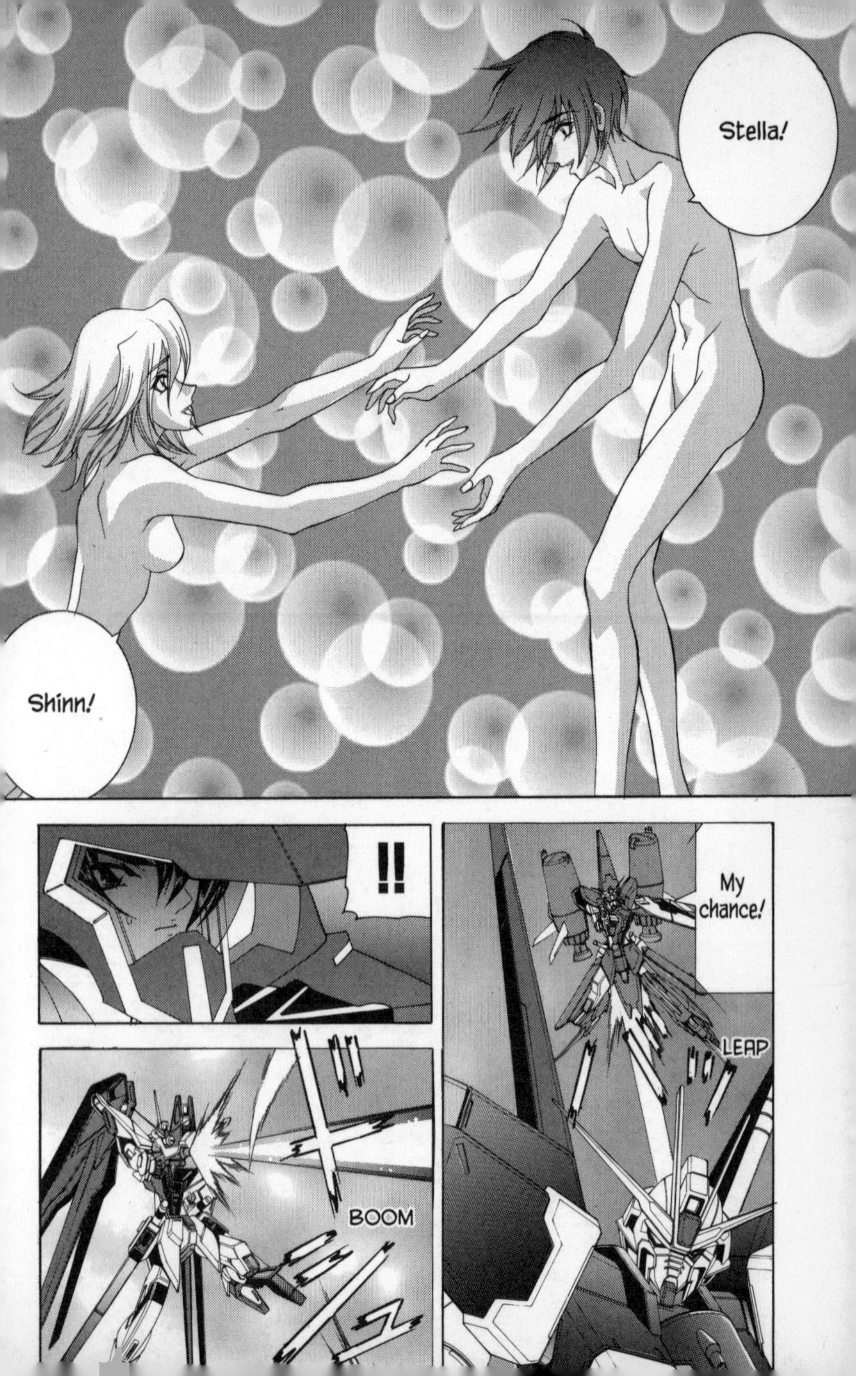
Stella!
Shinn!
My chance!
LEAP
!!
BOOM

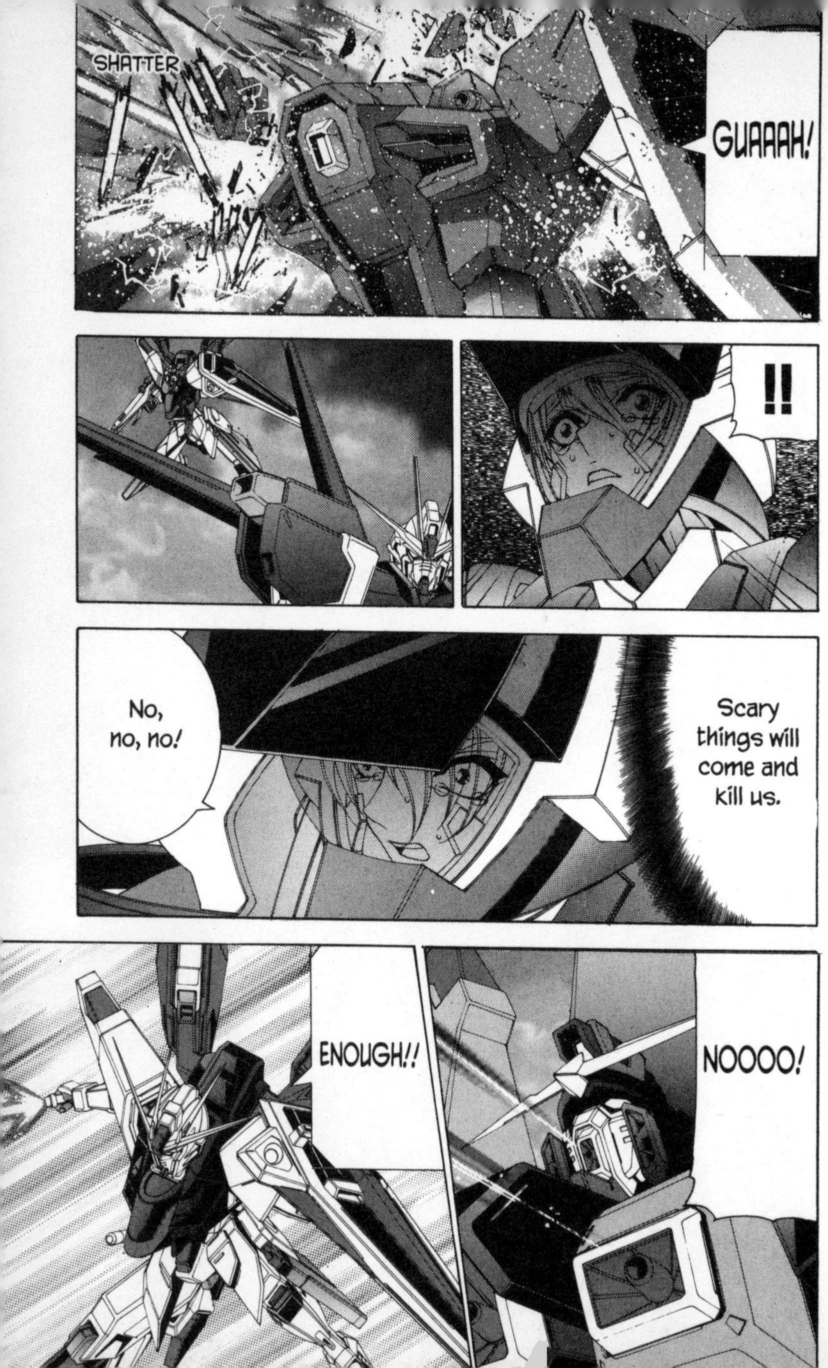
GUAAAH!
SHATTER
!!
Scary things will come and kill us.
No, no, no!
NOOOO!
ENOUGH!!

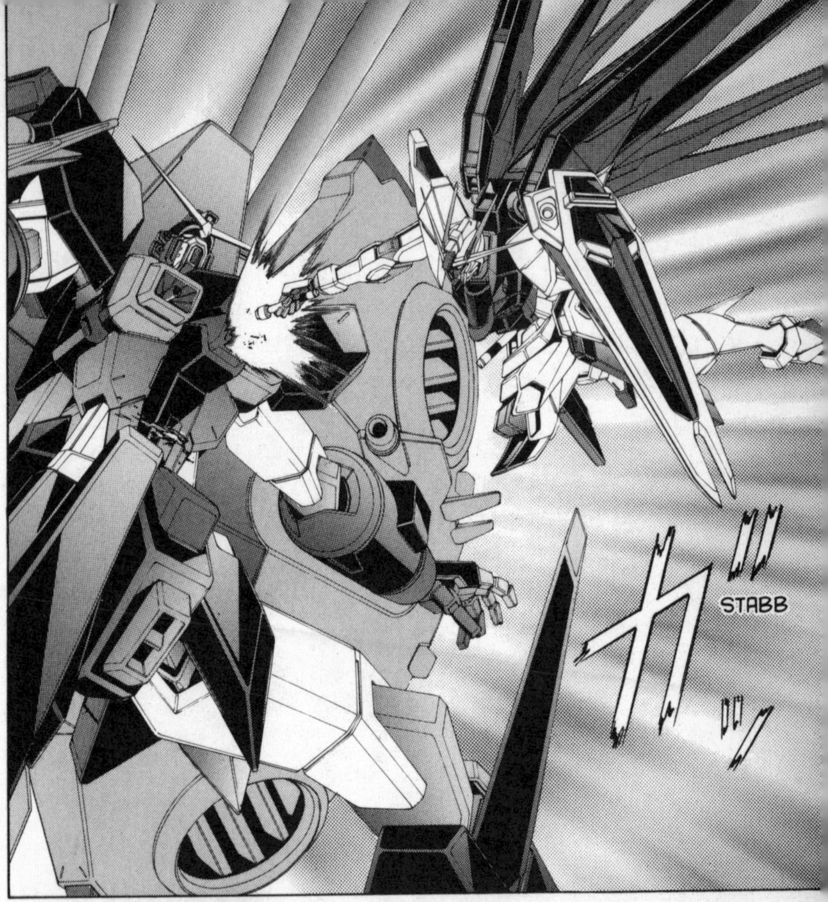
STABB
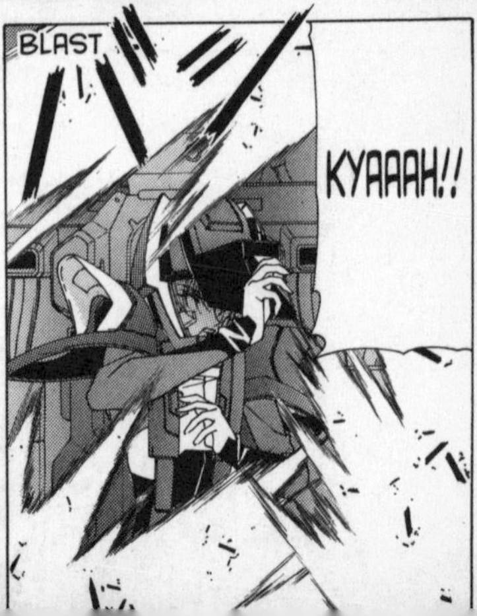
BLAST
KYAAAH!!
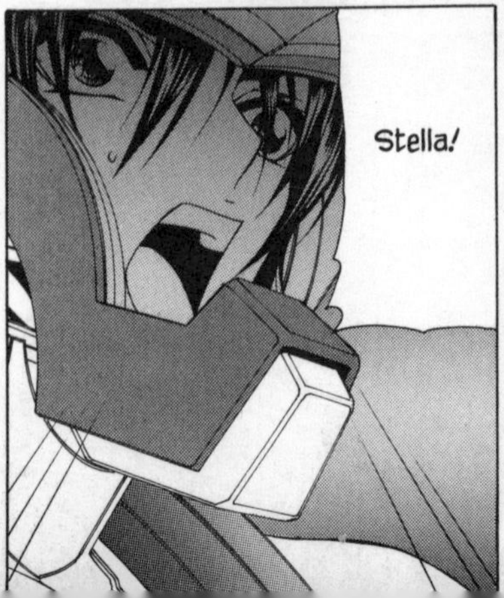
Stella!

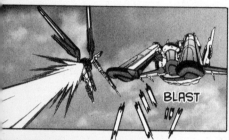

BLAST

URGH...

Stella!
Stella!!

Stella!
Wake up!

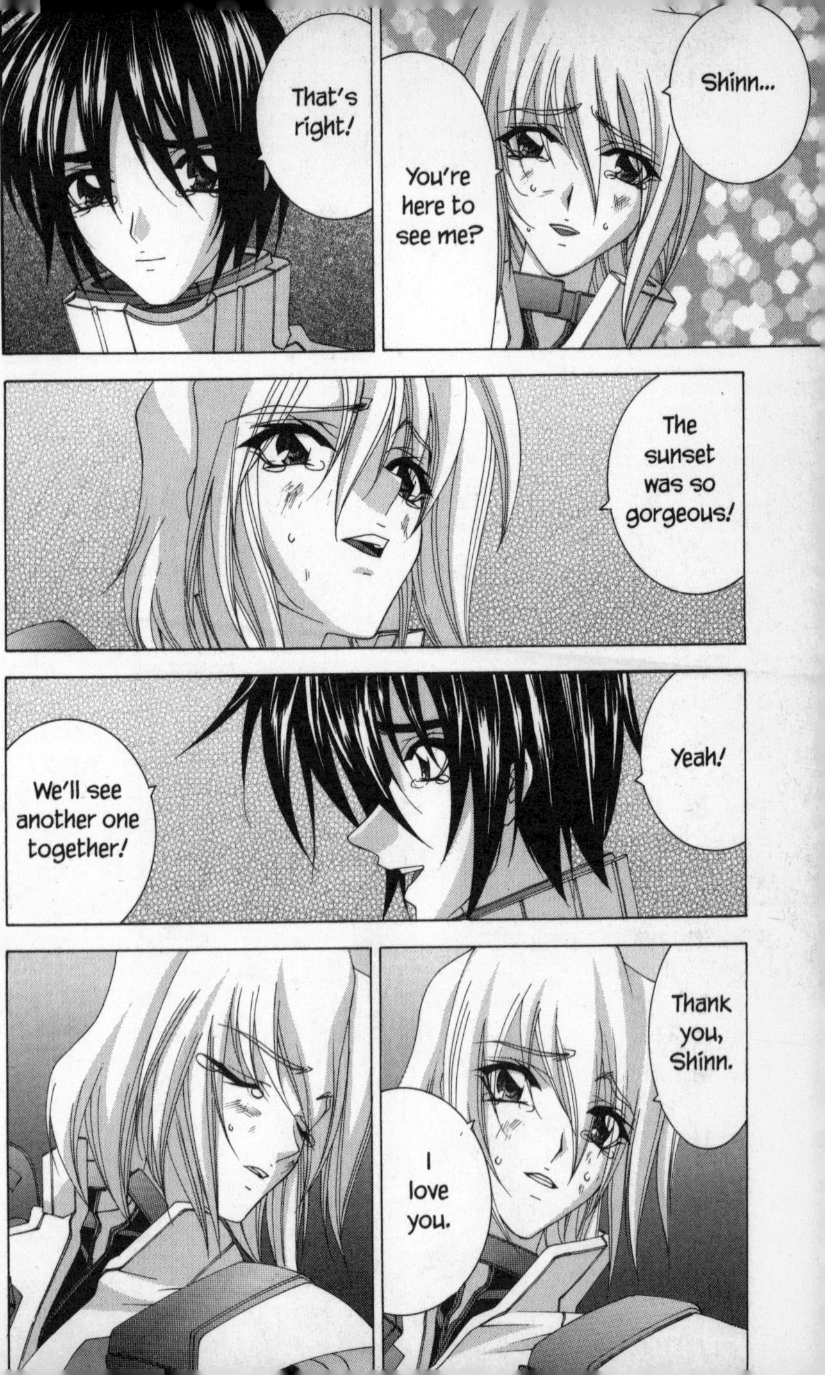
Shinn...
You're here to see me?
That's right!
The sunset was so gorgeous!
Yeah!
We'll see another one together!
Thank you, Shinn.
I love you.

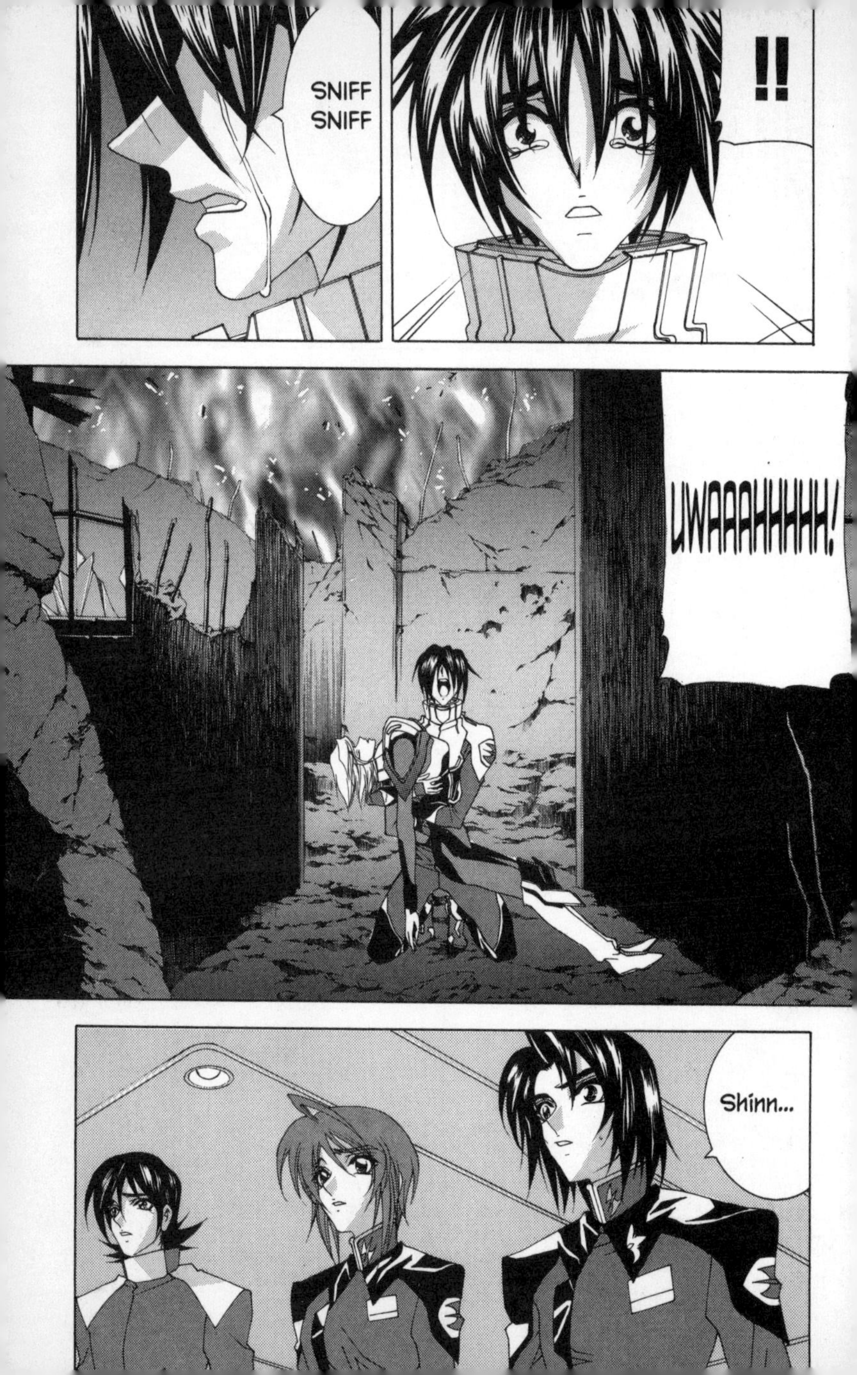
!!
SNIFF SNIFF
UWAAAHHHH!
Shinn...

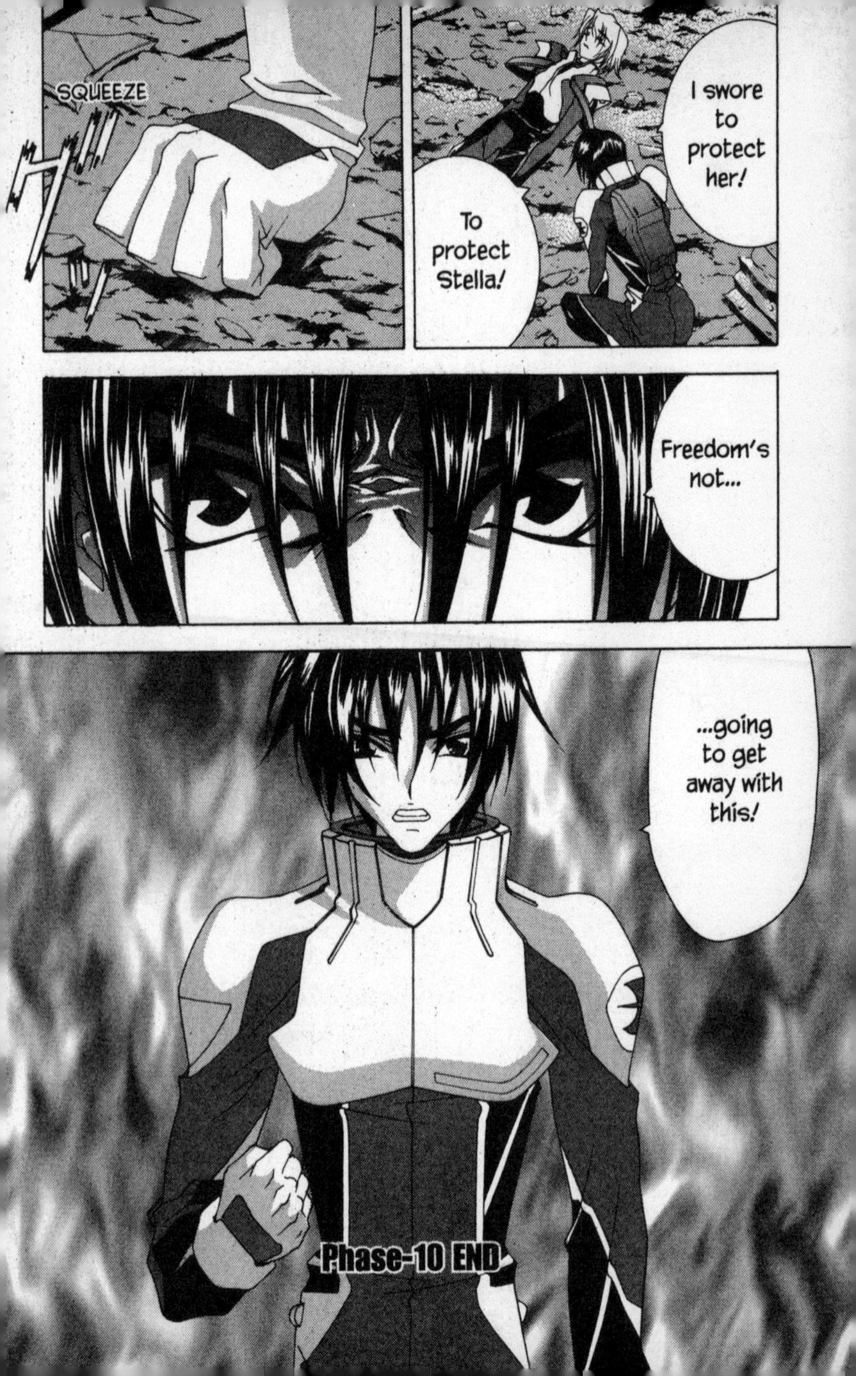
I swore to protect her!
To protect Stella!
SQUEEZE
Freedom's not...
...going to get away with this!
Phase-10 END

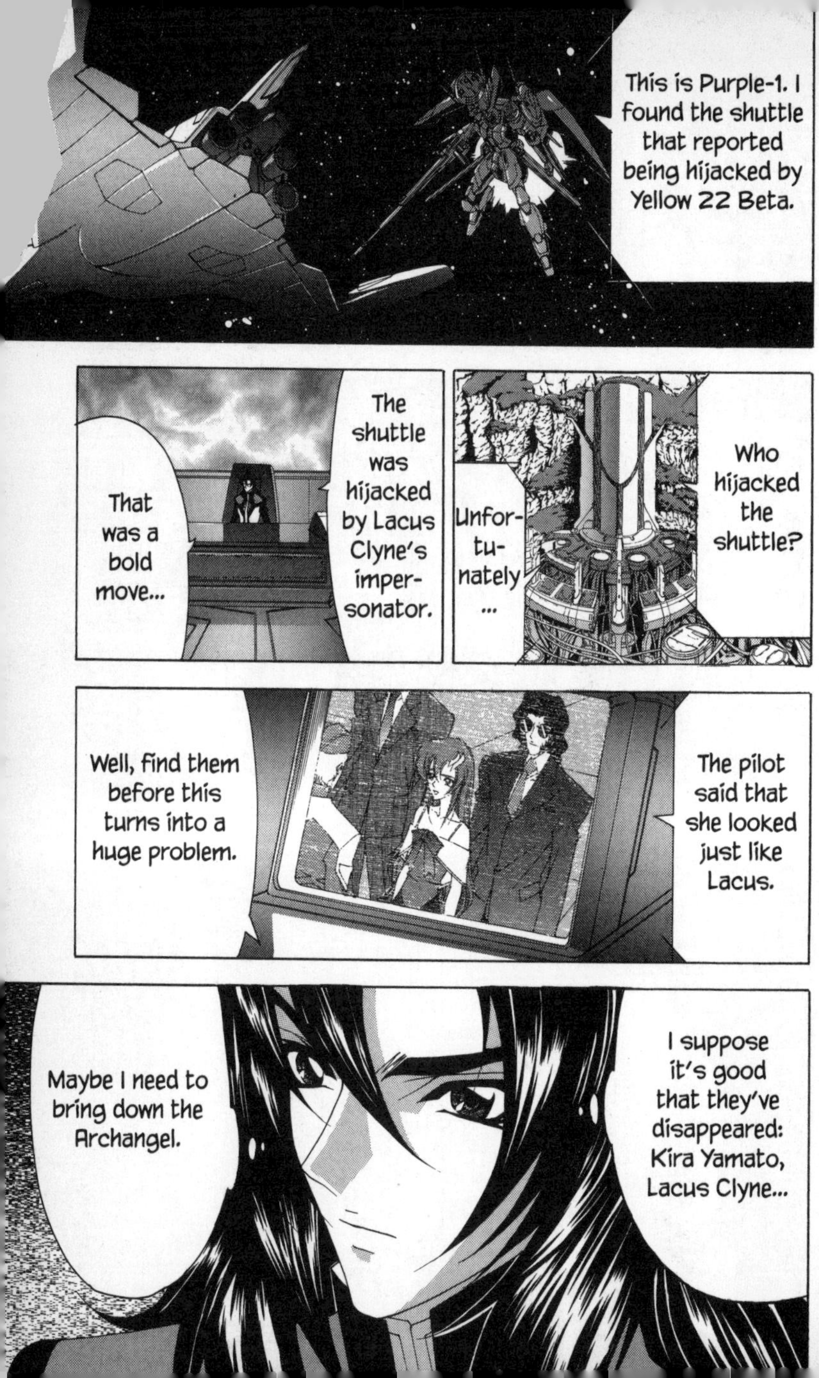
This is Purple-1. I found the shuttle that reported being hijacked by Yellow 22 Beta.
Who hijacked the shuttle?
Unfortunately...
The shuttle was hijacked by Lacus Clyne's impersonator.
That was a bold move...
The pilot said that she looked just like Lacus.
Well, find them before this turns into a huge problem.
I suppose it's good that they've disappeared: Kira Yamato, Lacus Clyne...
Maybe I need to bring down the Archangel.

Phase-11 Seen by the World

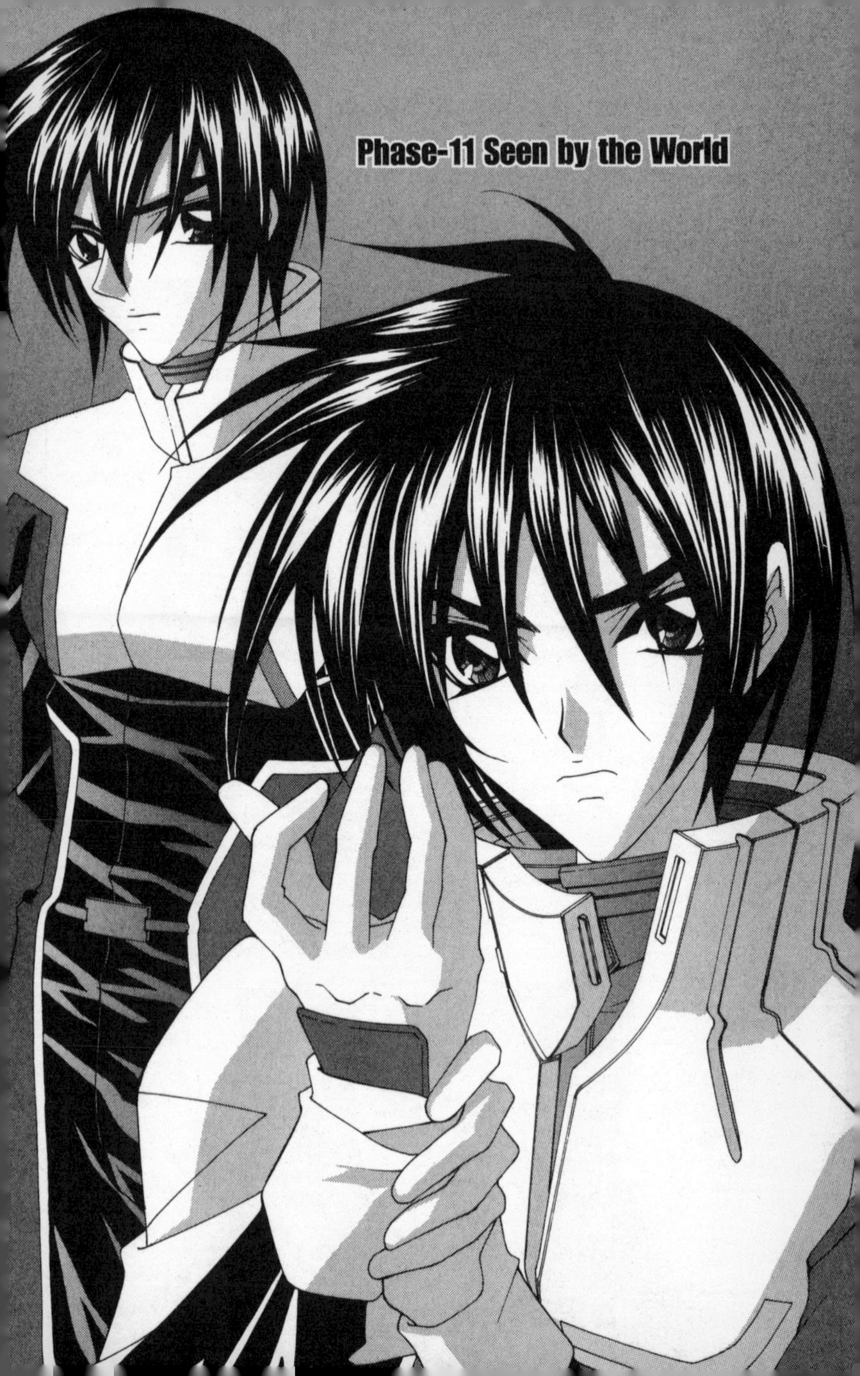

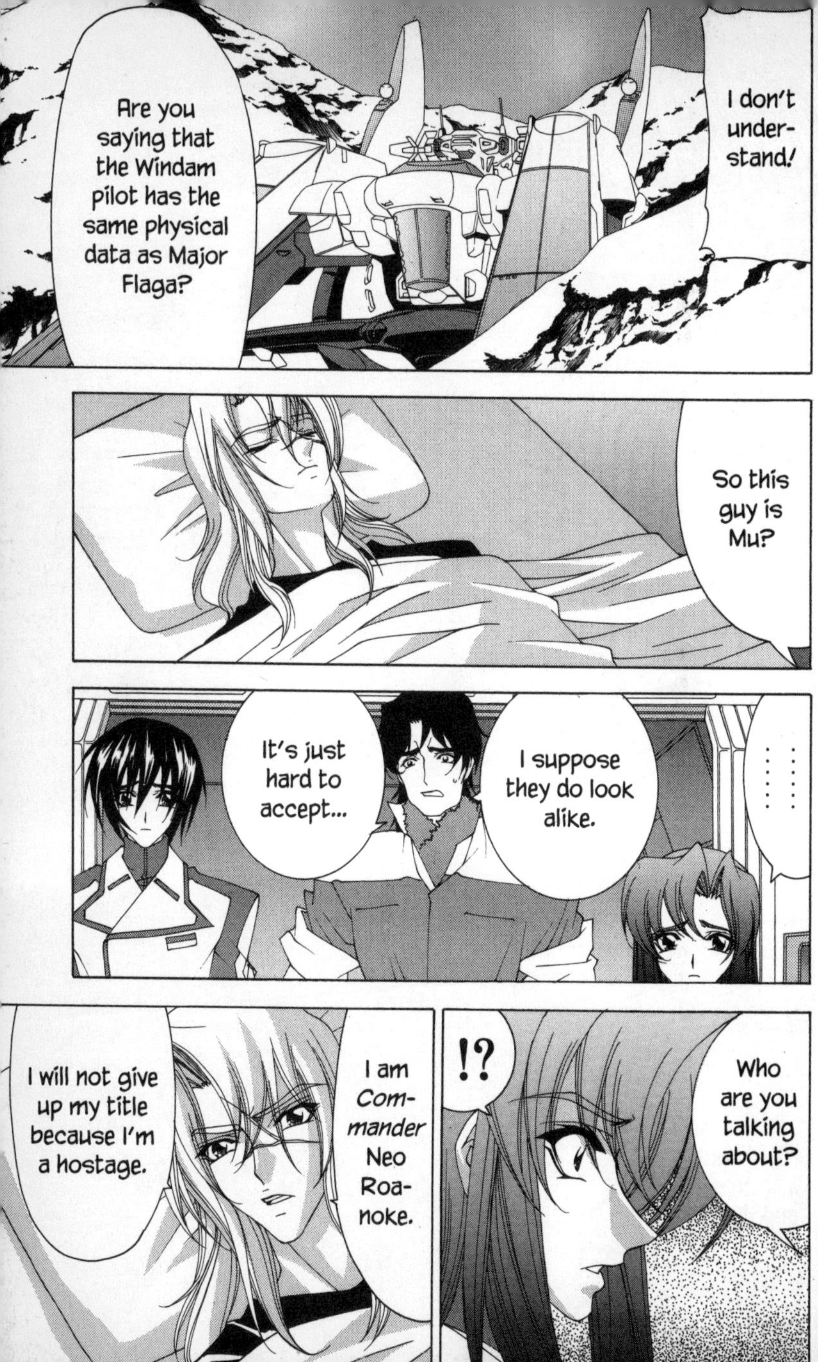
I don't under-stand!
Are you saying that the Windam pilot has the same physical data as Major Flaga?
So this guy is Mu?
......
I suppose they do look alike.
It's just hard to accept...
Who are you talking about?
!?
I am *Commander* Neo Roanoke.
I will not give up my title because I'm a hostage.

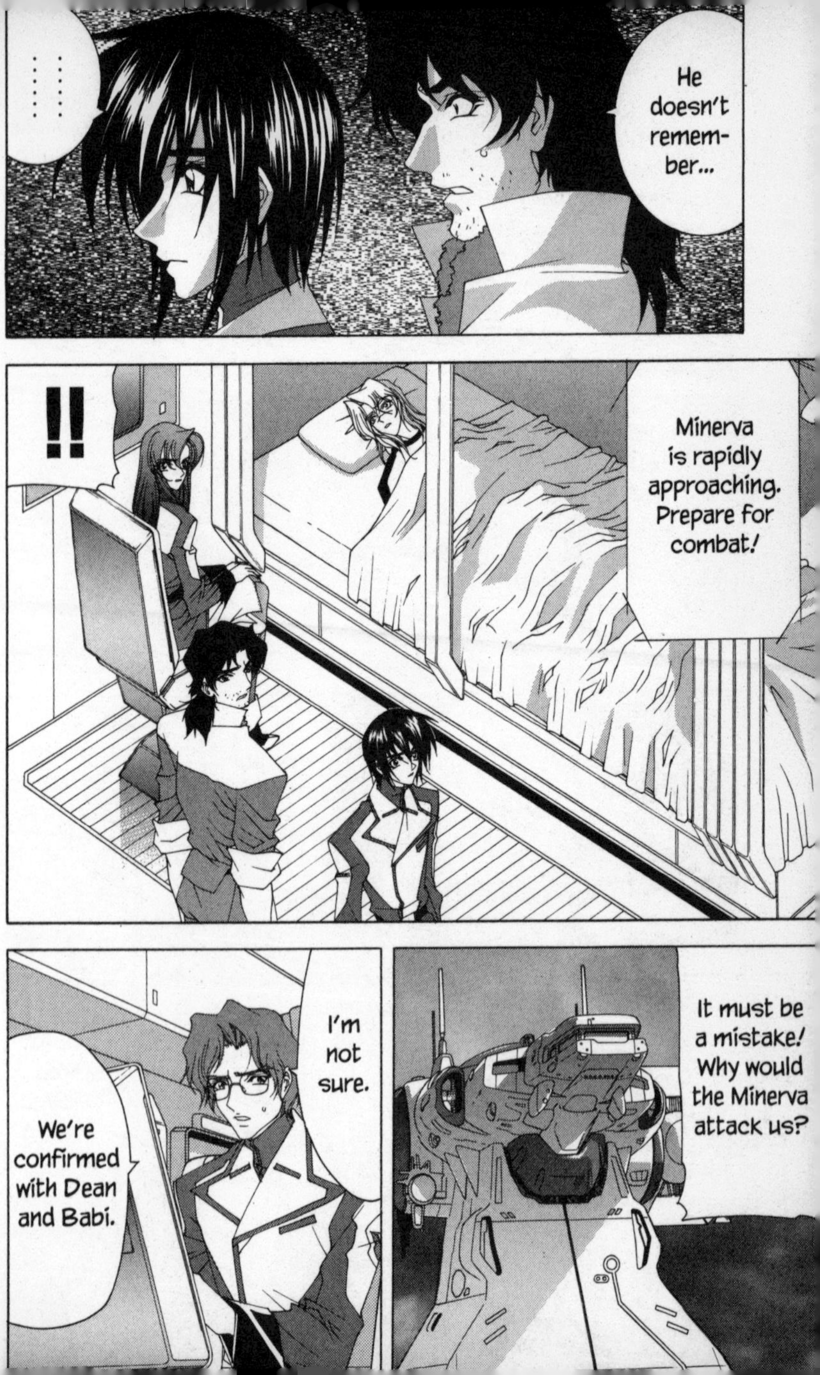
He doesn't remember...
......
Minerva is rapidly approaching. Prepare for combat!
!!
It must be a mistake! Why would the Minerva attack us?
I'm not sure.
We're confirmed with Dean and Babi.

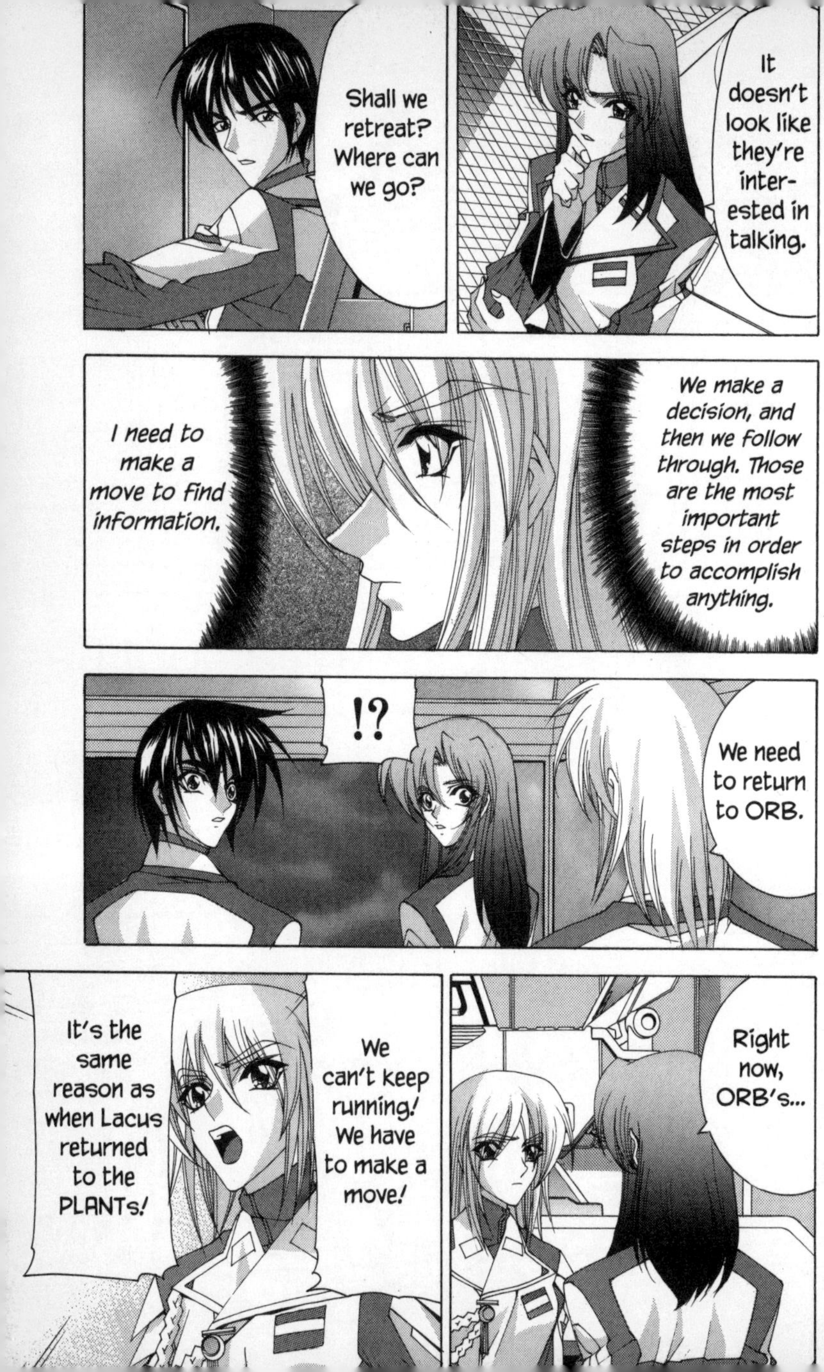
It doesn't look like they're interested in talking.
Shall we retreat? Where can we go?
We make a decision, and then we follow through. Those are the most important steps in order to accomplish anything.
I need to make a move to find information.
We need to return to ORB.
!?
Right now, ORB's...
We can't keep running! We have to make a move!
It's the same reason as when Lacus returned to the PLANTs!

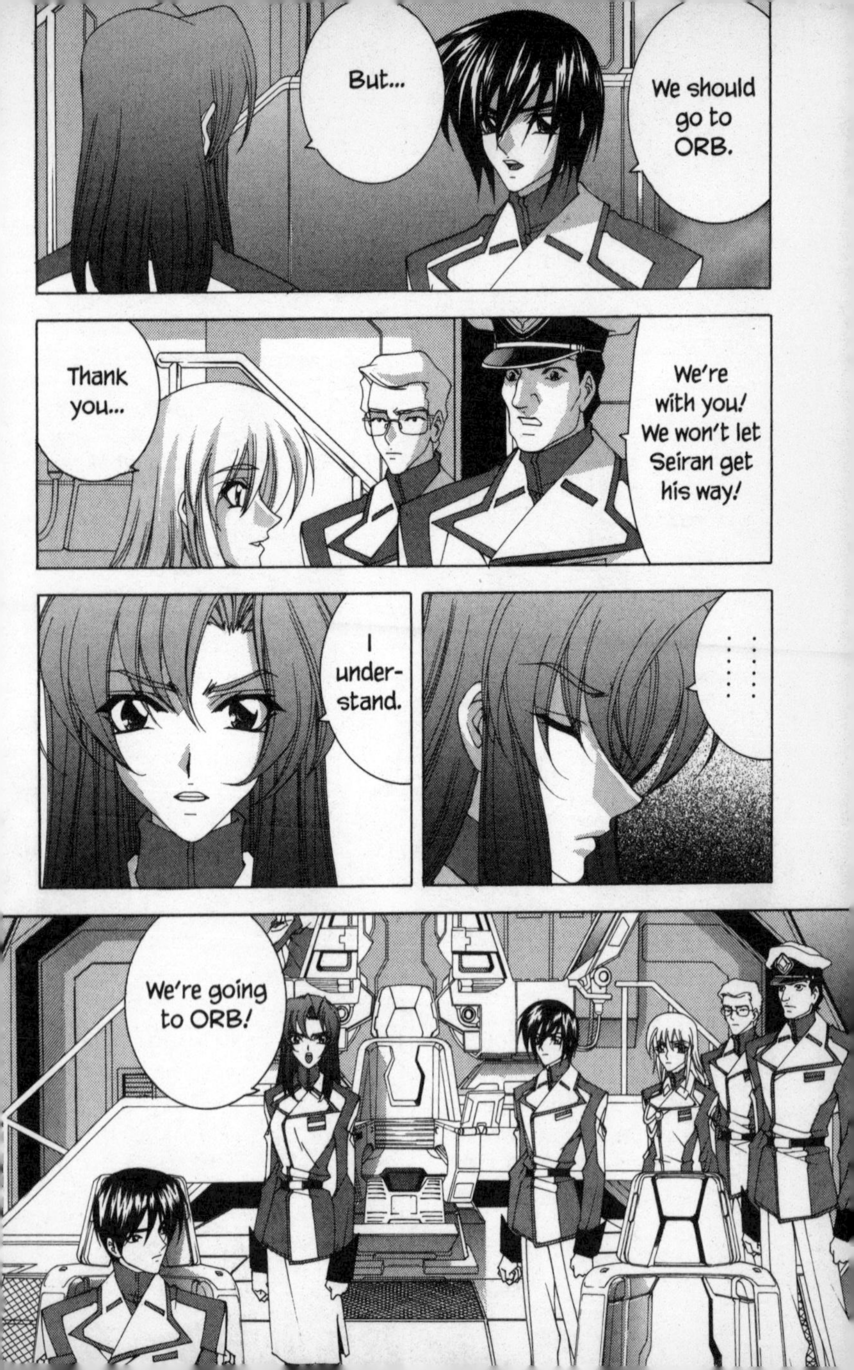
We should go to ORB.
But...
We're with you! We won't let Seiran get his way!
Thank you...
......
I under-stand.
We're going to ORB!

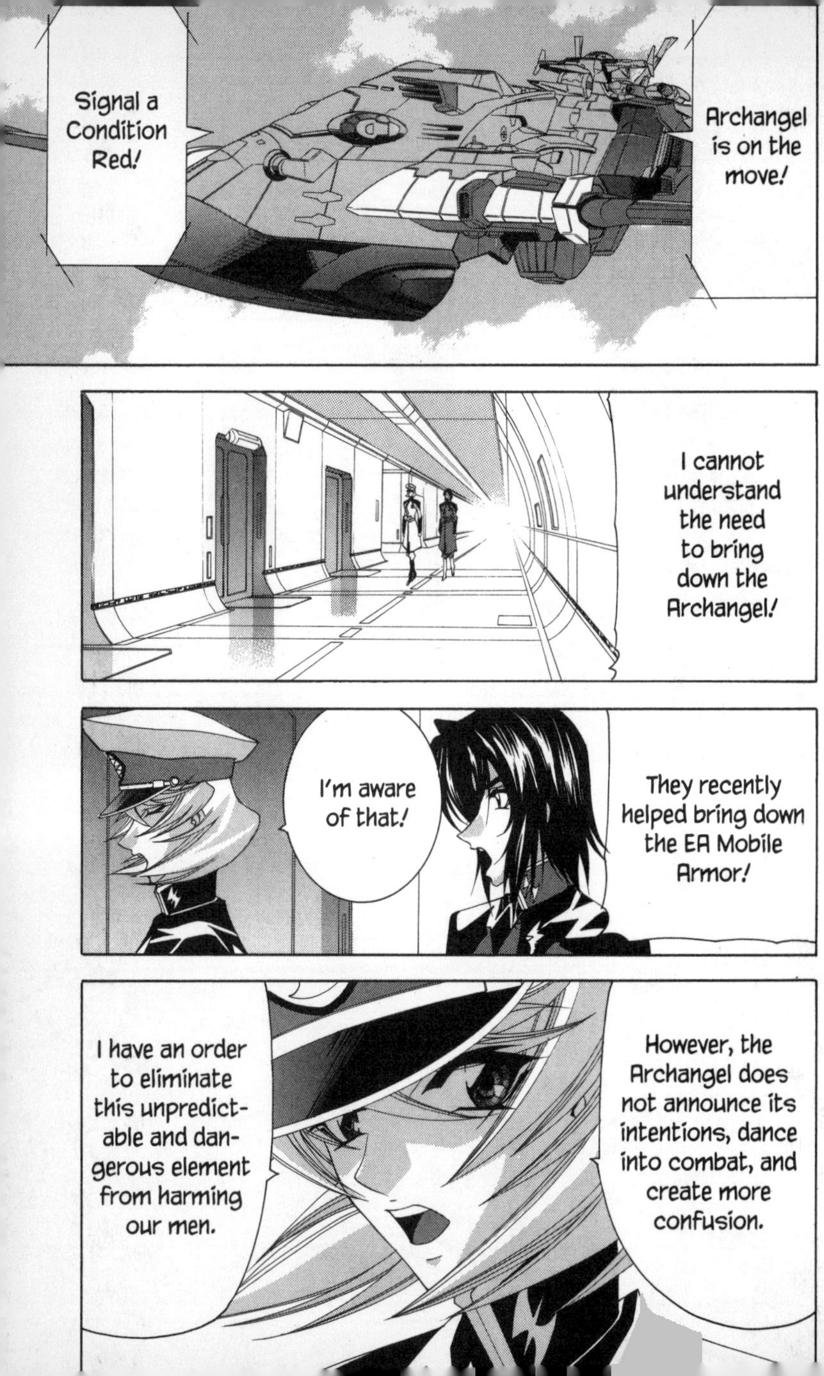
Archangel is on the move!
Signal a Condition Red!
I cannot understand the need to bring down the Archangel!
They recently helped bring down the EA Mobile Armor!
I'm aware of that!
However, the Archangel does not announce its intentions, dance into combat, and create more confusion.
I have an order to eliminate this unpredict-able and dan-gerous element from harming our men.

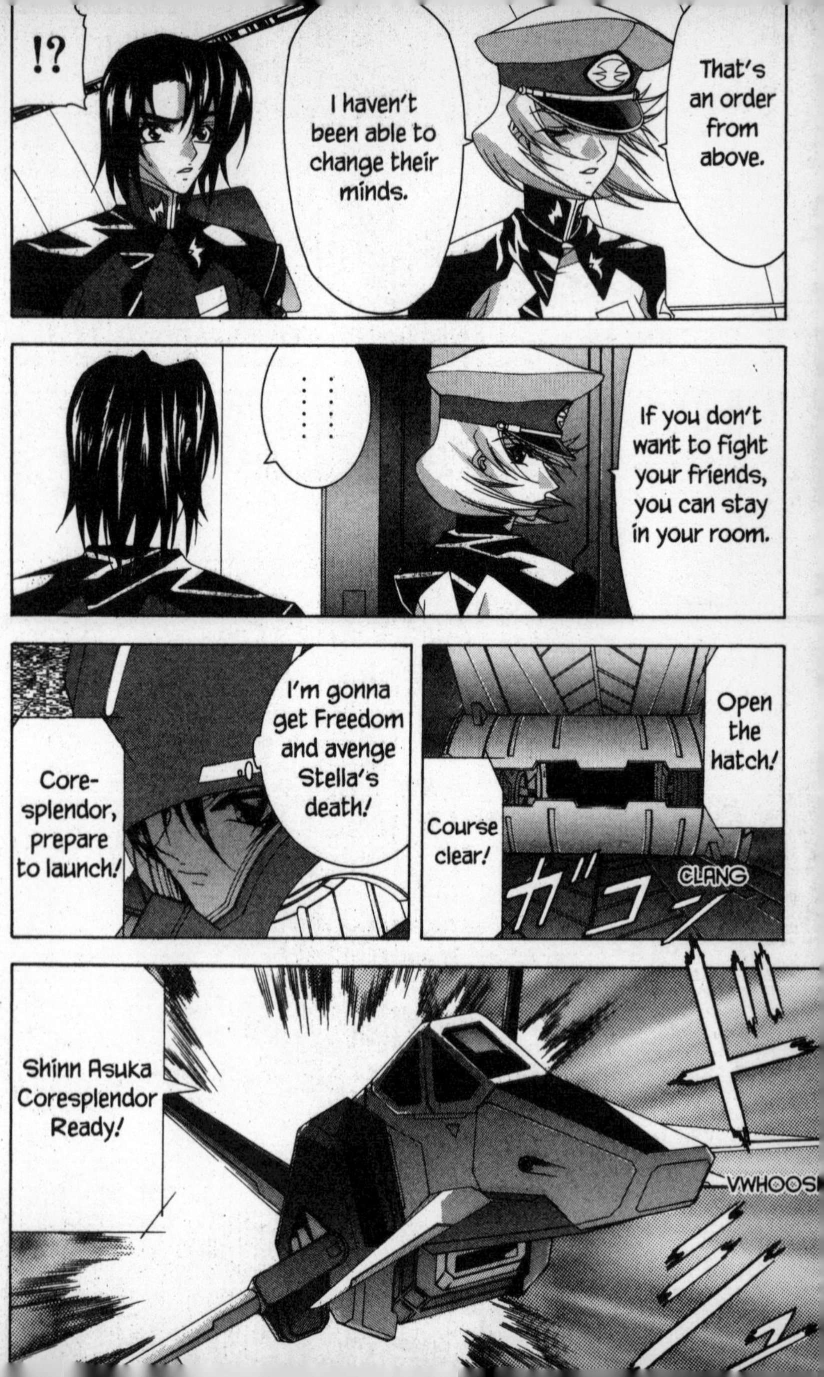
That's an order from above.
I haven't been able to change their minds.
!?
If you don't want to fight your friends, you can stay in your room.
......
Open the hatch!
Course clear!
ガコン
CLANG
I'm gonna get Freedom and avenge Stella's death!
Core-splendor, prepare to launch!
Shinn Asuka Coresplendor Ready!
VWHOOS

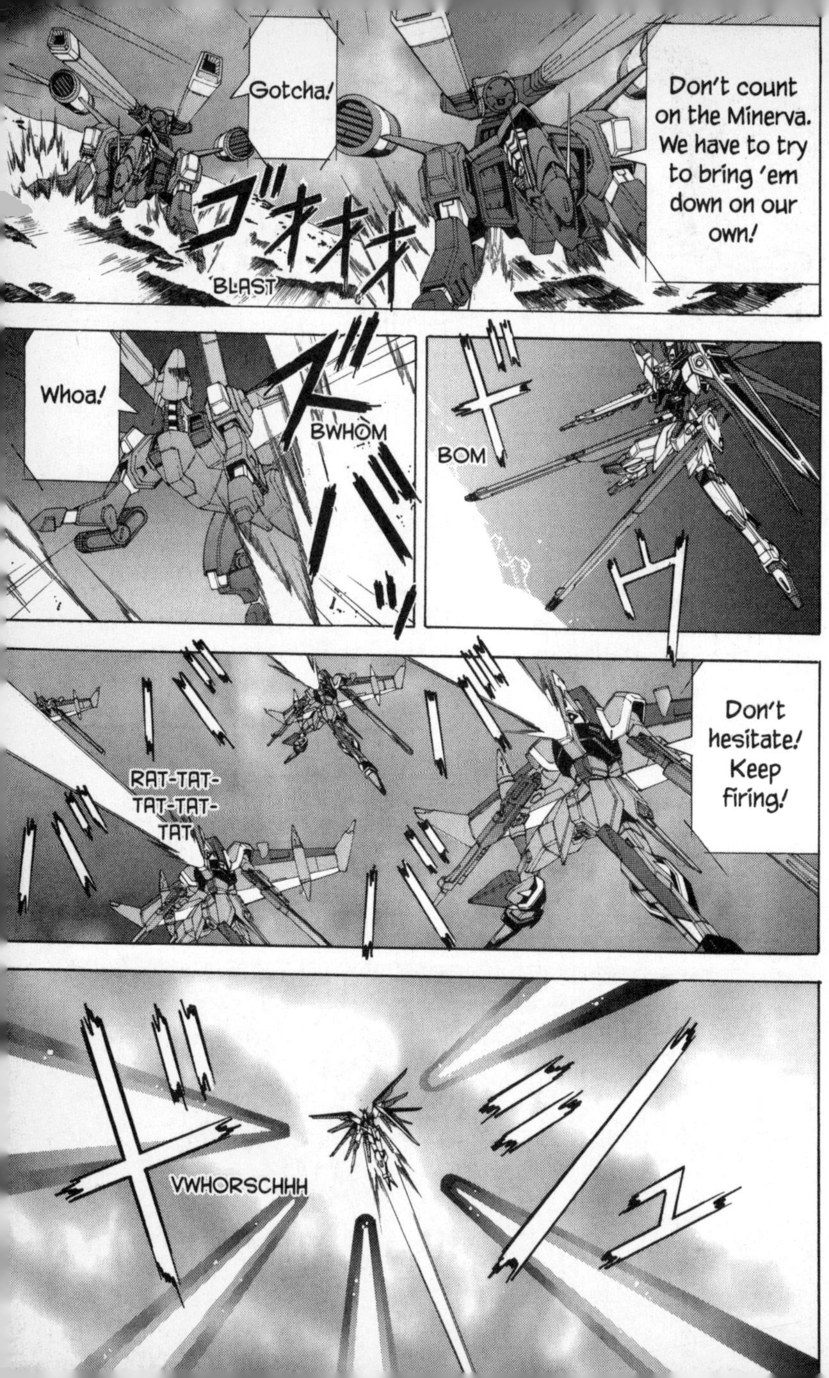

Don't count on the Minerva. We have to try to bring 'em down on our own!
Gotcha!
BLAST
BOM
BWHOM
Whoa!
Don't hesitate! Keep firing!
RAT-TAT-TAT-TAT-TAT
VWHORSCHHH

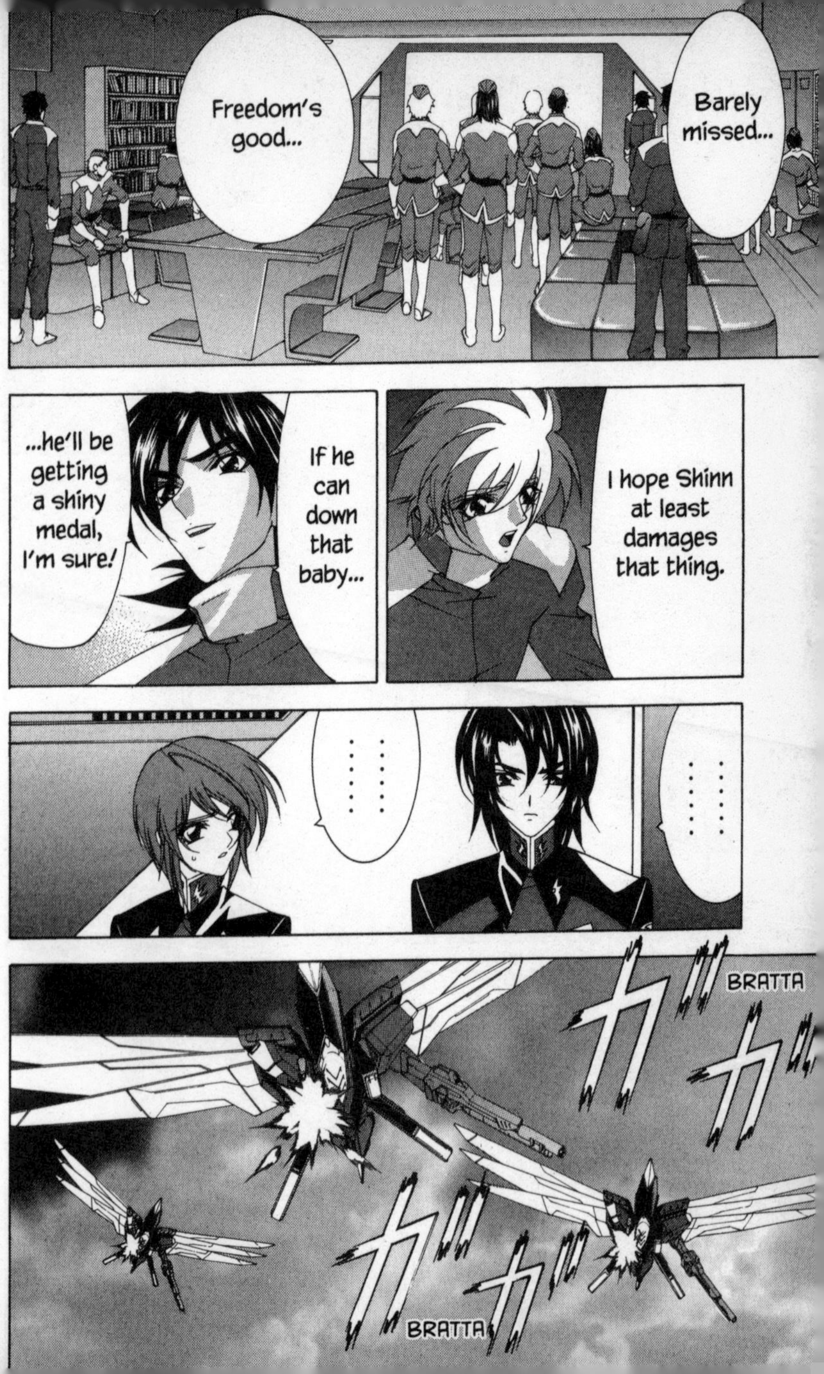
Barely missed...
Freedom's good...
I hope Shinn at least damages that thing.
If he can down that baby...
...he'll be getting a shiny medal, I'm sure!
......
......
BRATTA
BRATTA

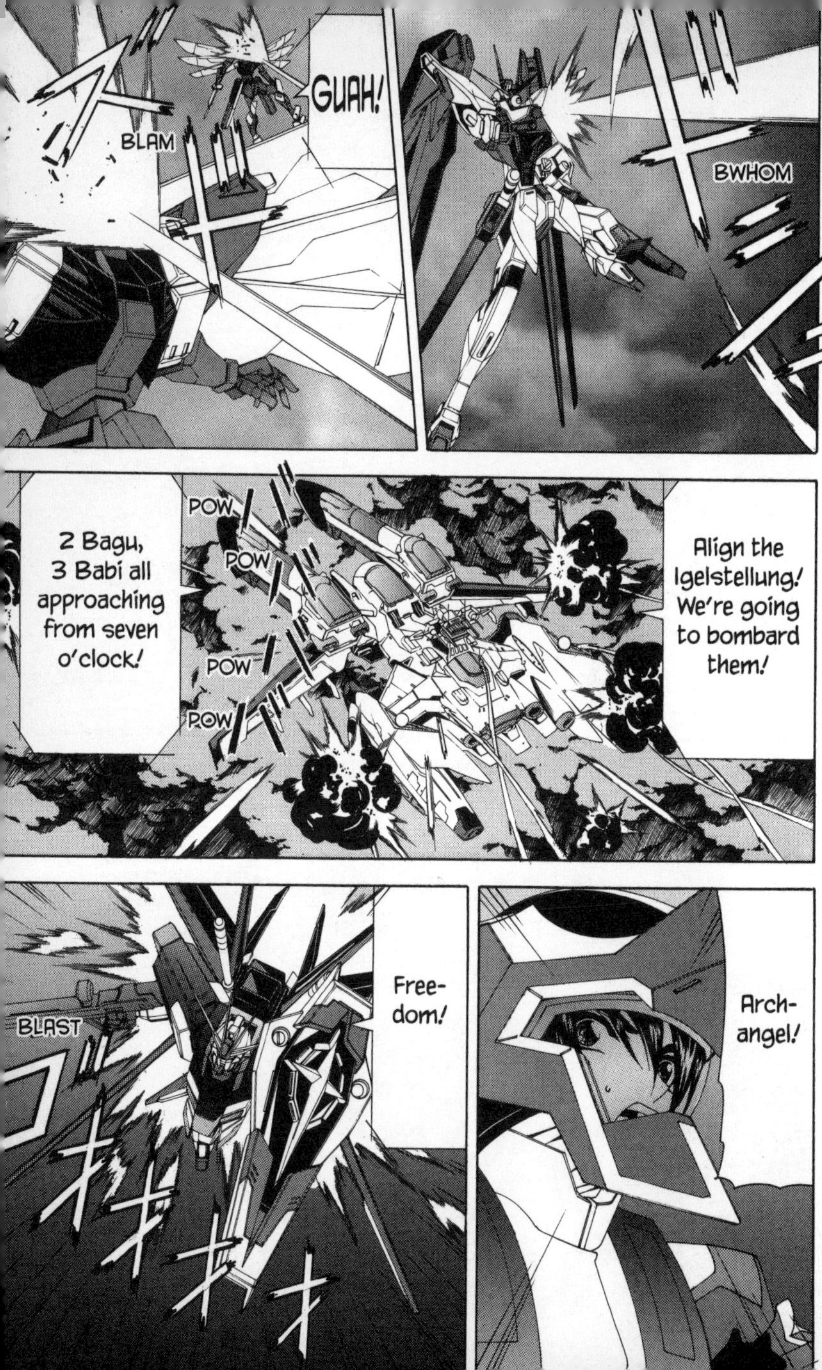
BWHOM
GUAH!
BLAM
Align the Igelstellung! We're going to bombard them!
POW
POW
POW
POW
2 Bagu, 3 Babi all approaching from seven o'clock!
Arch-angel!
Free-dom!
BLAST

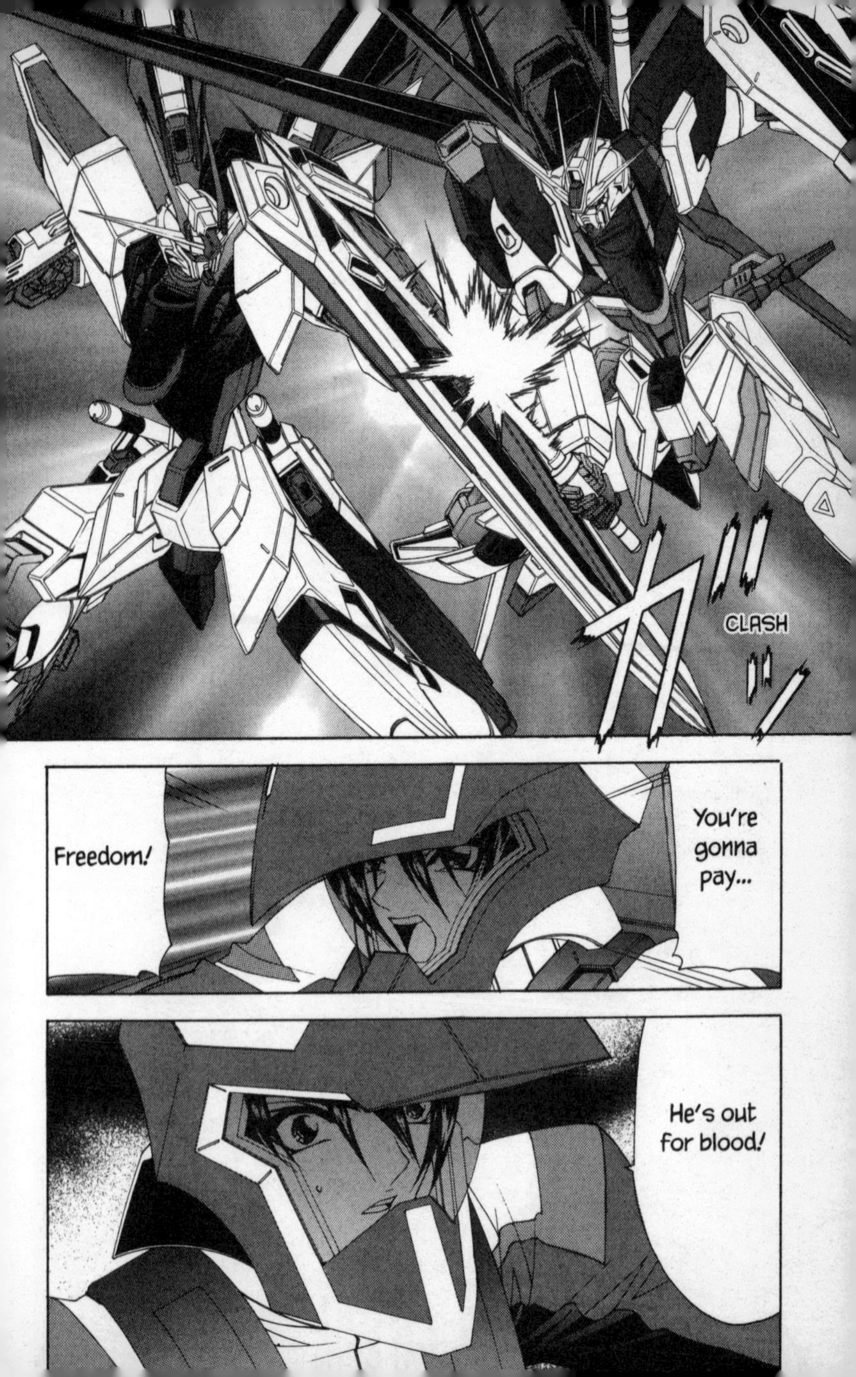
CLASH
You're gonna pay...
Freedom!
He's out for blood!

Meyrin, I want to communicate with the ship.

I am currently acting on orders to eliminate the Archangel.

This is Captain Talia Gladys of the Minerva. Can you hear me?

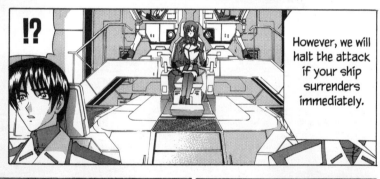

!?

However, we will halt the attack if your ship surrenders immediately.

This is Captain Murrue Ramius of the Arch-angel.

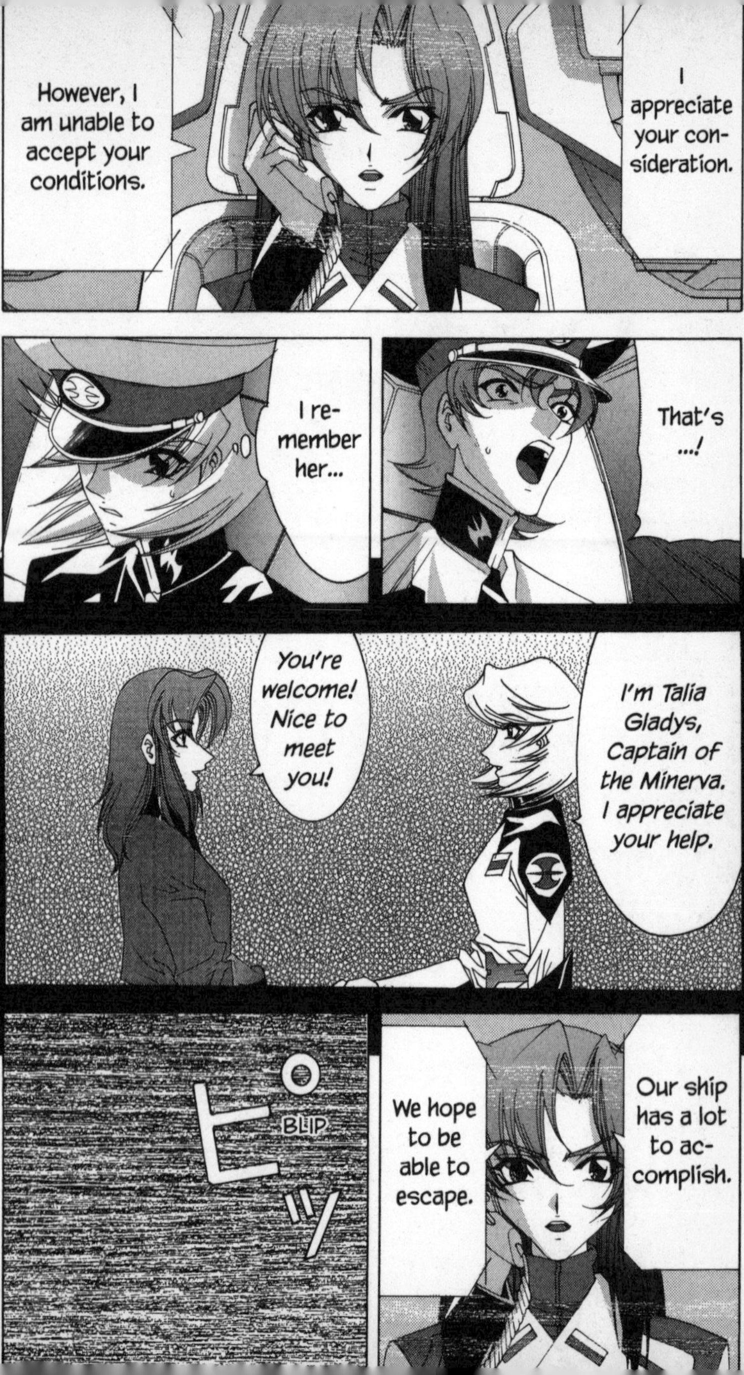
I appreciate your consideration.
However, I am unable to accept your conditions.
That's ...!
I remember her...
I'm Talia Gladys, Captain of the Minerva. I appreciate your help.
You're welcome! Nice to meet you!
Our ship has a lot to accomplish.
We hope to be able to escape.
BLIP

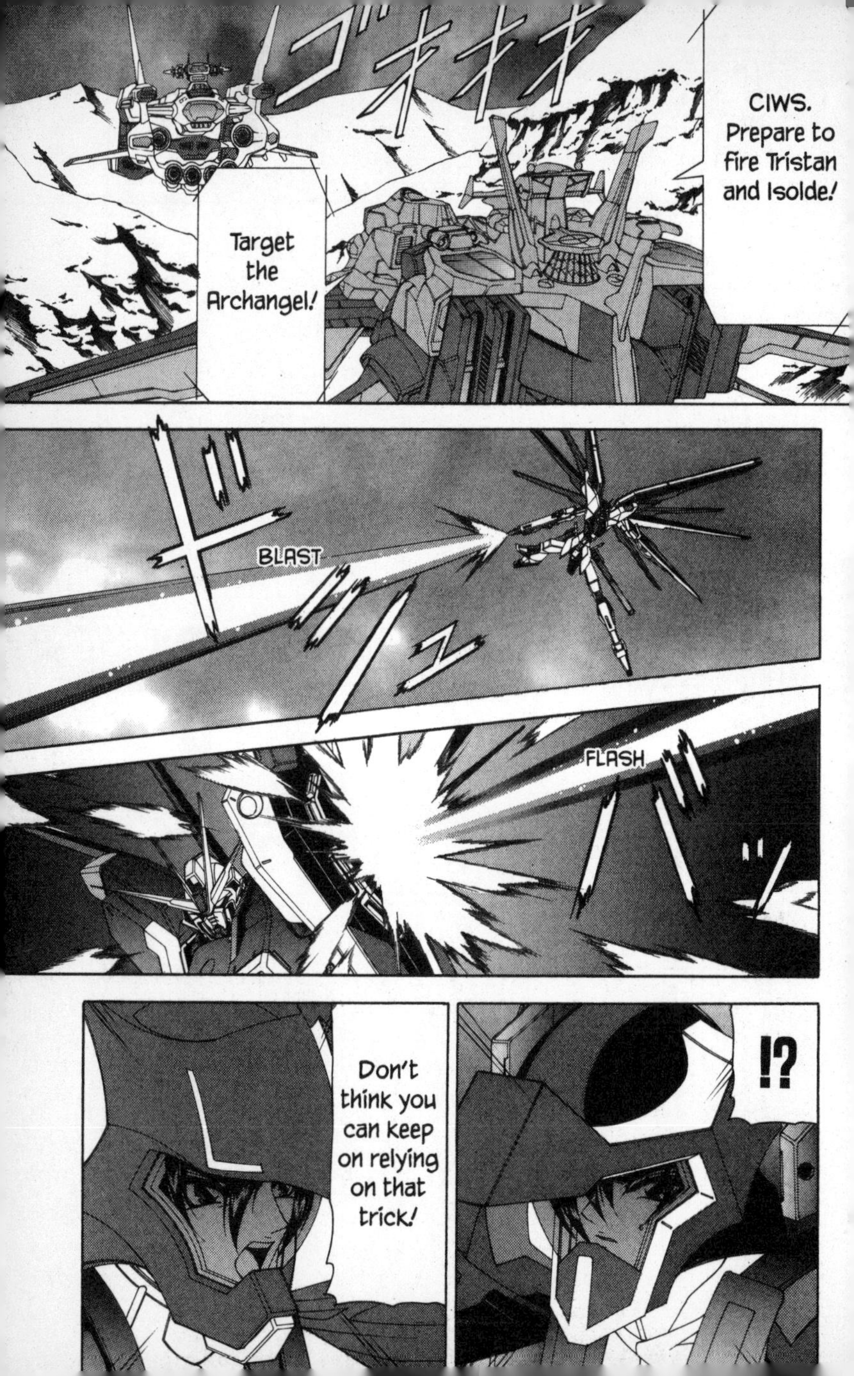
ゴオオオ
CIWS. Prepare to fire Tristan and Isolde!
Target the Archangel!
BLAST
FLASH
!?
Don't think you can keep on relying on that trick!

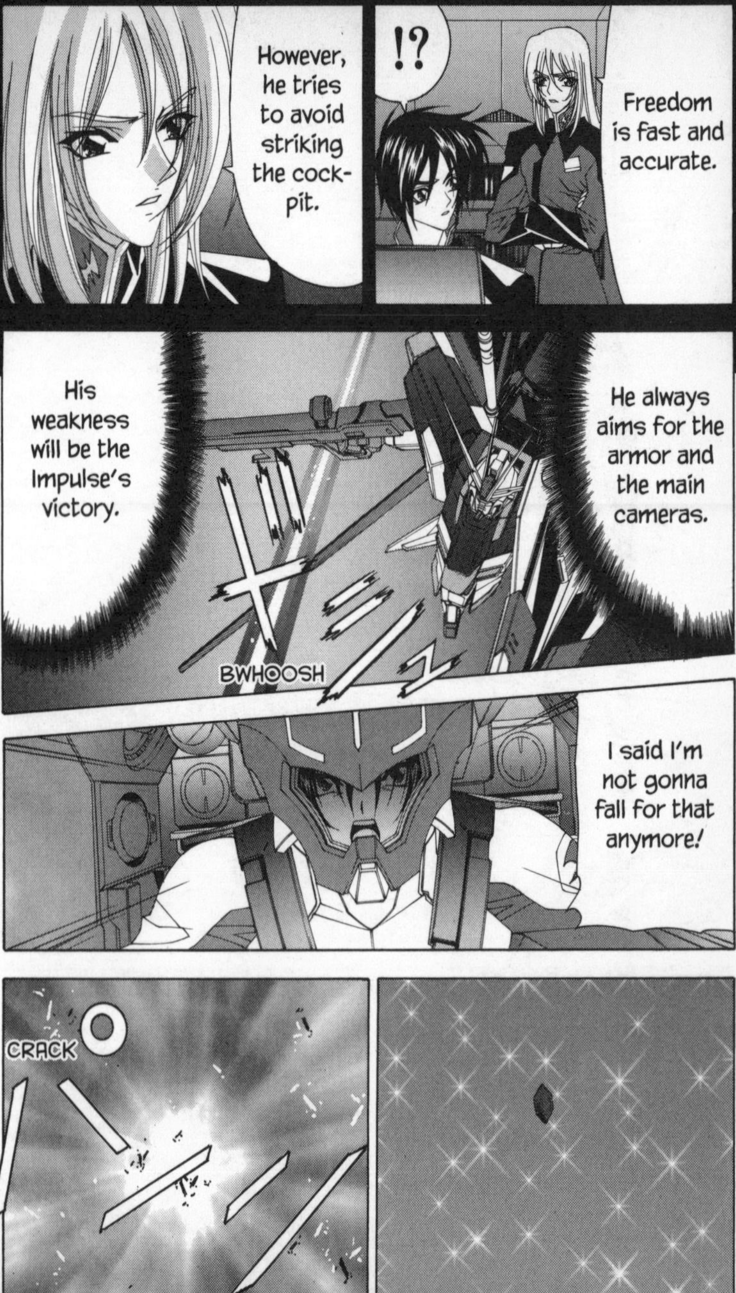
!?
Freedom is fast and accurate.
However, he tries to avoid striking the cock-pit.
He always aims for the armor and the main cameras.
His weakness will be the Impulse's victory.
BWHOOSH
I said I'm not gonna fall for that anymore!
CRACK

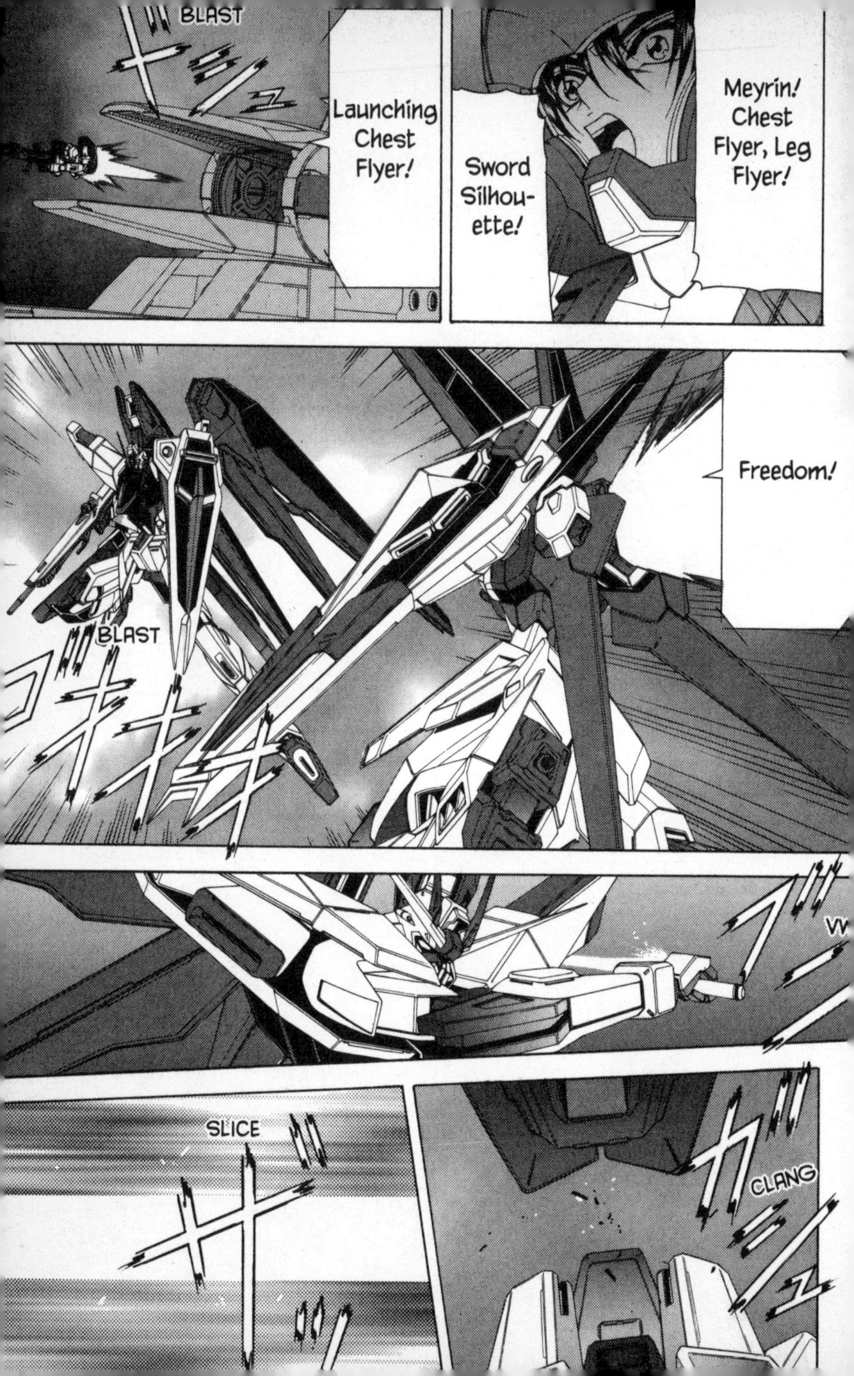
Meyrin! Chest Flyer, Leg Flyer!
Sword Silhou-ette!
BLAST
Launching Chest Flyer!
Freedom!
BLAST
CLANG
SLICE

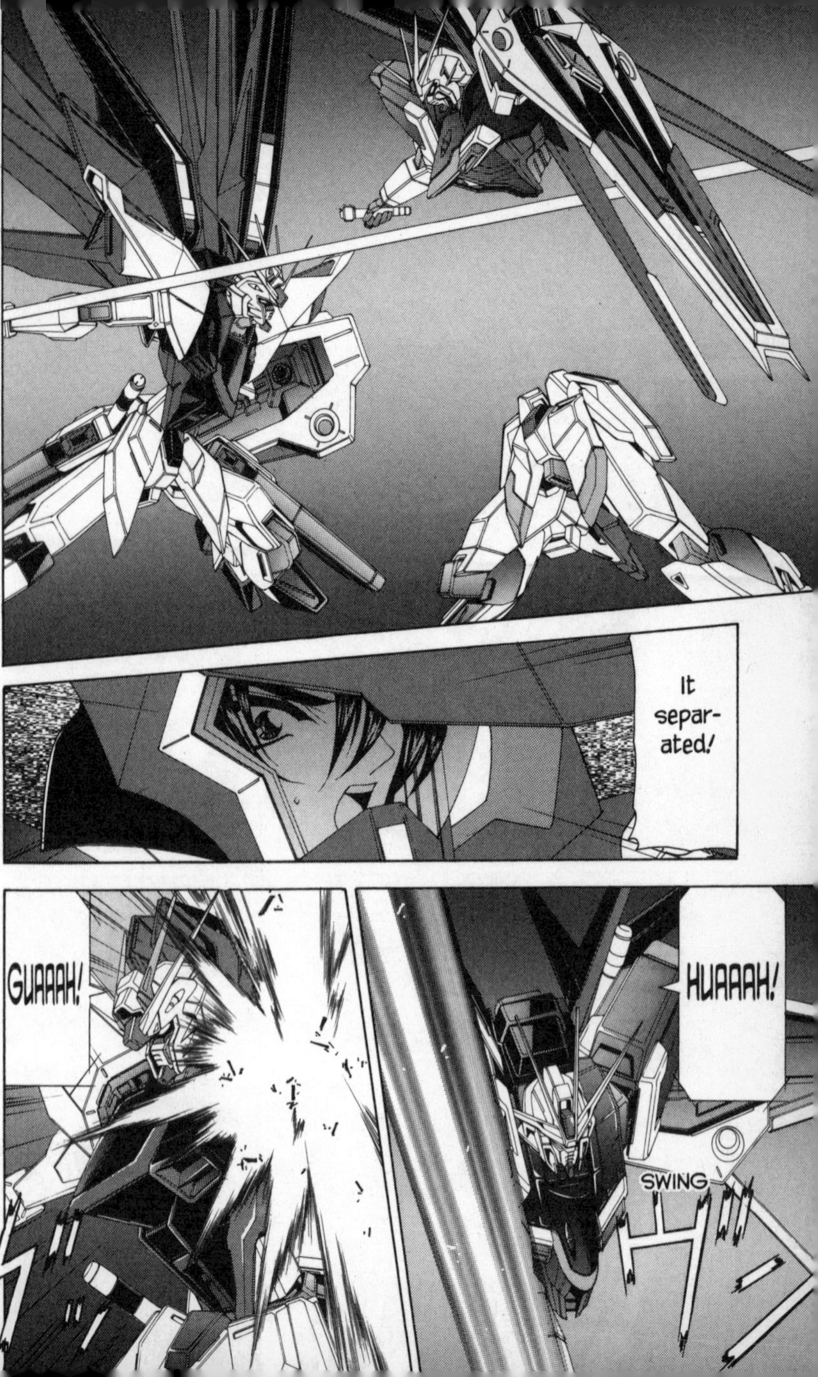
It separated!
HUAAAH!
SWING
GUAAAH!

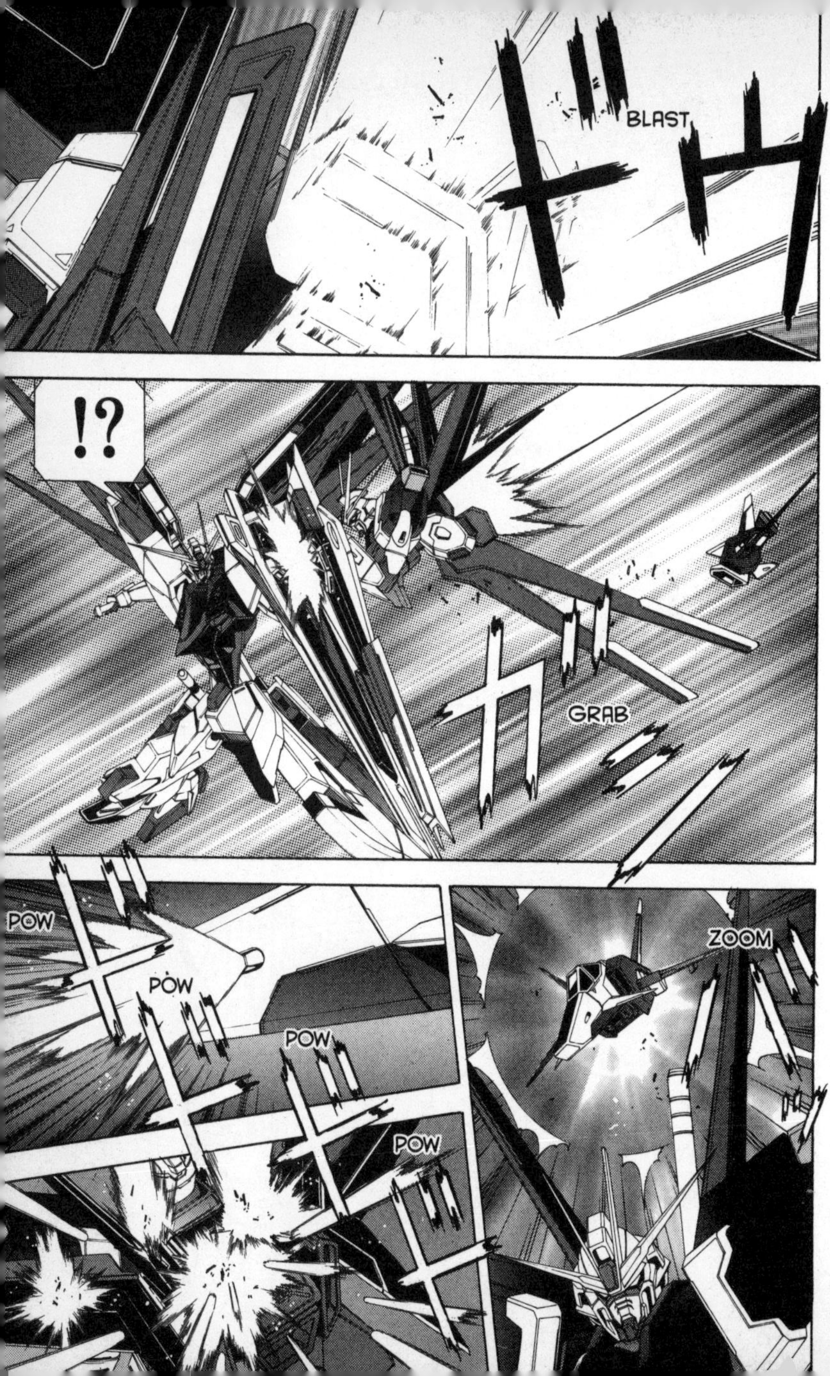
BLAST
!?
GRAB
ZOOM
POW
POW
POW
POW

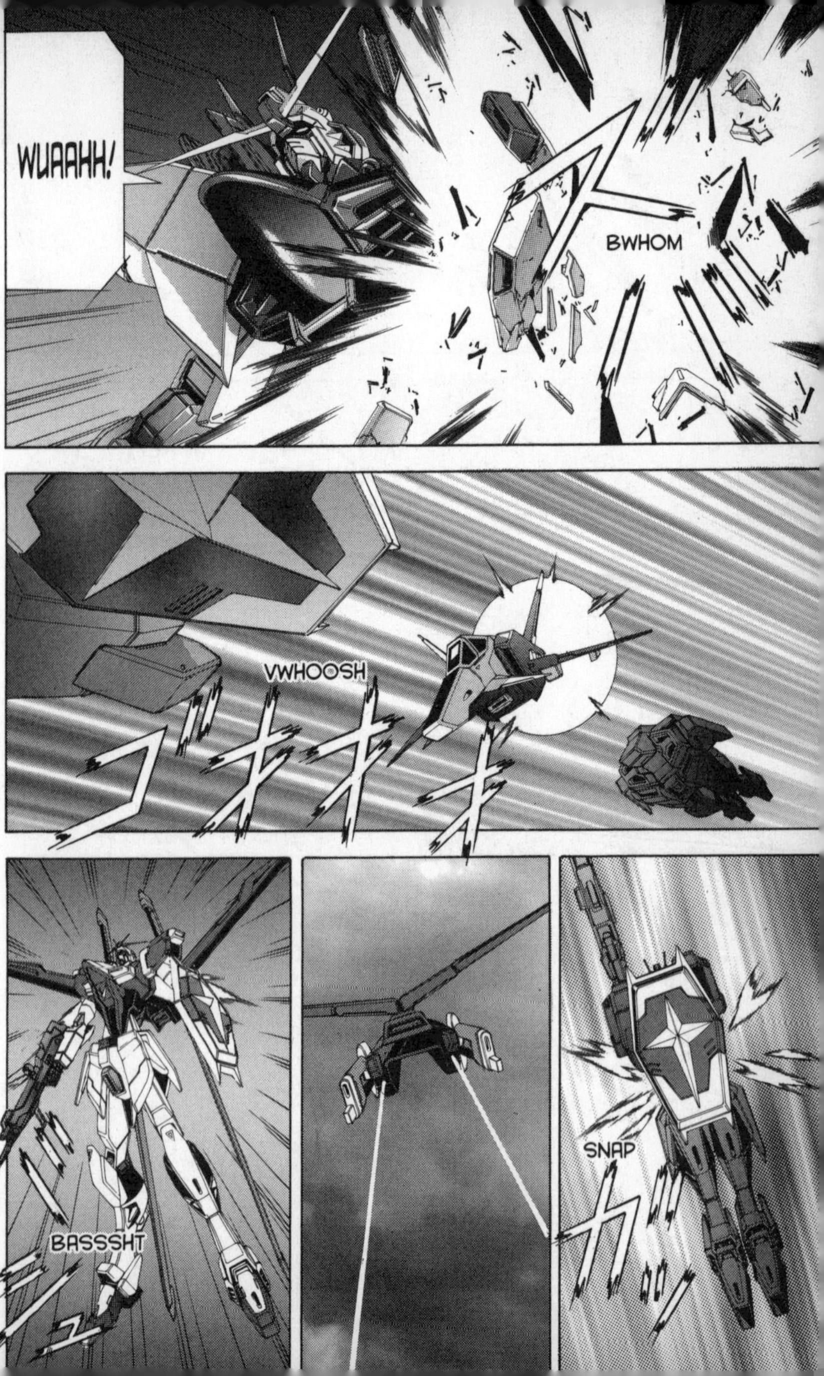
WUAAHH!
BWHOM
VWHOOSH
SNAP
BASSSHT

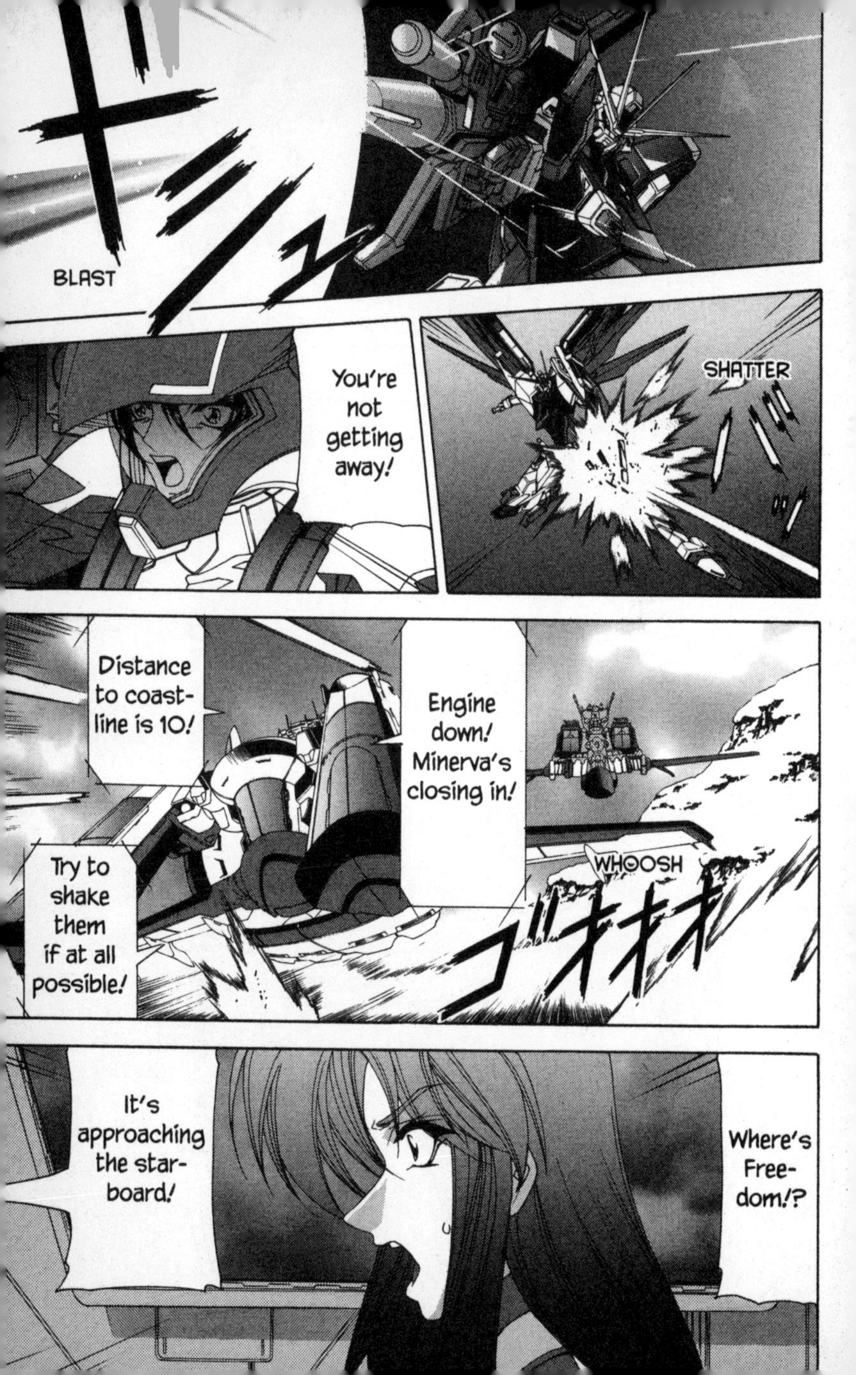
BLAST
SHATTER
You're not getting away!
Engine down! Minerva's closing in!
Distance to coast-line is 10!
WHOOSH
Try to shake them if at all possible!
Where's Free-dom!?
It's approaching the star-board!

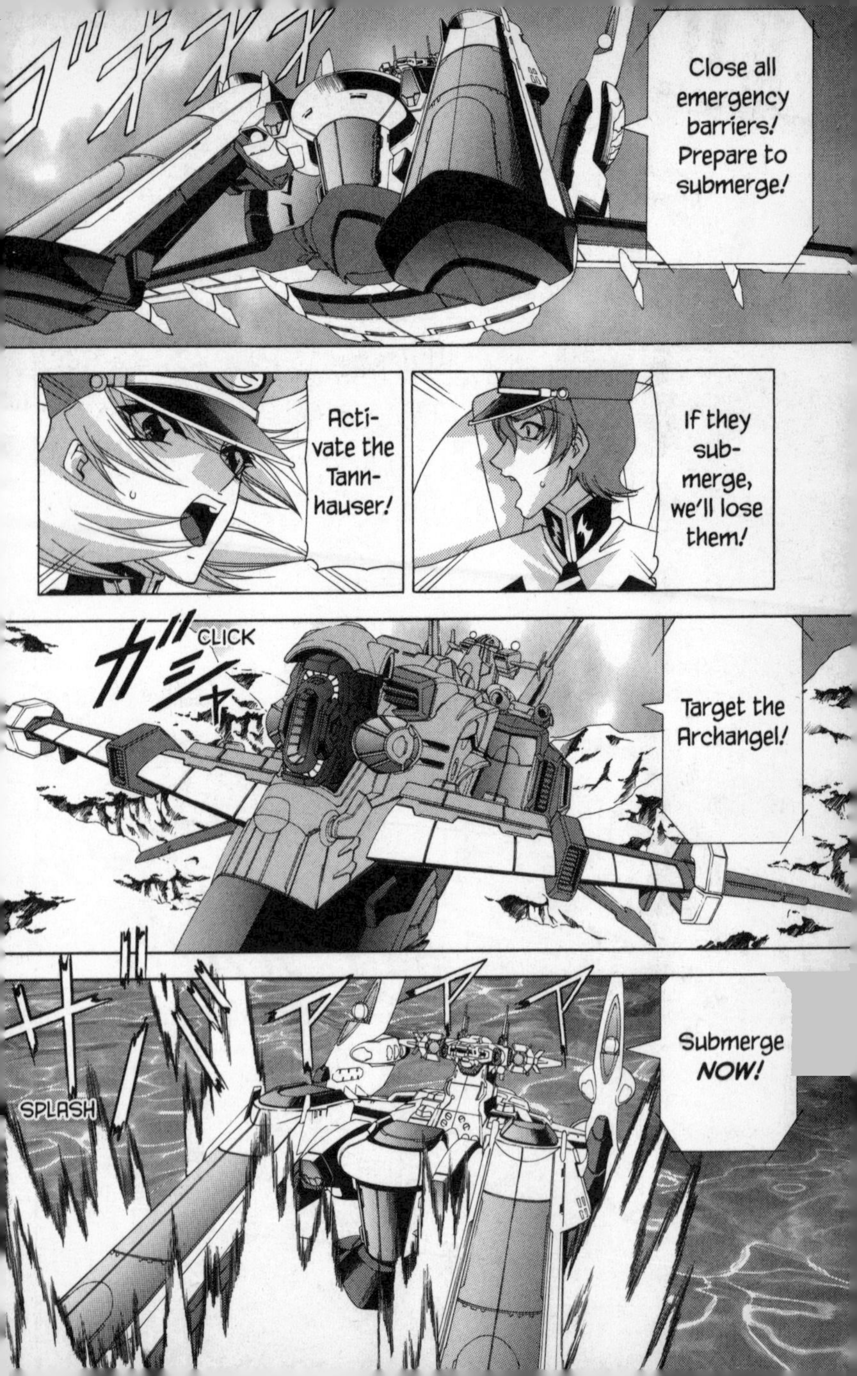

Close all emergency barriers! Prepare to submerge!
If they sub-merge, we'll lose them!
Acti-vate the Tann-hauser!
CLICK
Target the Archangel!
SPLASH
Submerge NOW!

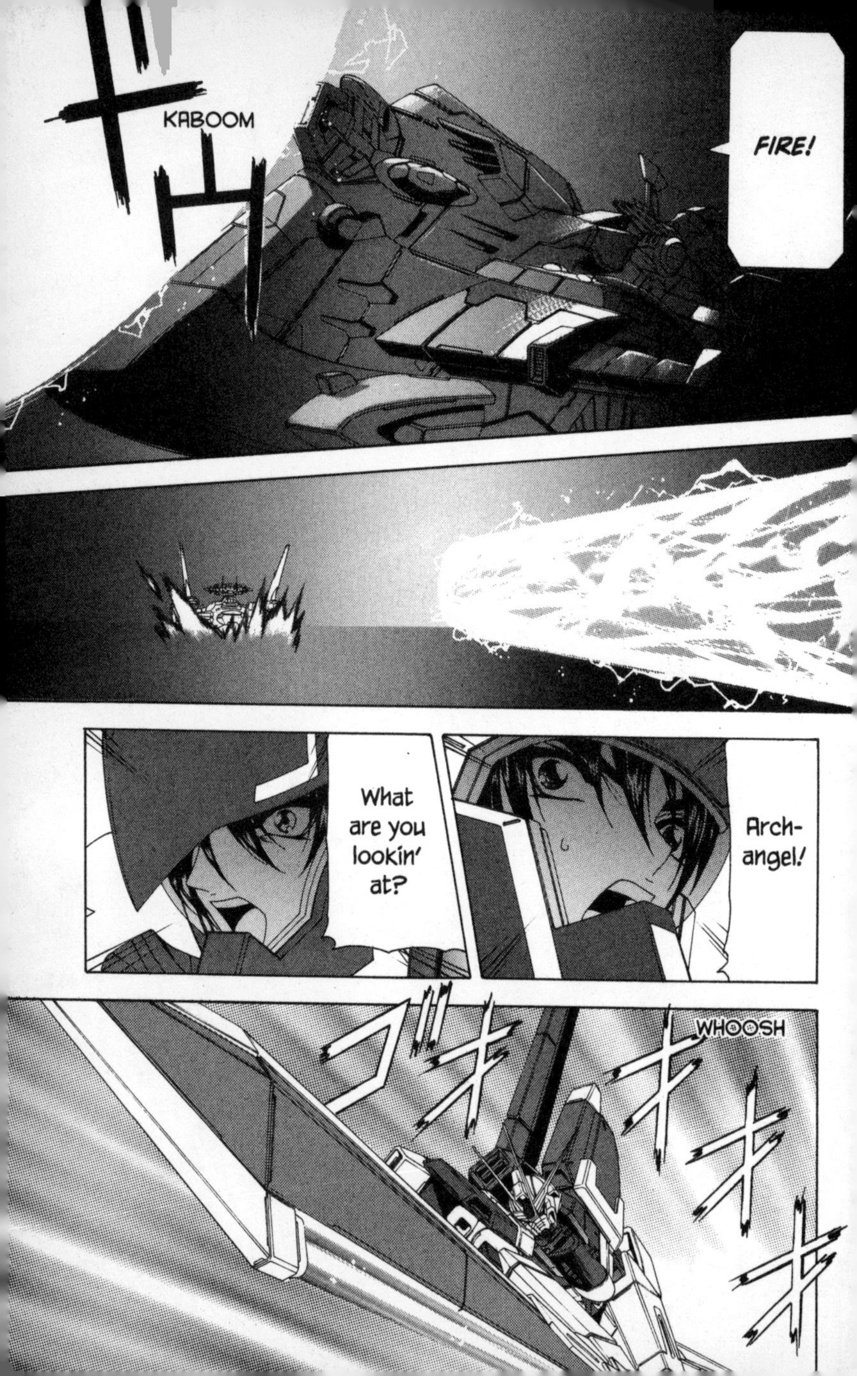
FIRE!
KABOOM
Arch-angel!
What are you lookin' at?
WHOOSH

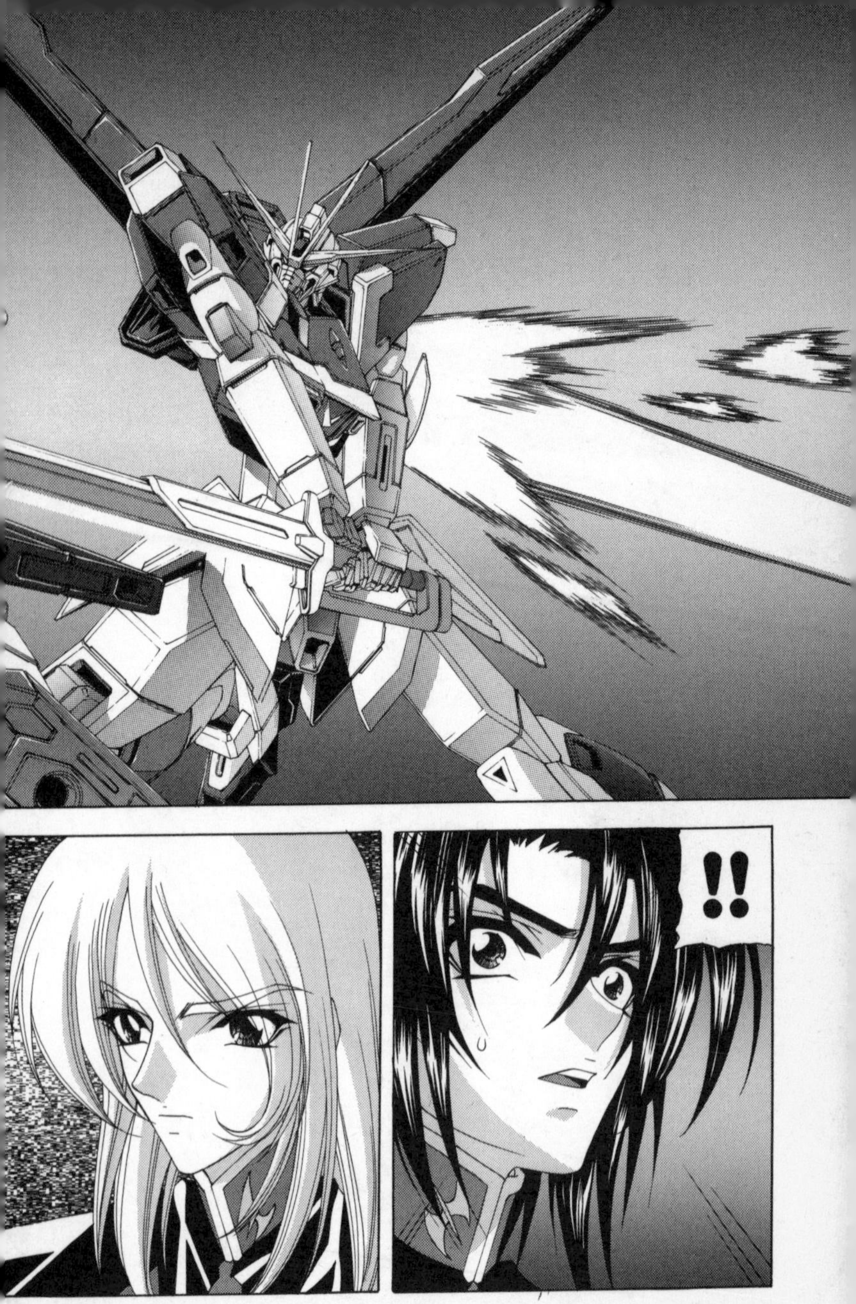
!!

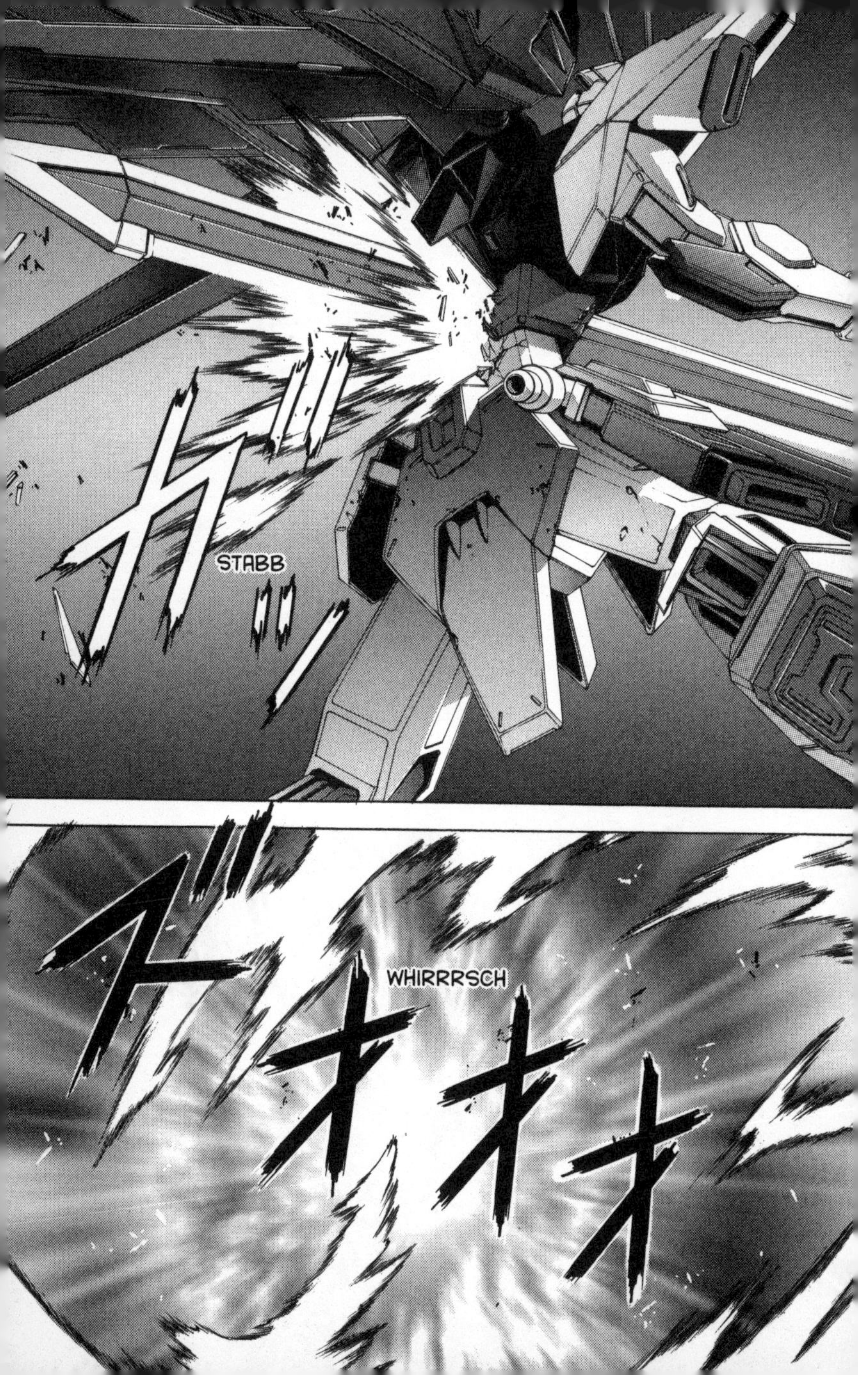
STABB
WHIRRRSCH

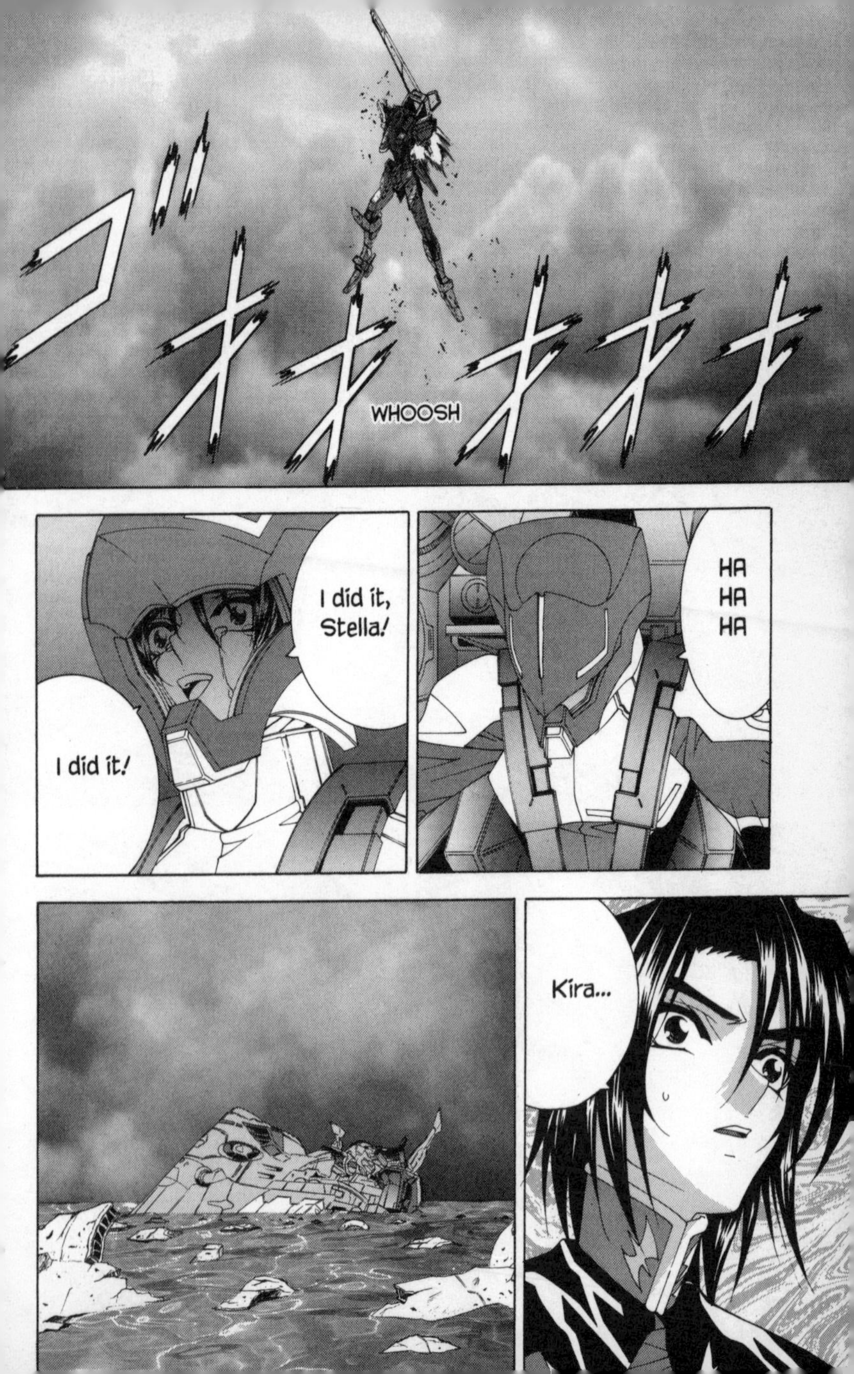
ゴオオオオオ
WHOOSH
HA HA HA
I did it, Stella!
I did it!
Kira...

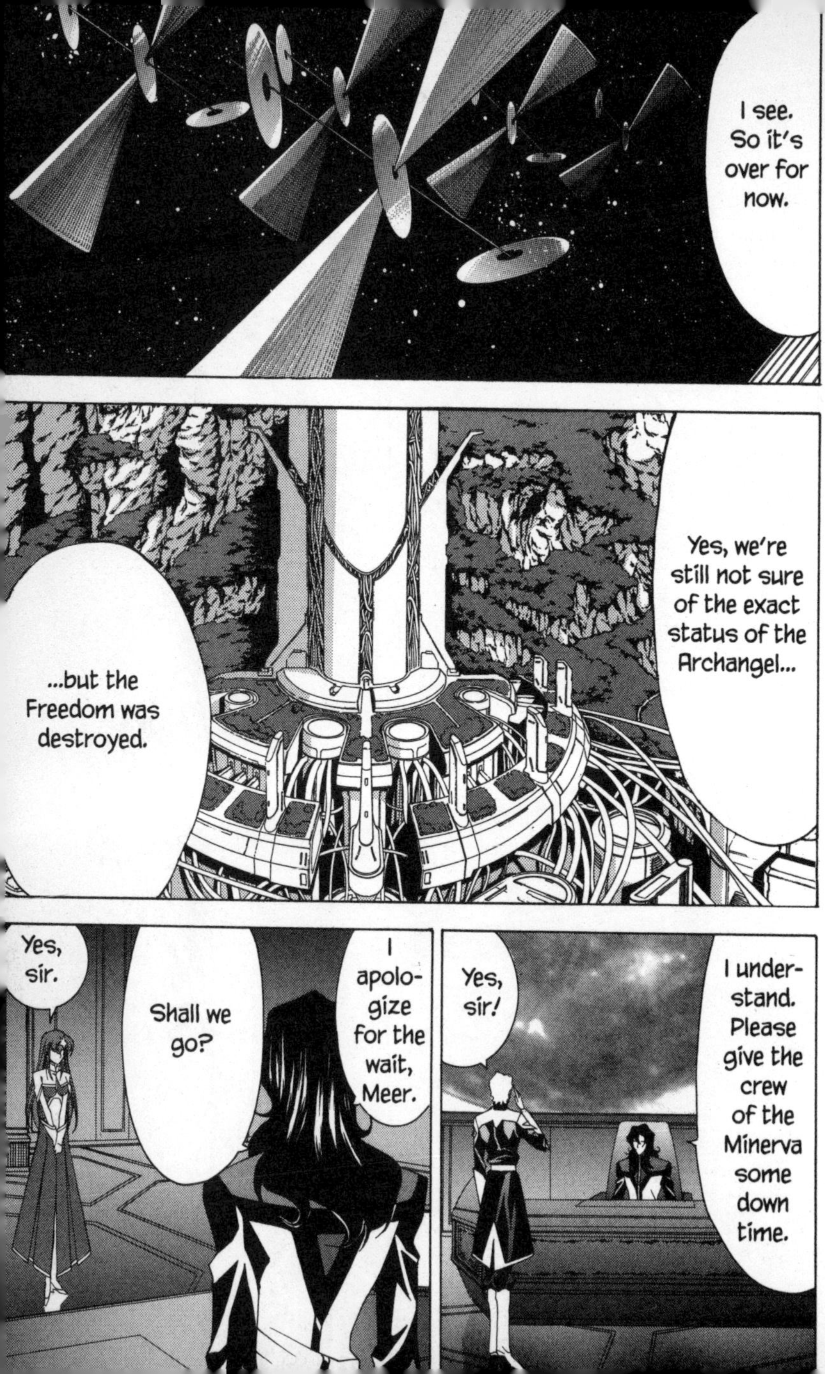
I see. So it's over for now.
Yes, we're still not sure of the exact status of the Archangel...
...but the Freedom was destroyed.
I under-stand. Please give the crew of the Minerva some down time.
Yes, sir!
I apolo-gize for the wait, Meer.
Shall we go?
Yes, sir.

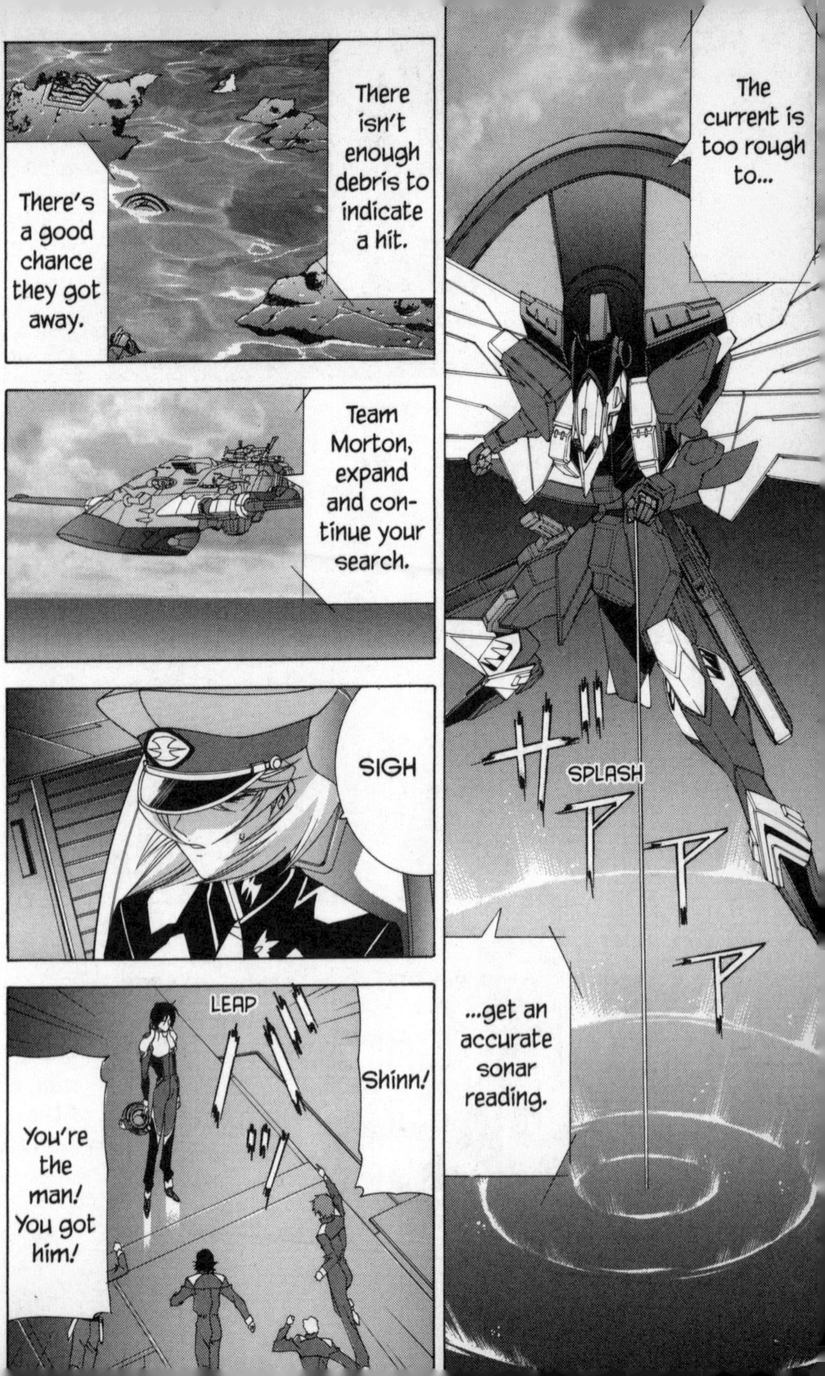
The current is too rough to...
SPLASH
...get an accurate sonar reading.
There isn't enough debris to indicate a hit.
There's a good chance they got away.
Team Morton, expand and continue your search.
SIGH
LEAP
Shinn!
You're the man! You got him!

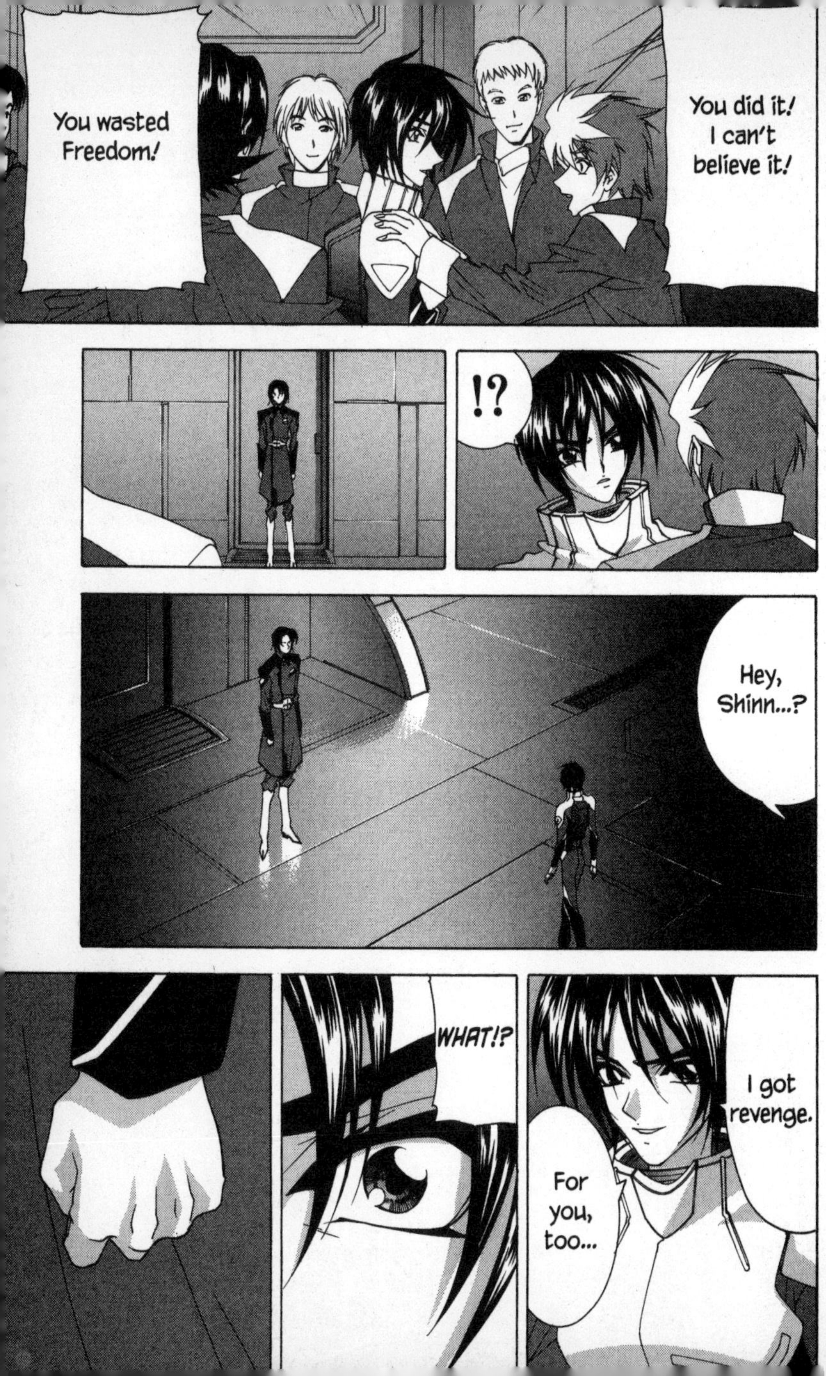
You did it! I can't believe it!
You wasted Freedom!
!?
Hey, Shinn...?
I got revenge.
For you, too...
WHAT!?

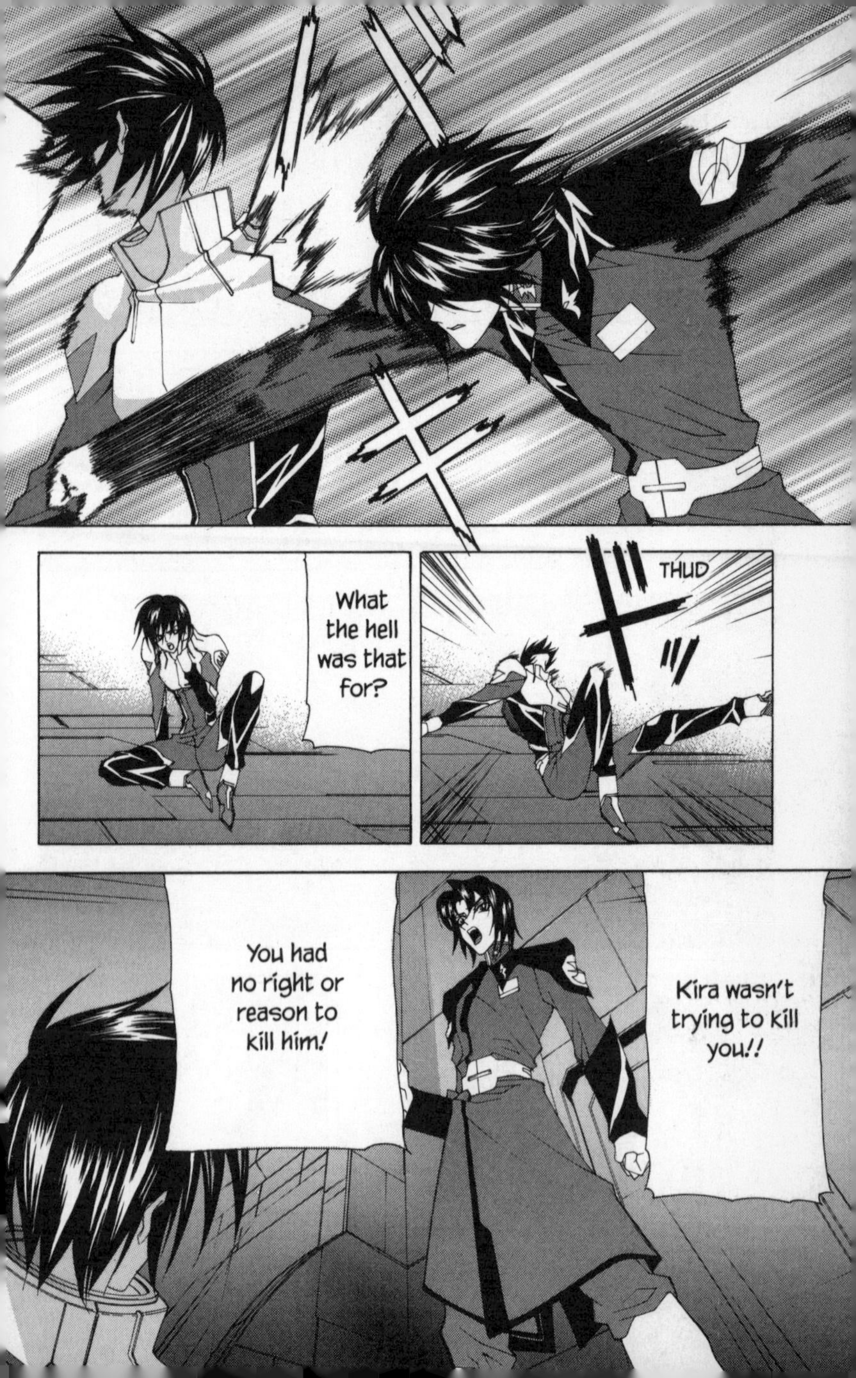
THUD
What the hell was that for?
Kira wasn't trying to kill you!!
You had no right or reason to kill him!

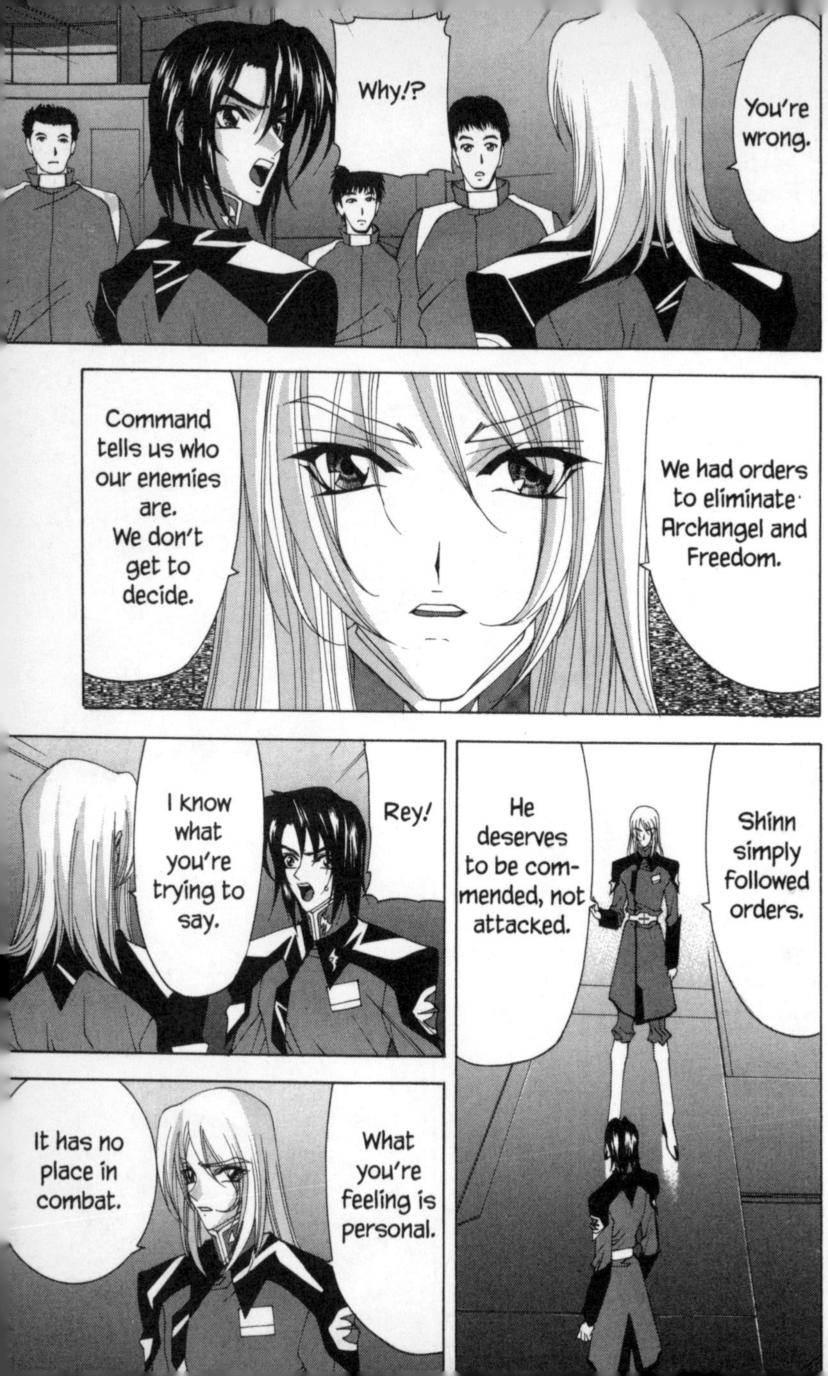

You're wrong.
Why!?
We had orders to eliminate Archangel and Freedom.
Command tells us who our enemies are. We don't get to decide.
Shinn simply followed orders.
He deserves to be commended, not attacked.
Rey!
I know what you're trying to say.
What you're feeling is personal.
It has no place in combat.

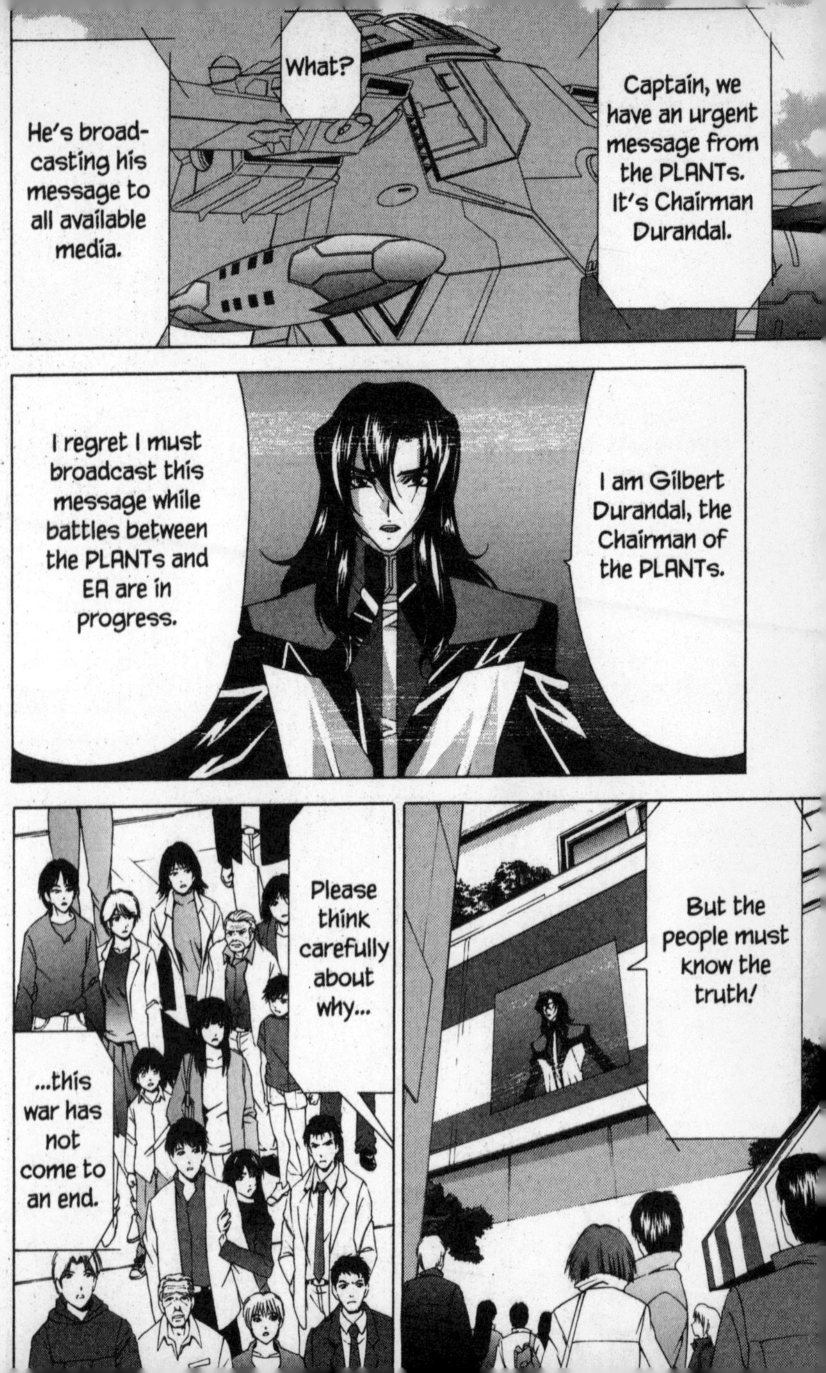
Captain, we have an urgent message from the PLANTs. It's Chairman Durandal.
What?
He's broad-casting his message to all available media.
I am Gilbert Durandal, the Chairman of the PLANTs.
I regret I must broadcast this message while battles between the PLANTs and EA are in progress.
But the people must know the truth!
Please think carefully about why...
...this war has not come to an end.

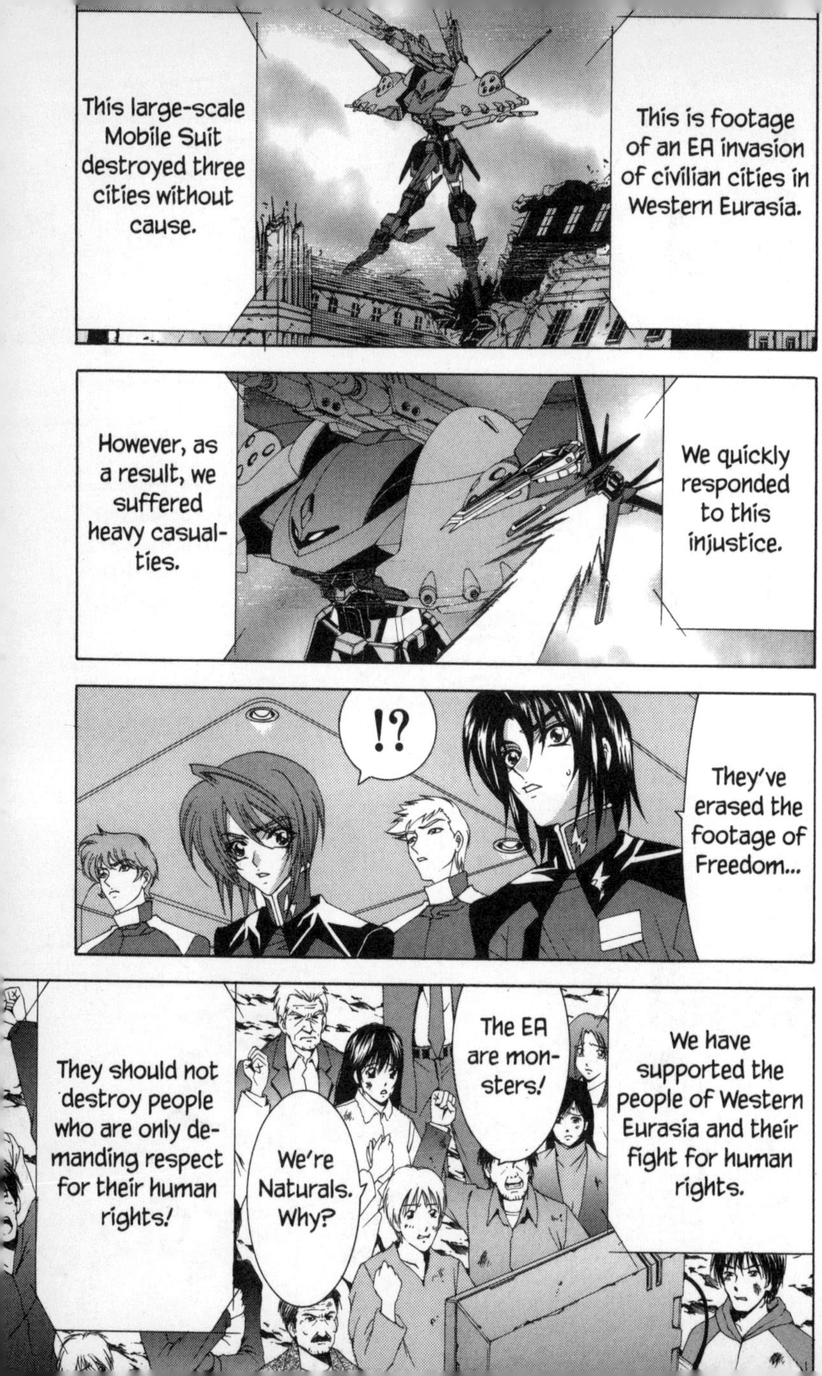
This is footage of an EA invasion of civilian cities in Western Eurasia.
This large-scale Mobile Suit destroyed three cities without cause.
We quickly responded to this injustice.
However, as a result, we suffered heavy casual-ties.
!?
They've erased the footage of Freedom...
We have supported the people of Western Eurasia and their fight for human rights.
The EA are mon-sters!
We're Naturals. Why?
They should not destroy people who are only de-manding respect for their human rights!

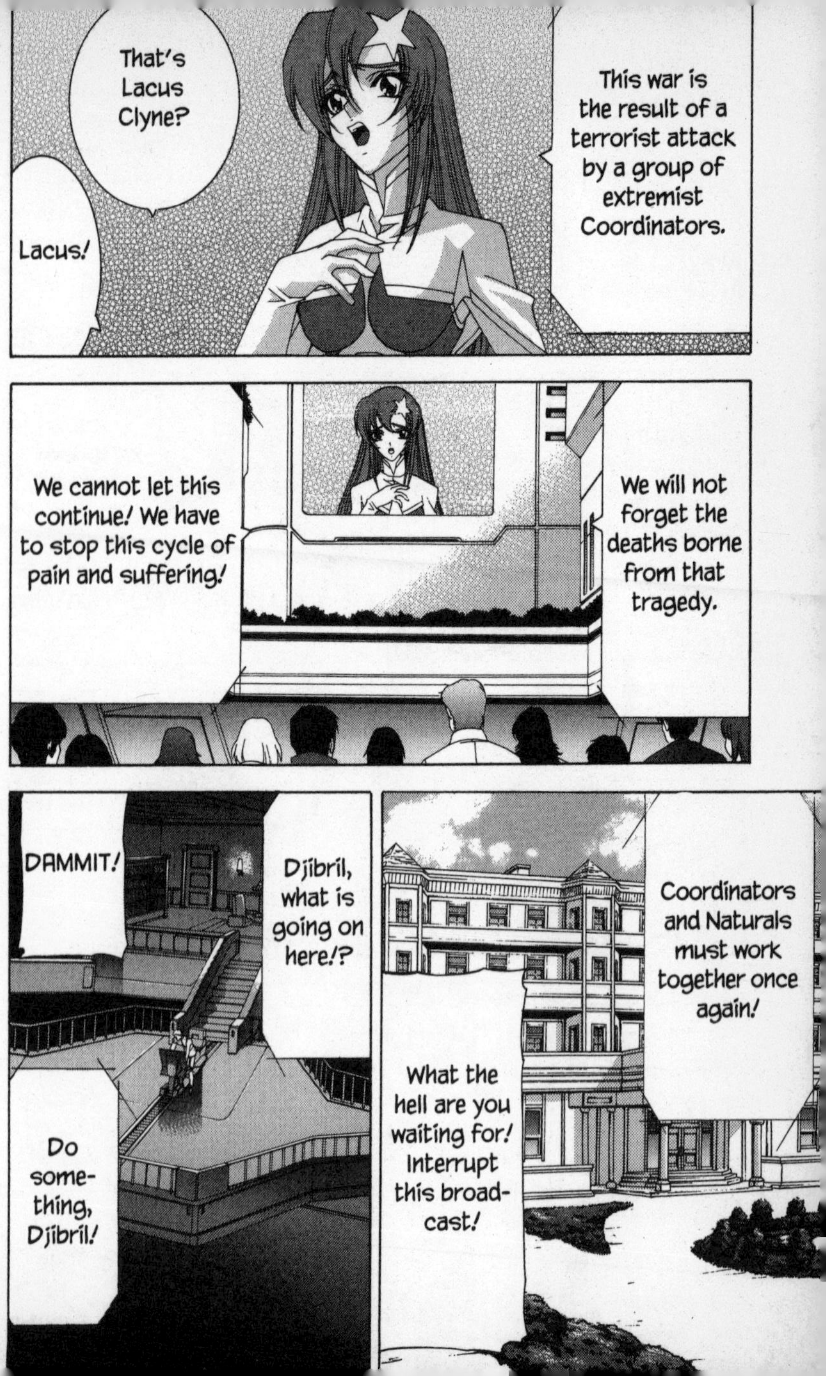

This war is the result of a terrorist attack by a group of extremist Coordinators.
That's Lacus Clyne?
Lacus!
We will not forget the deaths borne from that tragedy.
We cannot let this continue! We have to stop this cycle of pain and suffering!
Coordinators and Naturals must work together once again!
What the hell are you waiting for! Interrupt this broad-cast!
Djibril, what is going on here!?
DAMMIT!
Do some-thing, Djibril!

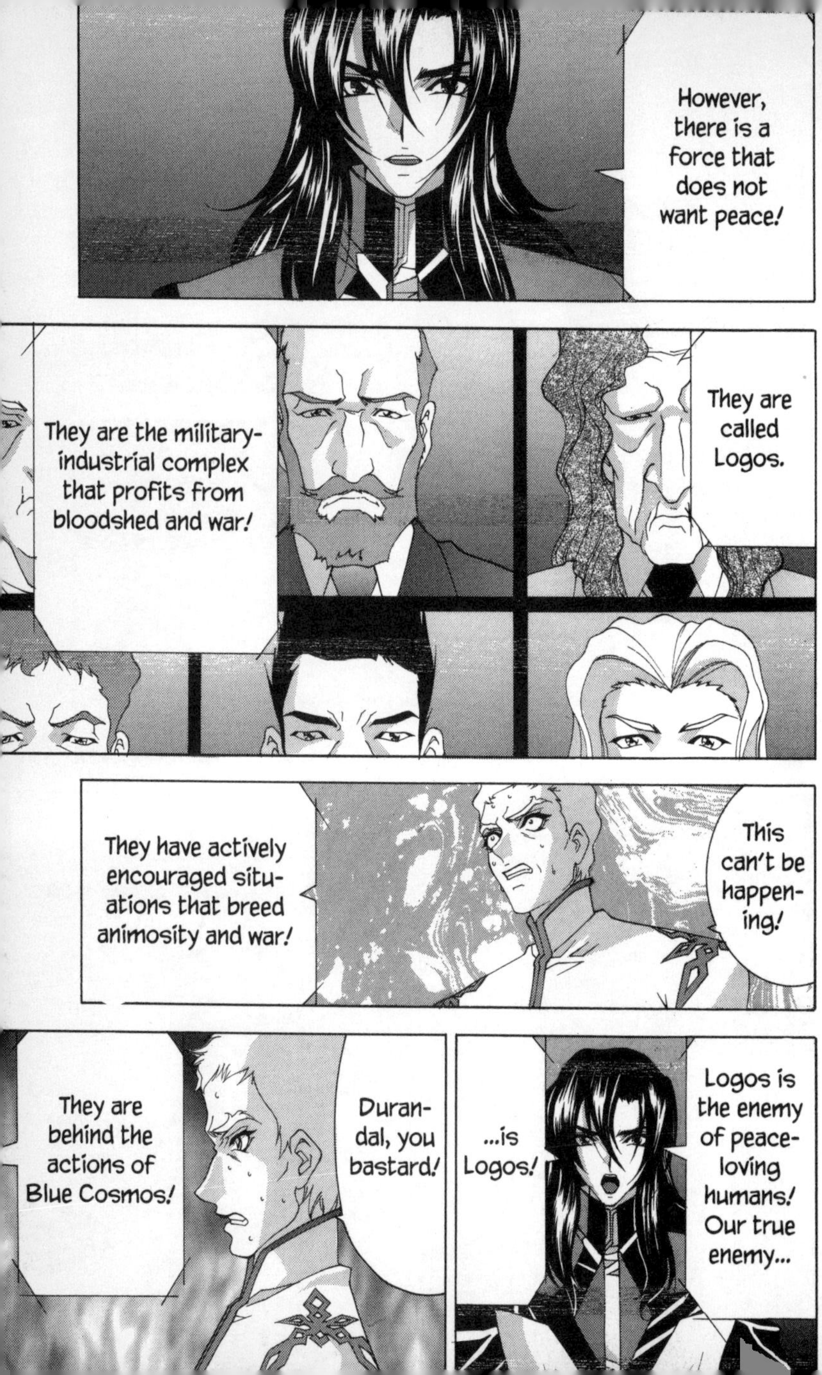
However, there is a force that does not want peace!
They are called Logos.
They are the military-industrial complex that profits from bloodshed and war!
This can't be happening!
They have actively encouraged situations that breed animosity and war!
Logos is the enemy of peace-loving humans! Our true enemy...
...is Logos!
Durandal, you bastard!
They are behind the actions of Blue Cosmos!

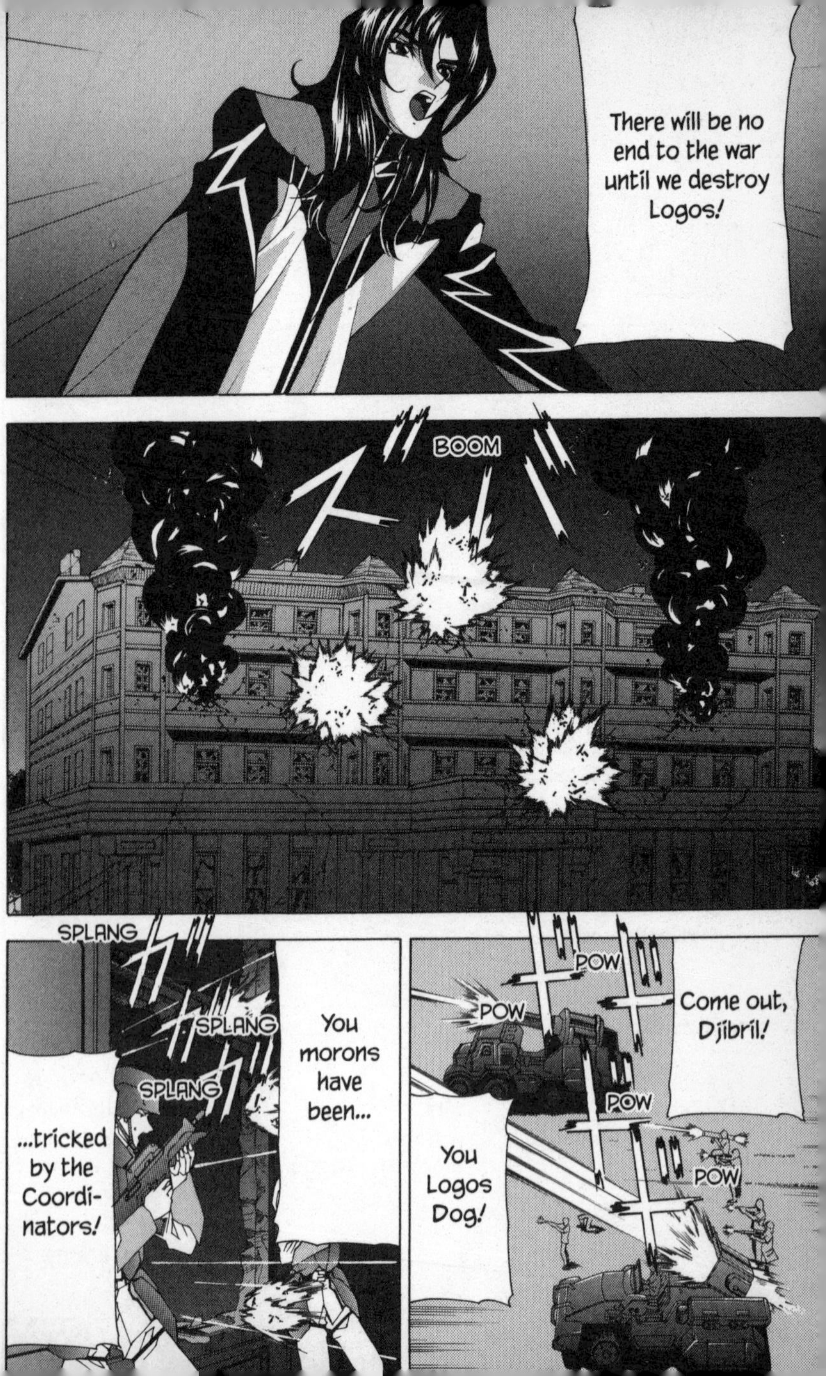
There will be no end to the war until we destroy Logos!
BOOM
POW
POW
Come out, Djibril!
POW
You Logos Dog!
POW
SPLANG
You morons have been...
SPLANG
SPLANG
...tricked by the Coordi-nators!

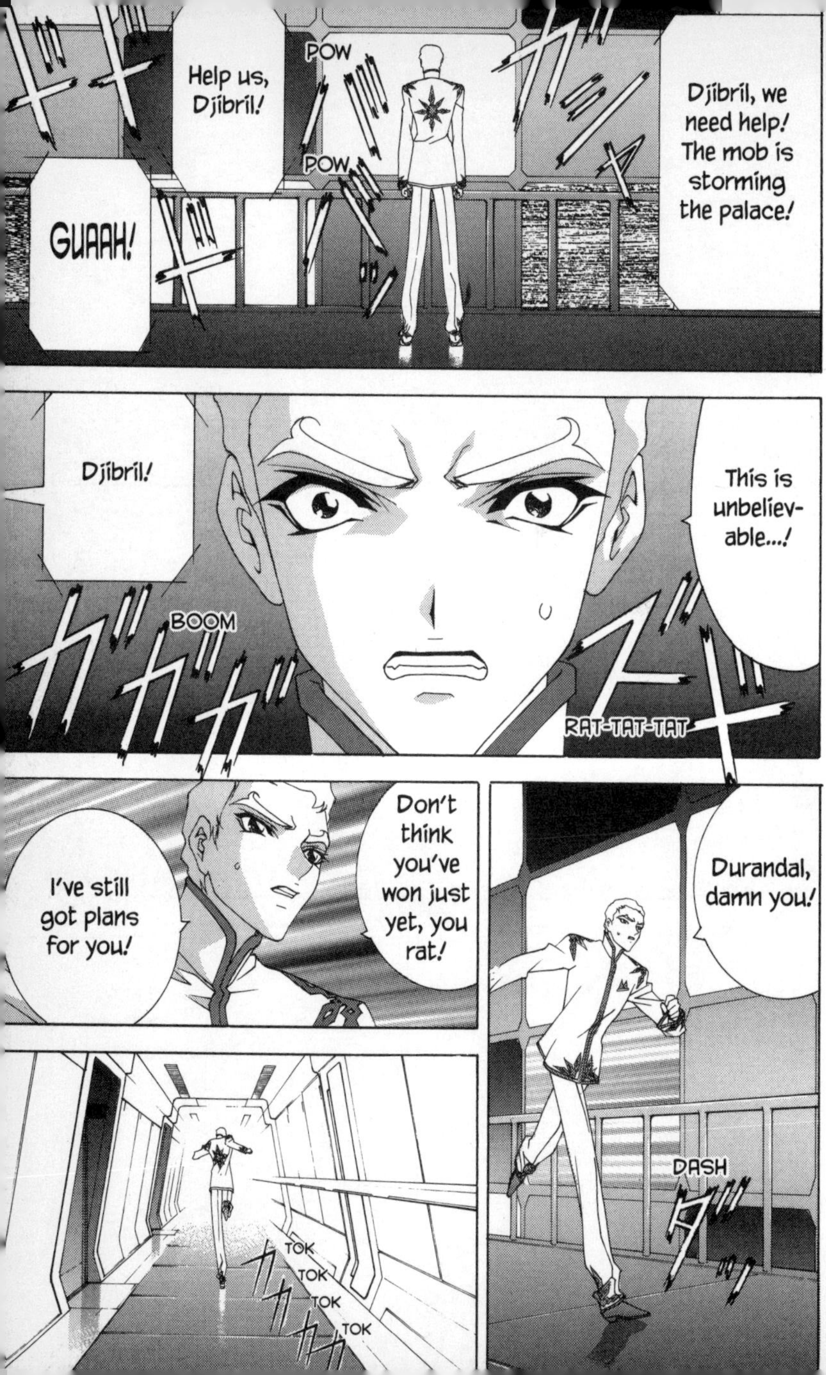
Djibril, we need help! The mob is storming the palace!
POW
Help us, Djibril!
POW
GUAAH!
This is unbelievable...!
Djibril!
RAT-TAT-TAT
BOOM
Durandal, damn you!
DASH
Don't think you've won just yet, you rat!
I've still got plans for you!
TOK
TOK
TOK
TOK

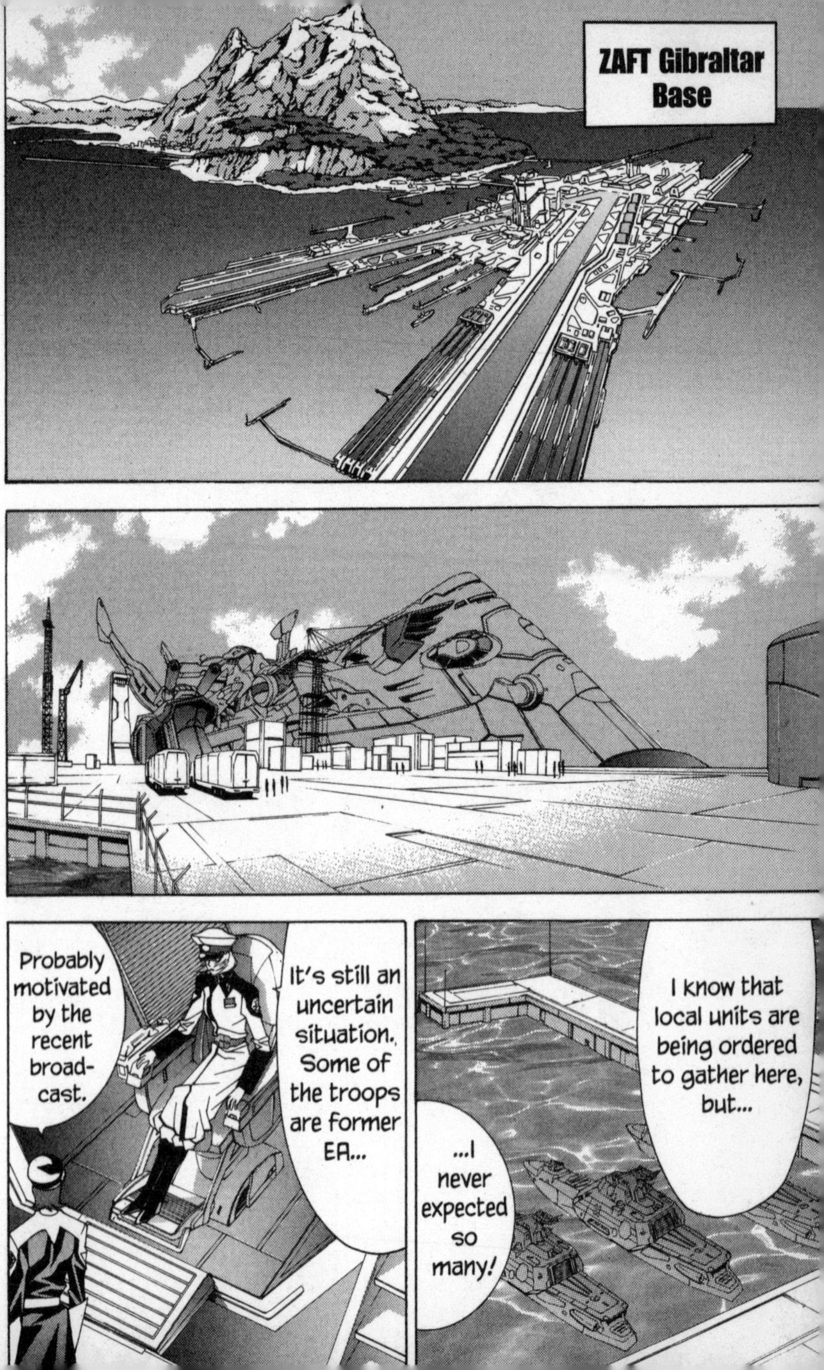
ZAFT Gibraltar Base
I know that local units are being ordered to gather here, but...
...I never expected so many!
It's still an uncertain situation. Some of the troops are former EA...
Probably motivated by the recent broadcast.

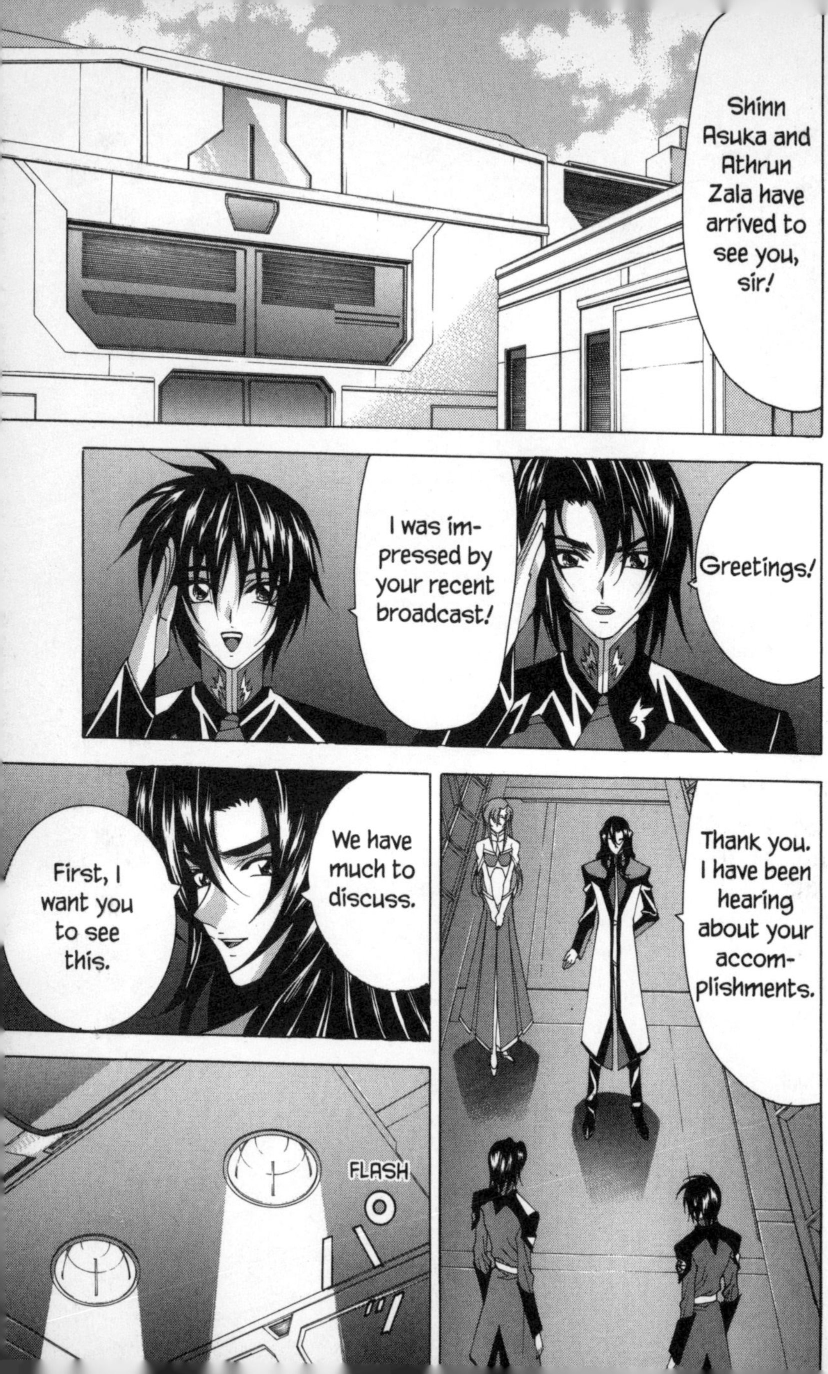
Shinn Asuka and Athrun Zala have arrived to see you, sir!
Greetings!
I was impressed by your recent broadcast!
Thank you. I have been hearing about your accomplishments.
We have much to discuss.
First, I want you to see this.
FLASH

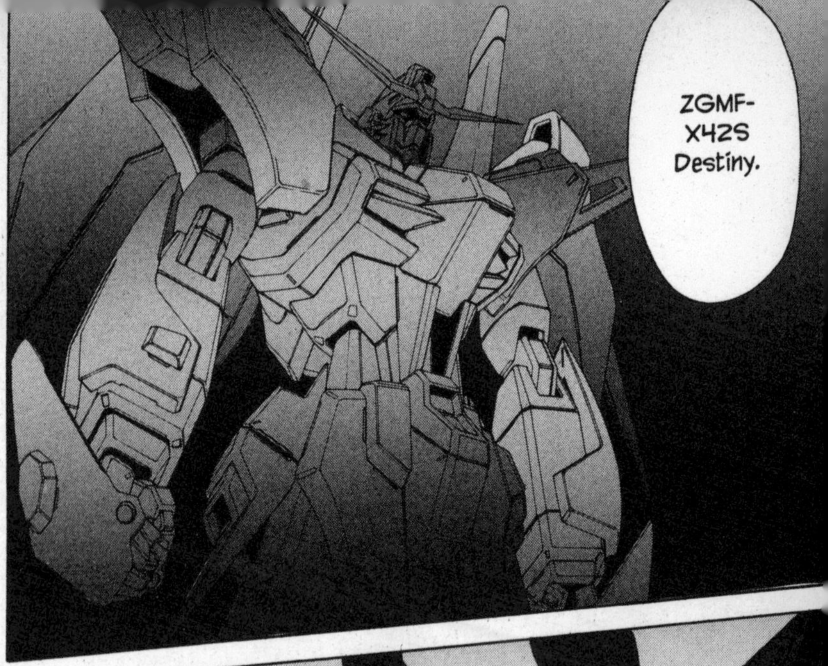
ZGMF-X42S Destiny.
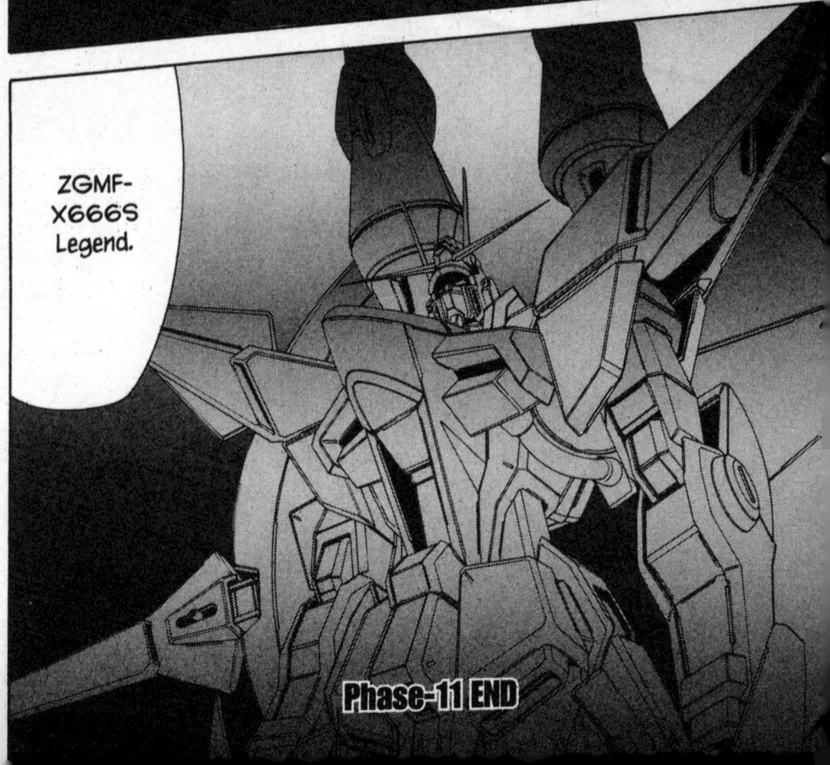
ZGMF-X666S Legend.
Phase-11 END

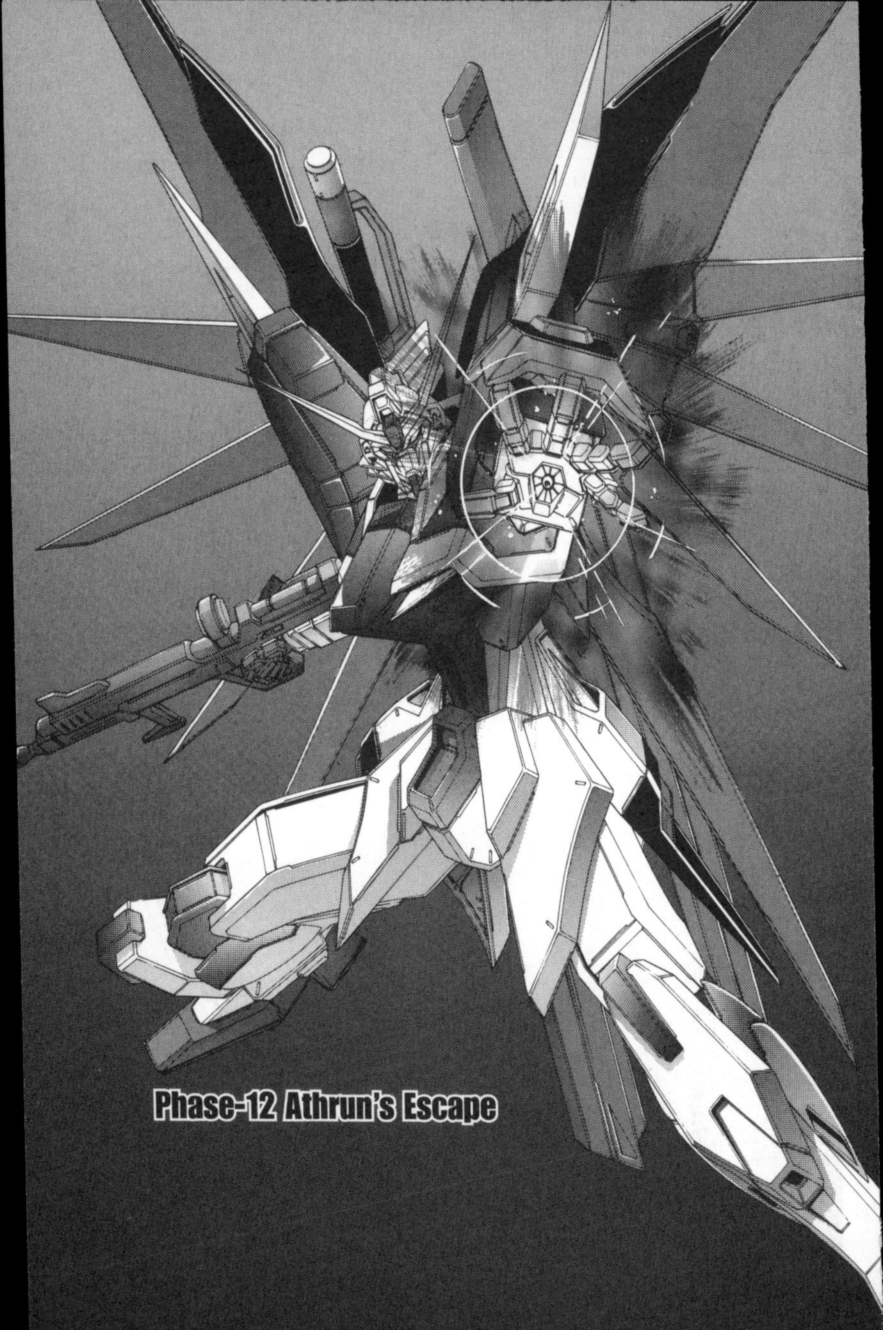

Phase-12 Athrun's Escape

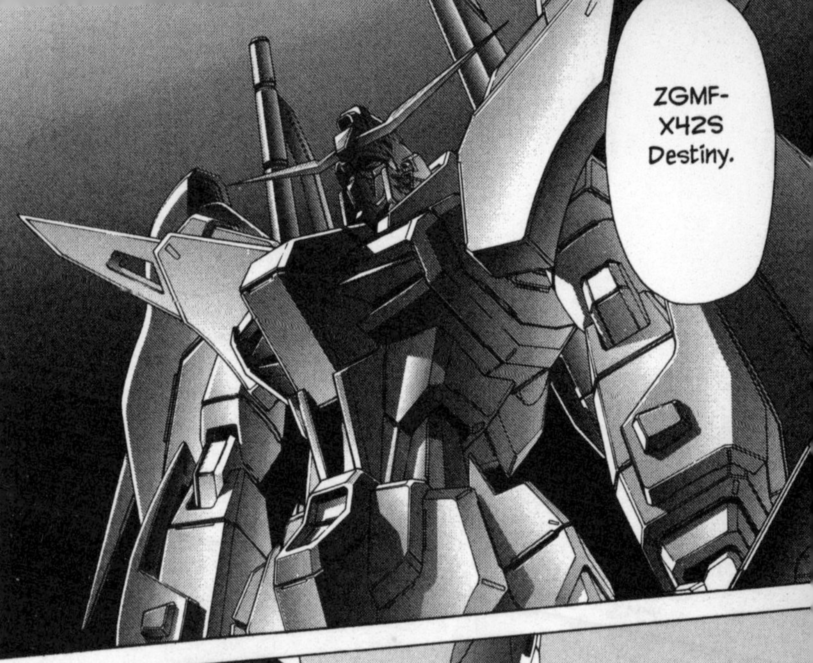
ZGMF-
X42S
Destiny.
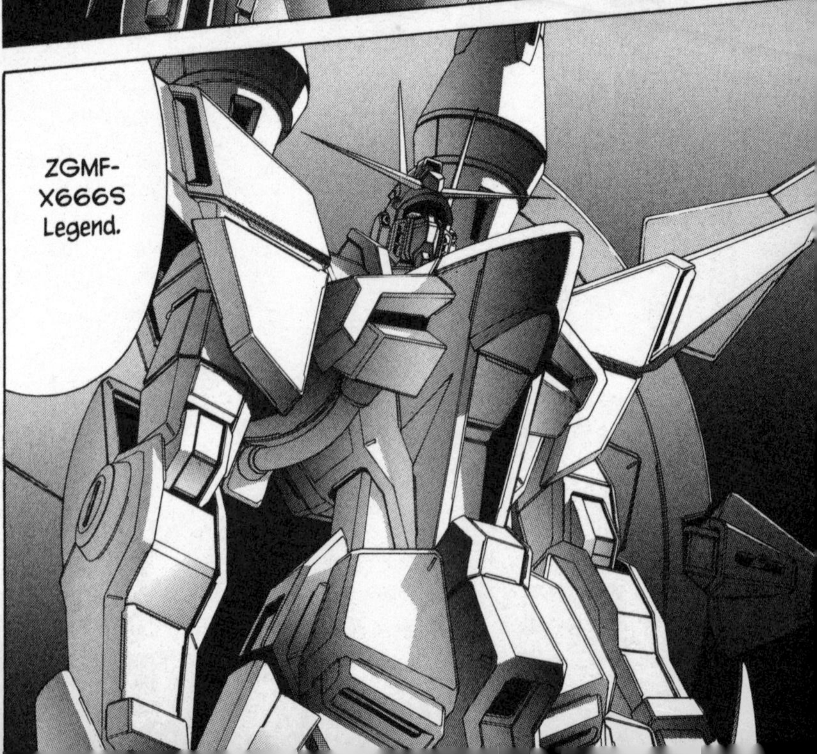
ZGMF-
X666S
Legend.

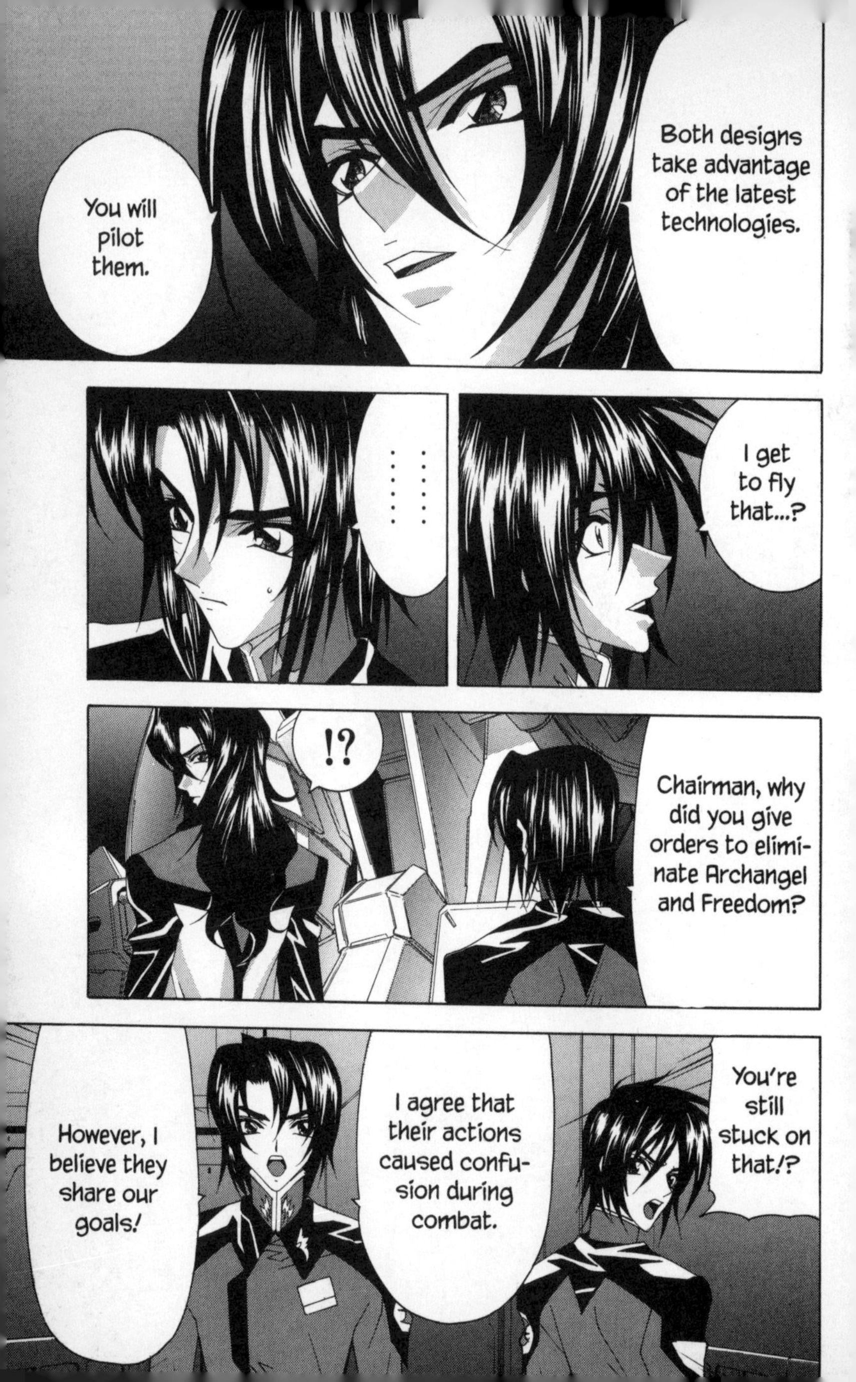
Both designs take advantage of the latest technologies.
You will pilot them.
I get to fly that...?
......
Chairman, why did you give orders to elimi-nate Archangel and Freedom?
!?
You're still stuck on that!?
I agree that their actions caused confu-sion during combat.
However, I believe they share our goals!

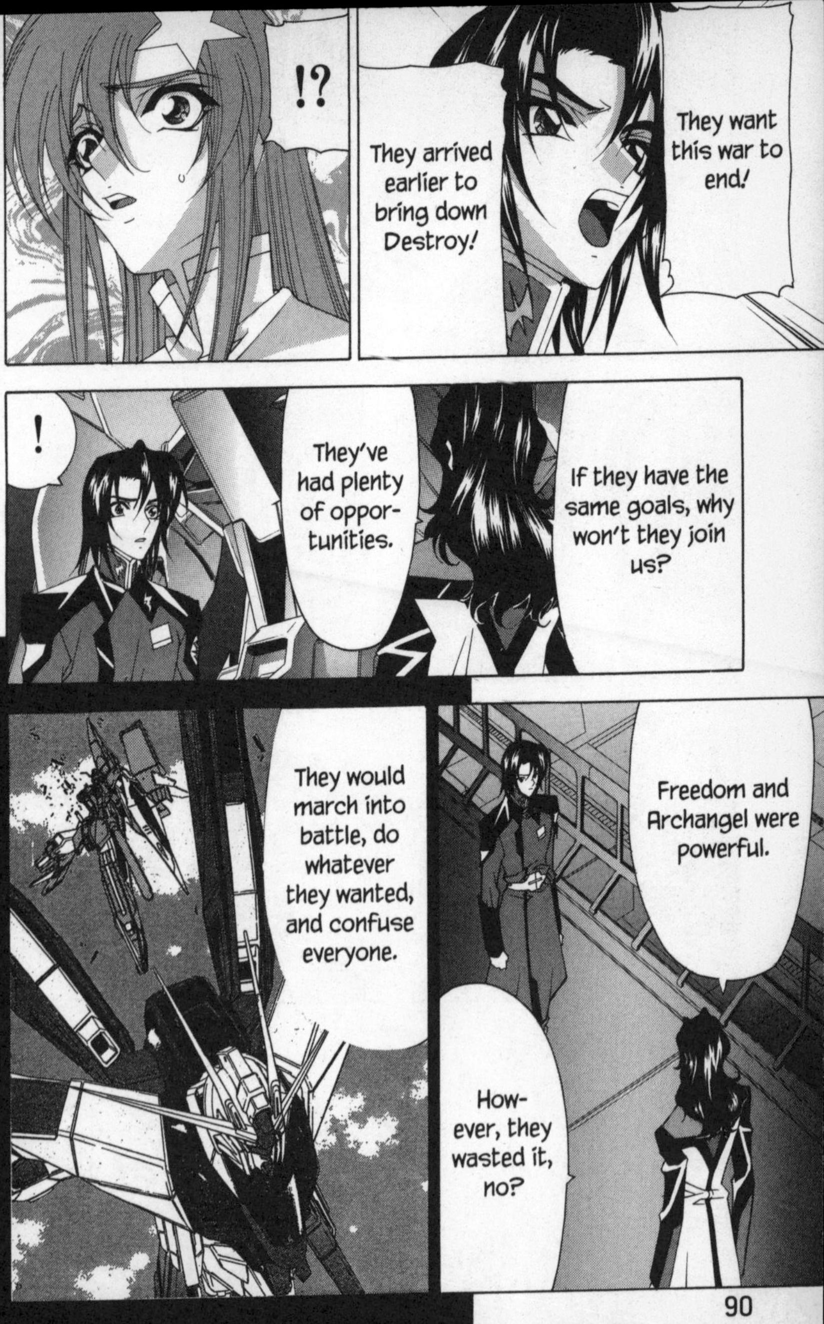
They want this war to end!
They arrived earlier to bring down Destroy!
!?
If they have the same goals, why won't they join us?
They've had plenty of opportunities.
!
Freedom and Archangel were powerful.
How-ever, they wasted it, no?
They would march into battle, do whatever they wanted, and confuse everyone.

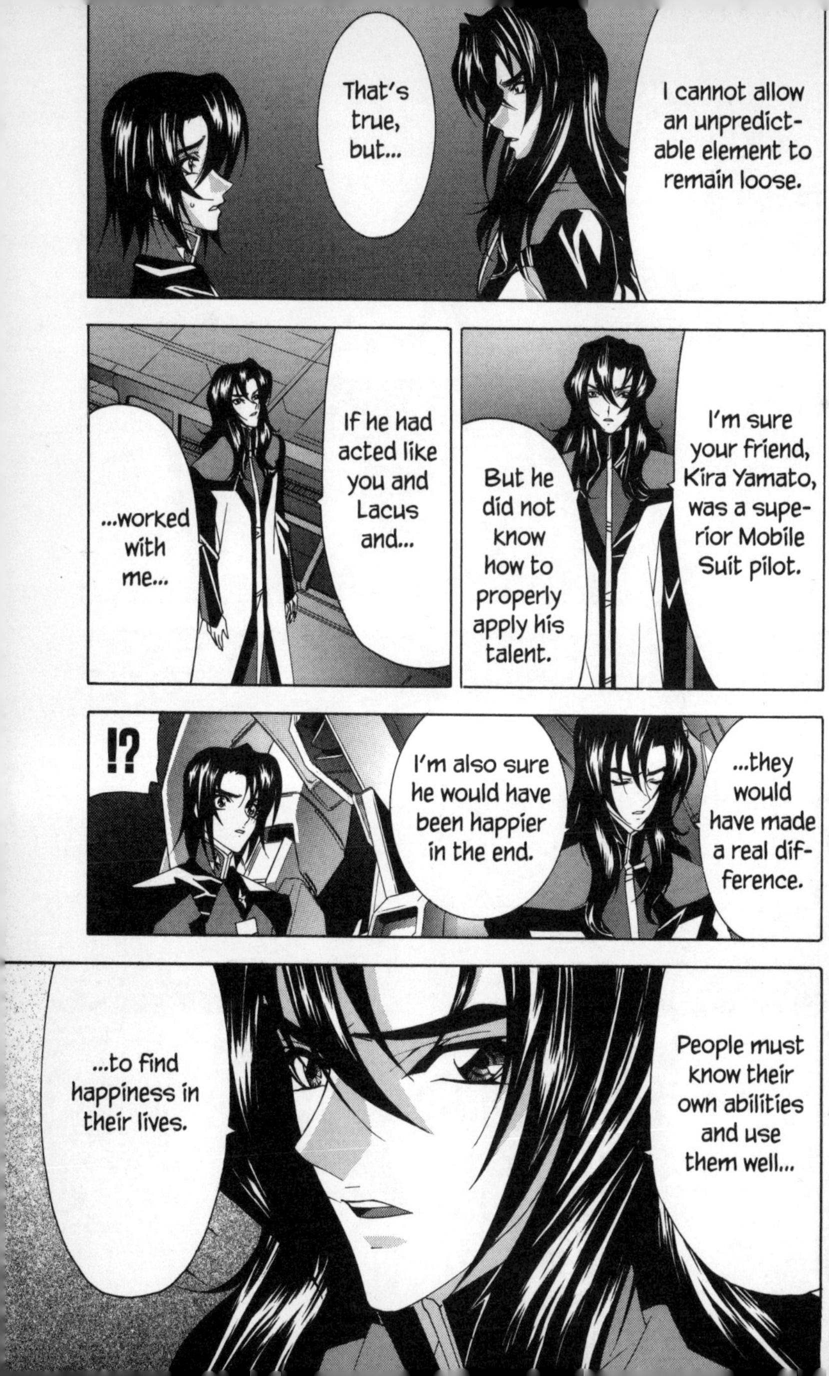
I cannot allow an unpredictable element to remain loose.
That's true, but...
I'm sure your friend, Kira Yamato, was a superior Mobile Suit pilot.
But he did not know how to properly apply his talent.
If he had acted like you and Lacus and...
...worked with me...
...they would have made a real difference.
I'm also sure he would have been happier in the end.
!?
People must know their own abilities and use them well...
...to find happiness in their lives.

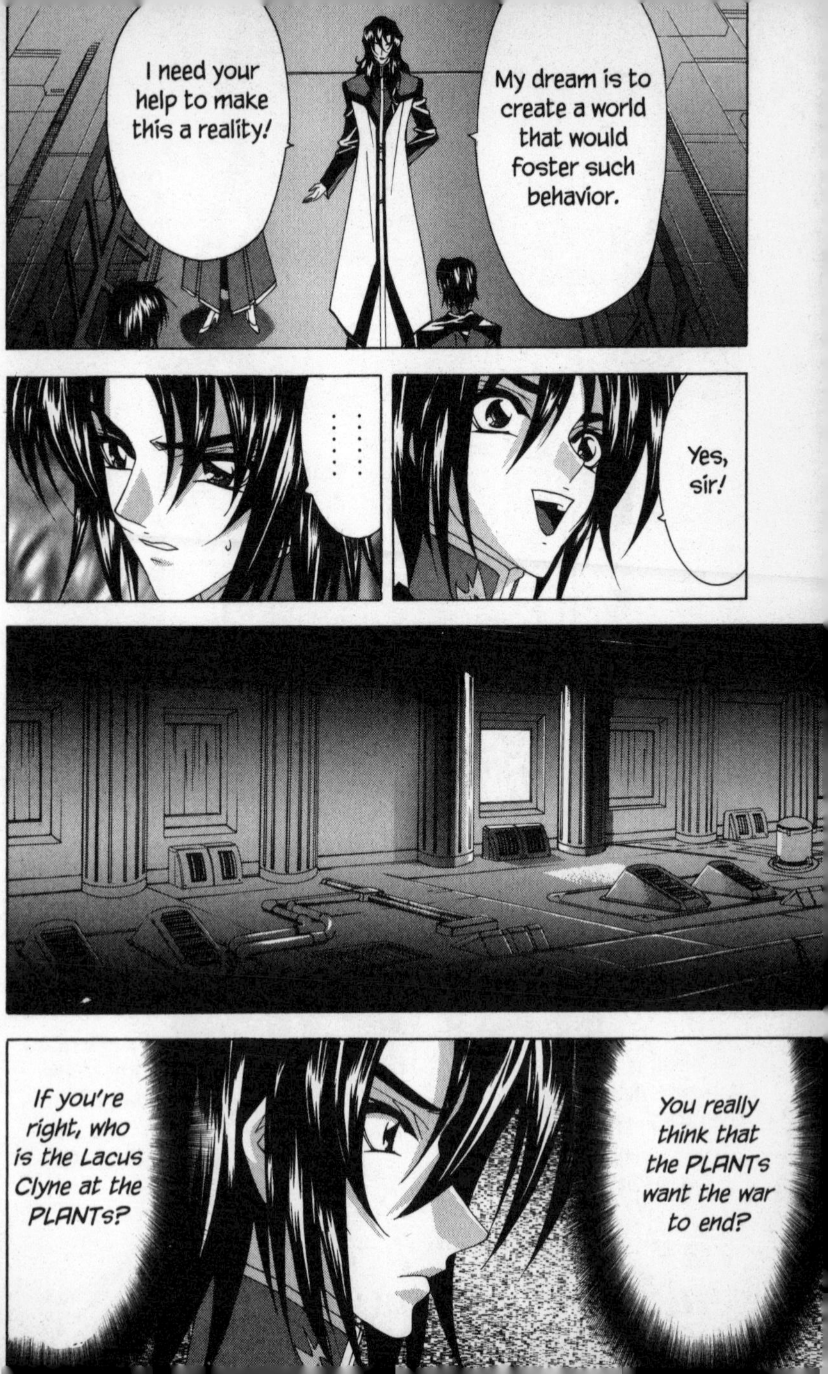
My dream is to create a world that would foster such behavior.
I need your help to make this a reality!
Yes, sir!
......
You really think that the PLANTs want the war to end?
If you're right, who is the Lacus Clyne at the PLANTs?

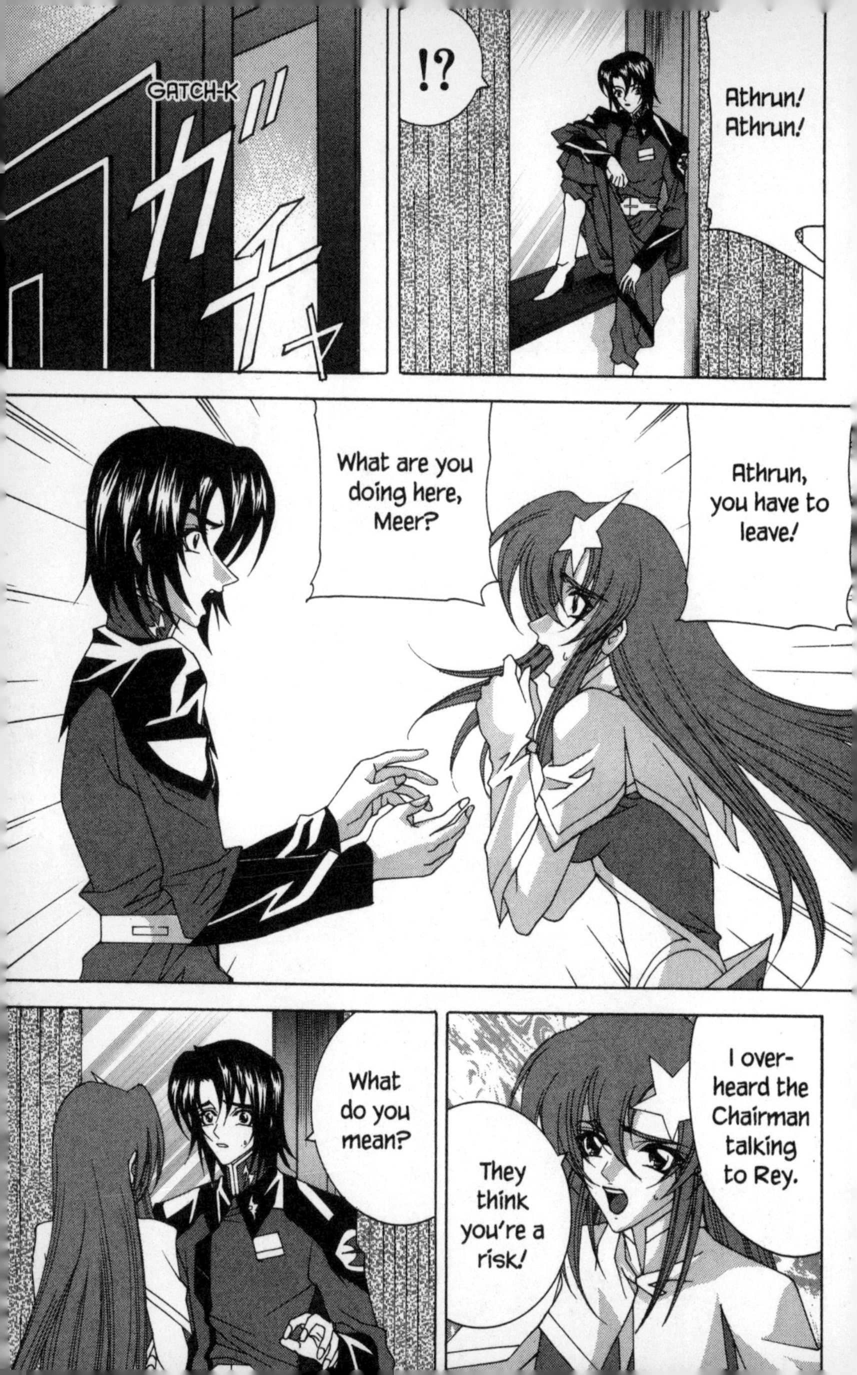
Athrun! Athrun!
!?
GATCH-K
ガチャ
Athrun, you have to leave!
What are you doing here, Meer?
I over-heard the Chairman talking to Rey.
They think you're a risk!
What do you mean?

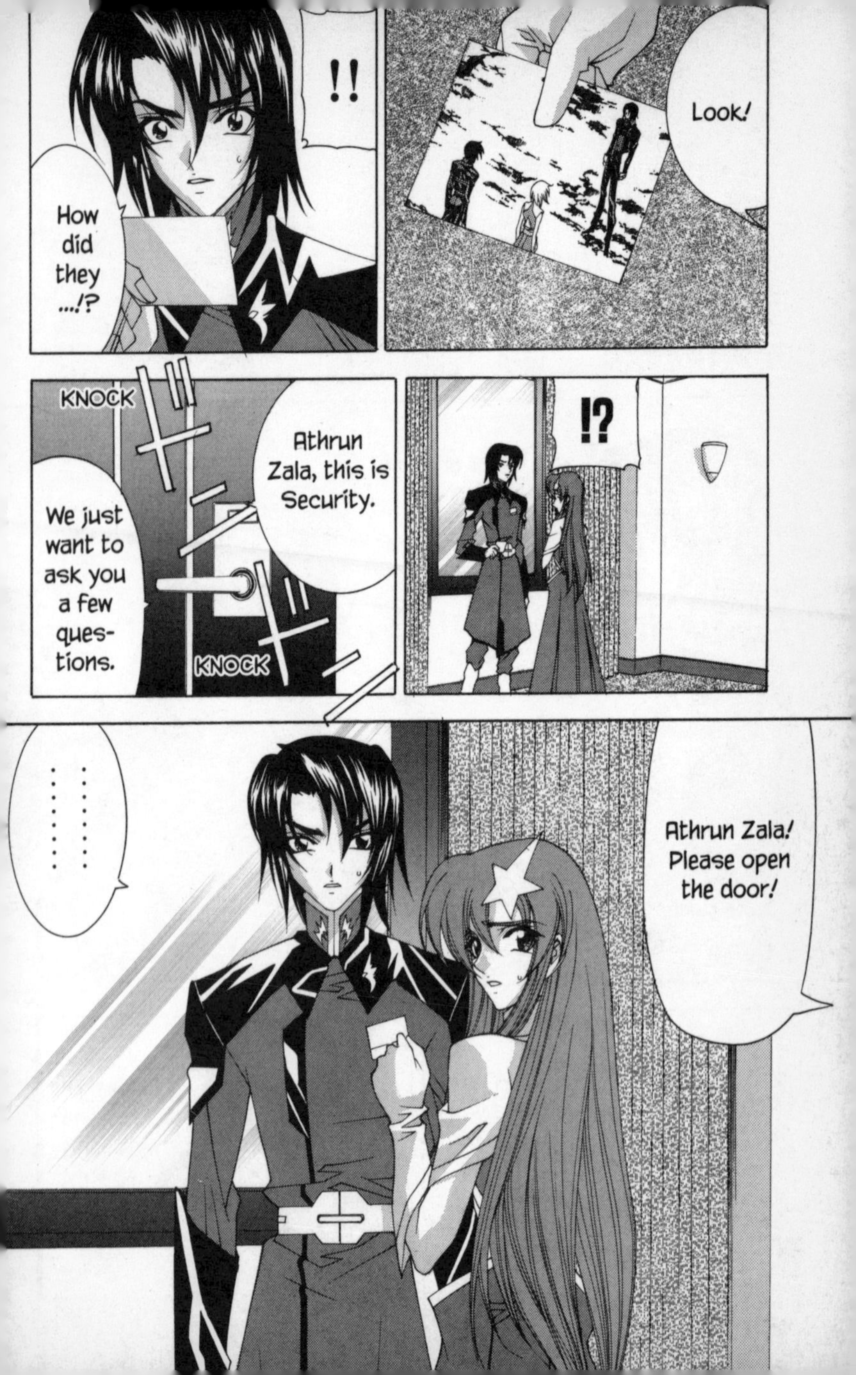
Look!
!!
How did they ...!?
!?
Athrun Zala, this is Security.
KNOCK
We just want to ask you a few questions.
KNOCK
Athrun Zala! Please open the door!
......

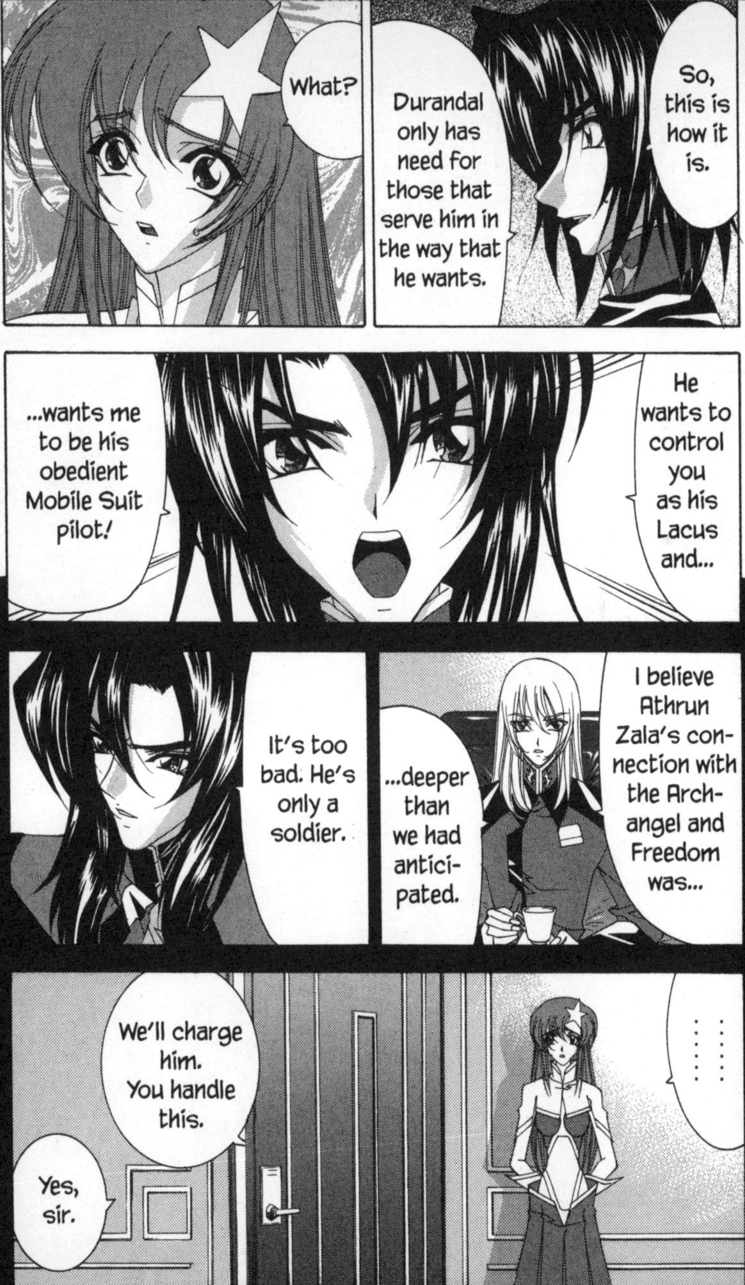
So, this is how it is.
Durandal only has need for those that serve him in the way that he wants.
What?
He wants to control you as his Lacus and...
...wants me to be his obedient Mobile Suit pilot!
I believe Athrun Zala's con-nection with the Arch-angel and Freedom was...
...deeper than we had antici-pated.
It's too bad. He's only a soldier.
......
We'll charge him. You handle this.
Yes, sir.

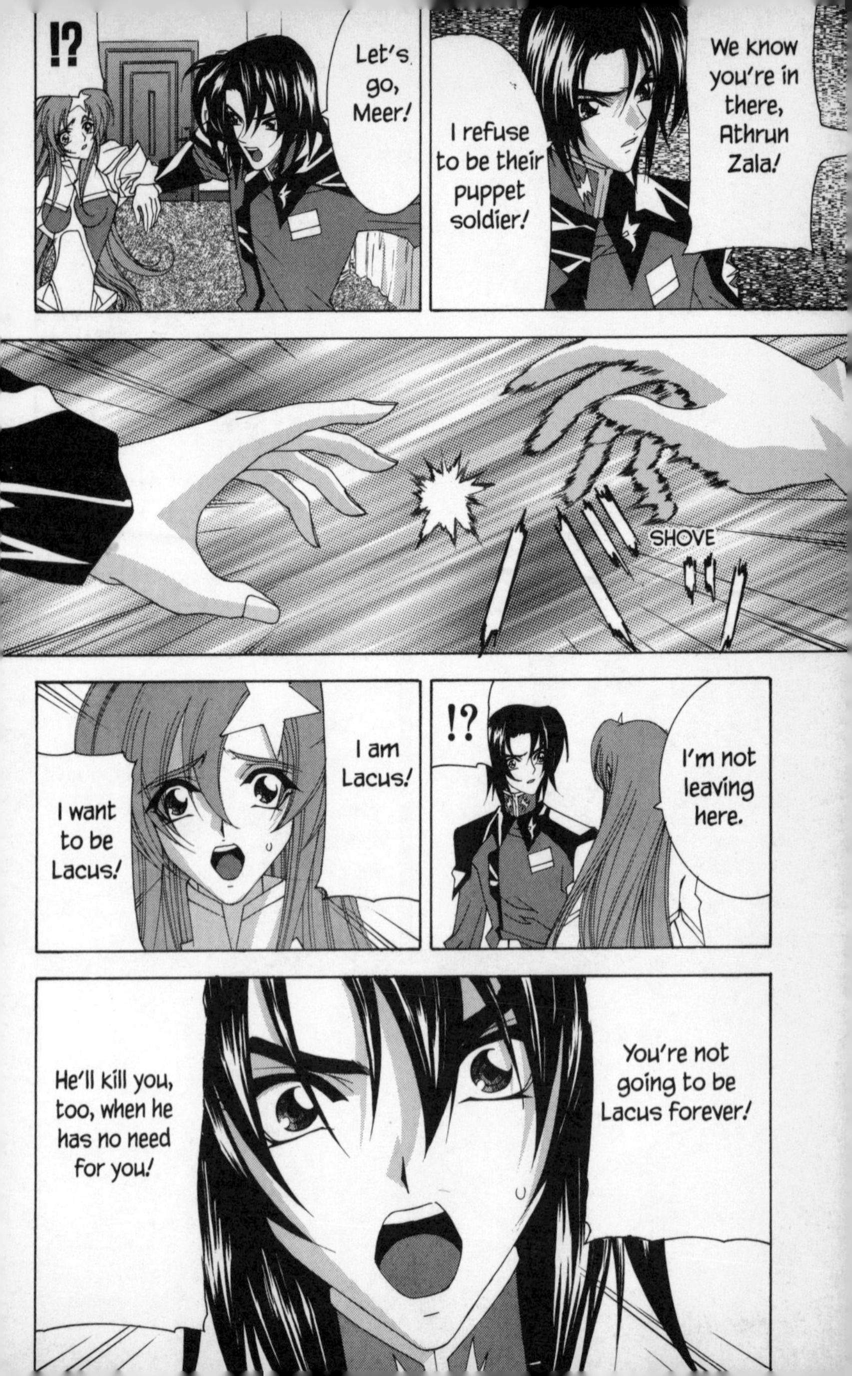
We know you're in there, Athrun Zala!
I refuse to be their puppet soldier!
Let's go, Meer!
!?
SHOVE
I'm not leaving here.
!?
I am Lacus!
I want to be Lacus!
You're not going to be Lacus forever!
He'll kill you, too, when he has no need for you!

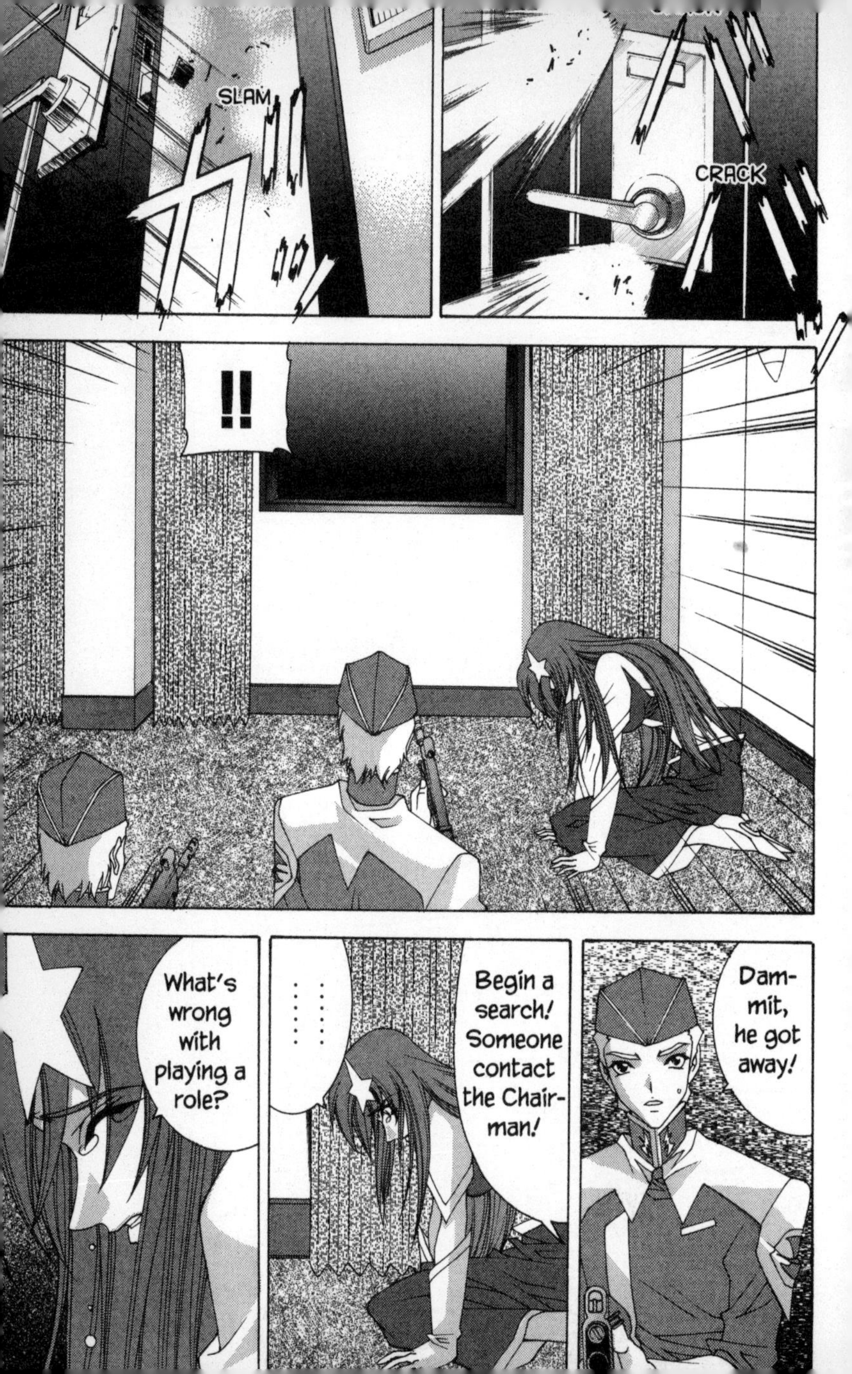
CRACK
SLAM
!!
Dam-mit, he got away!
Begin a search! Someone contact the Chair-man!
......
What's wrong with playing a role?

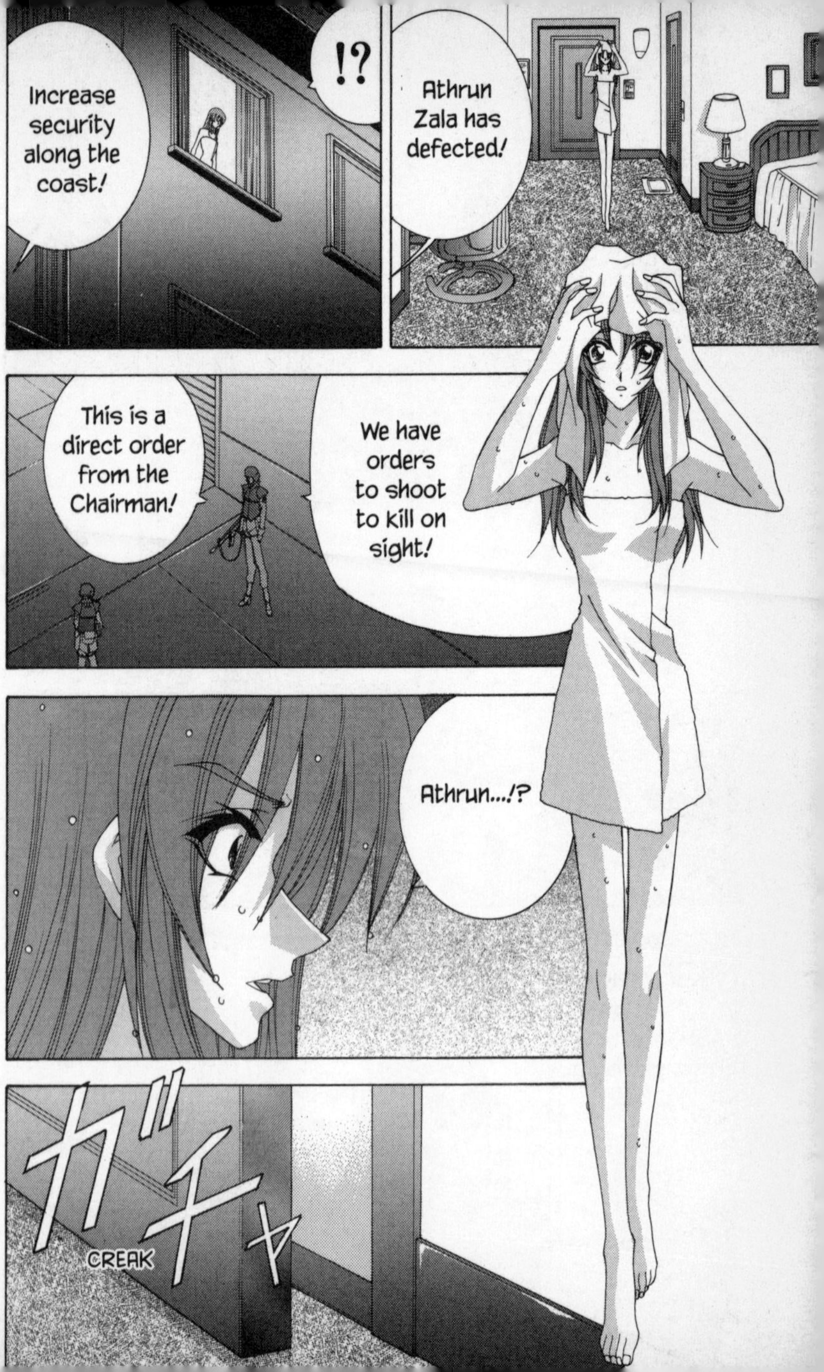

Athrun Zala has defected!
!?
Increase security along the coast!
We have orders to shoot to kill on sight!
This is a direct order from the Chairman!
Athrun...!?
ガチャ
CREAK

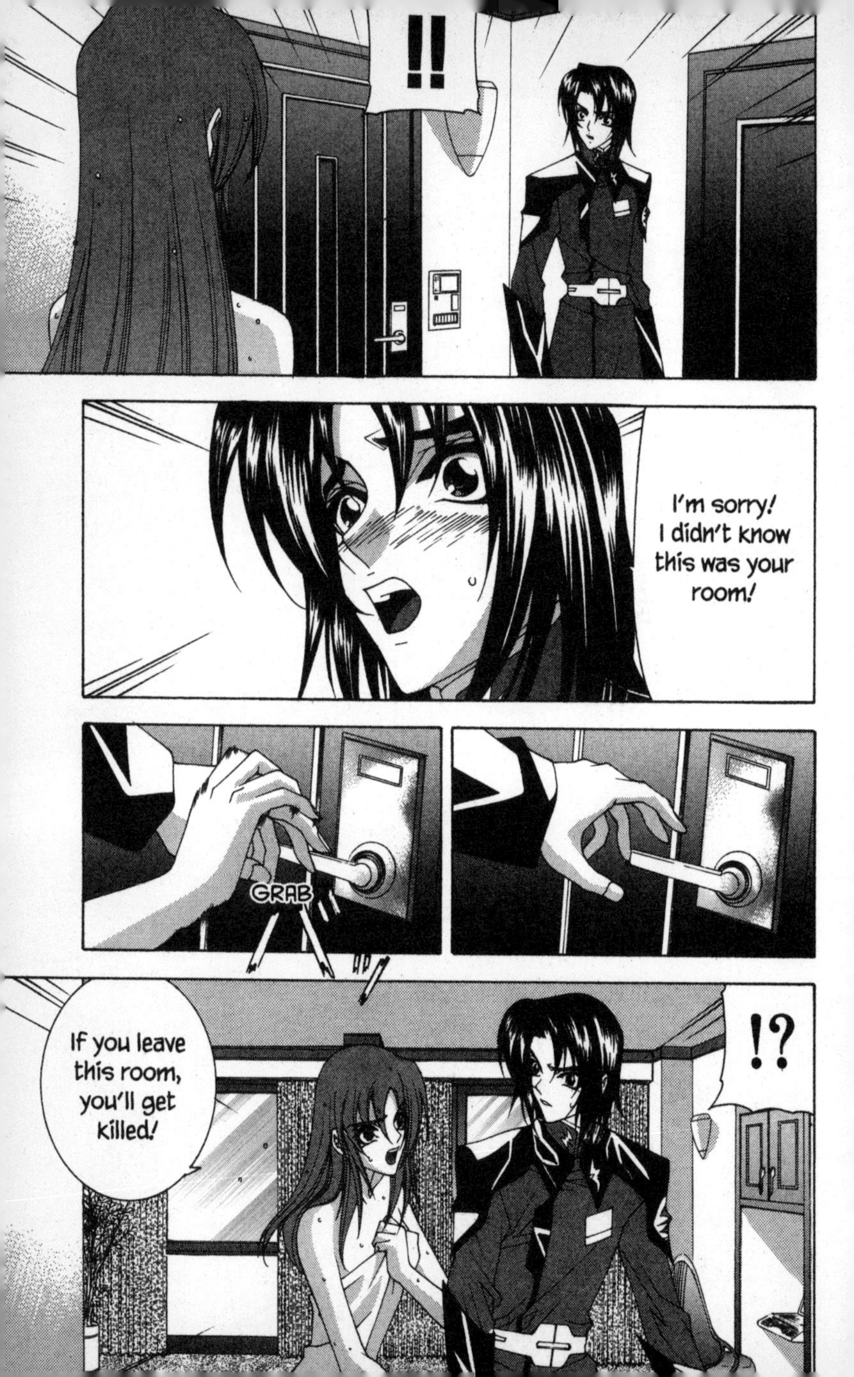
!!
I'm sorry! I didn't know this was your room!
GRAB
!?
If you leave this room, you'll get killed!

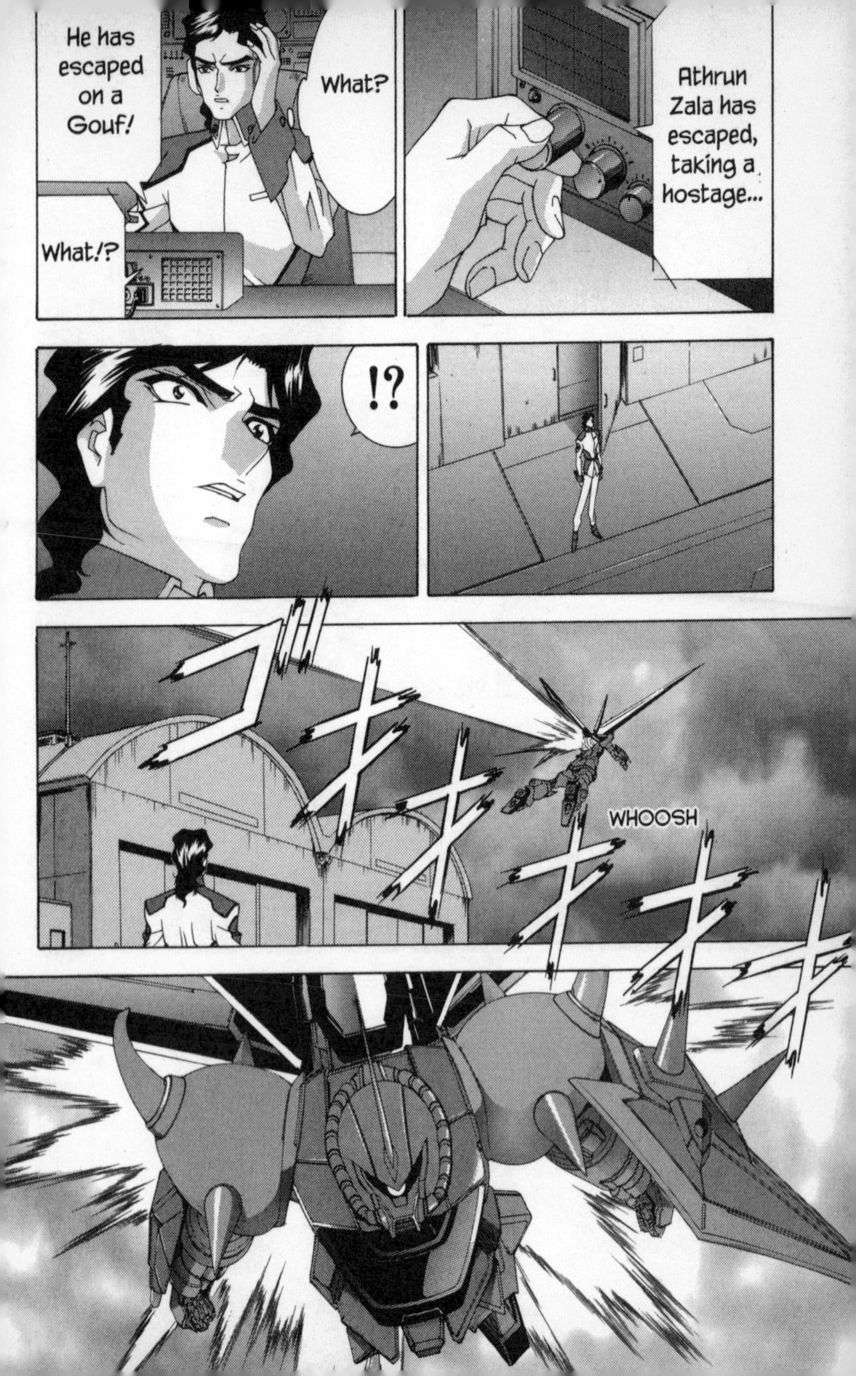

Athrun Zala has escaped, taking a hostage...
What?
He has escaped on a Gouf!
What!?
!?
ゴオオオオオ
WHOOSH

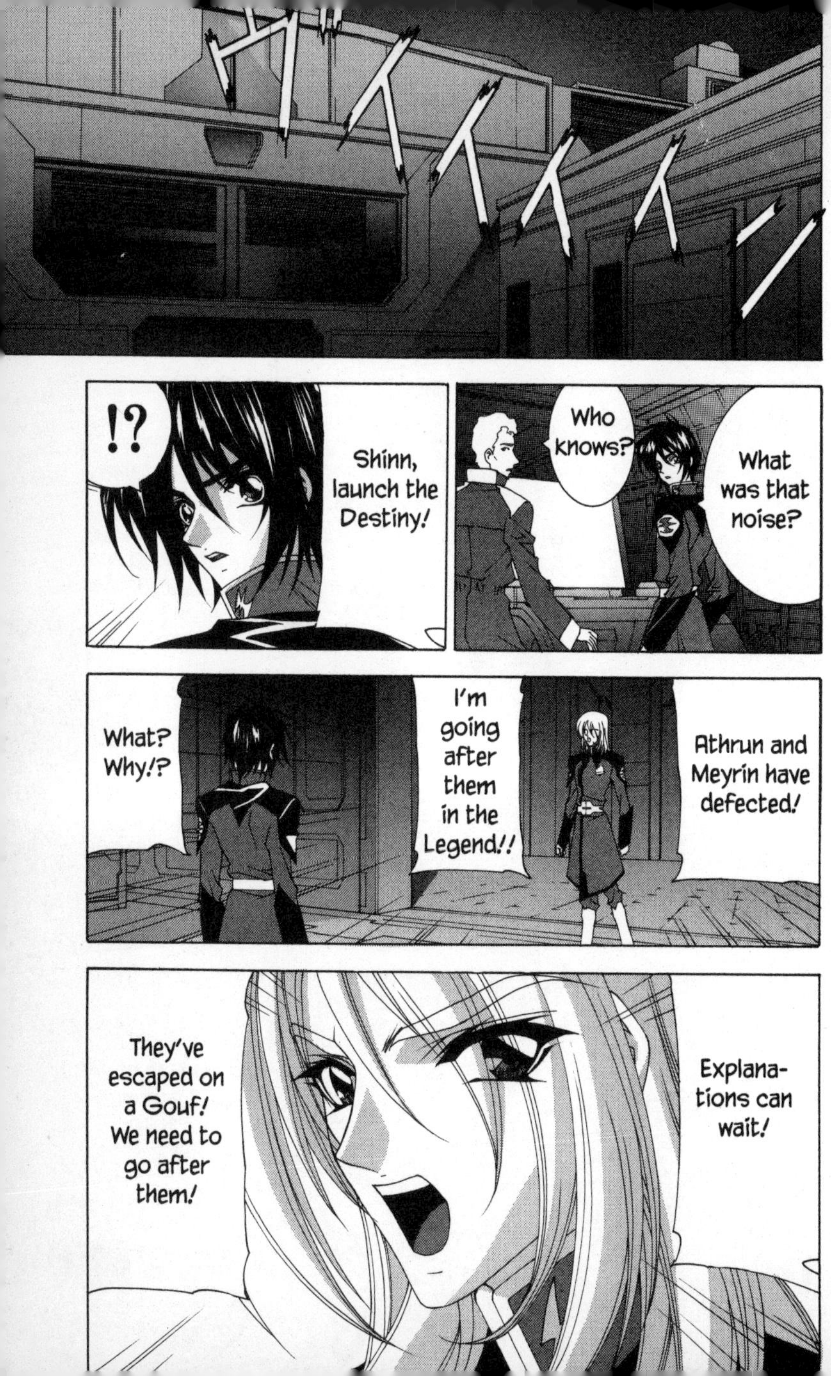
What was that noise?
Who knows?
Shinn, launch the Destiny!
!?
Athrun and Meyrin have defected!
I'm going after them in the Legend!!
What? Why!?
Explana-tions can wait!
They've escaped on a Gouf! We need to go after them!

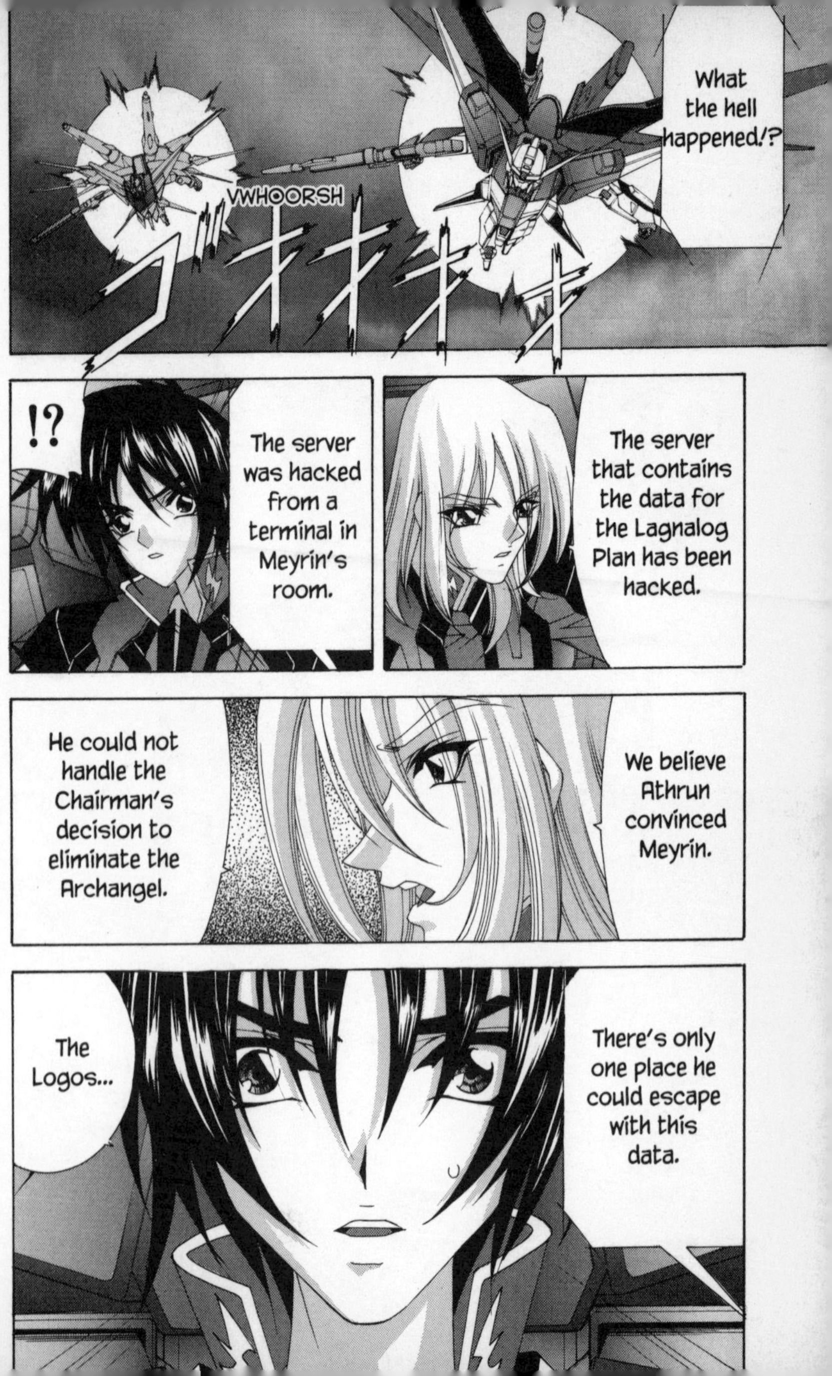
What the hell happened!?
VWHOORSH
ゴオオオオ
The server that contains the data for the Lagnalog Plan has been hacked.
!?
The server was hacked from a terminal in Meyrin's room.
We believe Athrun convinced Meyrin.
He could not handle the Chairman's decision to eliminate the Archangel.
There's only one place he could escape with this data.
The Logos...

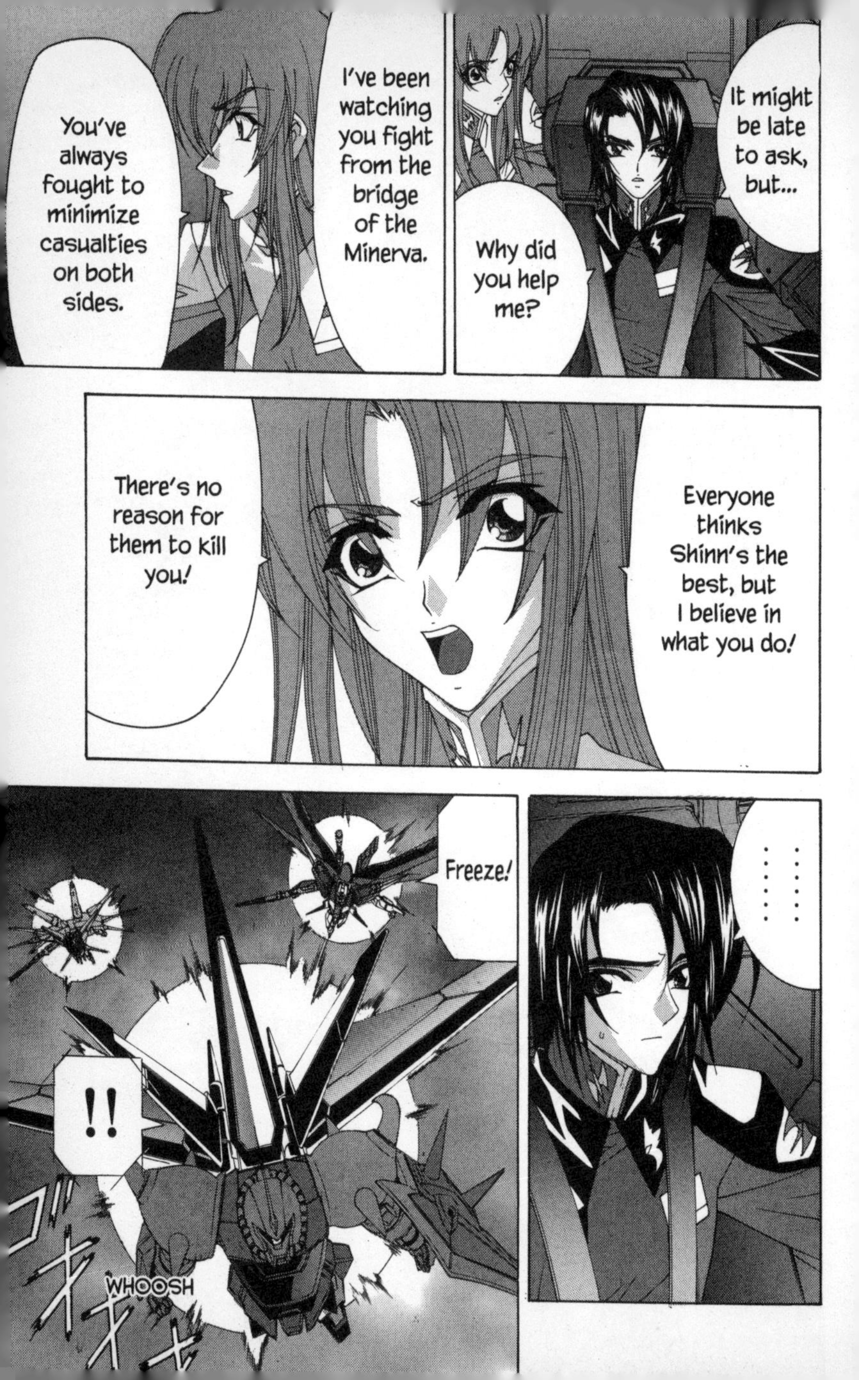
It might be late to ask, but...
Why did you help me?
I've been watching you fight from the bridge of the Minerva.
You've always fought to minimize casualties on both sides.
Everyone thinks Shinn's the best, but I believe in what you do!
There's no reason for them to kill you!
......
Freeze!
!!
WHOOSH

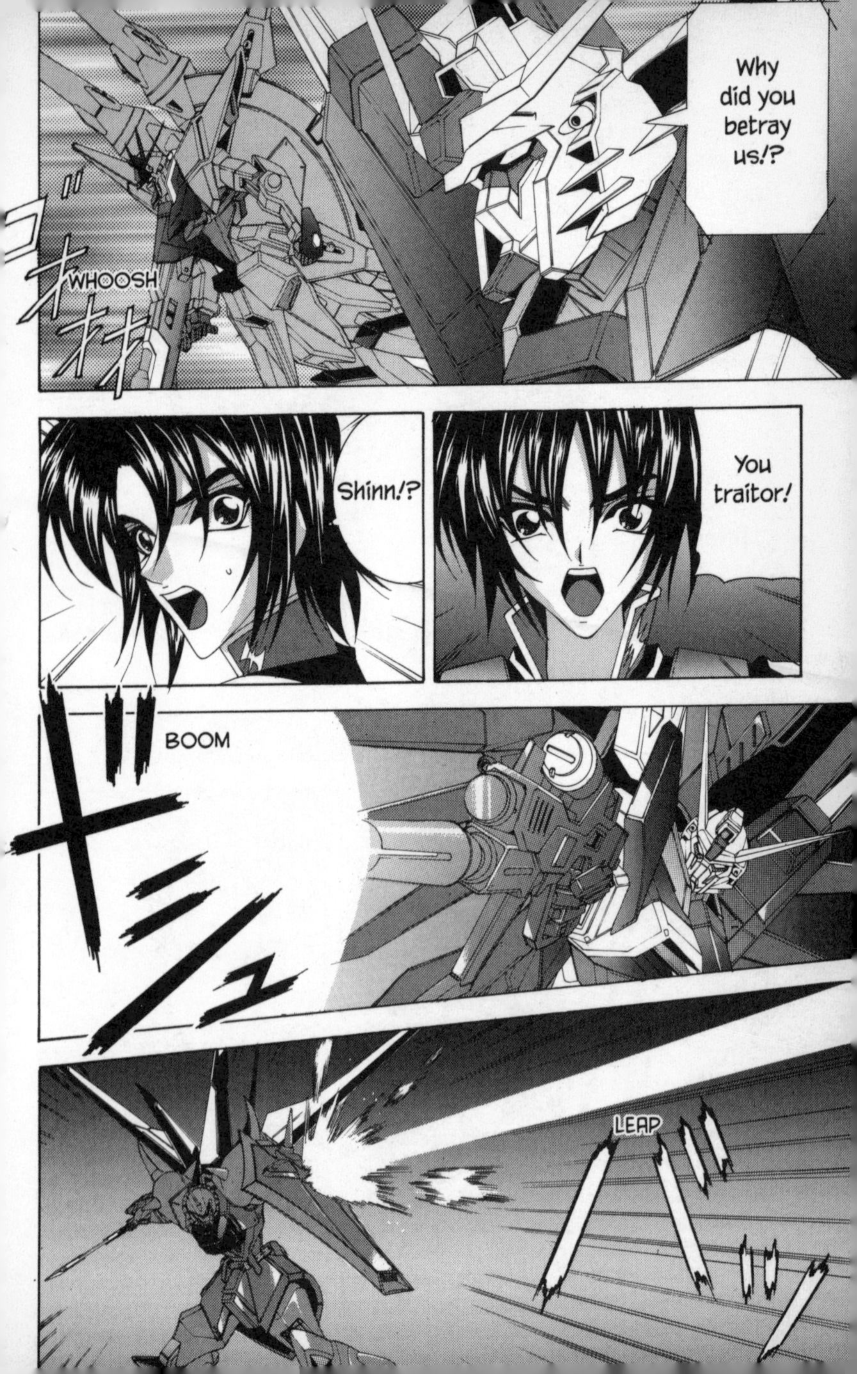
Why did you betray us!?
WHOOSH
You traitor!
Shinn!?
BOOM
LEAP

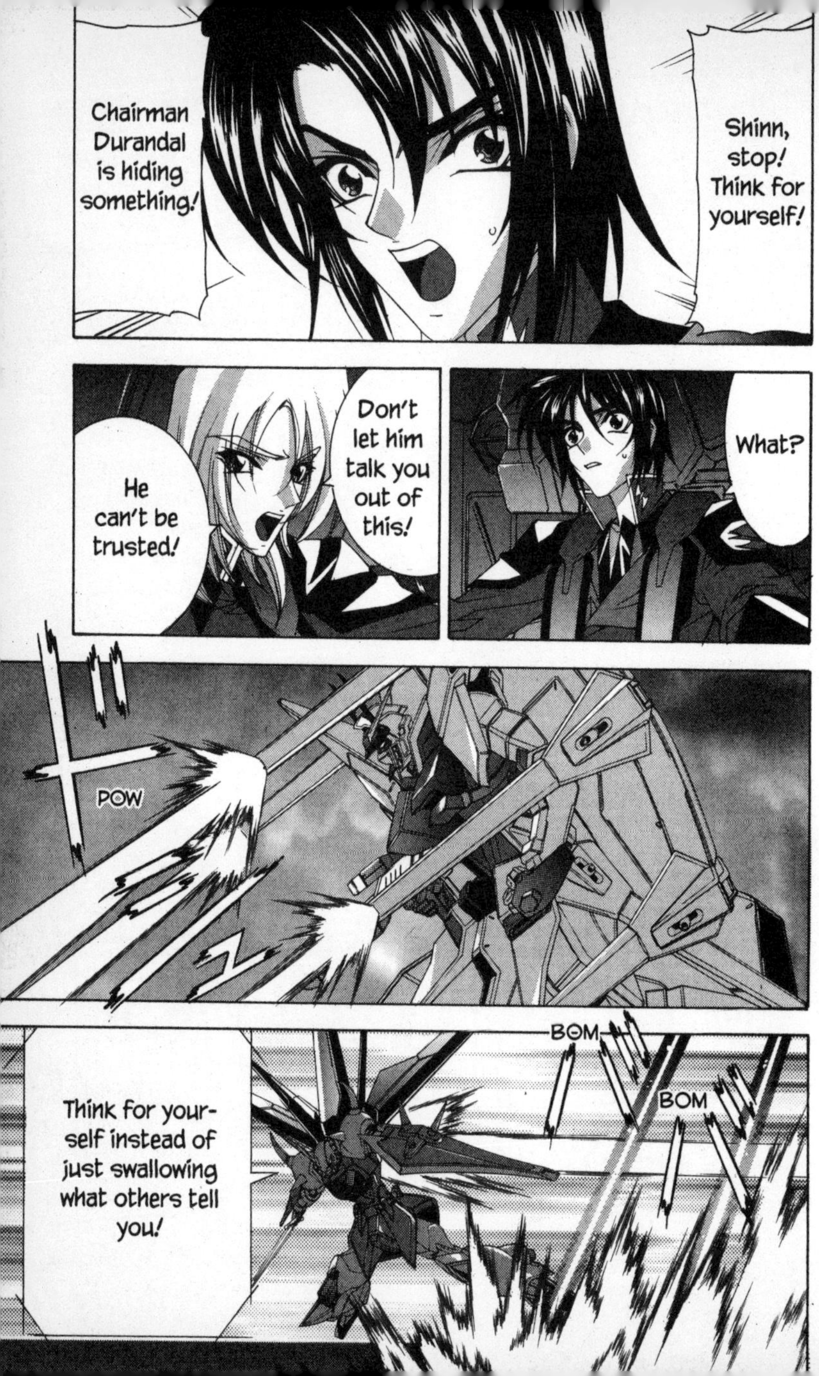
Shinn, stop! Think for yourself!
Chairman Durandal is hiding something!
What?
Don't let him talk you out of this!
He can't be trusted!
POW
BOM
BOM
Think for your-self instead of just swallowing what others tell you!

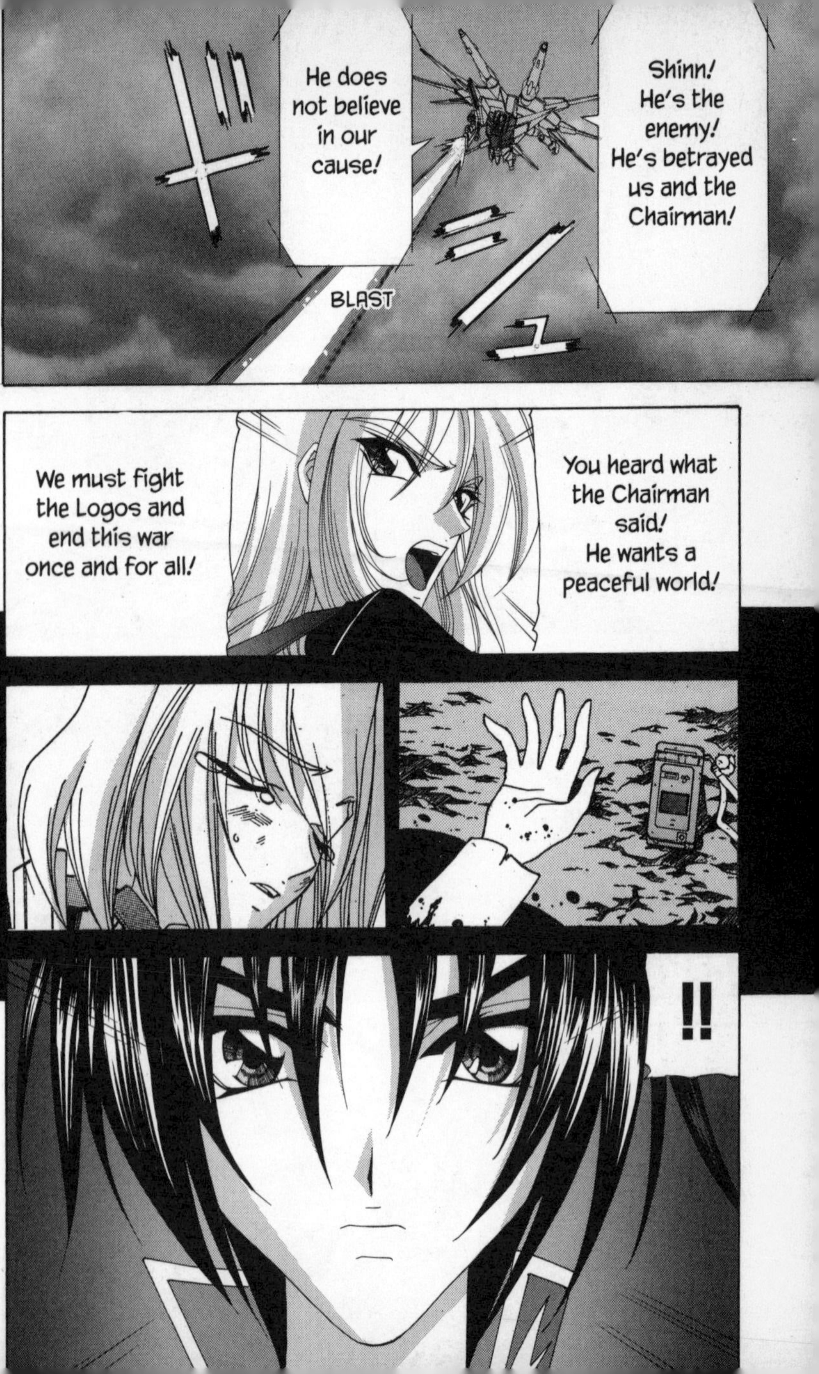
Shinn! He's the enemy! He's betrayed us and the Chairman!
He does not believe in our cause!
BLAST
You heard what the Chairman said! He wants a peaceful world!
We must fight the Logos and end this war once and for all!
!!

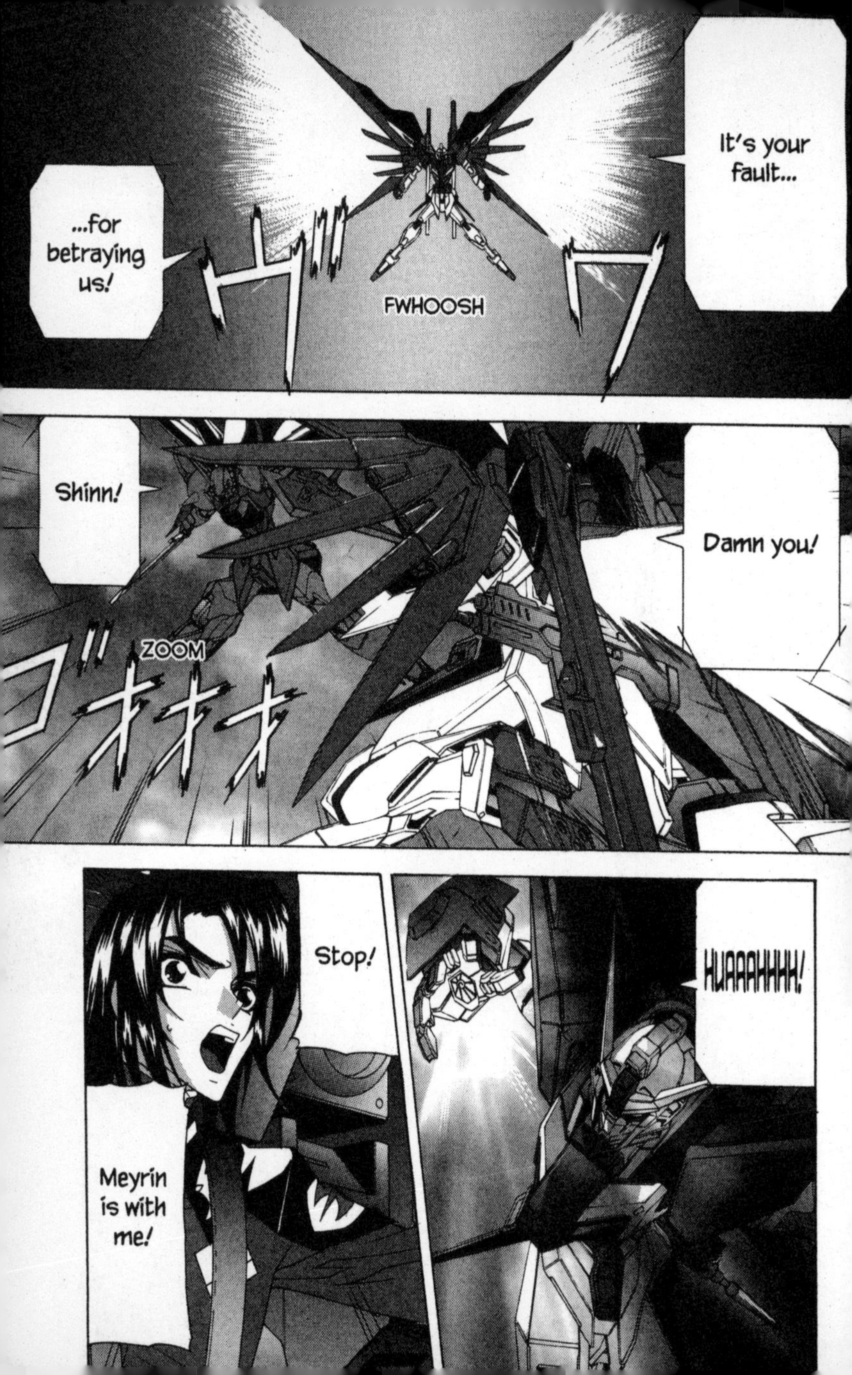
It's your fault...
...for betraying us!
FWHOOSH
Damn you!
Shinn!
ZOOM
HUAAAHHHH!
Stop!
Meyrin is with me!

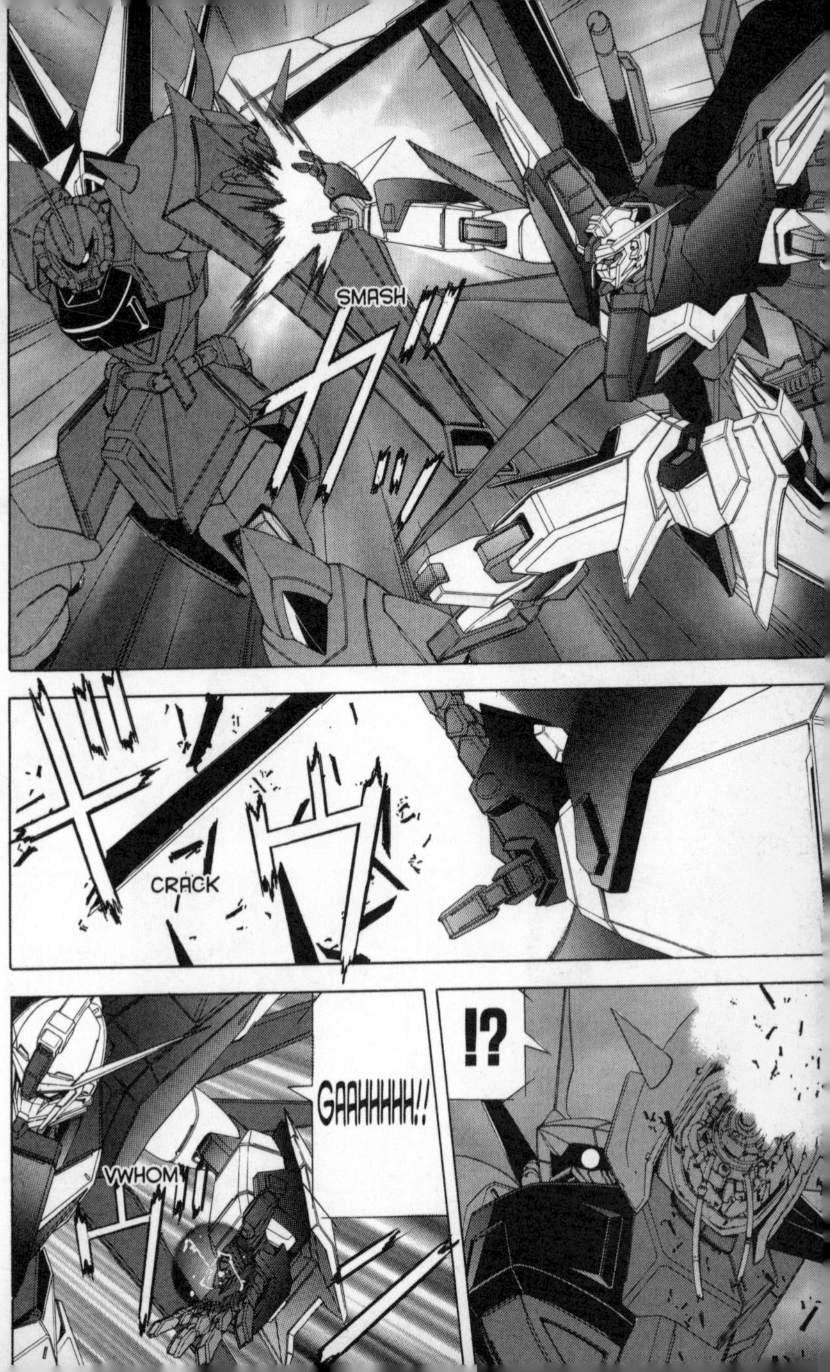
SMASH
CRACK
!?
GAAHHHH!!
VWHOM

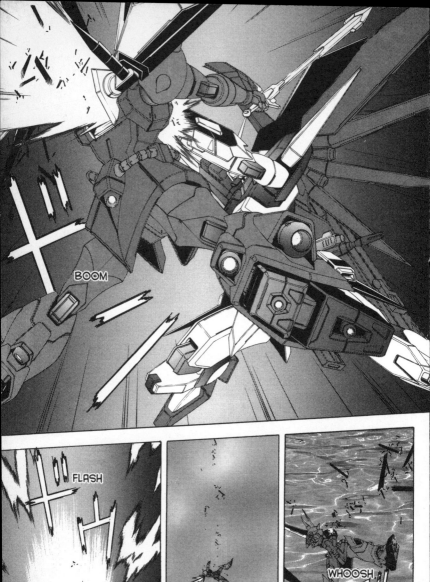

BOOM

FLASH

WHOOSH

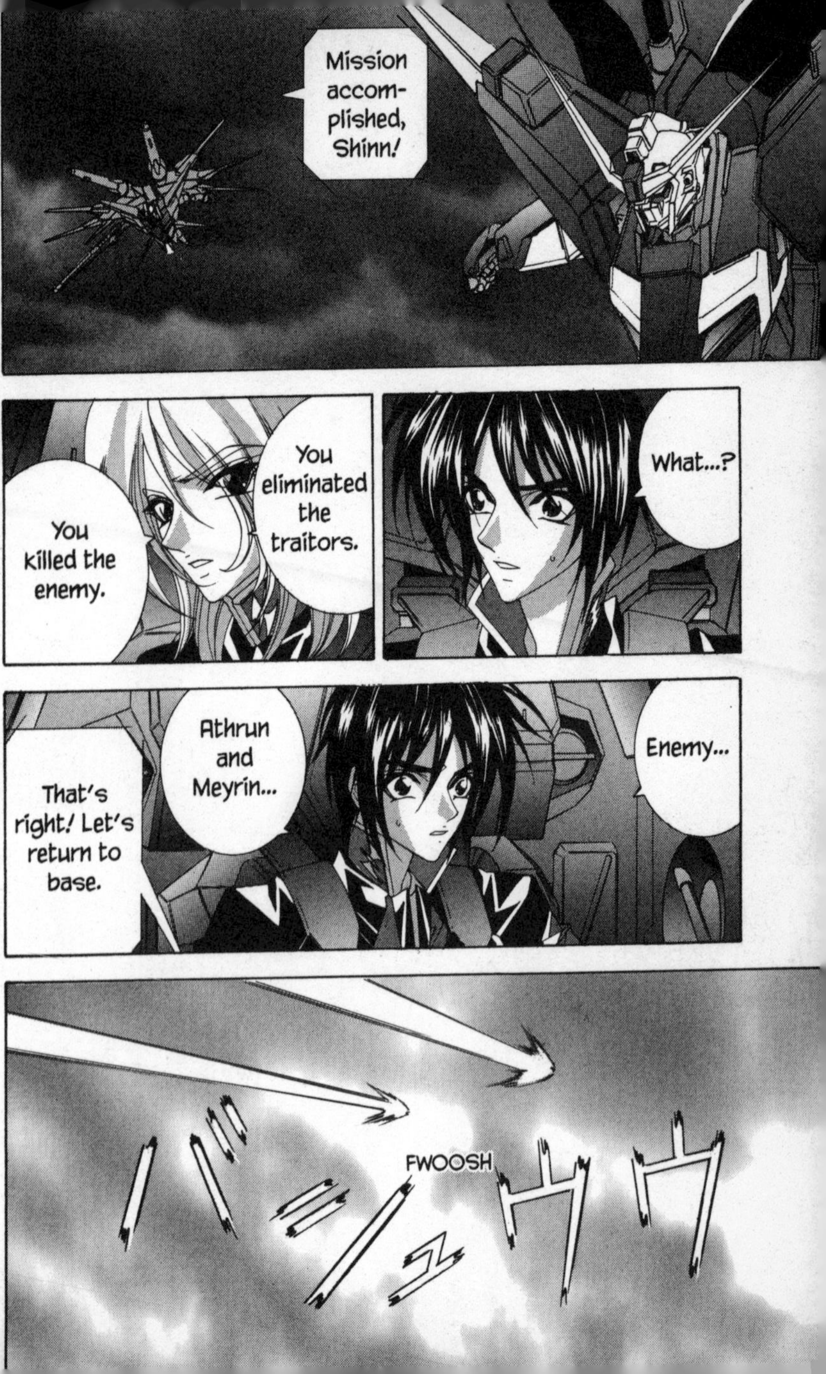
Mission accom-plished, Shinn!
What...?
You eliminated the traitors.
You killed the enemy.
Enemy...
Athrun and Meyrin...
That's right! Let's return to base.
FWOOSH

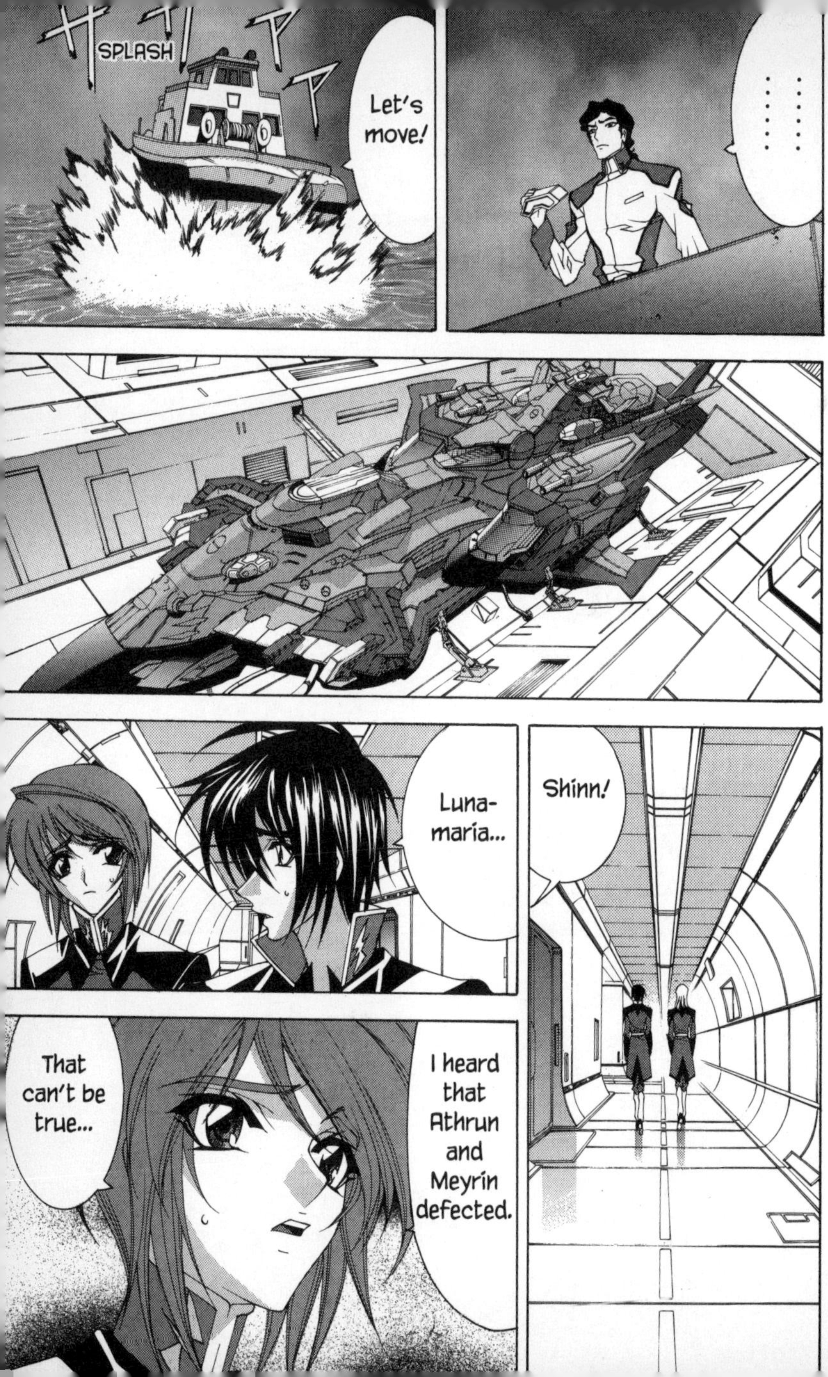
......
SPLASH
Let's move!
Shinn!
Luna-maria...
I heard that Athrun and Meyrin defected.
That can't be true...

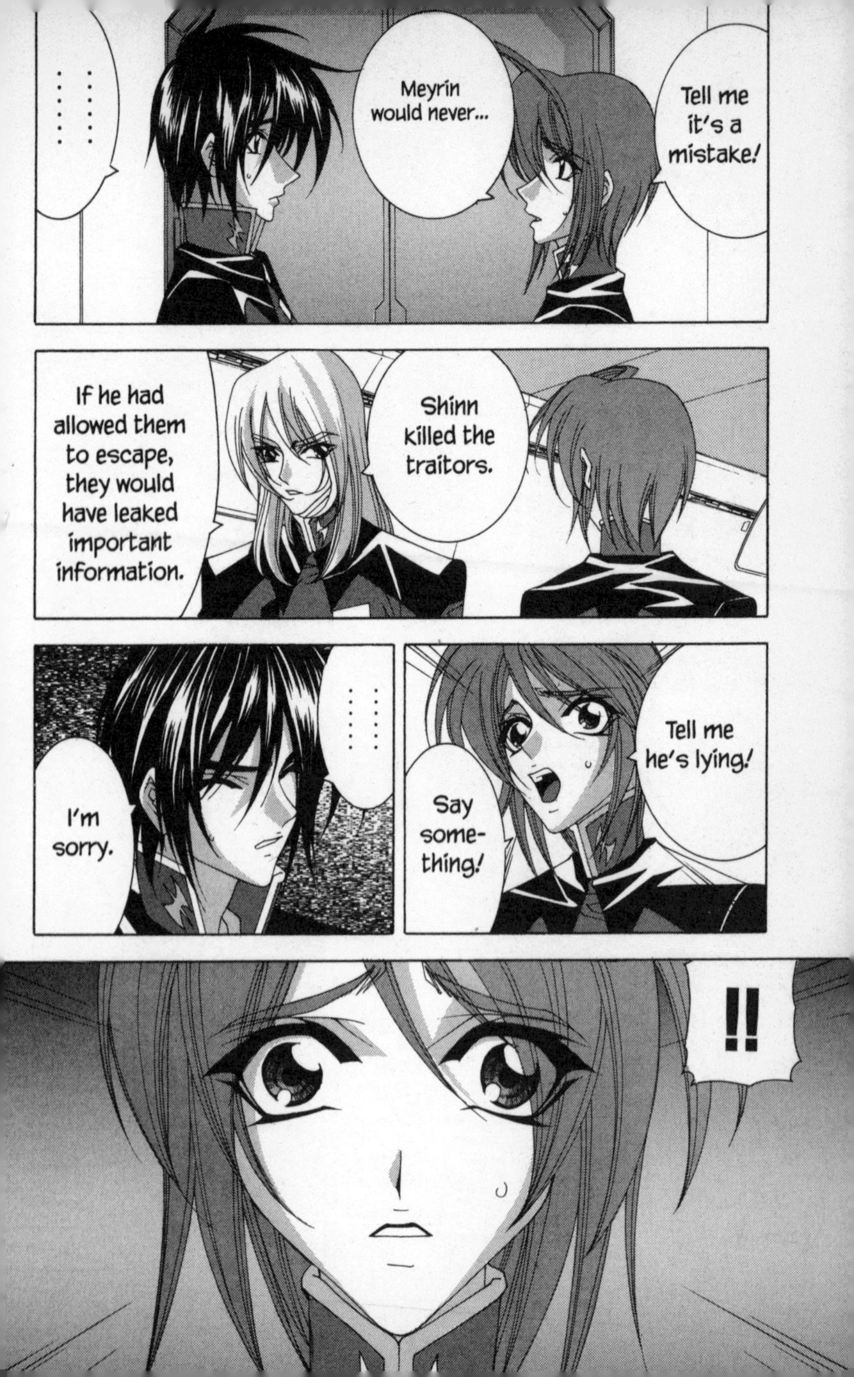
Tell me it's a mistake!
Meyrin would never...
......
Shinn killed the traitors.
If he had allowed them to escape, they would have leaked important information.
Tell me he's lying!
Say some-thing!
......
I'm sorry.
!!

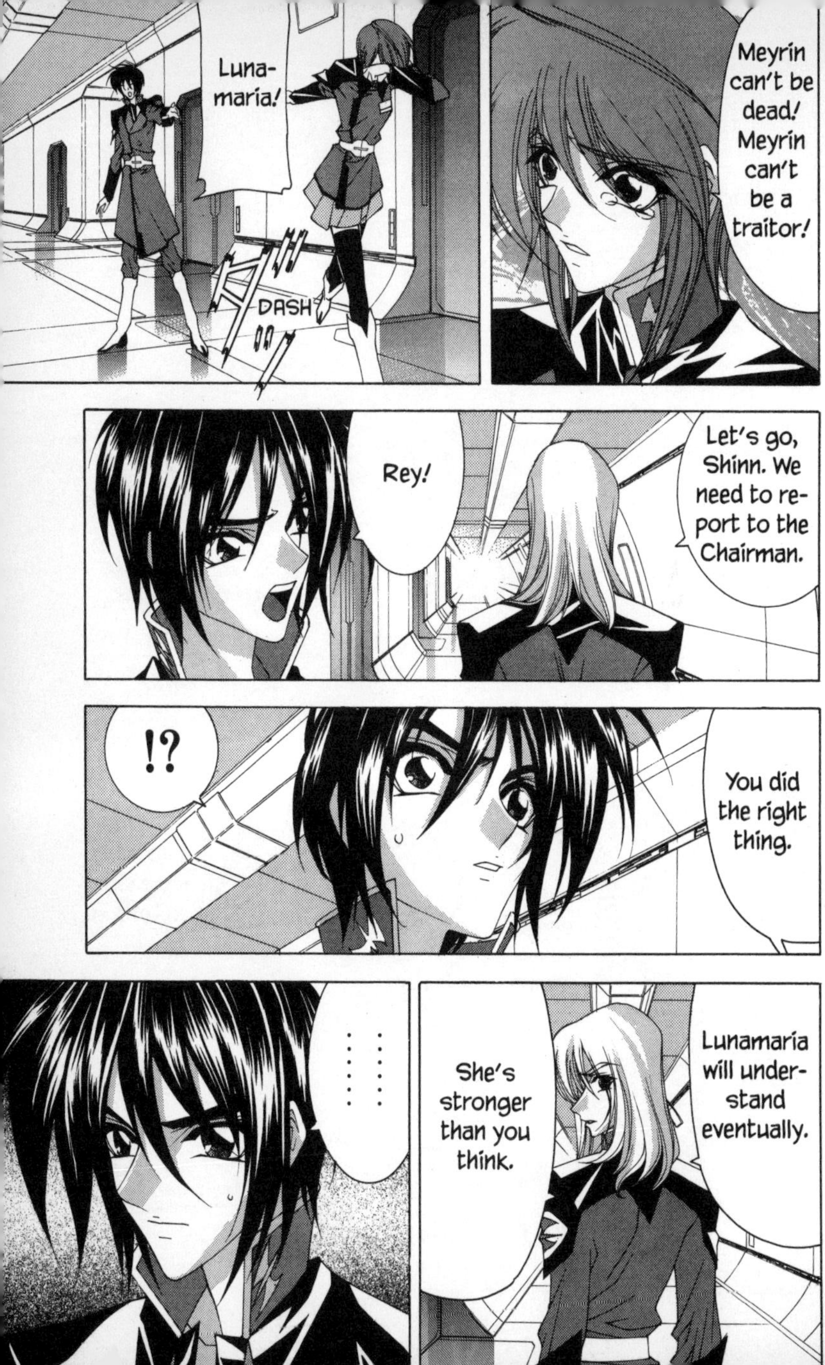
Meyrin can't be dead! Meyrin can't be a traitor!
Luna-maria!
DASH
Let's go, Shinn. We need to re-port to the Chairman.
Rey!
You did the right thing.
!?
Lunamaria will under-stand eventually.
She's stronger than you think.
......

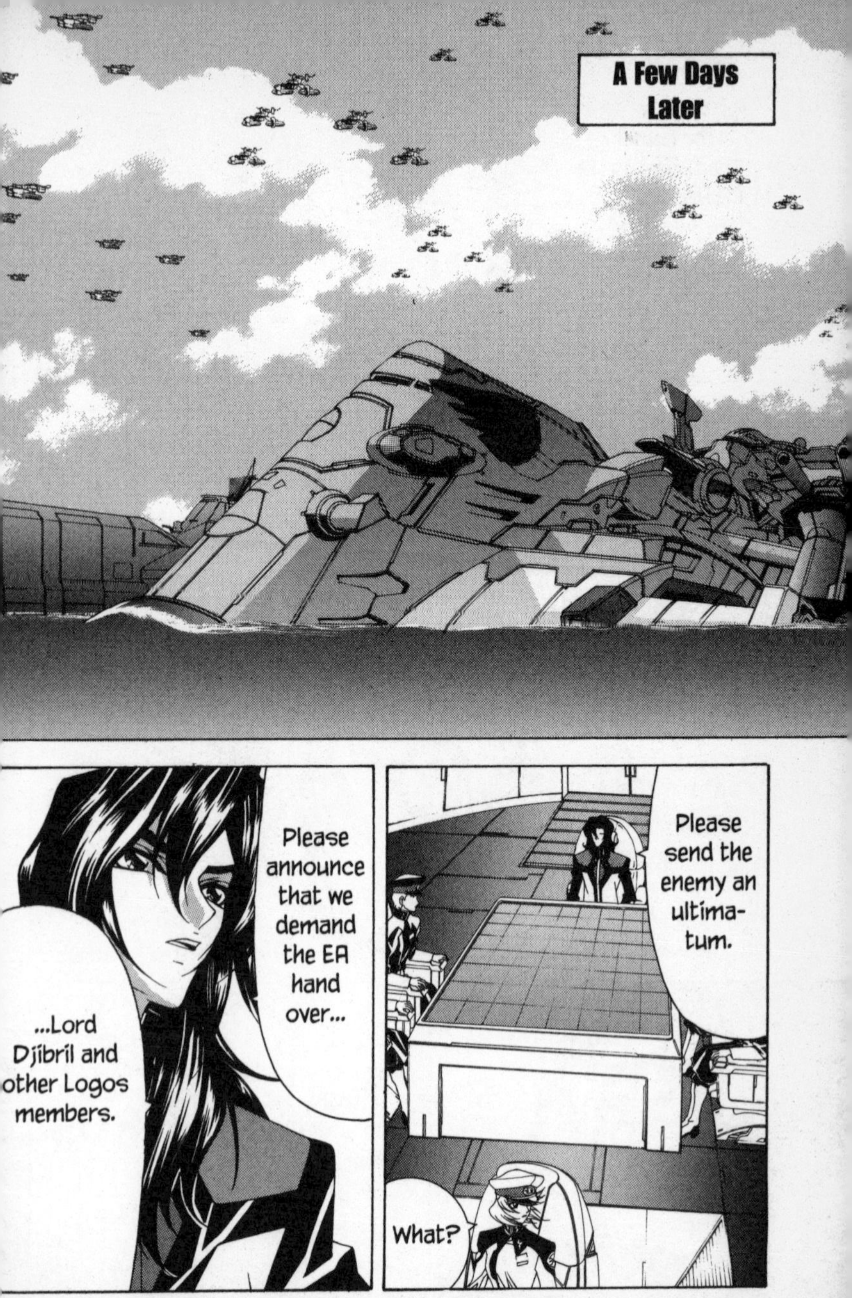
A Few Days Later
Please send the enemy an ultimatum.
What?
Please announce that we demand the EA hand over...
...Lord Djibril and other Logos members.

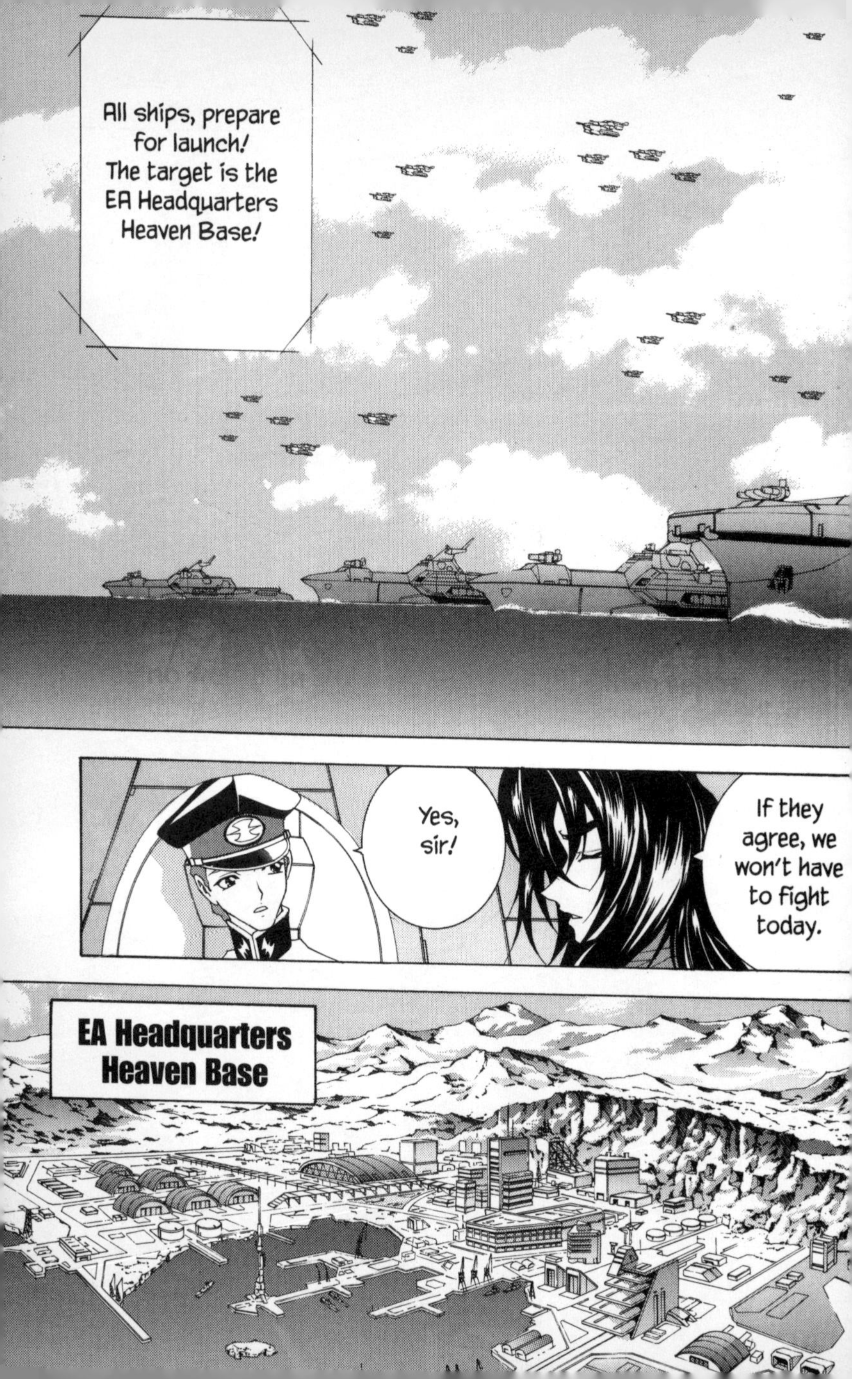
All ships, prepare for launch! The target is the EA Headquarters Heaven Base!
If they agree, we won't have to fight today.
Yes, sir!
EA Headquarters Heaven Base

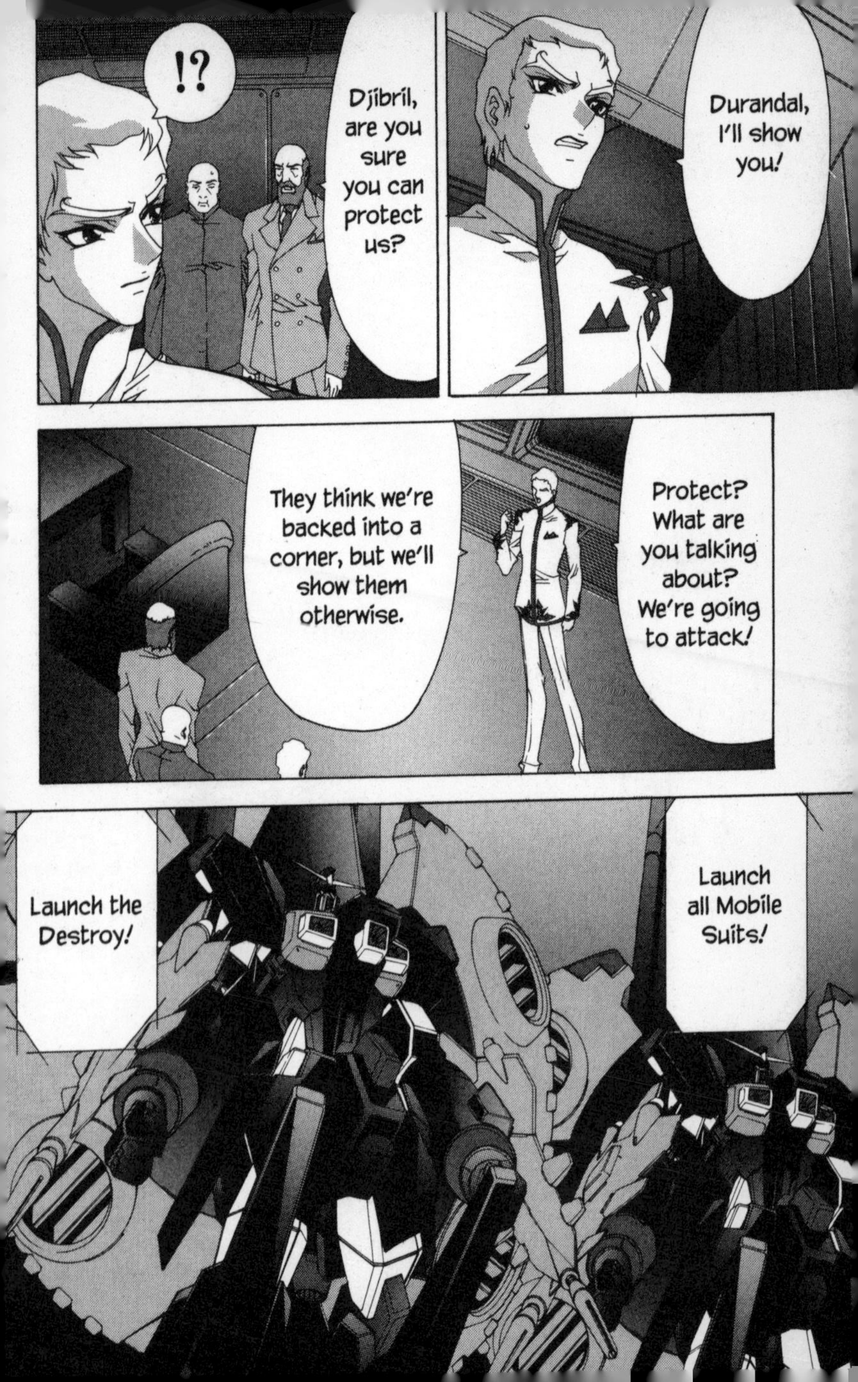
Durandal, I'll show you!
Djibril, are you sure you can protect us?
!?
Protect? What are you talking about? We're going to attack!
They think we're backed into a corner, but we'll show them otherwise.
Launch all Mobile Suits!
Launch the Destroy!

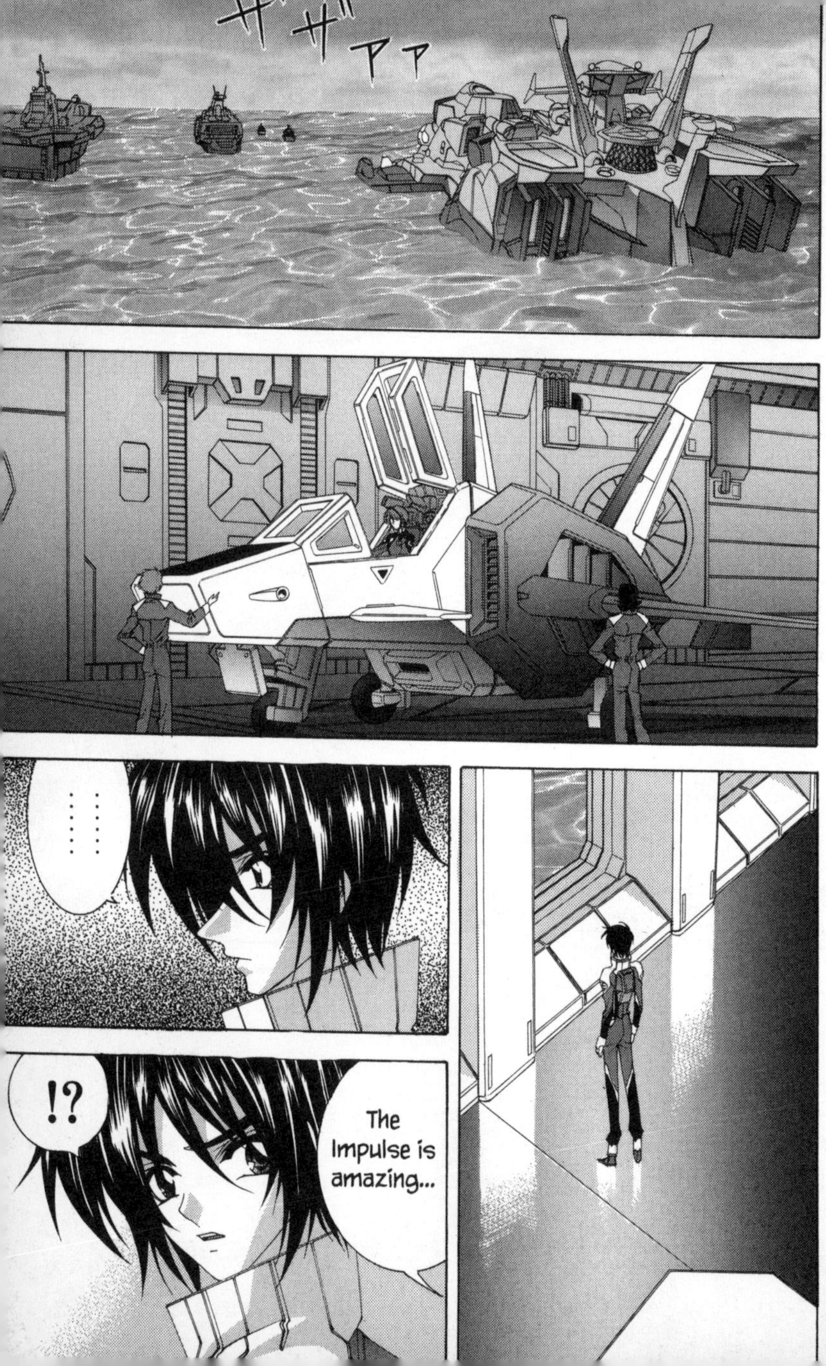
ザザァァ
......
!?
The Impulse is amazing...

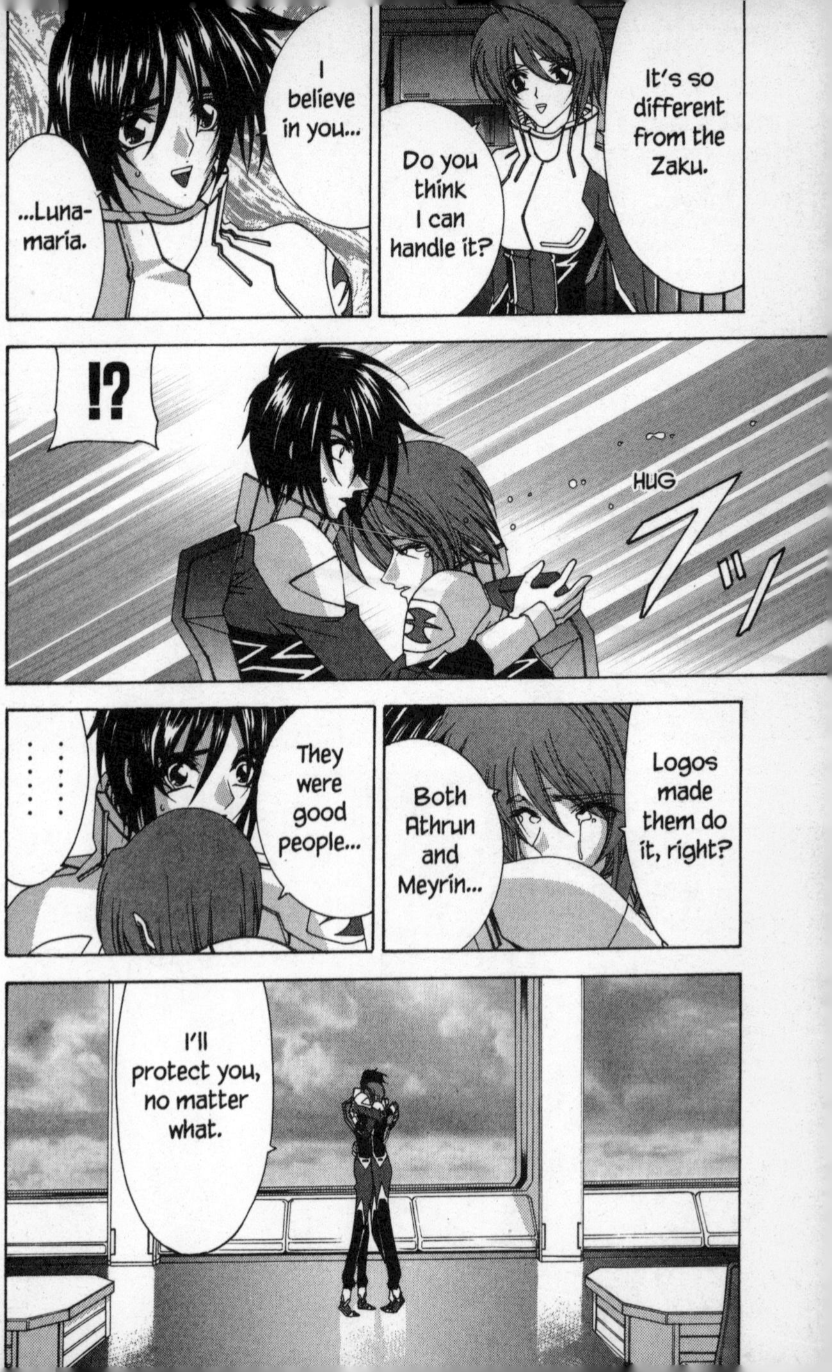
It's so different from the Zaku.
Do you think I can handle it?
I believe in you...
...Luna-maria.
!?
HUG
Logos made them do it, right?
Both Athrun and Meyrin...
They were good people...
......
I'll protect you, no matter what.

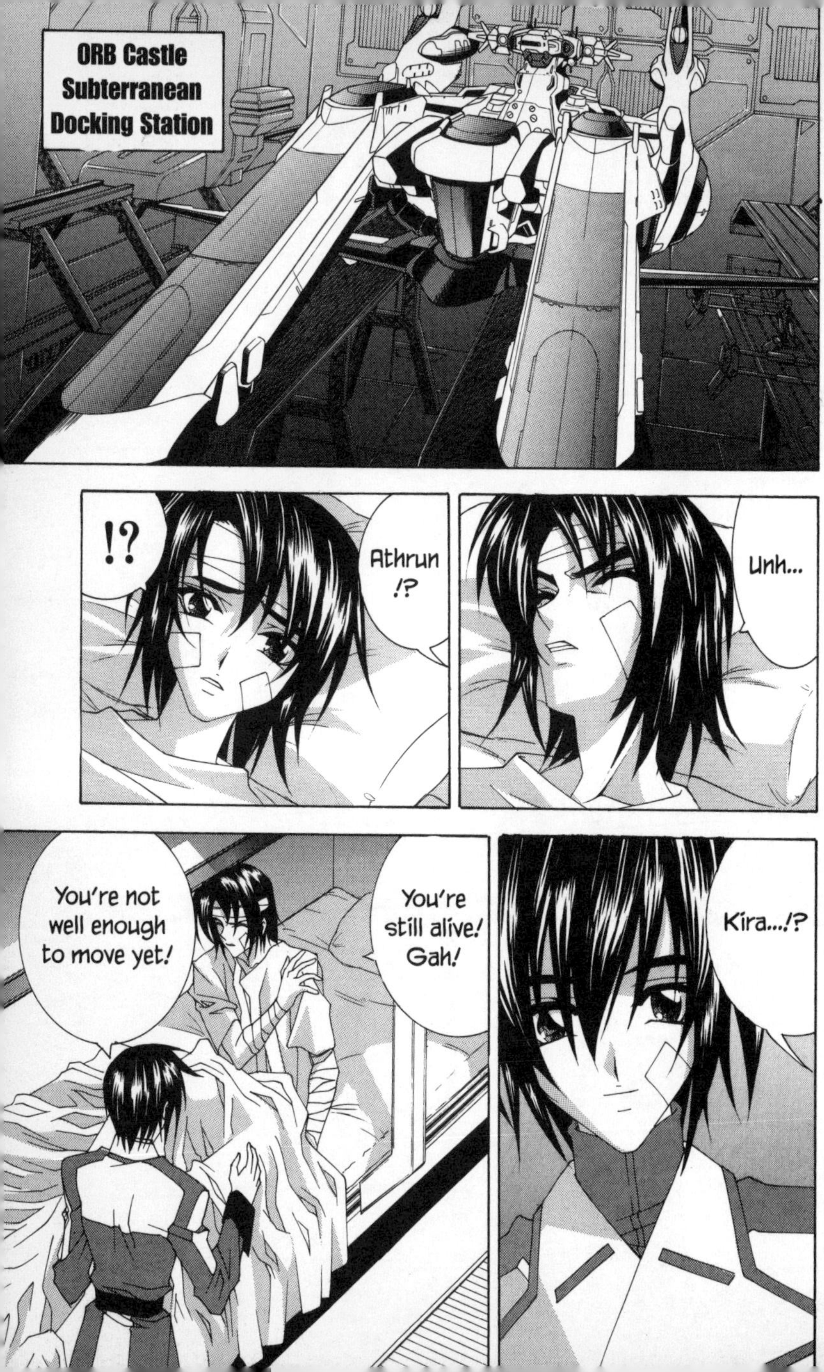
ORB Castle Subterranean Docking Station
Unh...
Athrun !?
!?
Kira...!?
You're still alive! Gah!
You're not well enough to move yet!

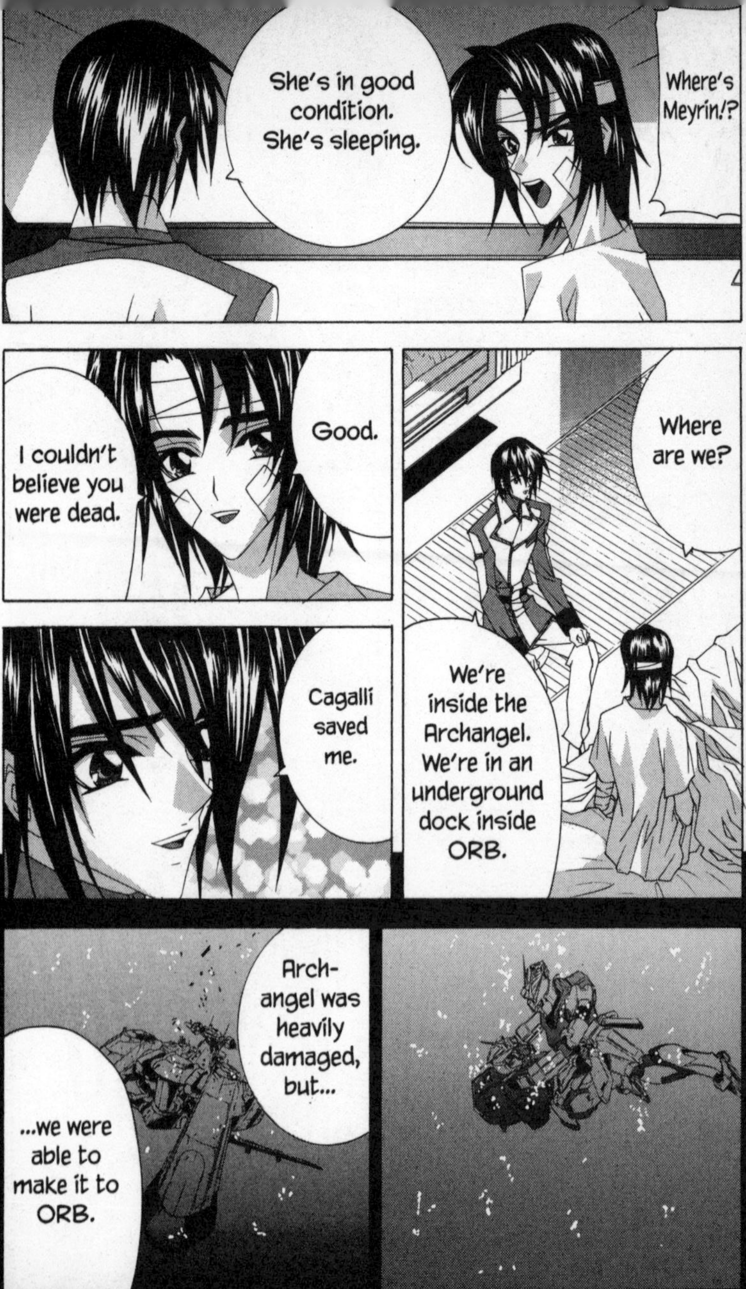

Where's Meyrin!?
She's in good condition. She's sleeping.
Where are we?
We're inside the Archangel. We're in an underground dock inside ORB.
Good.
I couldn't believe you were dead.
Cagalli saved me.
Arch-angel was heavily damaged, but...
...we were able to make it to ORB.

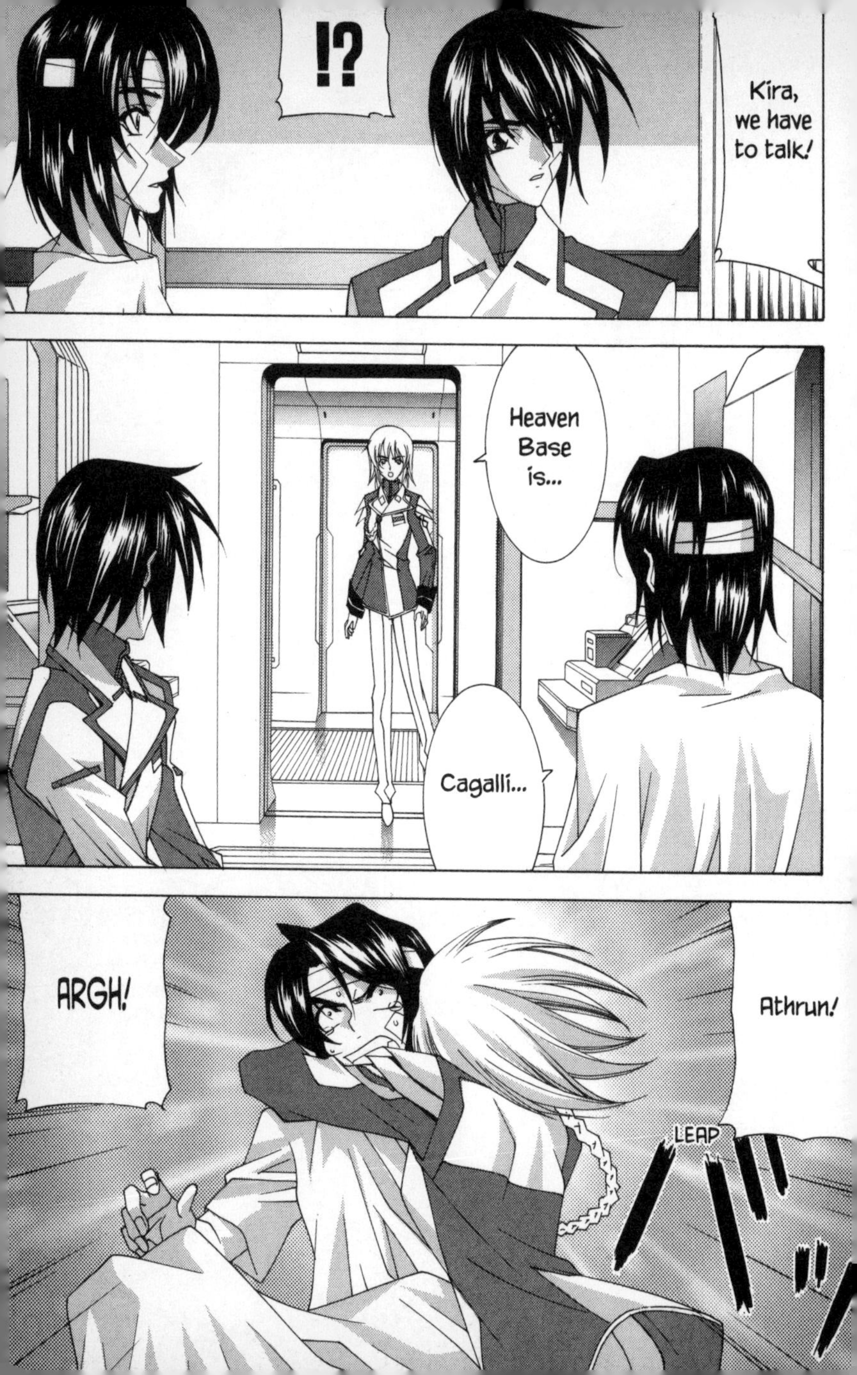

Kira, we have to talk!
!?
Heaven Base is...
Cagalli...
Athrun!
LEAP
ARGH!

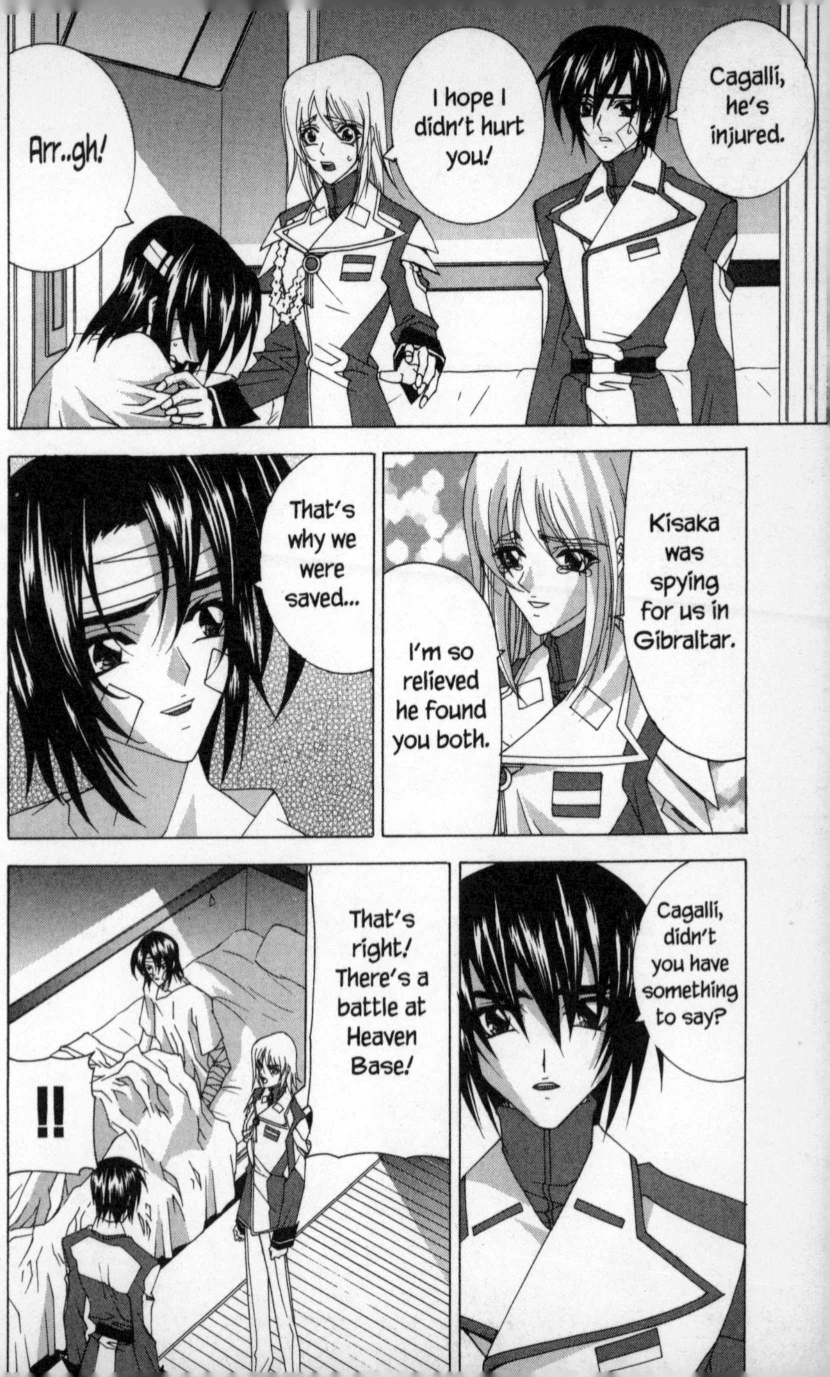
Cagalli, he's injured.
I hope I didn't hurt you!
Arr..gh!
Kisaka was spying for us in Gibraltar.
I'm so relieved he found you both.
That's why we were saved...
Cagalli, didn't you have something to say?
That's right! There's a battle at Heaven Base!
!!

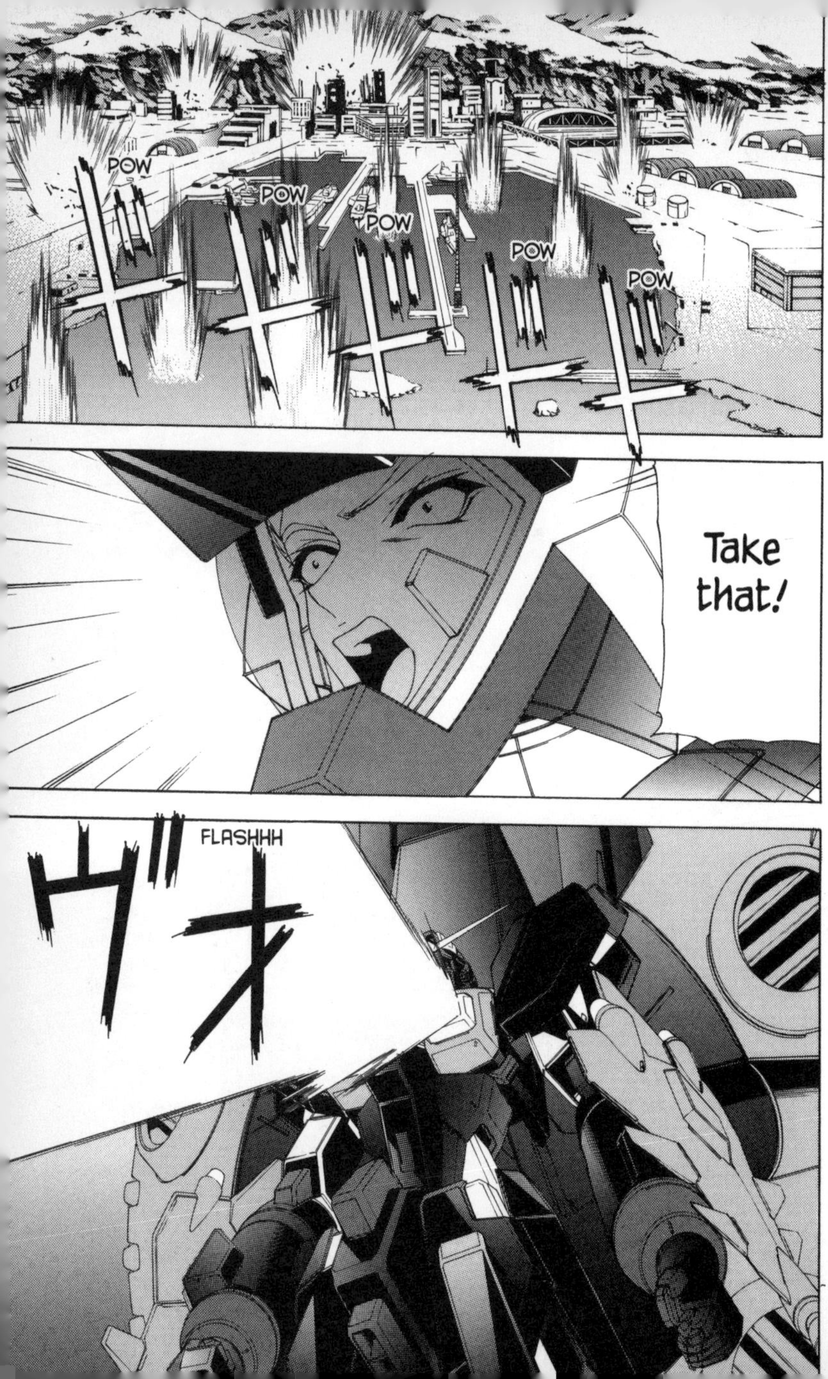
POW
POW
POW
POW
POW
Take that!
ヴオ
FLASHHH

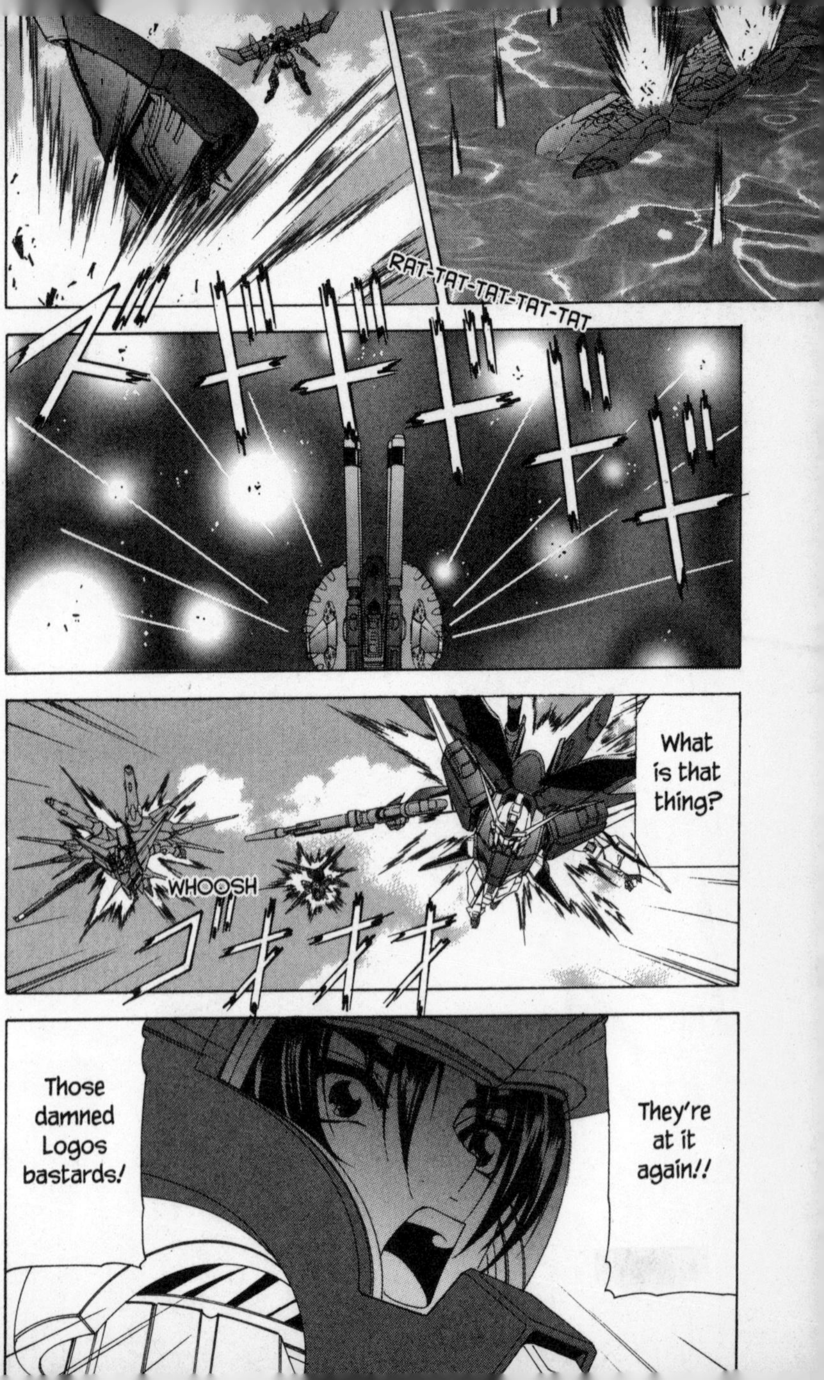
RAT-TAT-TAT-TAT-TAT
What is that thing?
WHOOSH
They're at it again!!
Those damned Logos bastards!

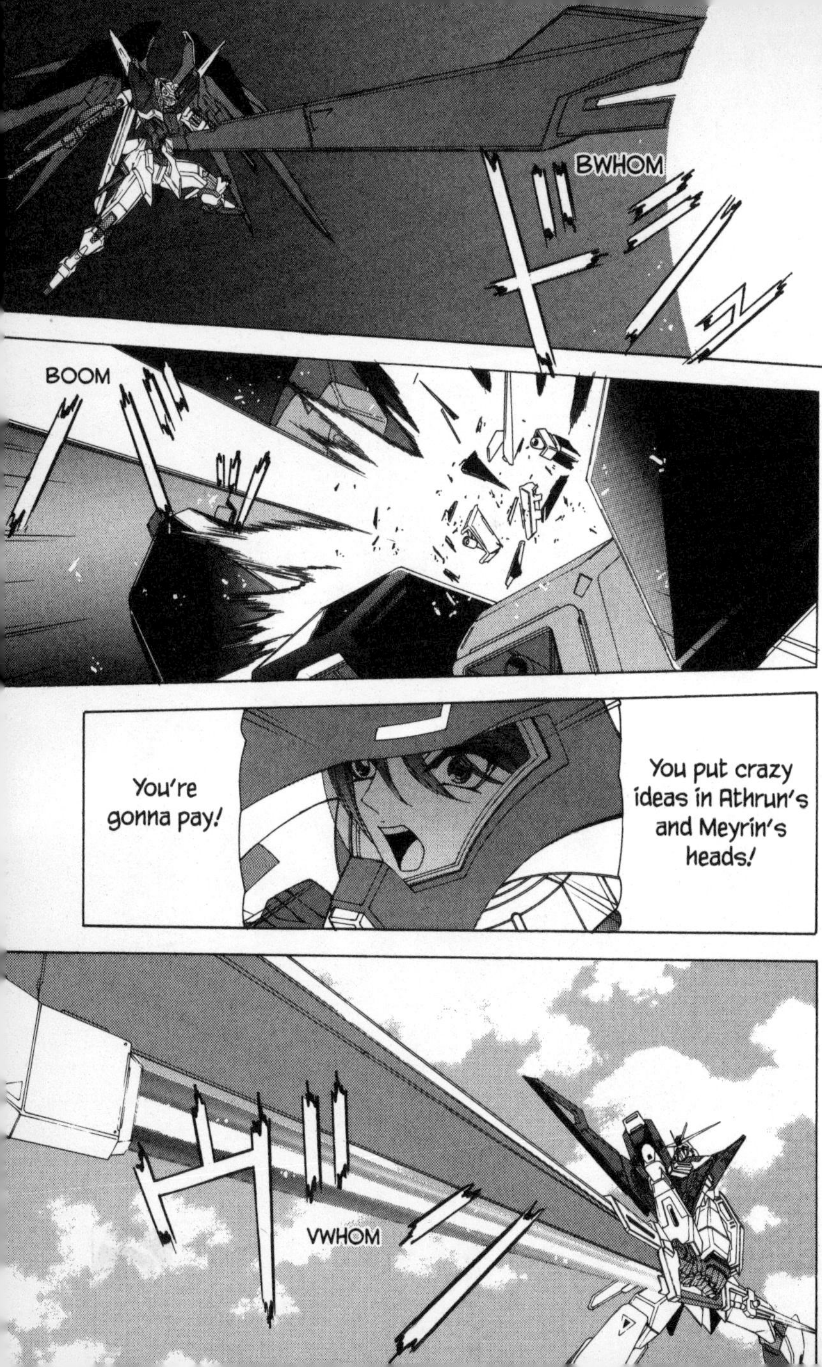
BWHOM
BOOM
You put crazy ideas in Athrun's and Meyrin's heads!
You're gonna pay!
VWHOM

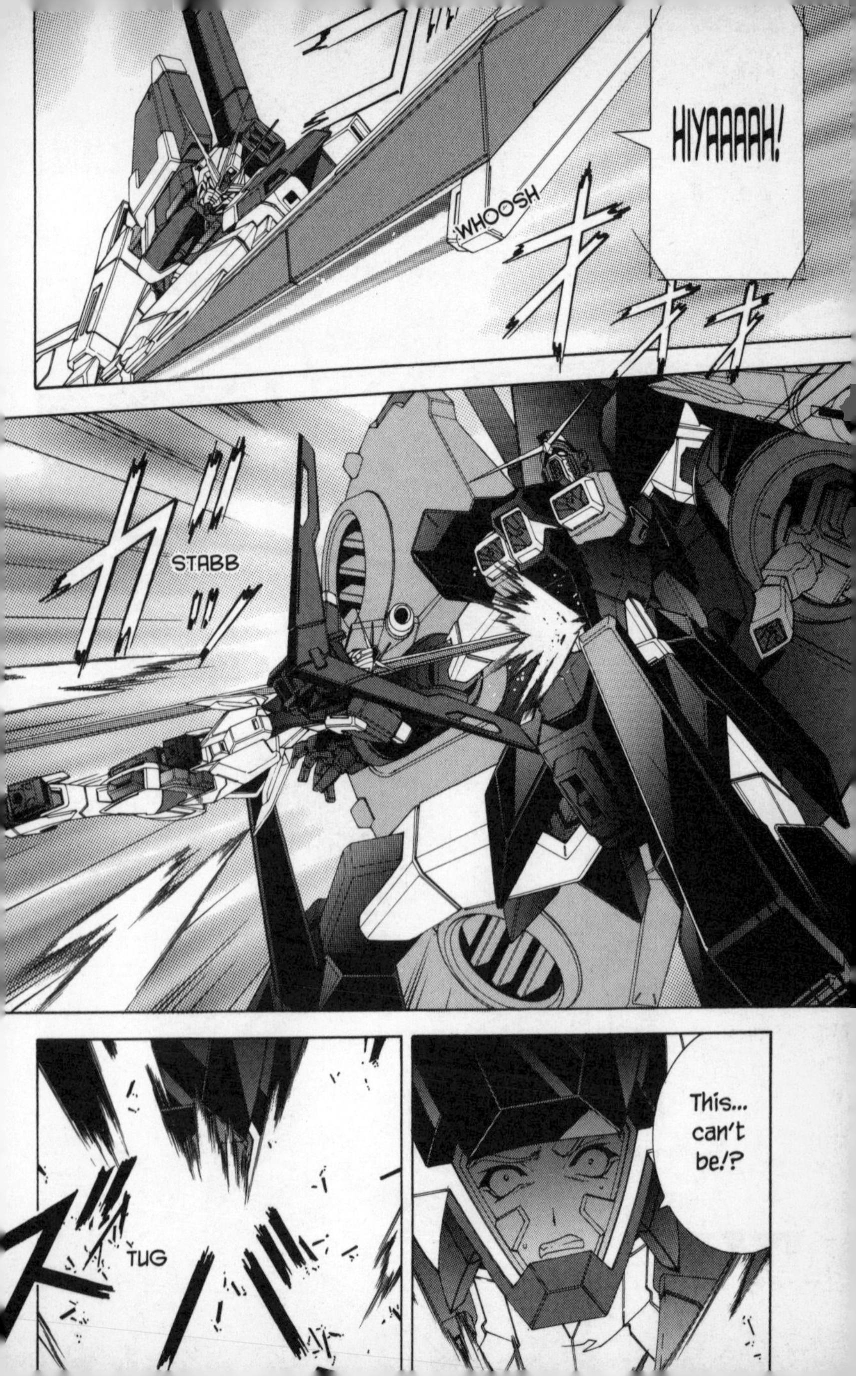
HIYAAAAH!
WHOOSH
STABB
This... can't be!?
TUG

YOOOO-OUUU!!
CRACK
BOOM
ズザオオ

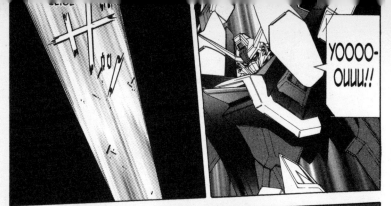

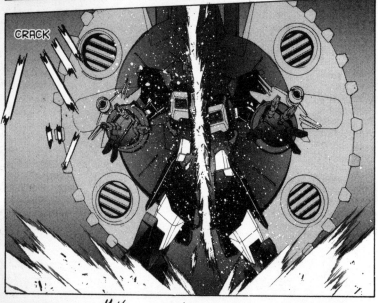

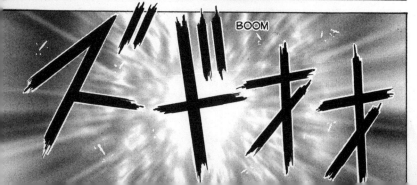

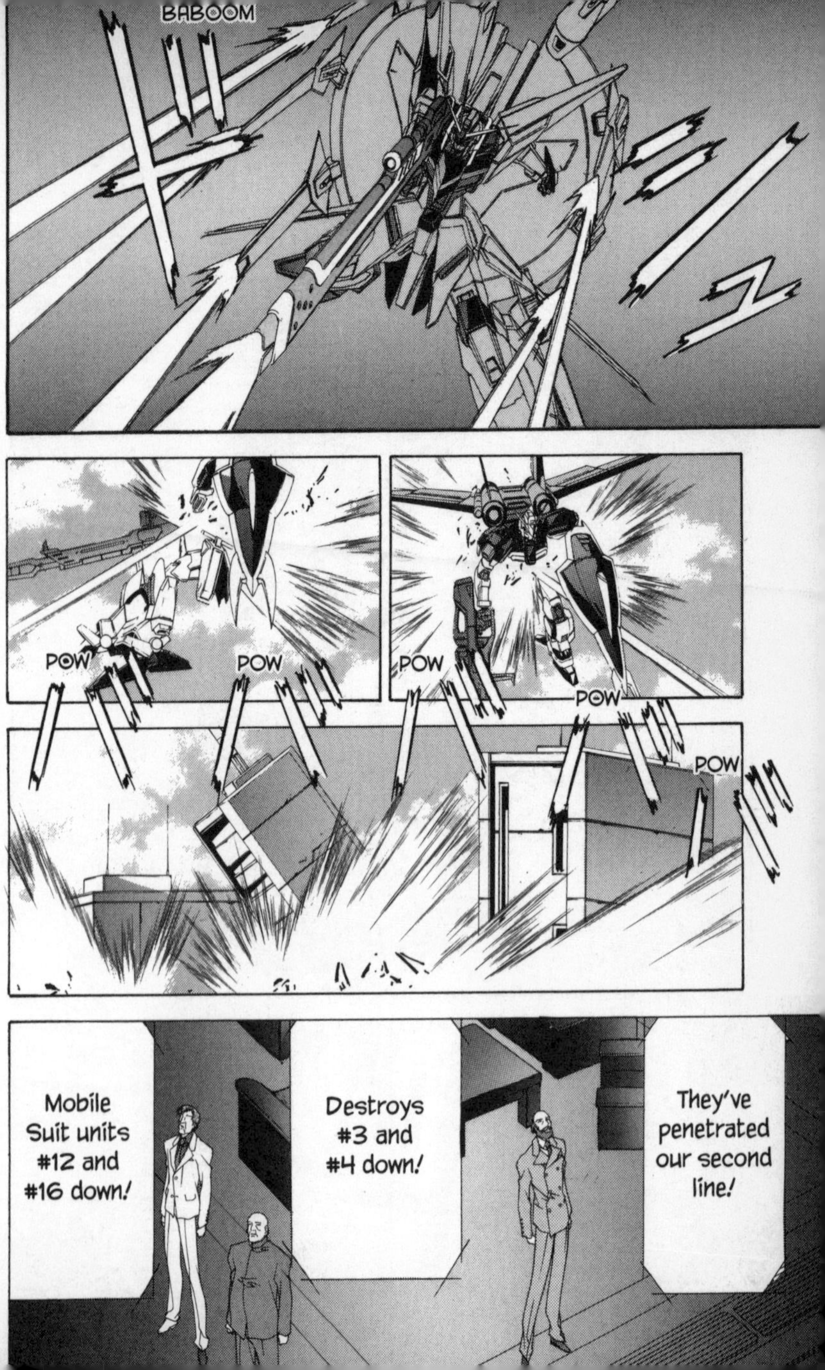
BABOOM
POW
POW
POW
POW
POW
They've penetrated our second line!
Destroys #3 and #4 down!
Mobile Suit units #12 and #16 down!

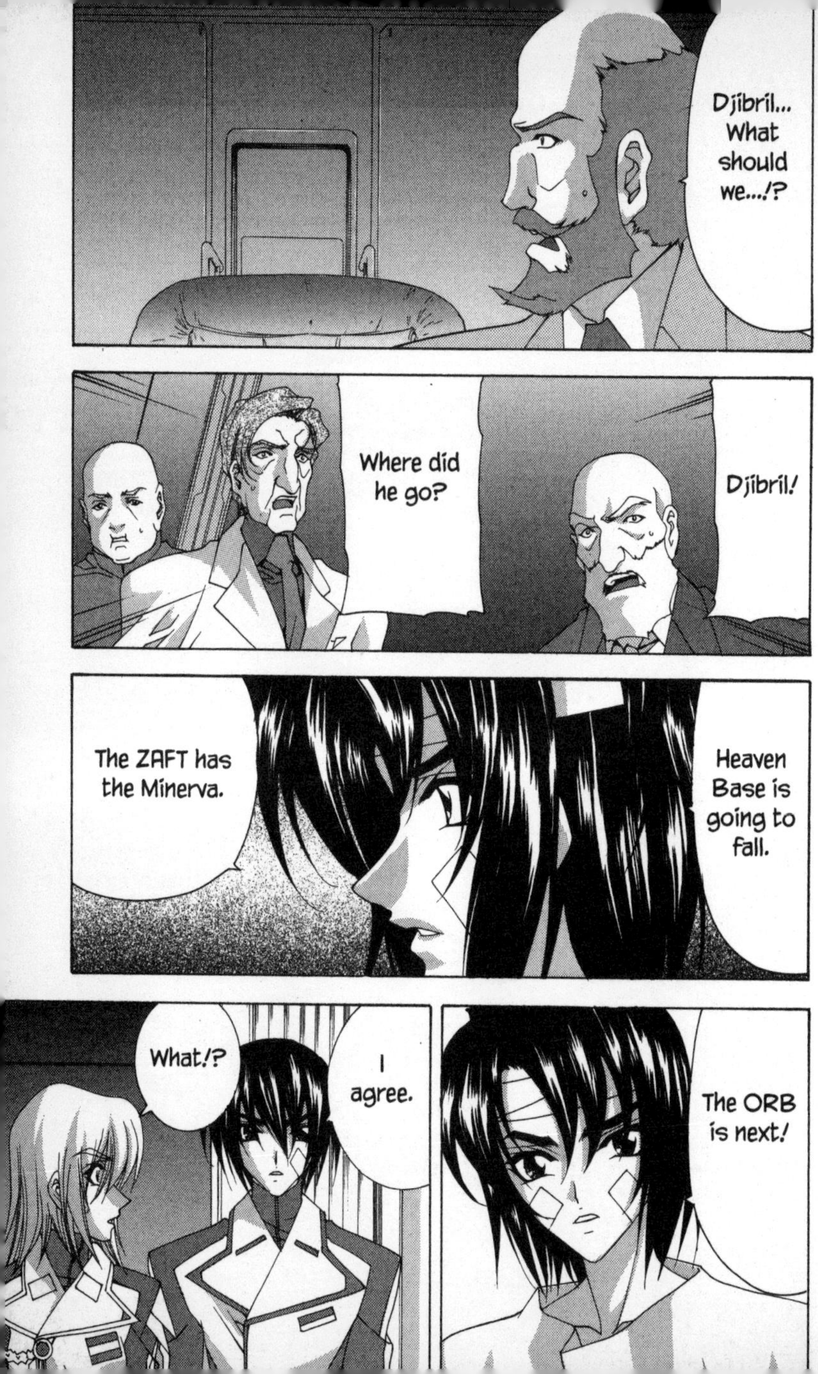
Djibril... What should we...!?
Djibril!
Where did he go?
Heaven Base is going to fall.
The ZAFT has the Minerva.
The ORB is next!
I agree.
What!?

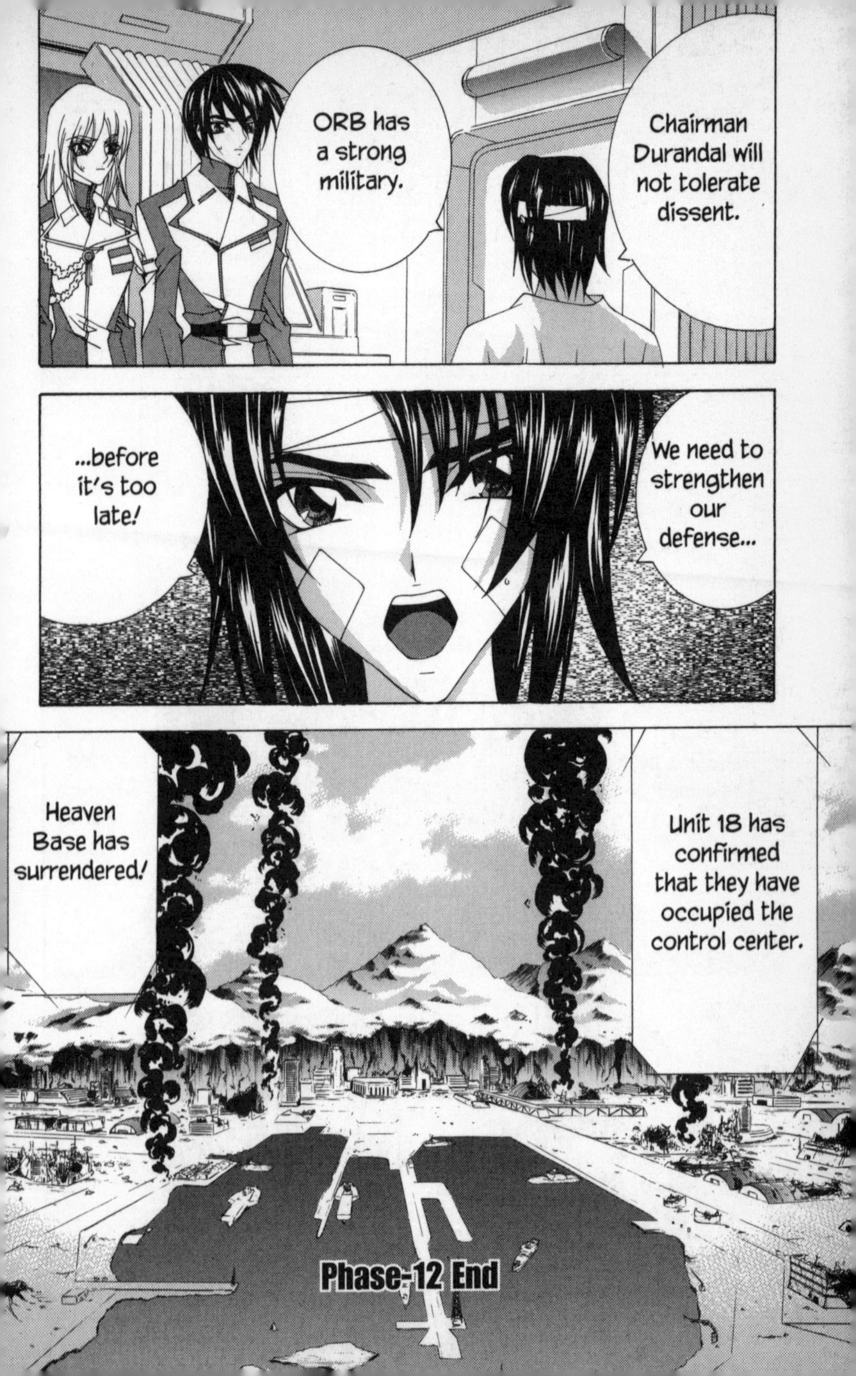
Chairman Durandal will not tolerate dissent.
ORB has a strong military.
We need to strengthen our defense...
...before it's too late!
Unit 18 has confirmed that they have occupied the control center.
Heaven Base has surrendered!
Phase-12 End

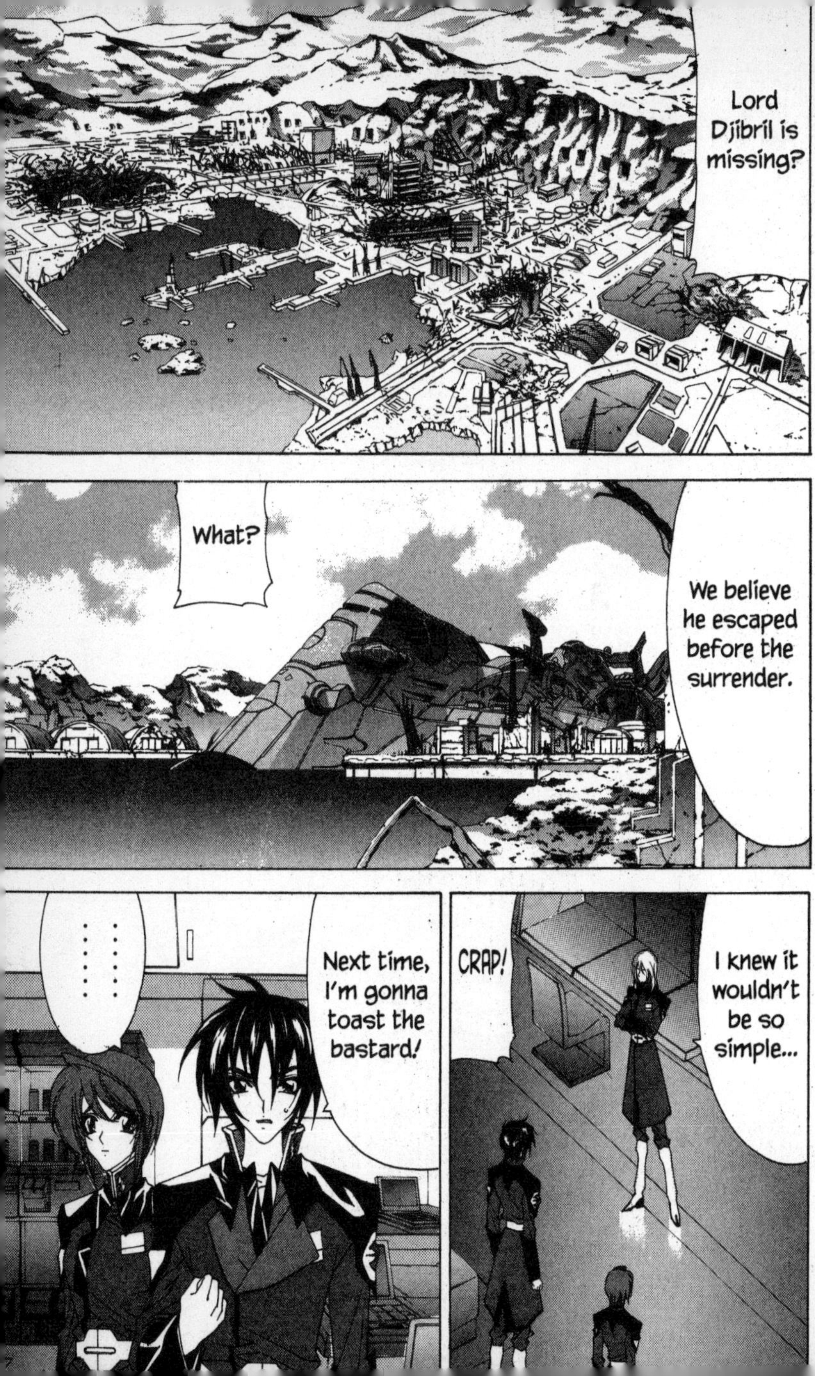
Lord Djibril is missing?
We believe he escaped before the surrender.
What?
I knew it wouldn't be so simple...
CRAP!
Next time, I'm gonna toast the bastard!
......

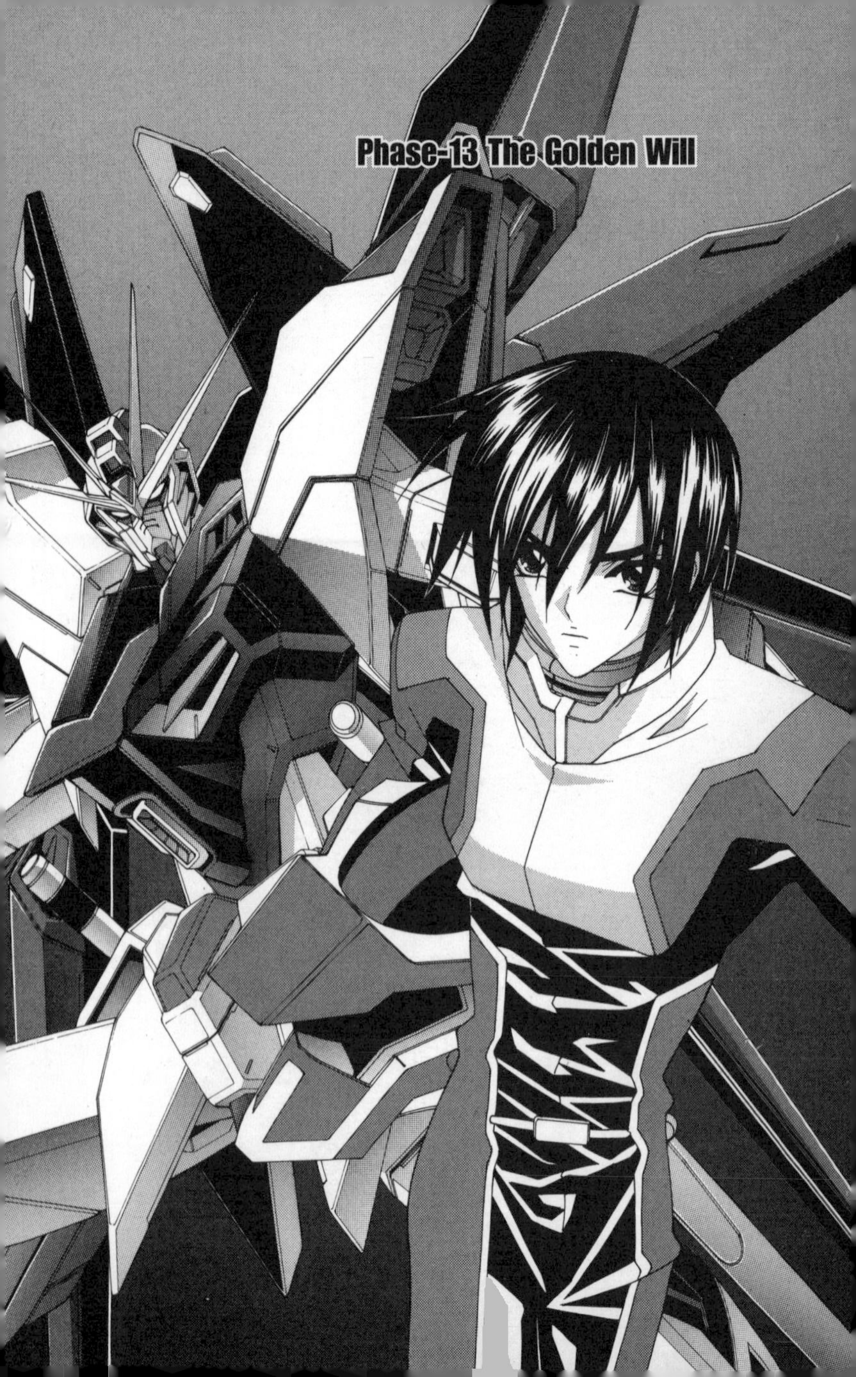
Phase-13 The Golden Will

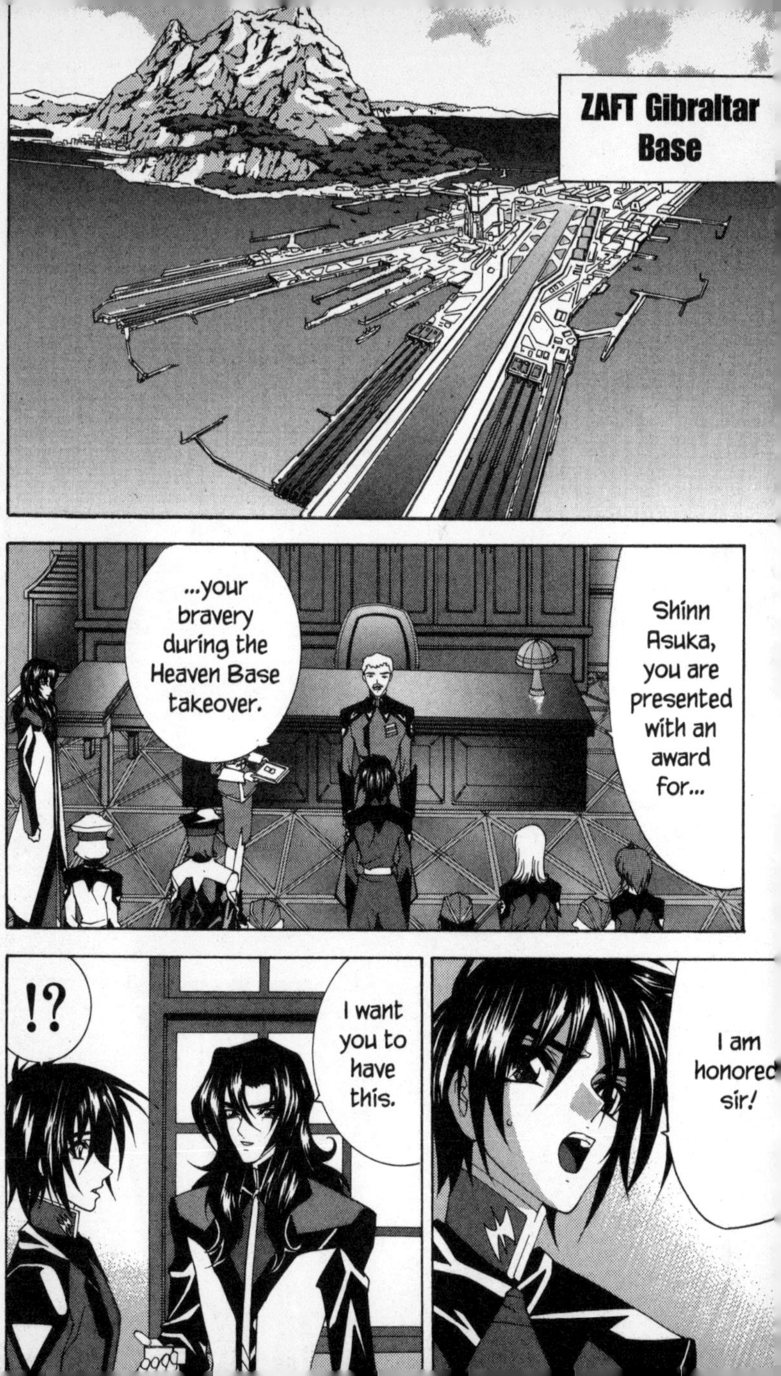
ZAFT Gibraltar Base
Shinn Asuka, you are presented with an award for...
...your bravery during the Heaven Base takeover.
I am honored sir!
I want you to have this.
!?

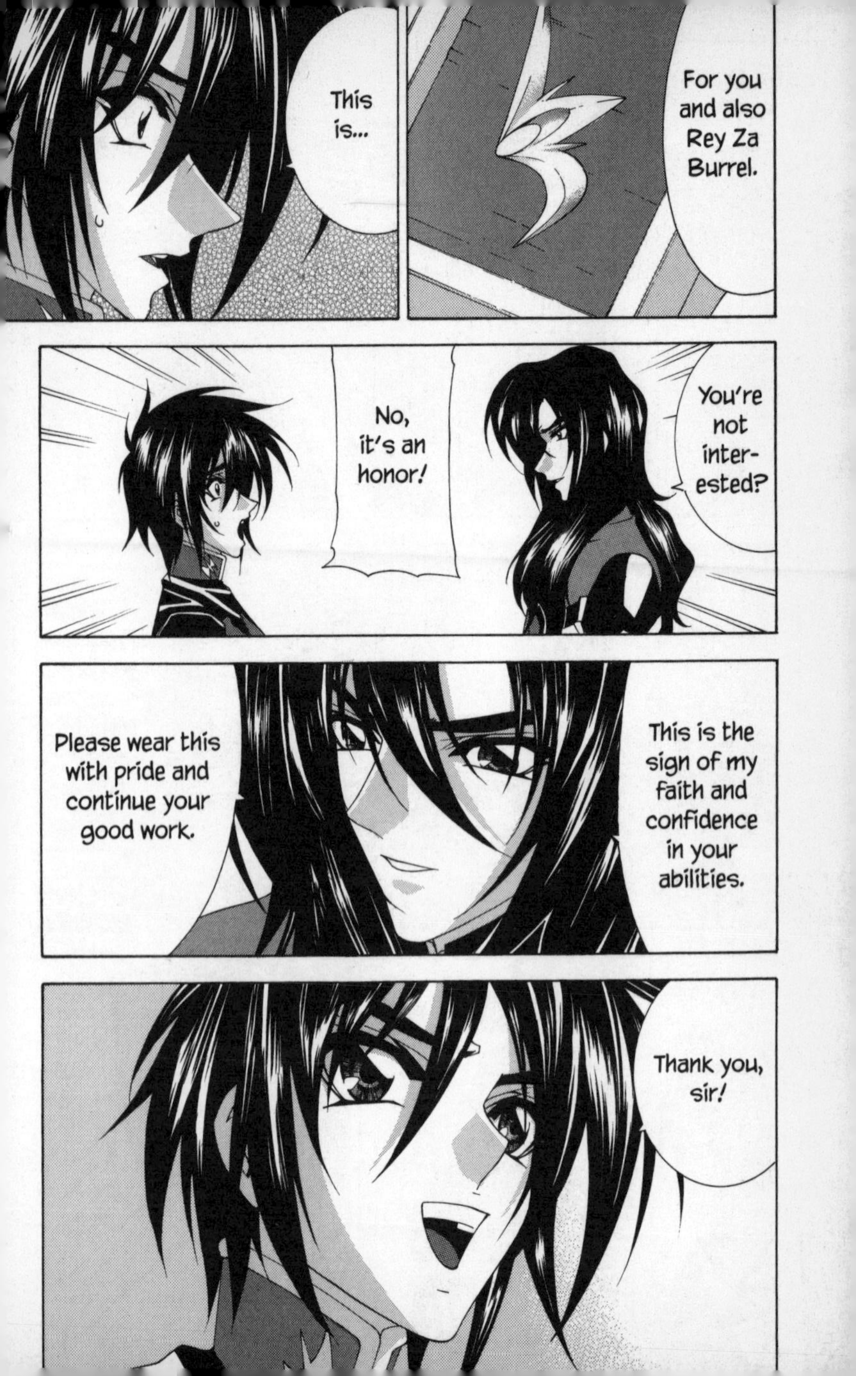
For you and also Rey Za Burrel.
This is...
You're not interested?
No, it's an honor!
This is the sign of my faith and confidence in your abilities.
Please wear this with pride and continue your good work.
Thank you, sir!

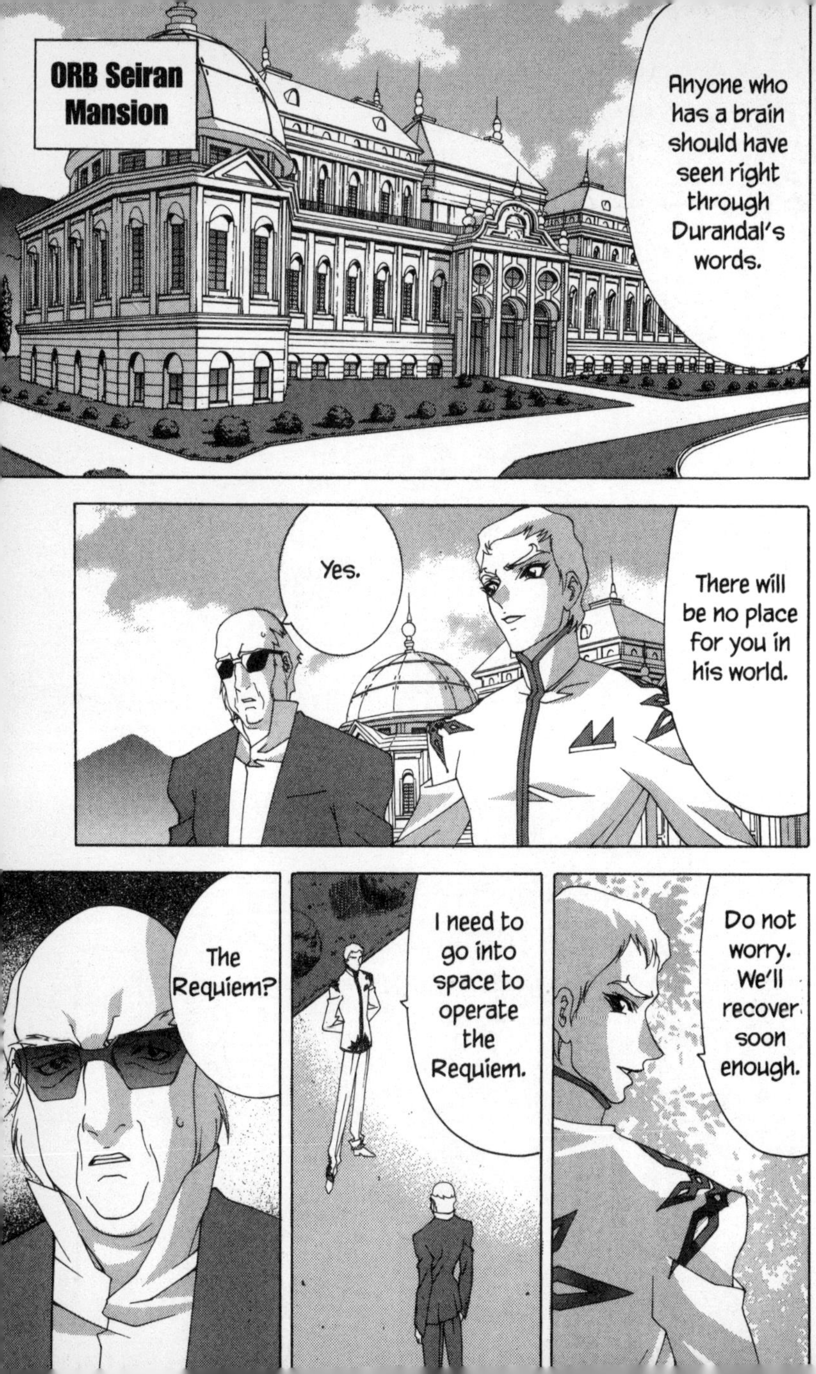
Anyone who has a brain should have seen right through Durandal's words.
ORB Seiran Mansion
There will be no place for you in his world.
Yes.
Do not worry. We'll recover soon enough.
I need to go into space to operate the Requiem.
The Requiem?

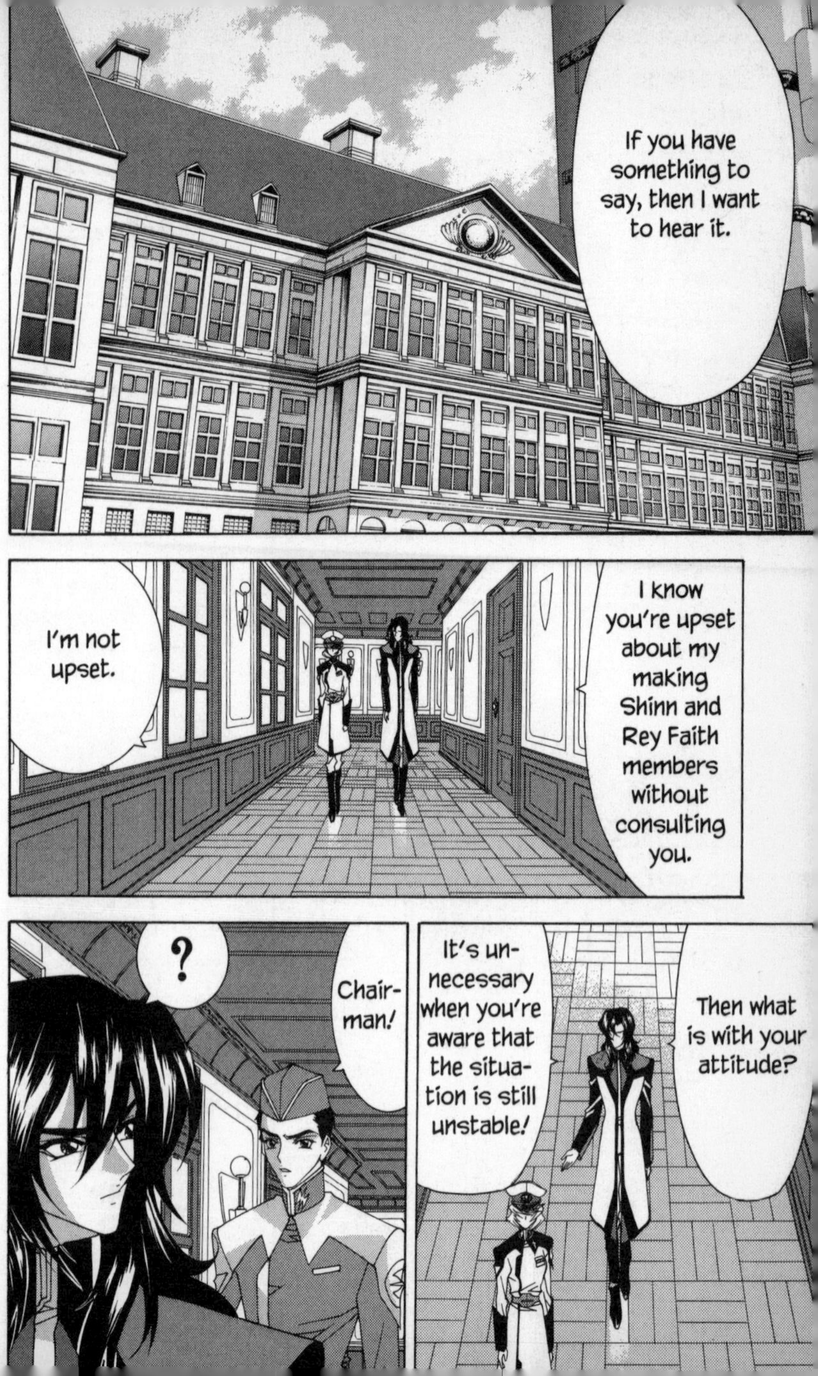
If you have something to say, then I want to hear it.
I know you're upset about my making Shinn and Rey Faith members without consulting you.
I'm not upset.
Then what is with your attitude?
It's un-necessary when you're aware that the situa-tion is still unstable!
Chair-man!
?

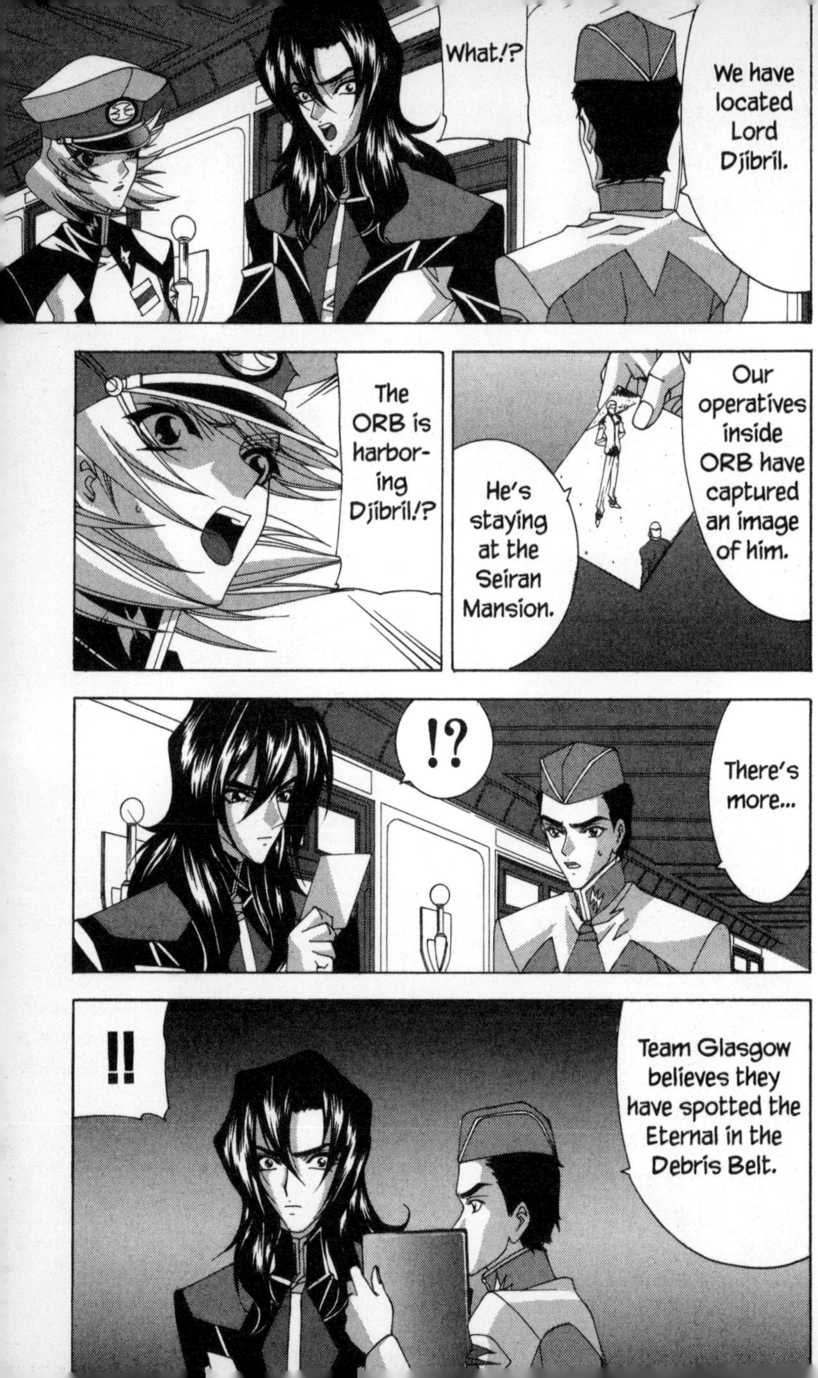
We have located Lord Djibril.
What!?
Our operatives inside ORB have captured an image of him.
He's staying at the Seiran Mansion.
The ORB is harbor-ing Djibril!?
There's more...
!?
Team Glasgow believes they have spotted the Eternal in the Debris Belt.
!!

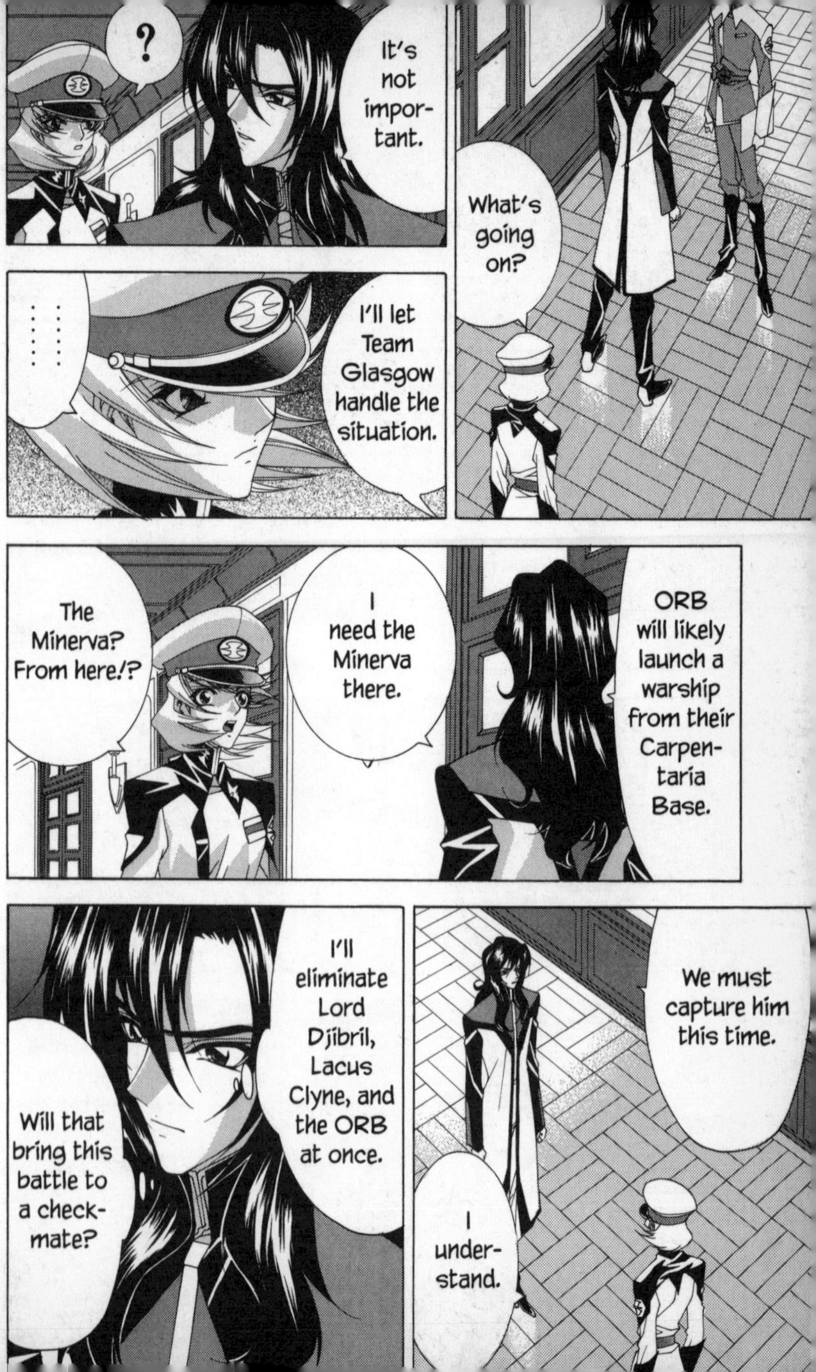
What's going on?
It's not important.
?
I'll let Team Glasgow handle the situation.
……
ORB will likely launch a warship from their Carpentaria Base.
I need the Minerva there.
The Minerva? From here!?
We must capture him this time.
I understand.
I'll eliminate Lord Djibril, Lacus Clyne, and the ORB at once.
Will that bring this battle to a checkmate?

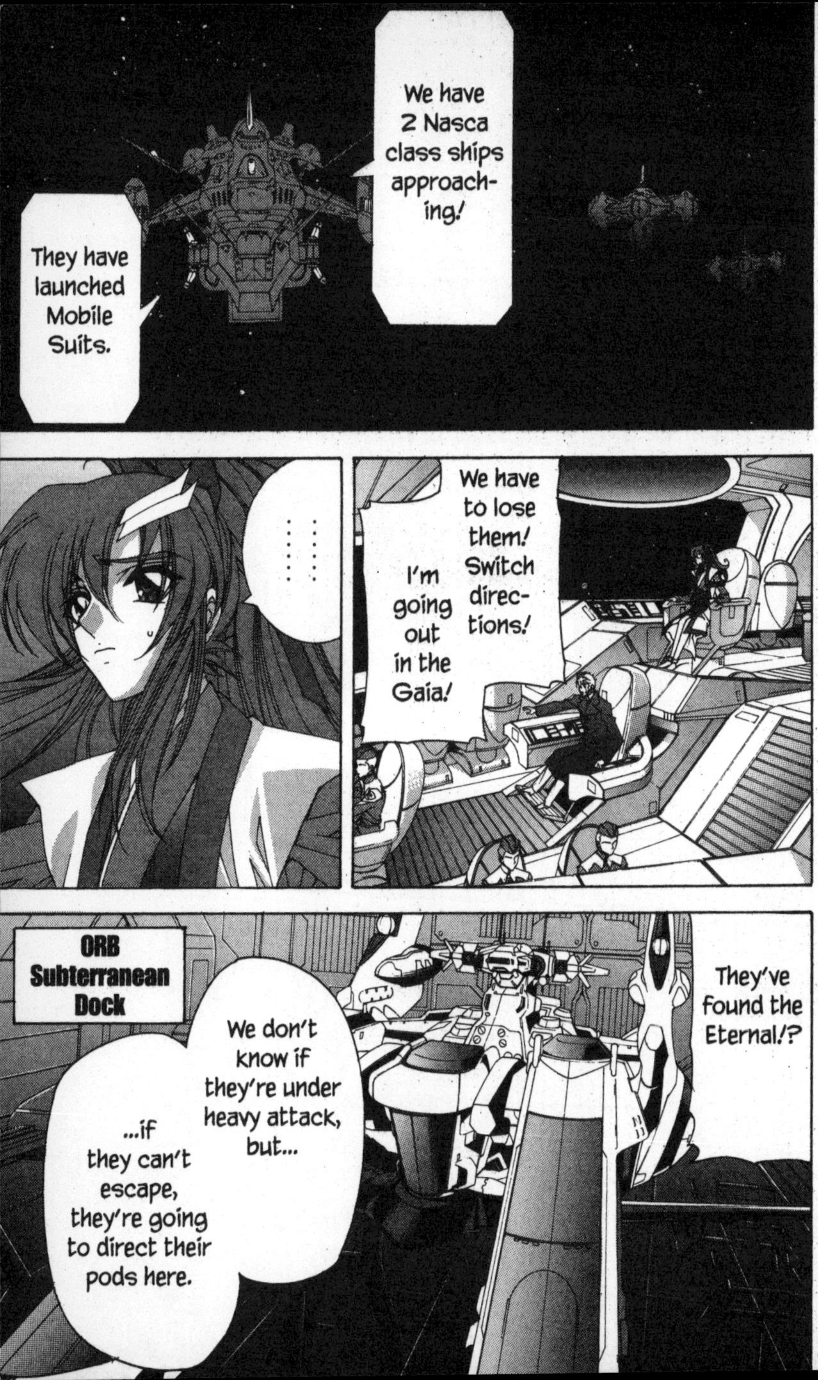
We have 2 Nasca class ships approaching!
They have launched Mobile Suits.
We have to lose them! Switch directions!
I'm going out in the Gaia!
......
They've found the Eternal!?
ORB Subterranean Dock
We don't know if they're under heavy attack, but...
...if they can't escape, they're going to direct their pods here.

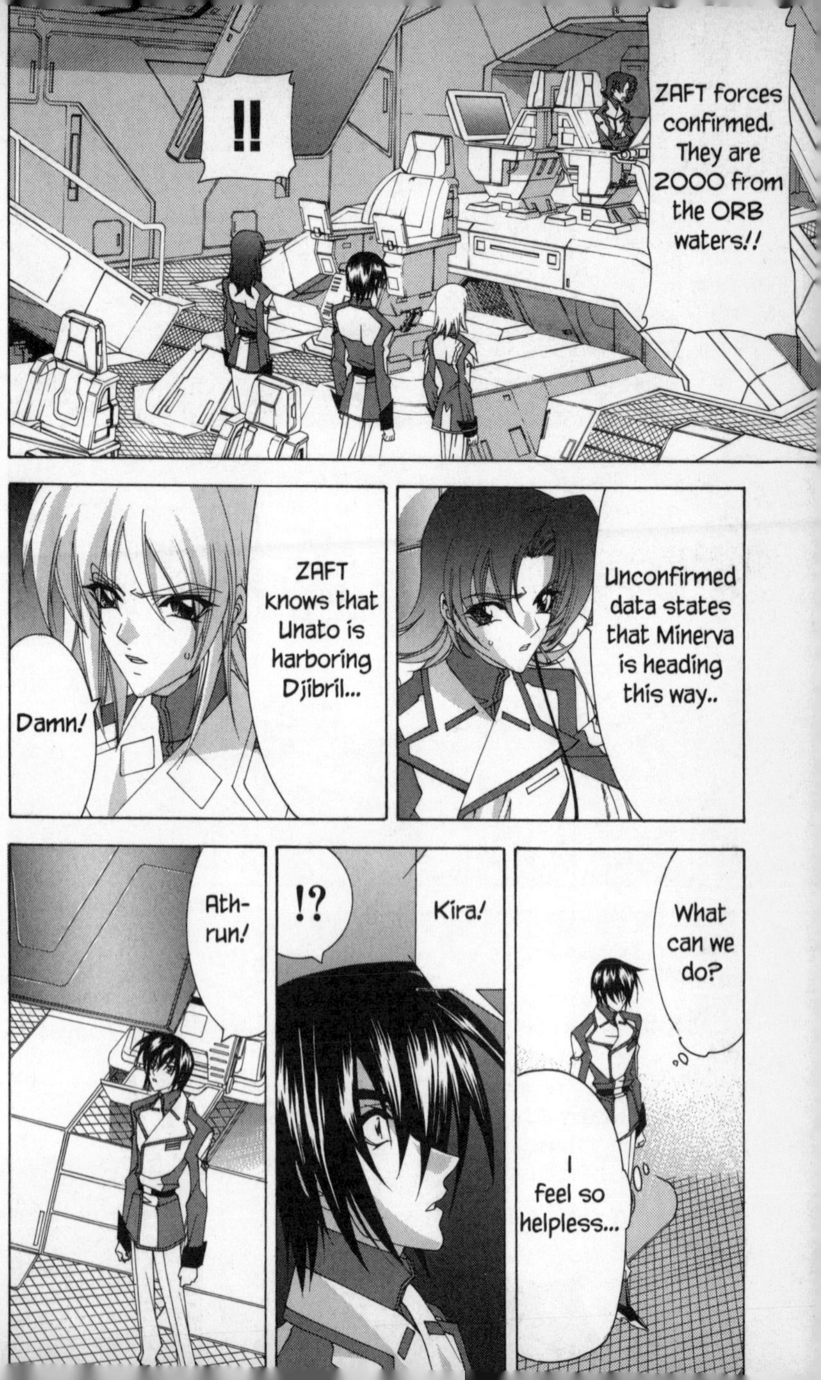
ZAFT forces confirmed. They are 2000 from the ORB waters!!
!!
Unconfirmed data states that Minerva is heading this way..
ZAFT knows that Unato is harboring Djibril...
Damn!
What can we do?
I feel so helpless...
Kira!
!?
Ath-run!

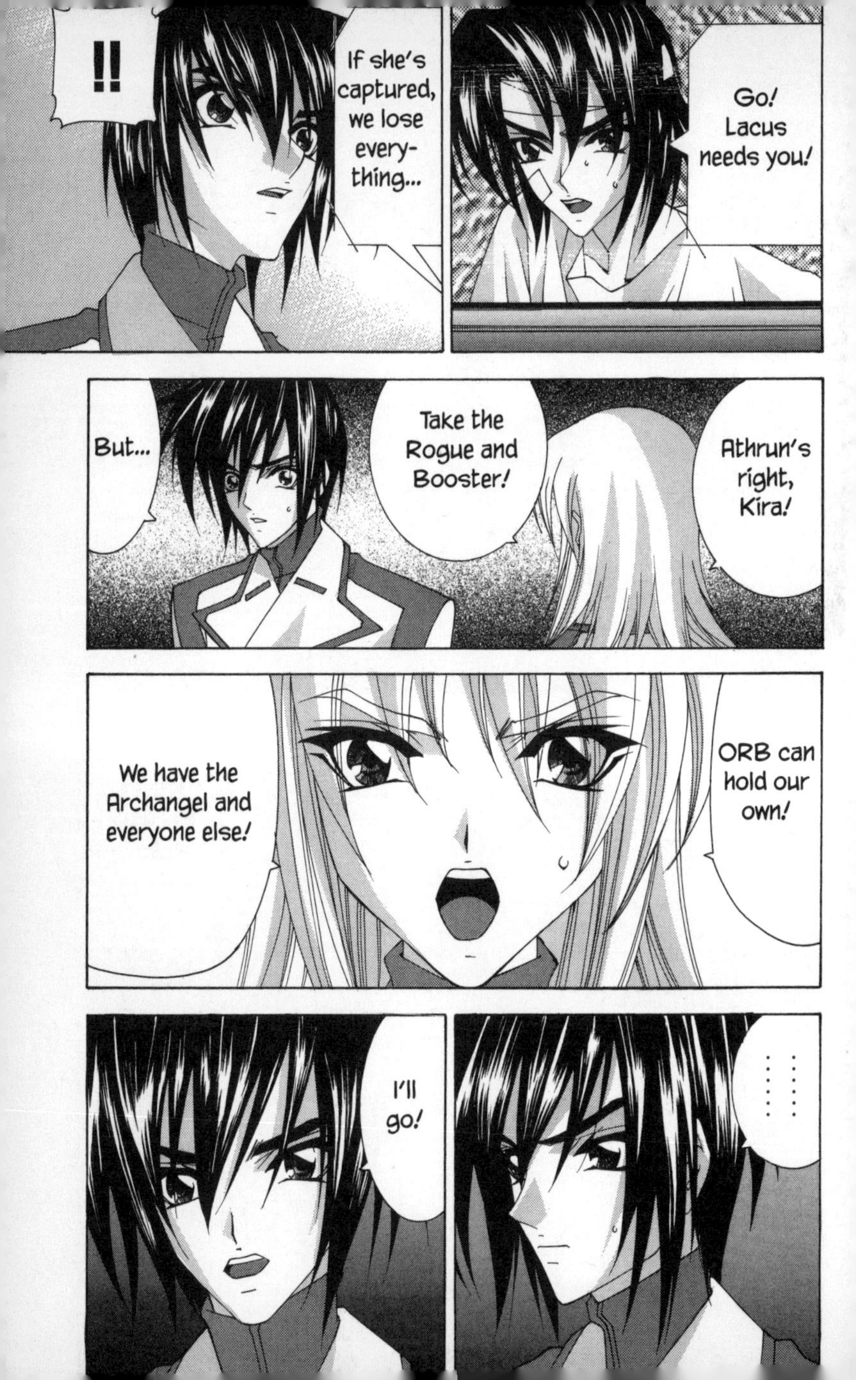
Go! Lacus needs you!
If she's captured, we lose every-thing...
!!
Athrun's right, Kira!
Take the Rogue and Booster!
But...
ORB can hold our own!
We have the Archangel and everyone else!
......
I'll go!

Path clear. Systems all green.

Strike Booster, proceed to the launch catapult.

Lacus, hold on. I'm on my way...

Launch!

Strike Booster Ready!

WHOOSH ゴォォォォ

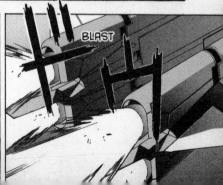

BLAST

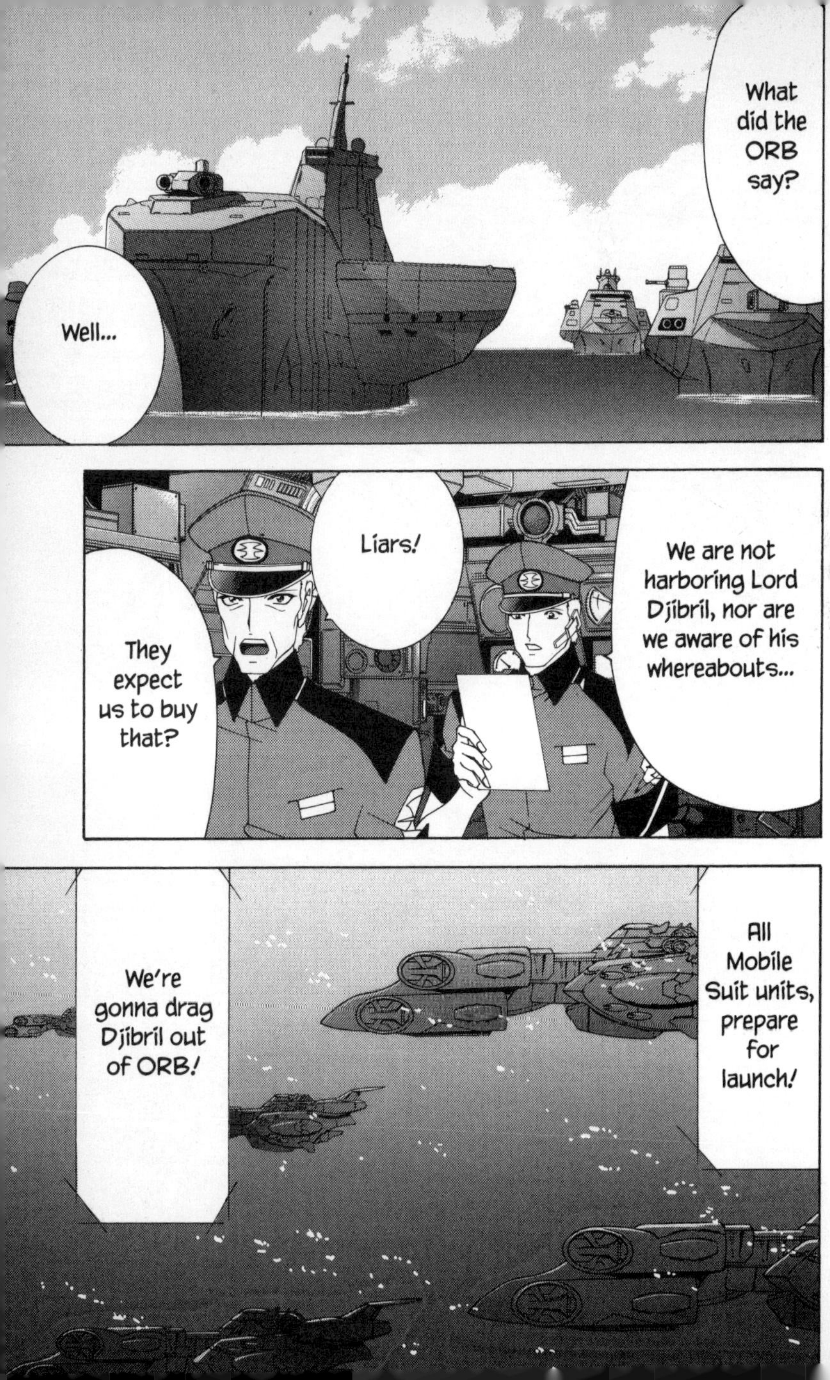
What did the ORB say?
Well...
We are not harboring Lord Djibril, nor are we aware of his whereabouts...
Liars!
They expect us to buy that?
All Mobile Suit units, prepare for launch!
We're gonna drag Djibril out of ORB!

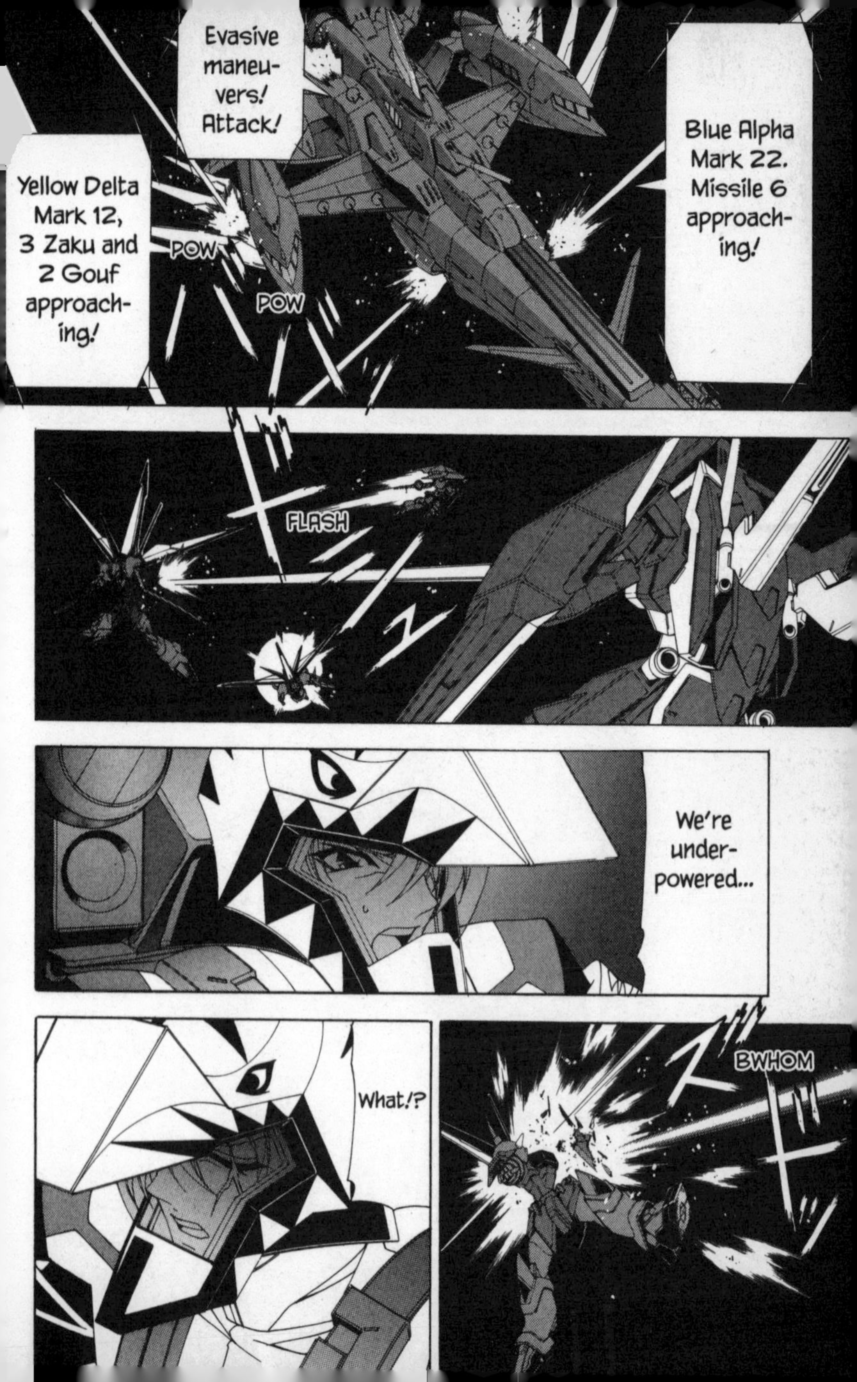
Blue Alpha Mark 22. Missile 6 approaching!
Evasive maneuvers! Attack!
Yellow Delta Mark 12, 3 Zaku and 2 Gouf approaching!
POW
POW
FLASH
We're underpowered...
BWHOM
What!?

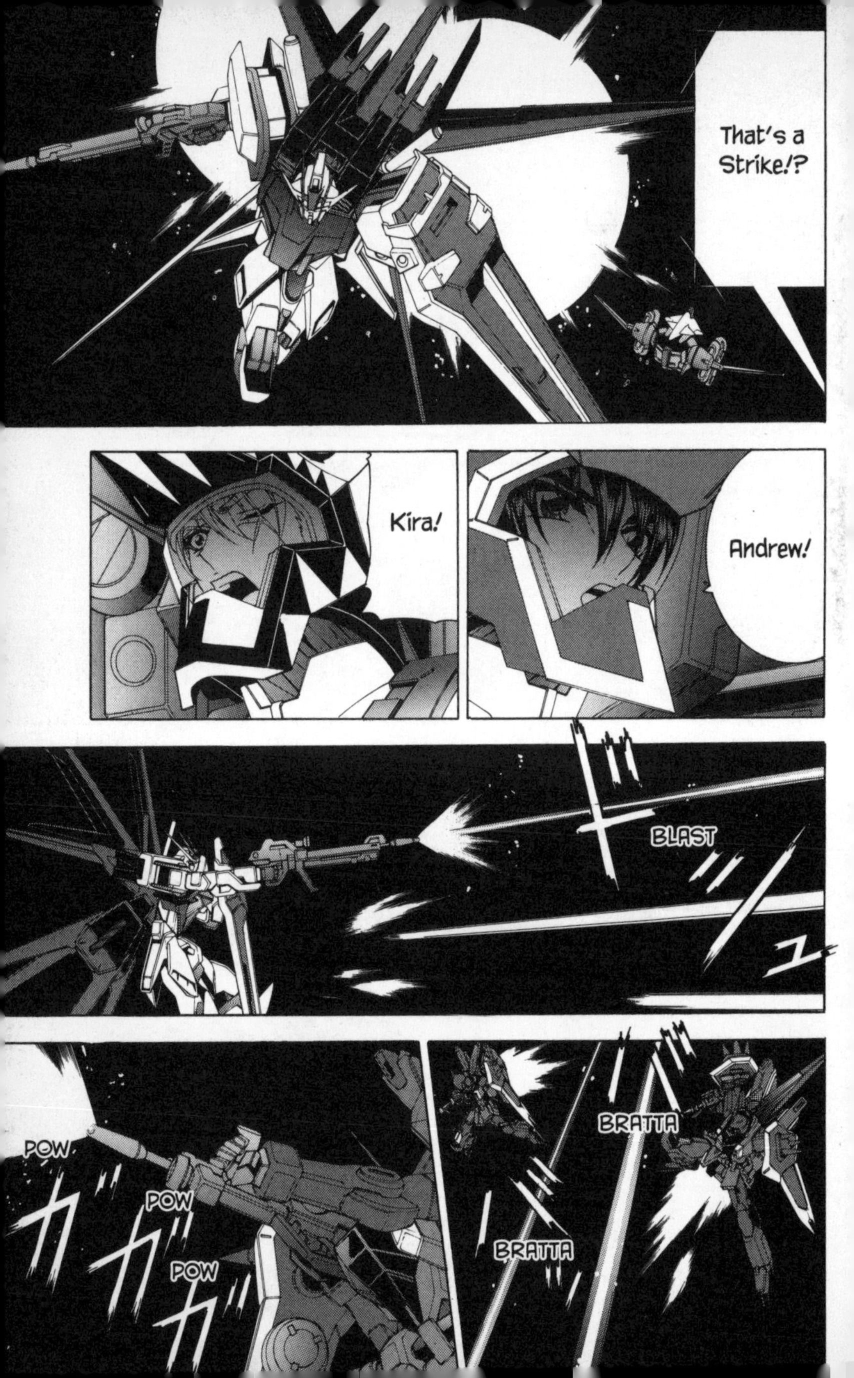
That's a Strike!?
Andrew!
Kira!
BLAST
BRATTA
BRATTA
POW
POW
POW

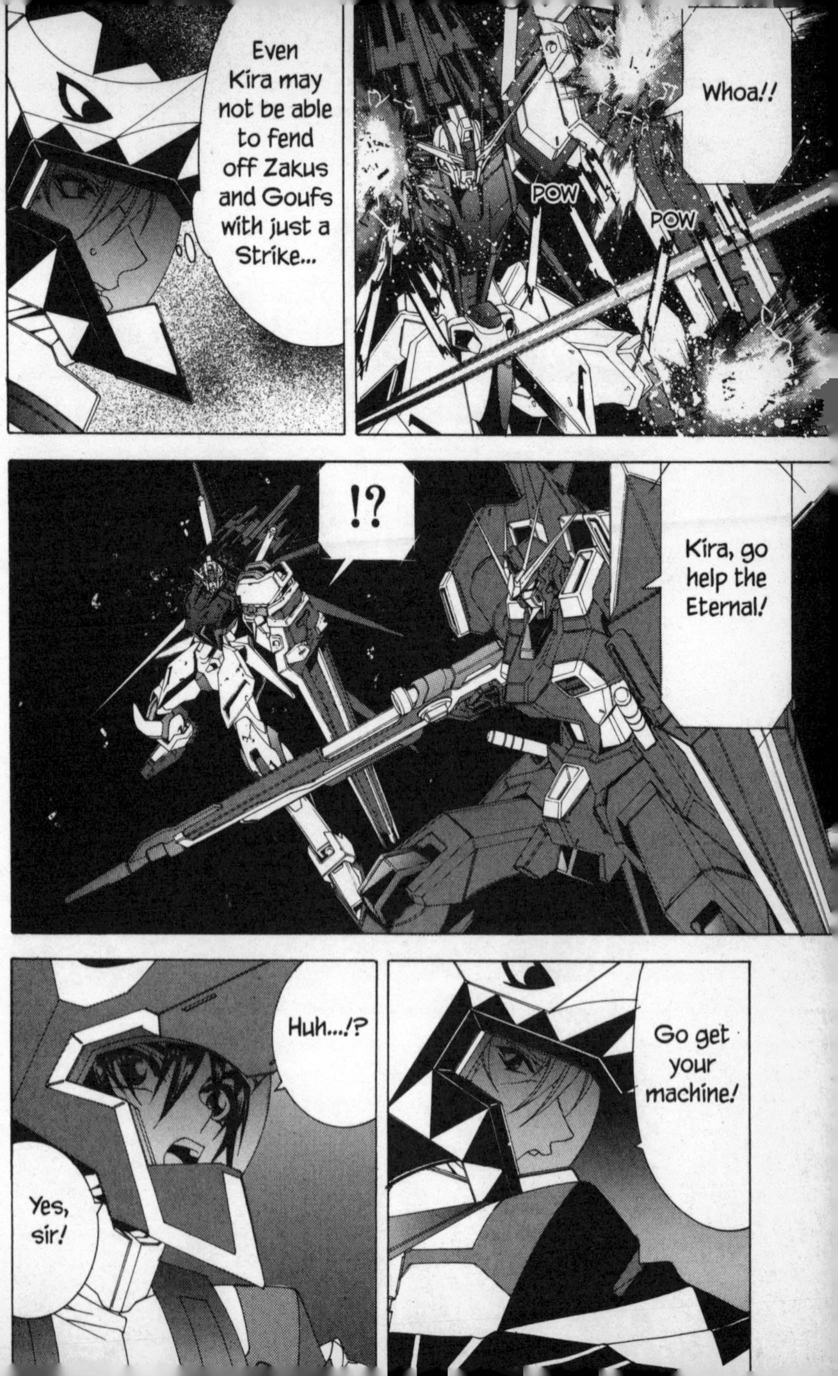
Whoa!!
POW
POW
Even Kira may not be able to fend off Zakus and Goufs with just a Strike...
Kira, go help the Eternal!
!?
Go get your machine!
Huh...!?
Yes, sir!

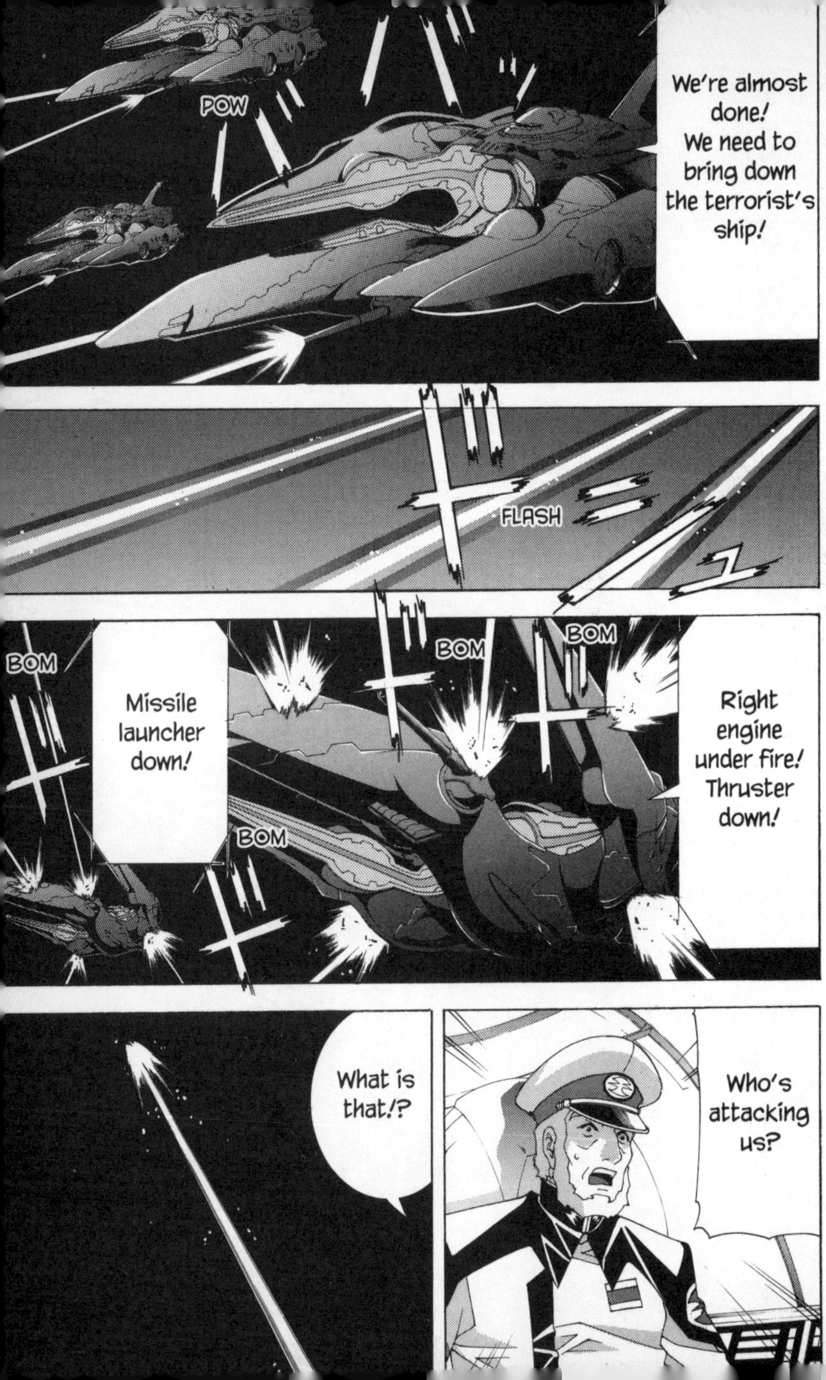
We're almost done! We need to bring down the terrorist's ship!
POW
FLASH
Right engine under fire! Thruster down!
BOM
BOM
BOM
Missile launcher down!
BOM
Who's attacking us?
What is that!?

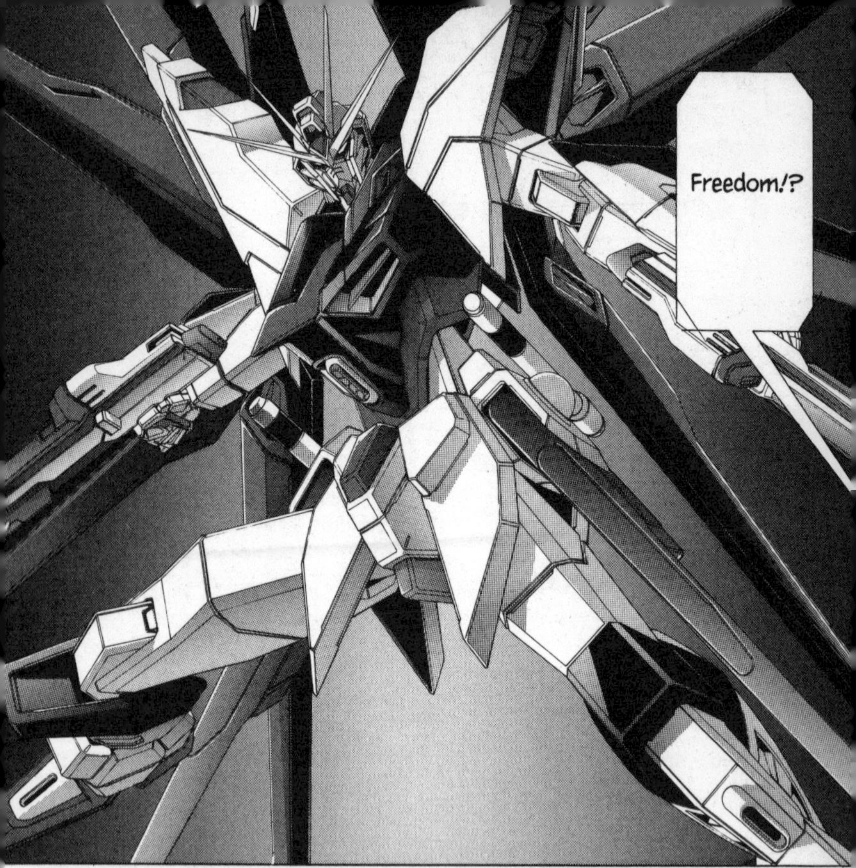
Freedom!?

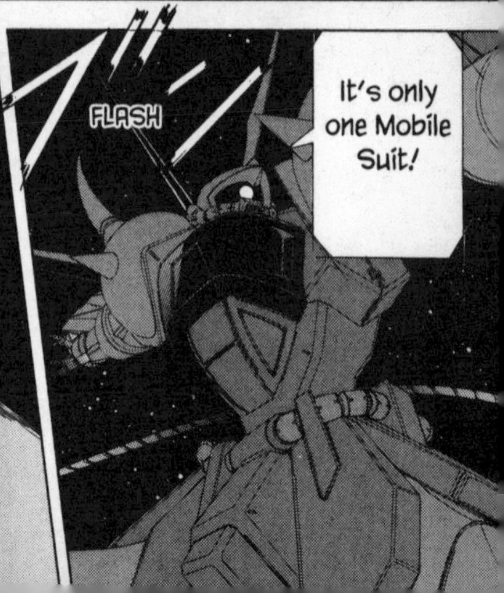
It's only one Mobile Suit!
FLASH

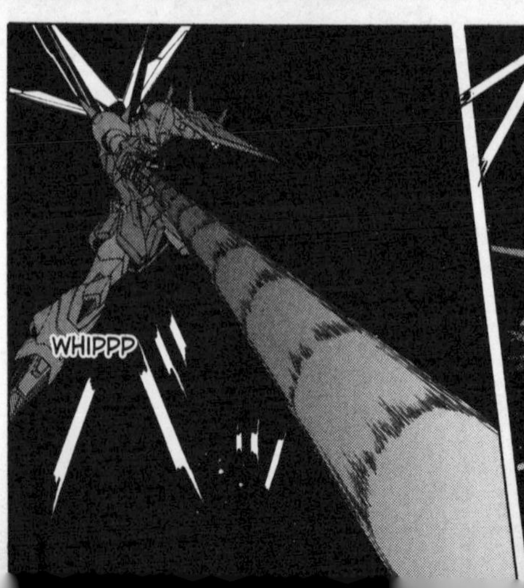
WHIPPP

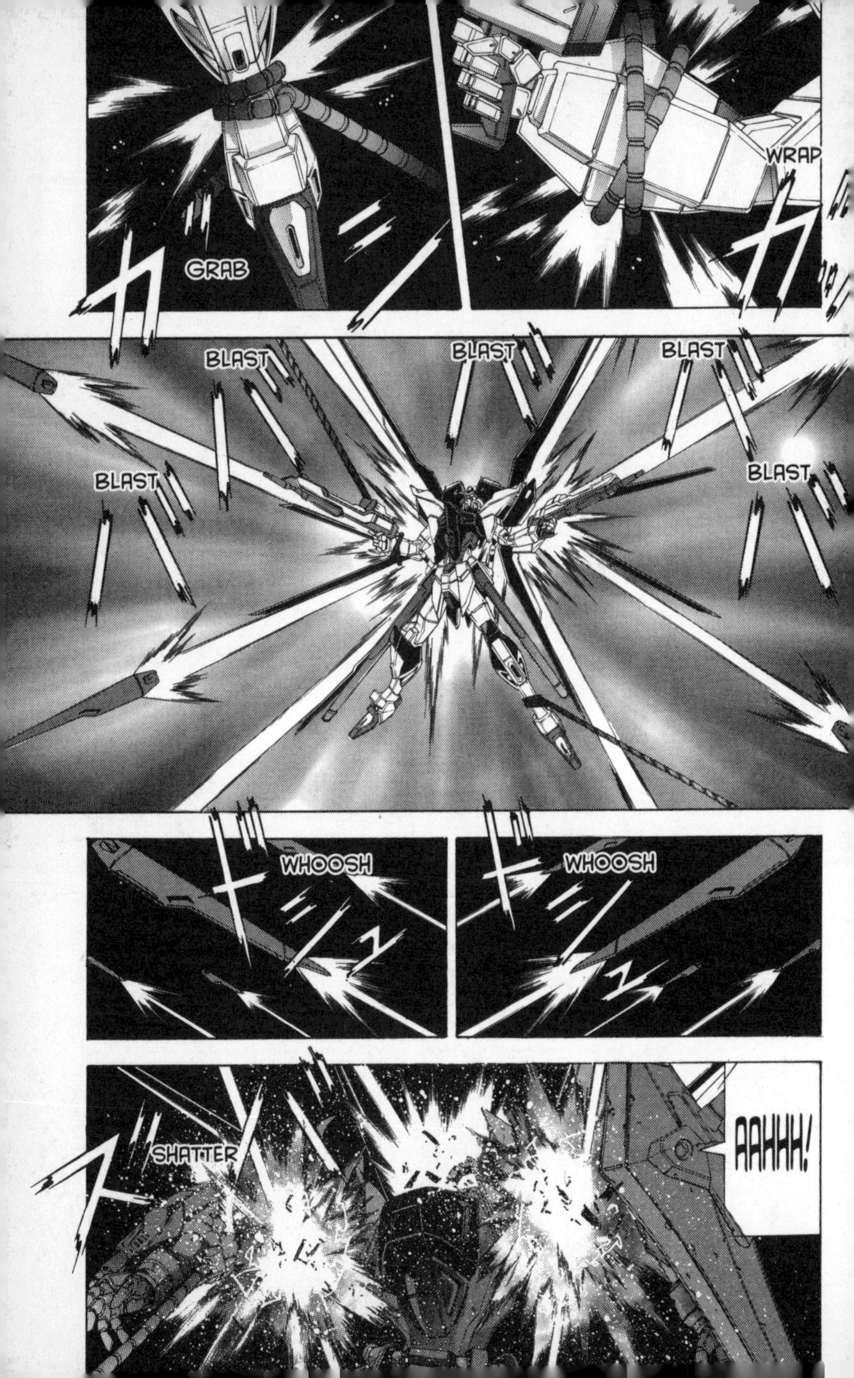
WRAP
GRAB
BLAST
BLAST
BLAST
BLAST
BLAST
WHOOSH
WHOOSH
AAHHH!
SHATTER

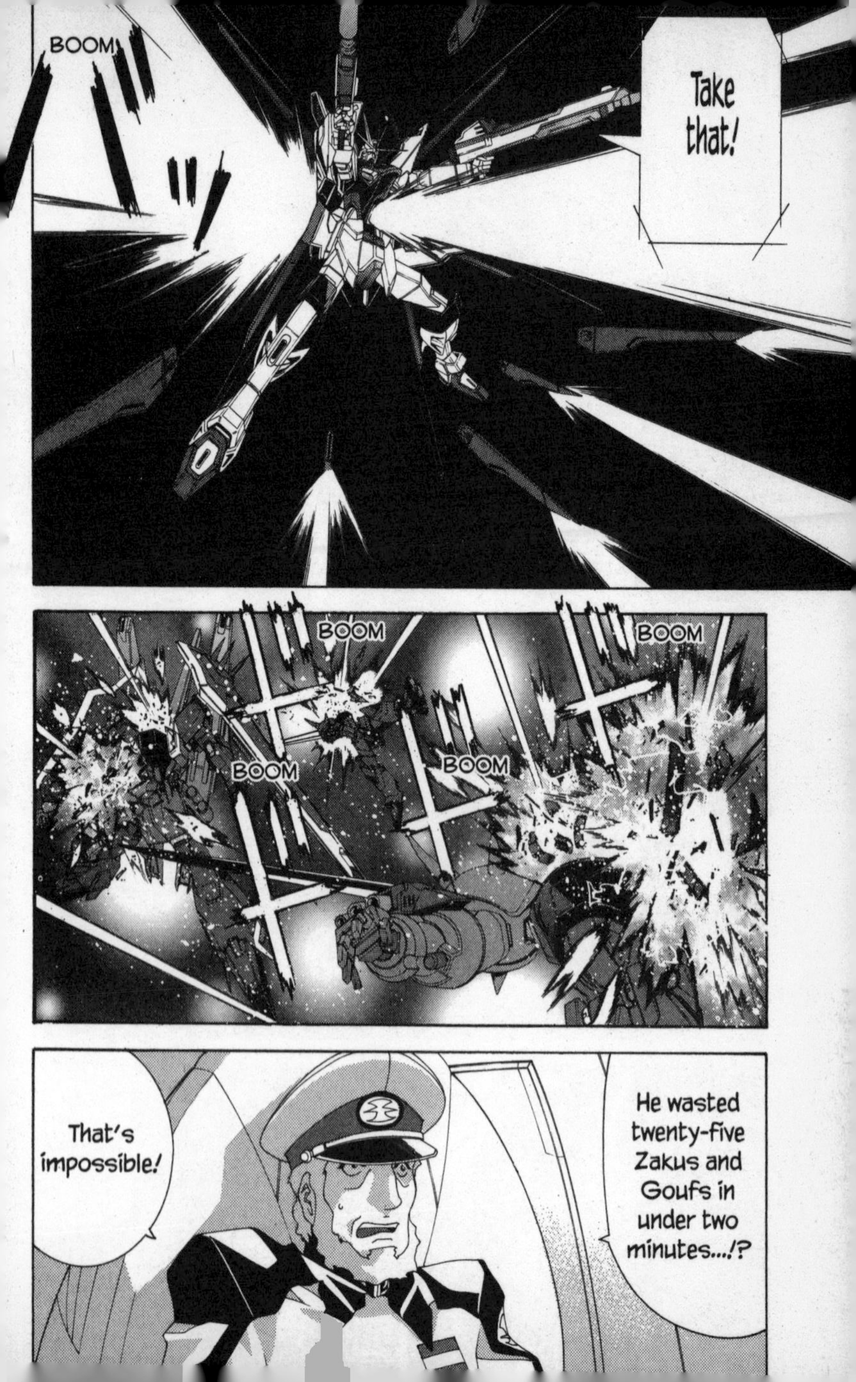
Take that!
BOOM
BOOM
BOOM
BOOM
BOOM
He wasted twenty-five Zakus and Goufs in under two minutes...!?
That's impossible!

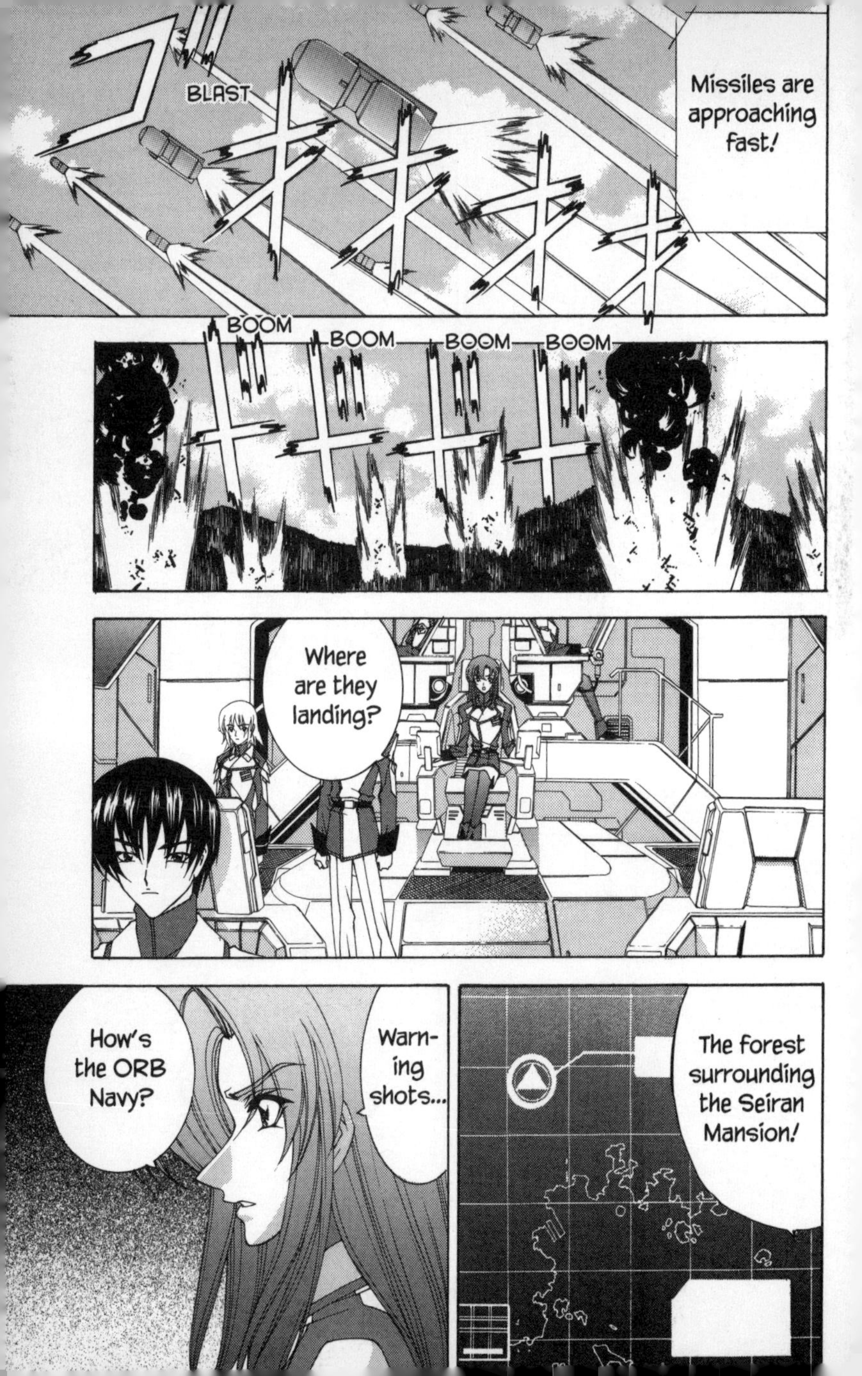
Missiles are approaching fast!
BLAST
BOOM
BOOM
BOOM
BOOM
Where are they landing?
The forest surrounding the Seiran Mansion!
Warn-ing shots...
How's the ORB Navy?

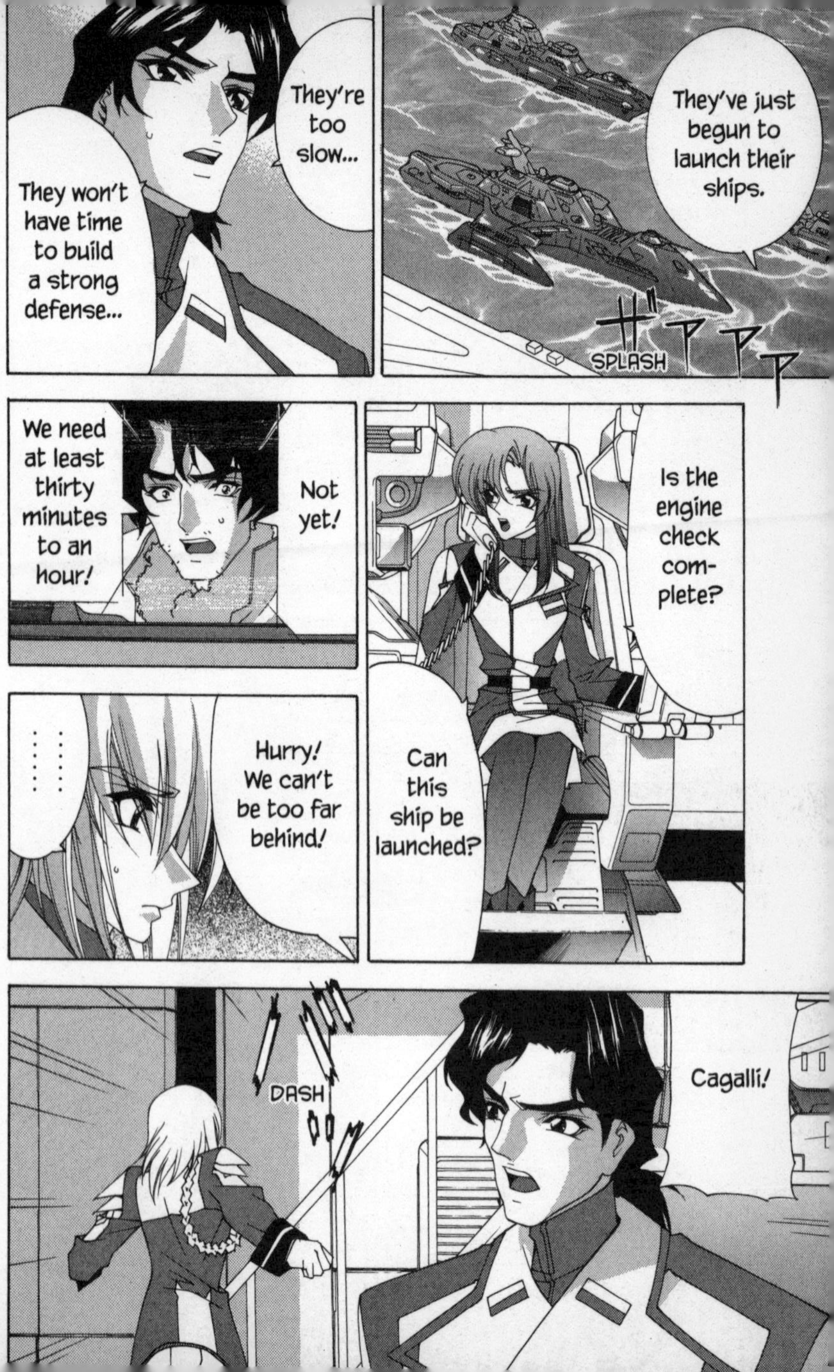
They've just begun to launch their ships.
SPLASH
They're too slow...
They won't have time to build a strong defense...
Is the engine check complete?
Can this ship be launched?
Not yet!
We need at least thirty minutes to an hour!
Hurry! We can't be too far behind!
......
Cagalli!
DASH

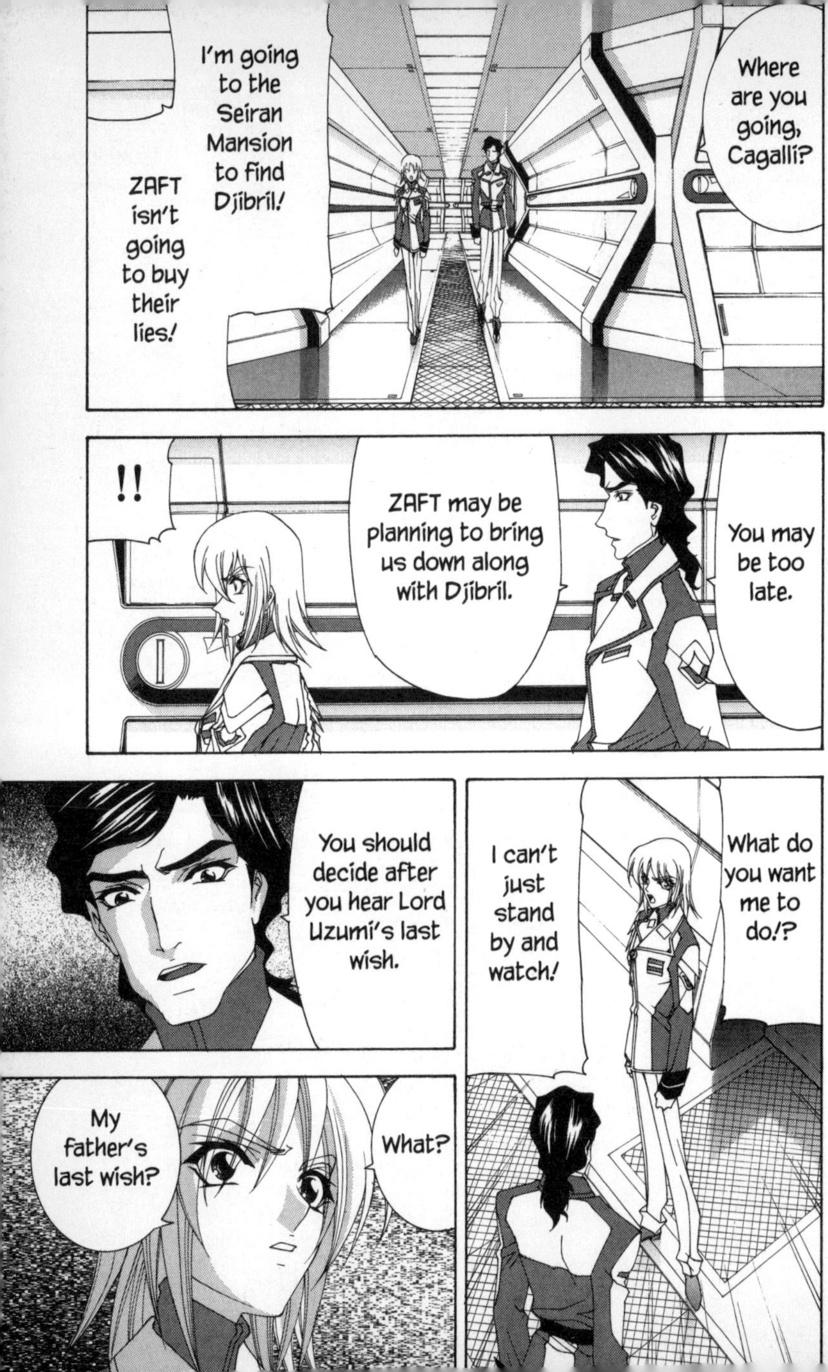
Where are you going, Cagalli?
I'm going to the Seiran Mansion to find Djibril!
ZAFT isn't going to buy their lies!
You may be too late.
ZAFT may be planning to bring us down along with Djibril.
!!
What do you want me to do!?
I can't just stand by and watch!
You should decide after you hear Lord Uzumi's last wish.
What?
My father's last wish?

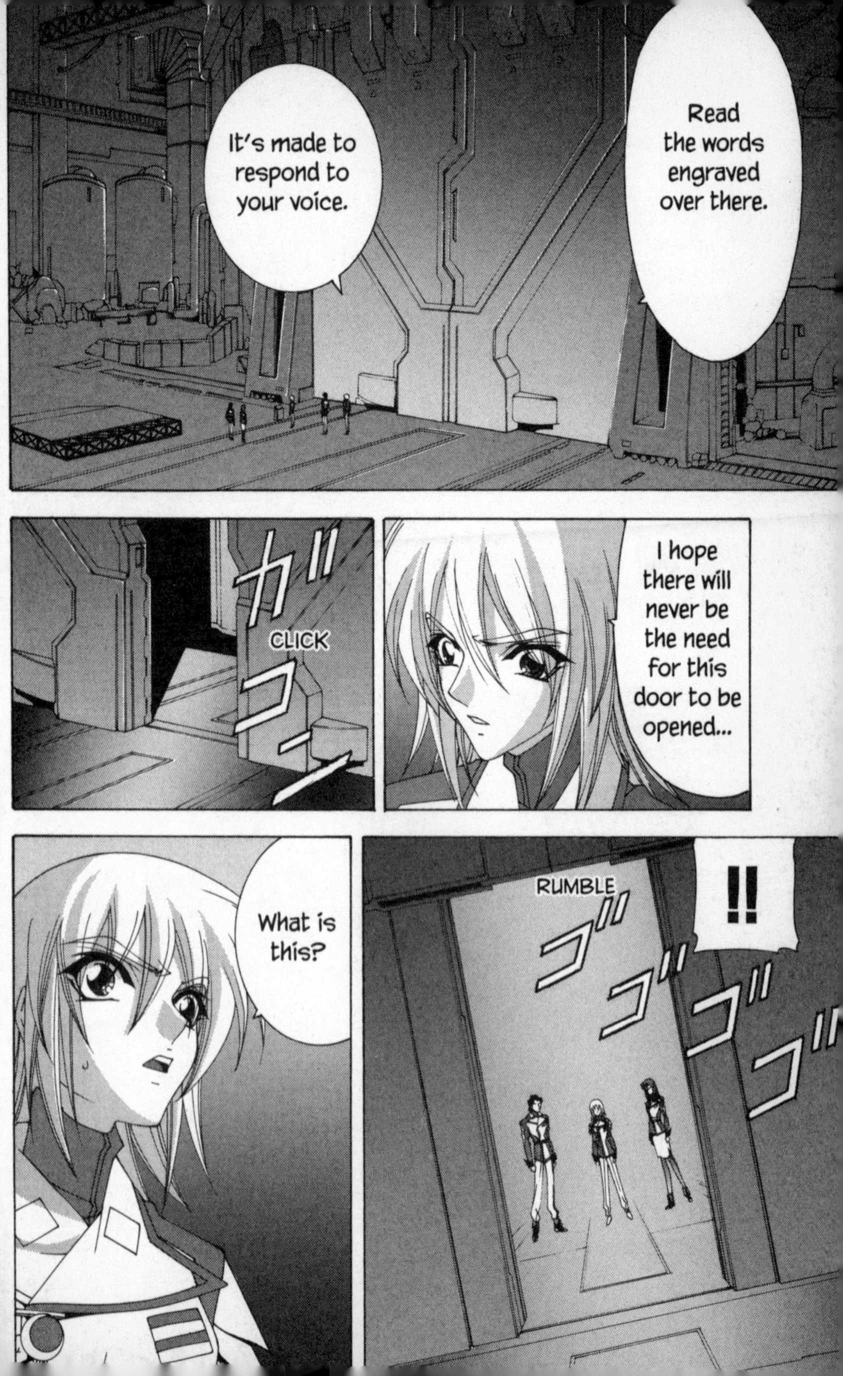
Read the words engraved over there.
It's made to respond to your voice.
I hope there will never be the need for this door to be opened...
ガコー
CLICK
!!
RUMBLE
ゴゴゴゴ
What is this?

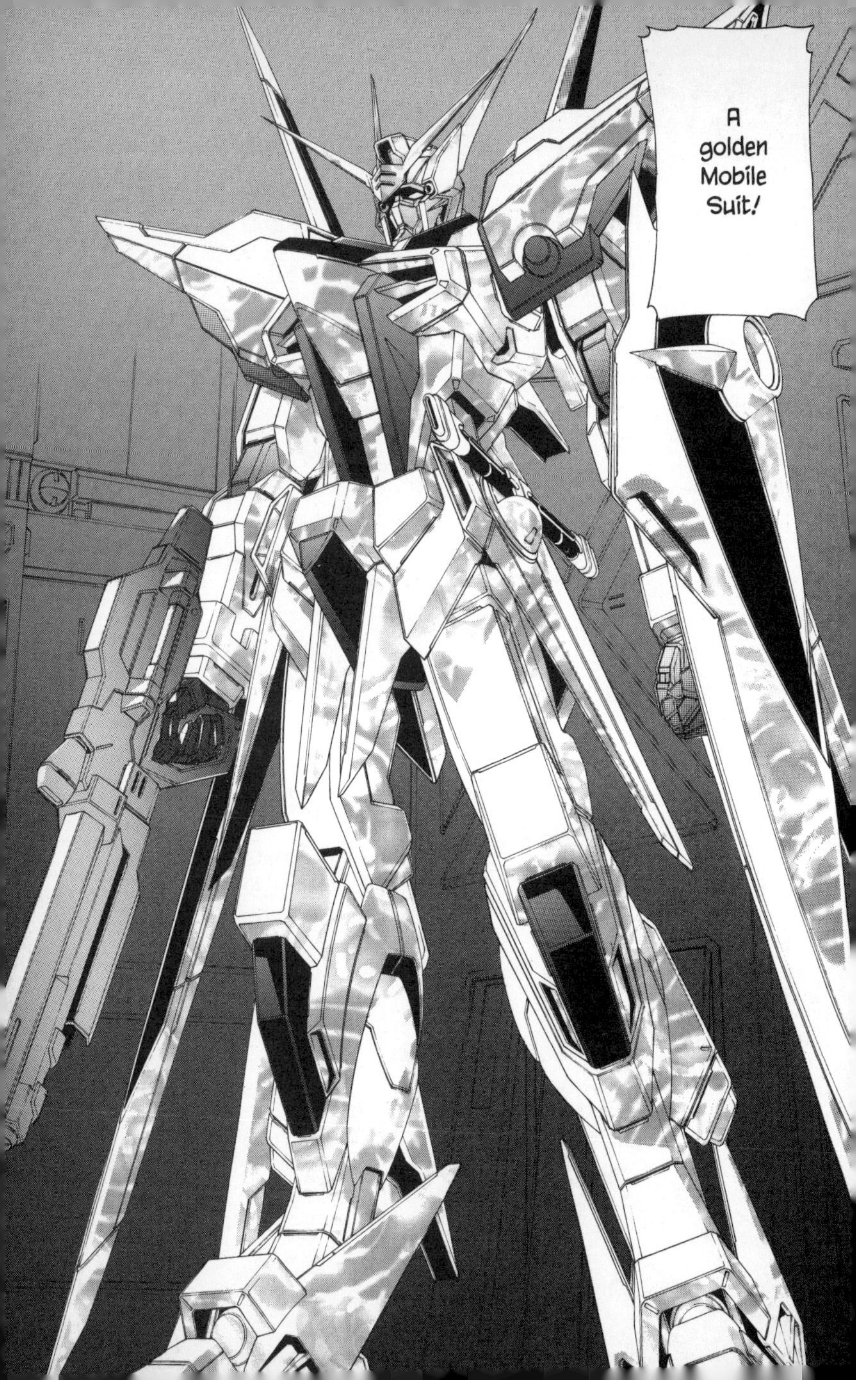
A golden Mobile Suit!

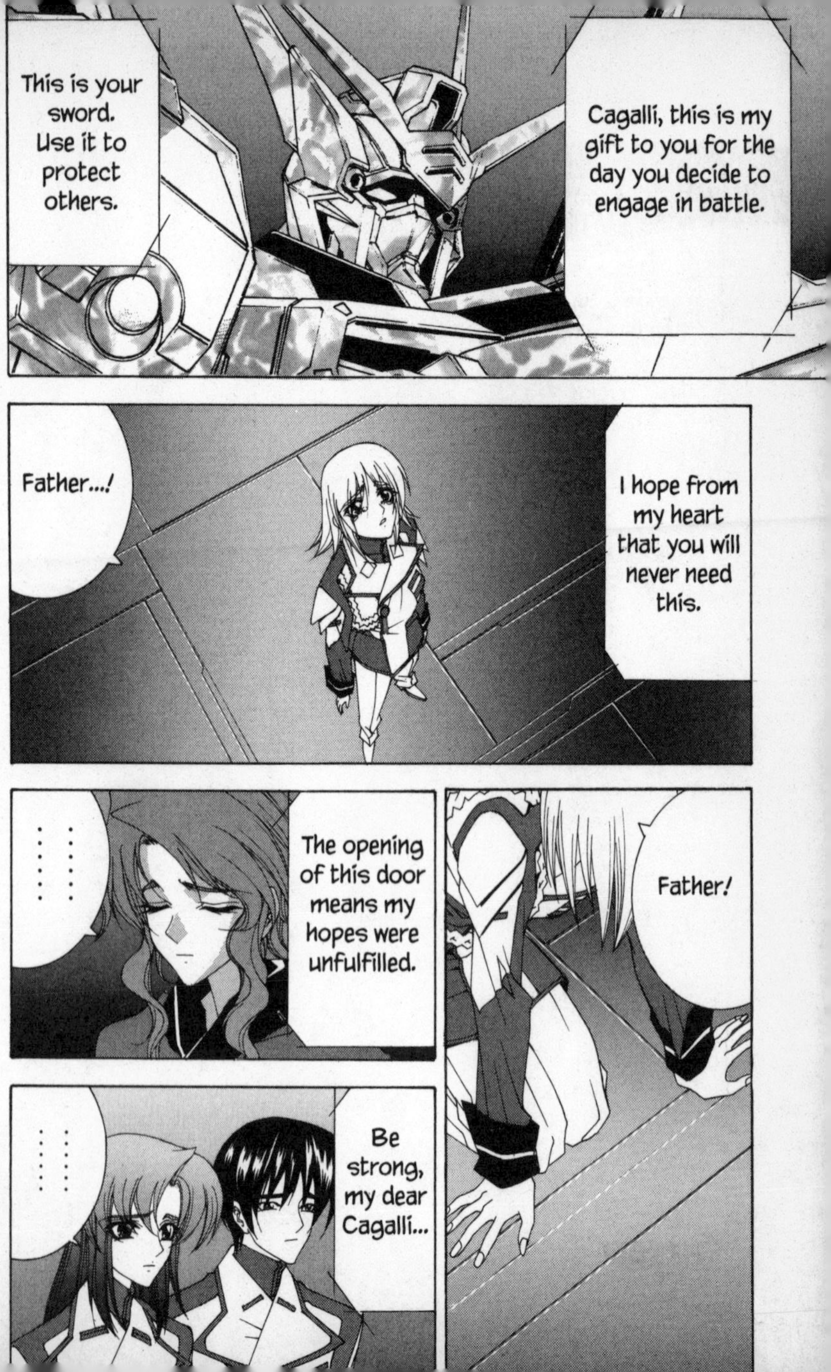
Cagalli, this is my gift to you for the day you decide to engage in battle.
This is your sword. Use it to protect others.
I hope from my heart that you will never need this.
Father...!
Father!
The opening of this door means my hopes were unfulfilled.
......
Be strong, my dear Cagalli...
......

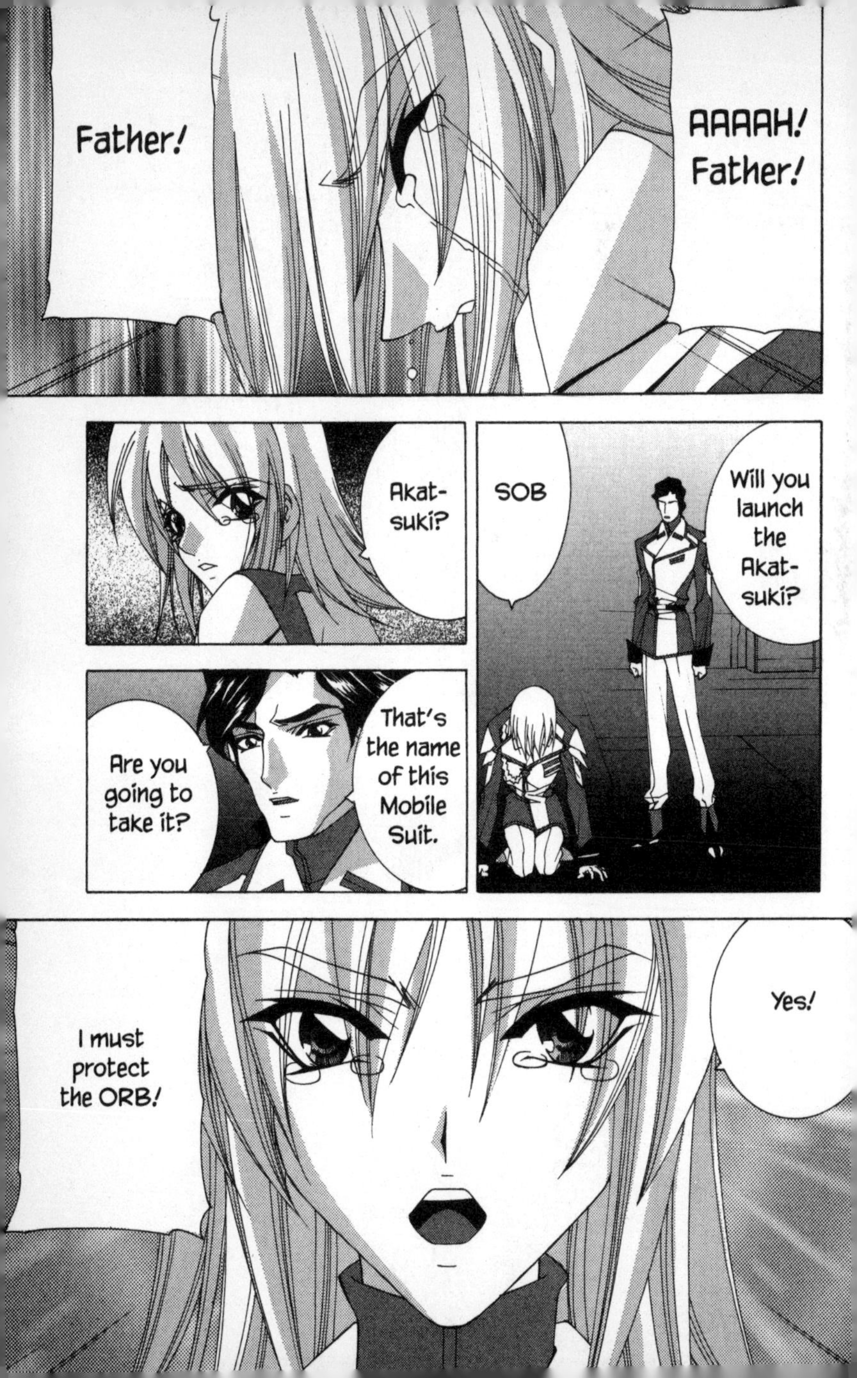
AAAAH! Father!
Father!
Will you launch the Akatsuki?
SOB
Akatsuki?
That's the name of this Mobile Suit.
Are you going to take it?
Yes!
I must protect the ORB!

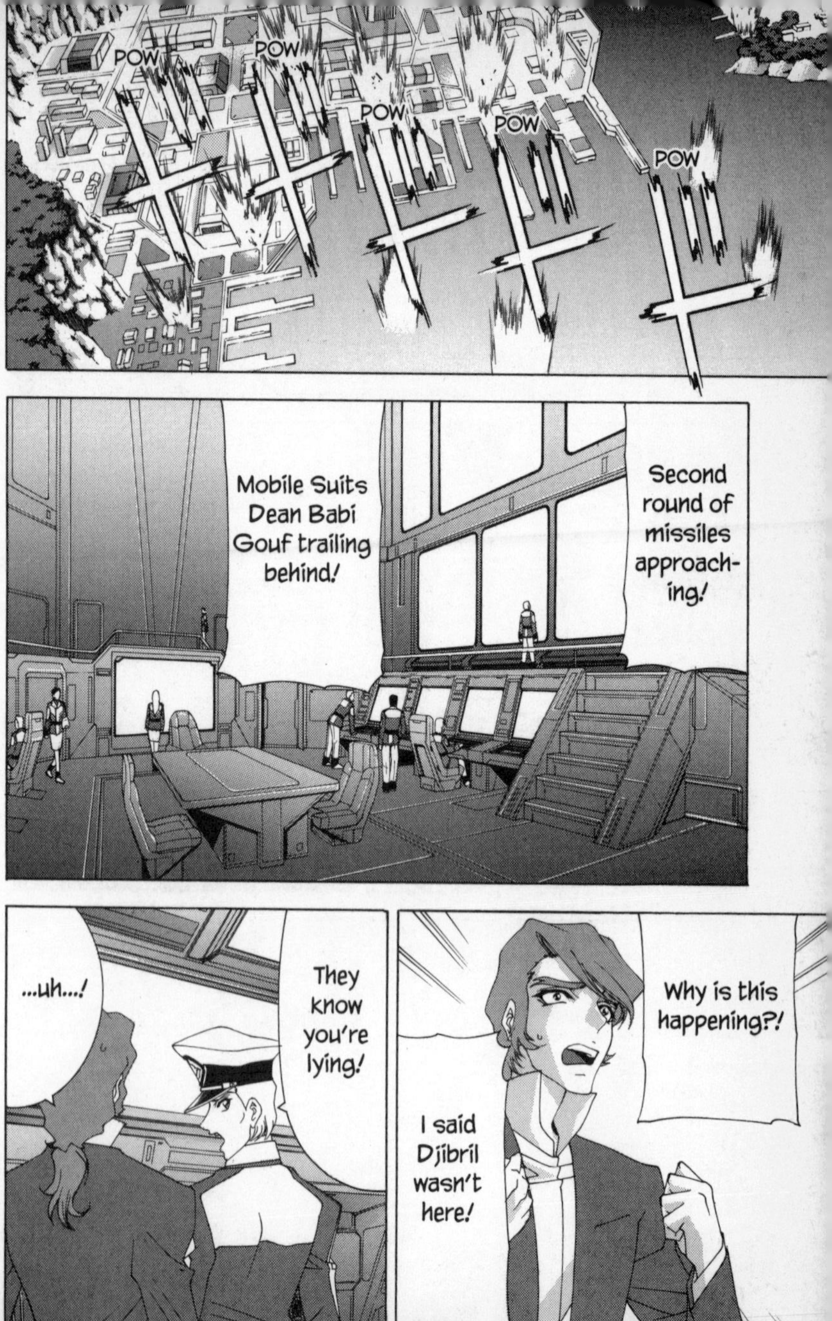
POW
POW
POW
POW
POW
Second round of missiles approaching!
Mobile Suits Dean Babi Gouf trailing behind!
Why is this happening?!
I said Djibril wasn't here!
They know you're lying!
...uh...!

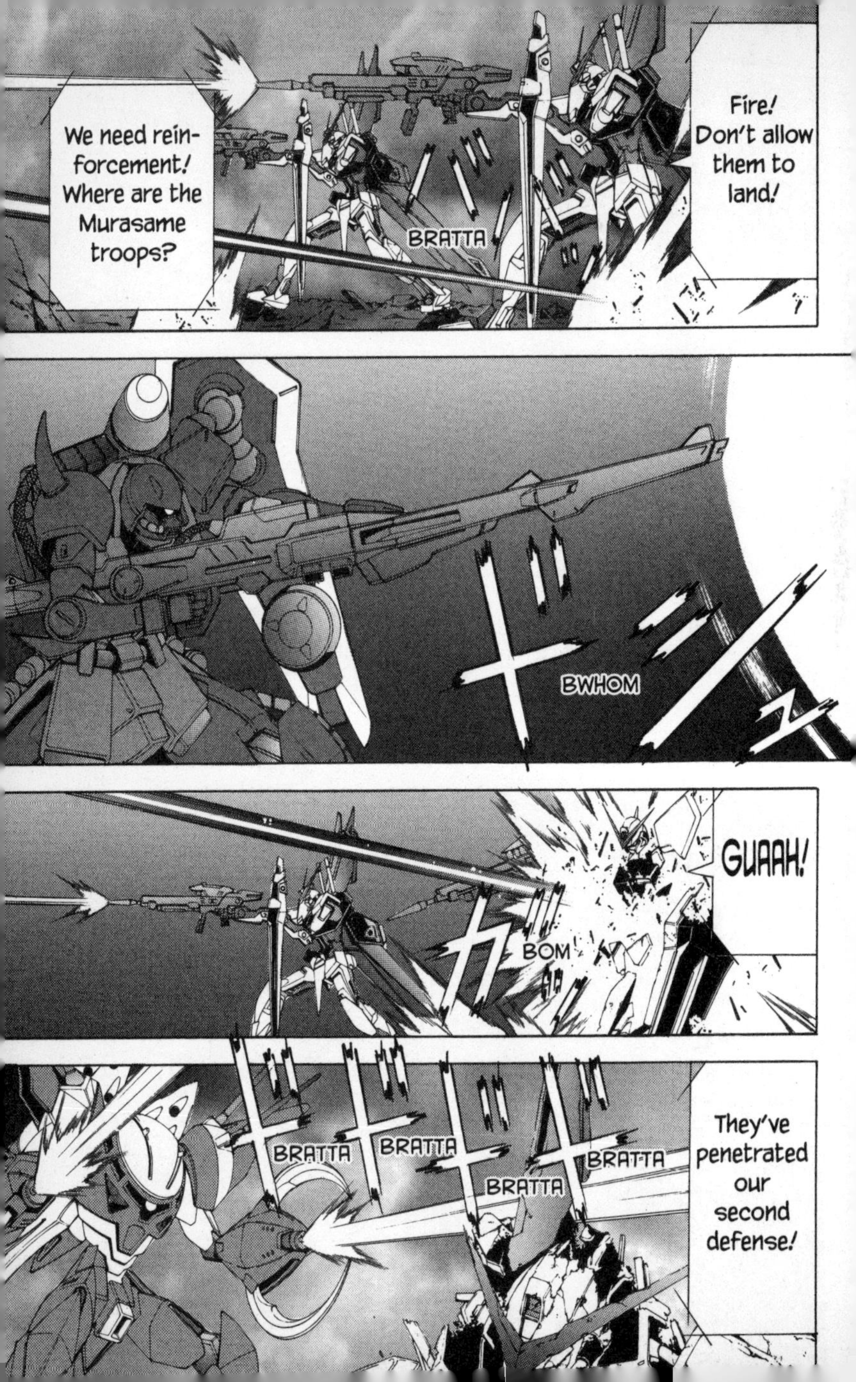
Fire! Don't allow them to land!
BRATTA
We need rein-forcement! Where are the Murasame troops?
BWHOM
GUAAH!
BOM
They've penetrated our second defense!
BRATTA
BRATTA
BRATTA
BRATTA

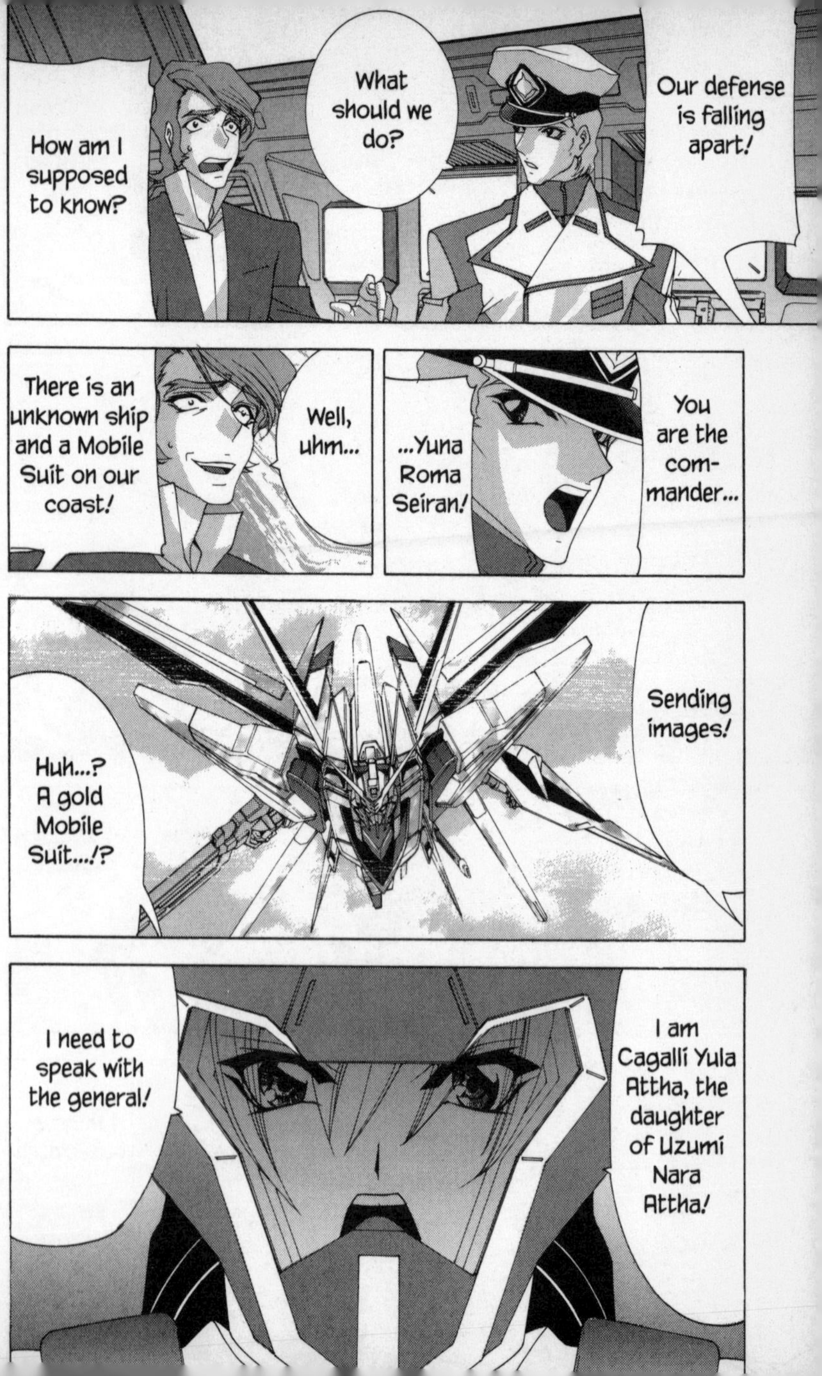
Our defense is falling apart!
What should we do?
How am I supposed to know?
You are the commander...
...Yuna Roma Seiran!
Well, uhm...
There is an unknown ship and a Mobile Suit on our coast!
Sending images!
Huh...? A gold Mobile Suit...!?
I am Cagalli Yula Attha, the daughter of Uzumi Nara Attha!
I need to speak with the general!

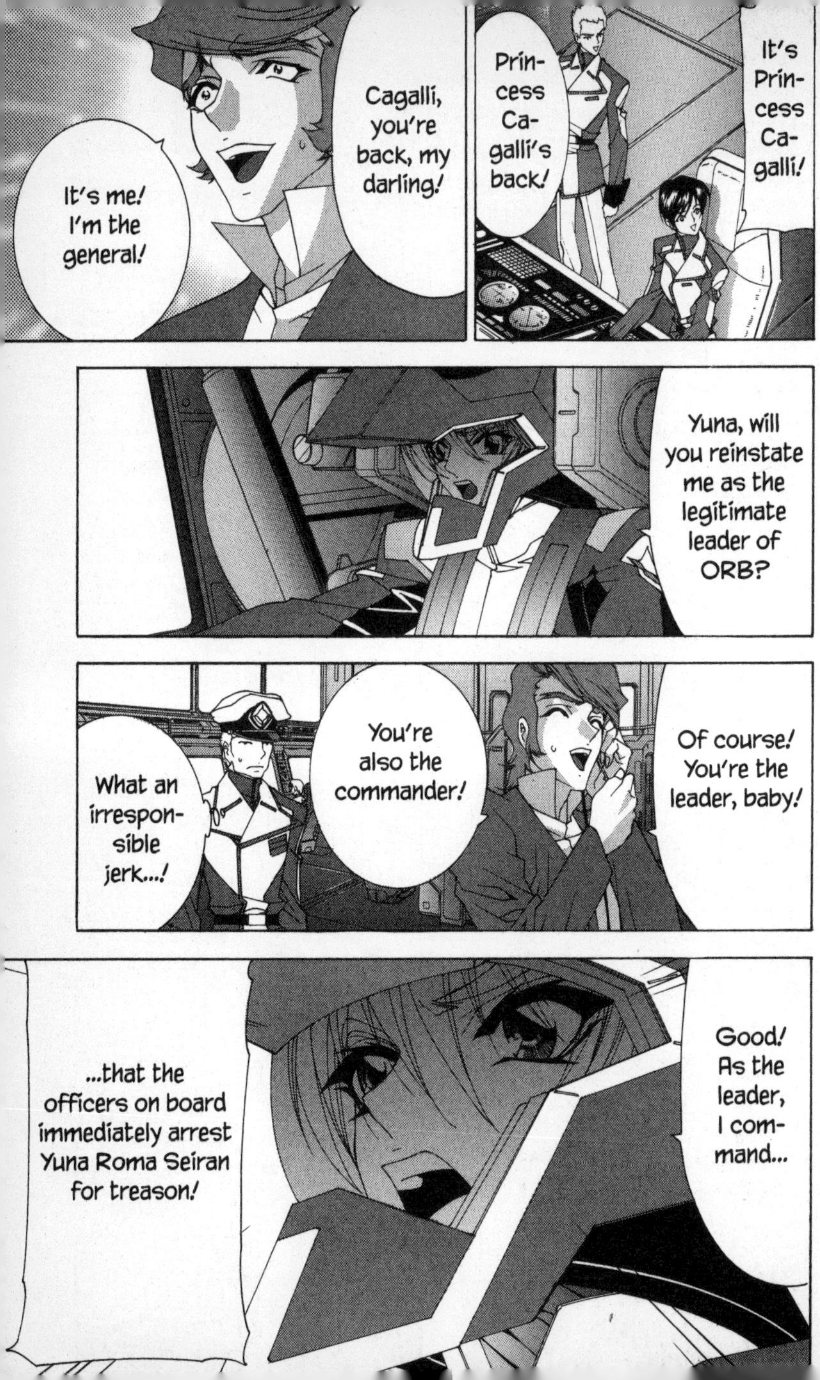
It's Princess Cagalli!
Princess Cagalli's back!
Cagalli, you're back, my darling!
It's me! I'm the general!
Yuna, will you reinstate me as the legitimate leader of ORB?
Of course! You're the leader, baby!
You're also the commander!
What an irresponsible jerk...!
Good! As the leader, I command...
...that the officers on board immediately arrest Yuna Roma Seiran for treason!

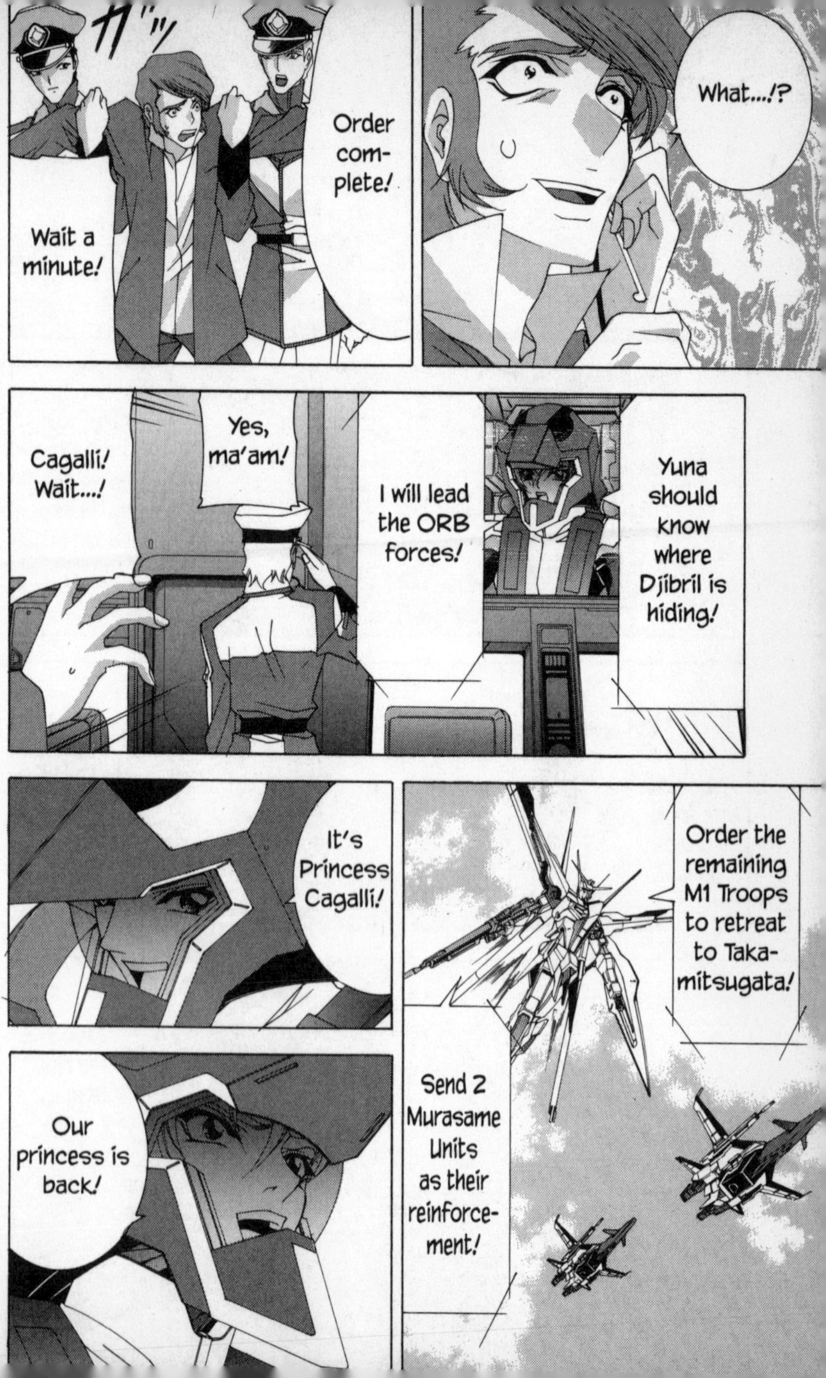
What...!?
Order complete!
ガッ
Wait a minute!
Yuna should know where Djibril is hiding!
I will lead the ORB forces!
Yes, ma'am!
Cagalli! Wait...!
Order the remaining M1 Troops to retreat to Takamitsugata!
Send 2 Murasame Units as their reinforcement!
It's Princess Cagalli!
Our princess is back!

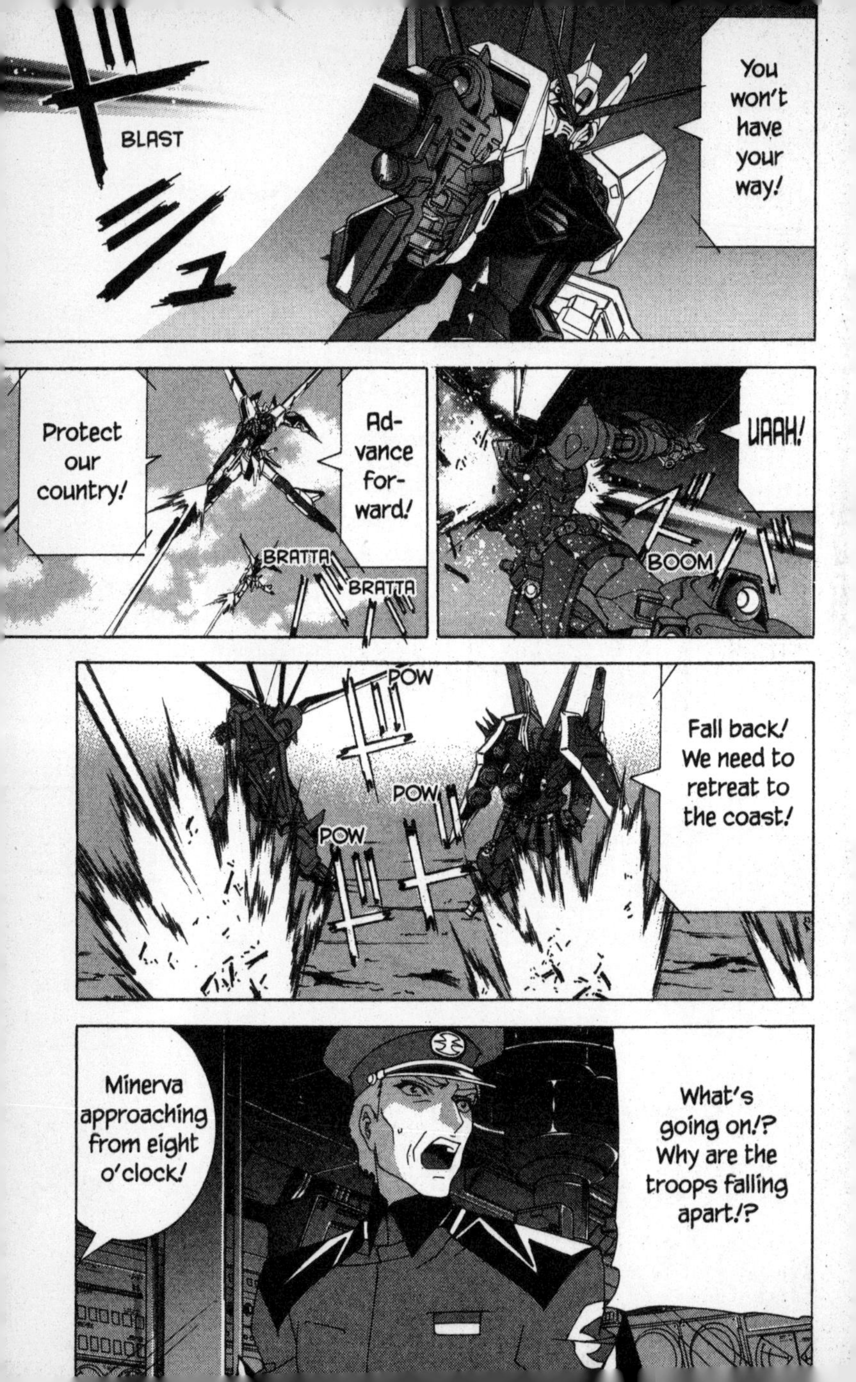
You won't have your way!
BLAST
UAAH!
BOOM
Ad- vance for- ward!
Protect our country!
BRATTA
BRATTA
Fall back! We need to retreat to the coast!
POW
POW
POW
What's going on!? Why are the troops falling apart!?
Minerva approaching from eight o'clock!

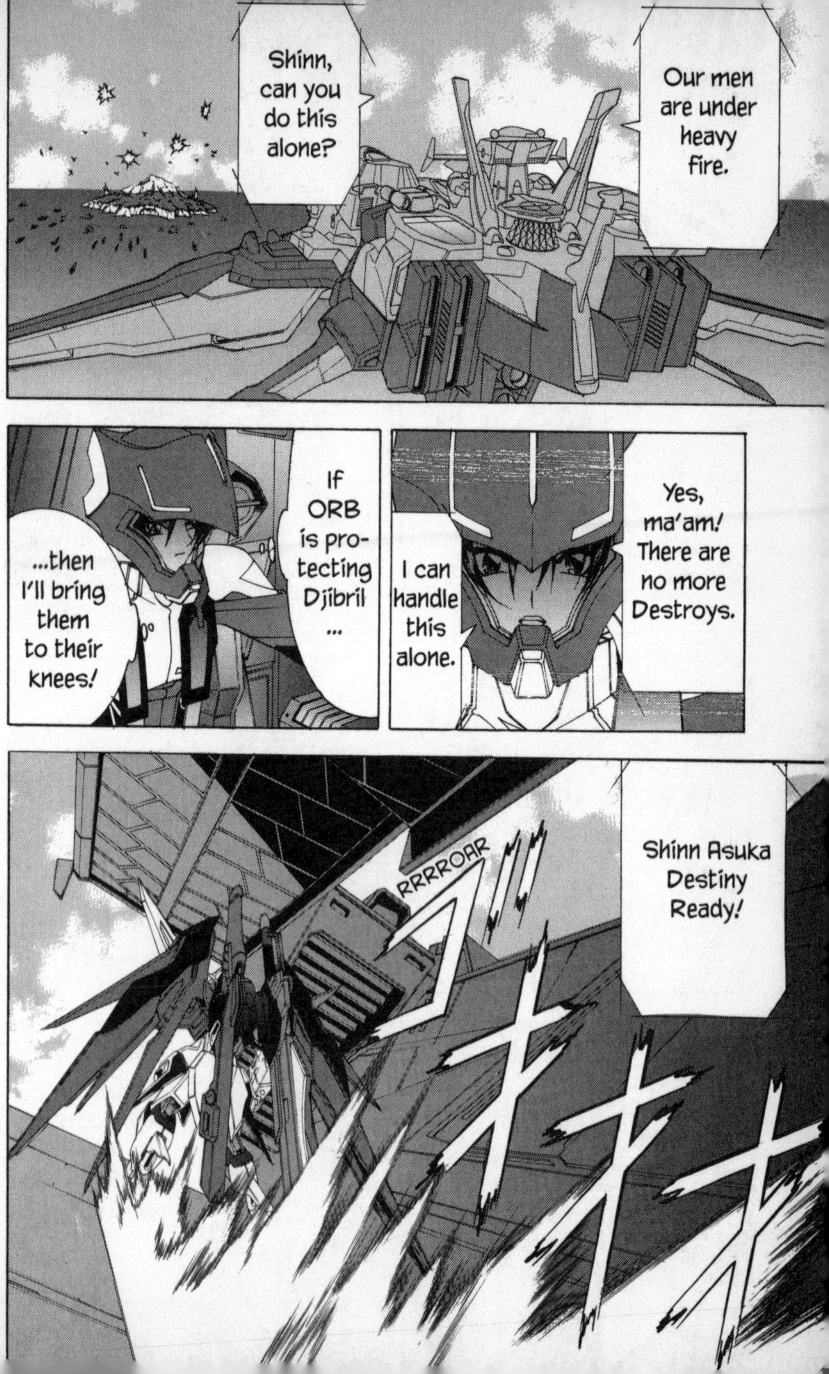
Our men are under heavy fire.
Shinn, can you do this alone?
Yes, ma'am! There are no more Destroys.
I can handle this alone.
If ORB is protecting Djibril ...
...then I'll bring them to their knees!
Shinn Asuka Destiny Ready!
RRRROAR

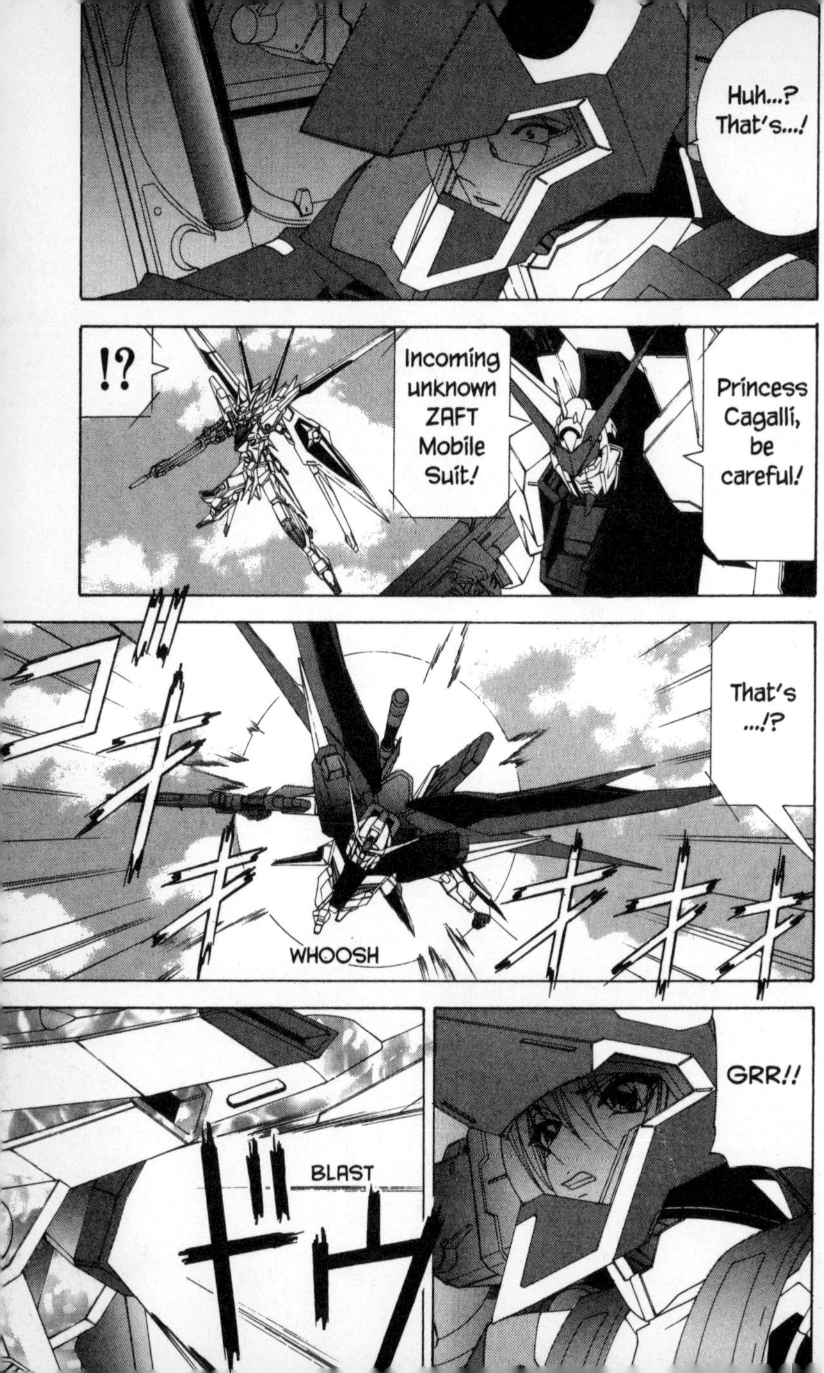
Huh...? That's...!
Princess Cagalli, be careful!
Incoming unknown ZAFT Mobile Suit!
!?
That's ...!?
WHOOSH
GRR!!
BLAST

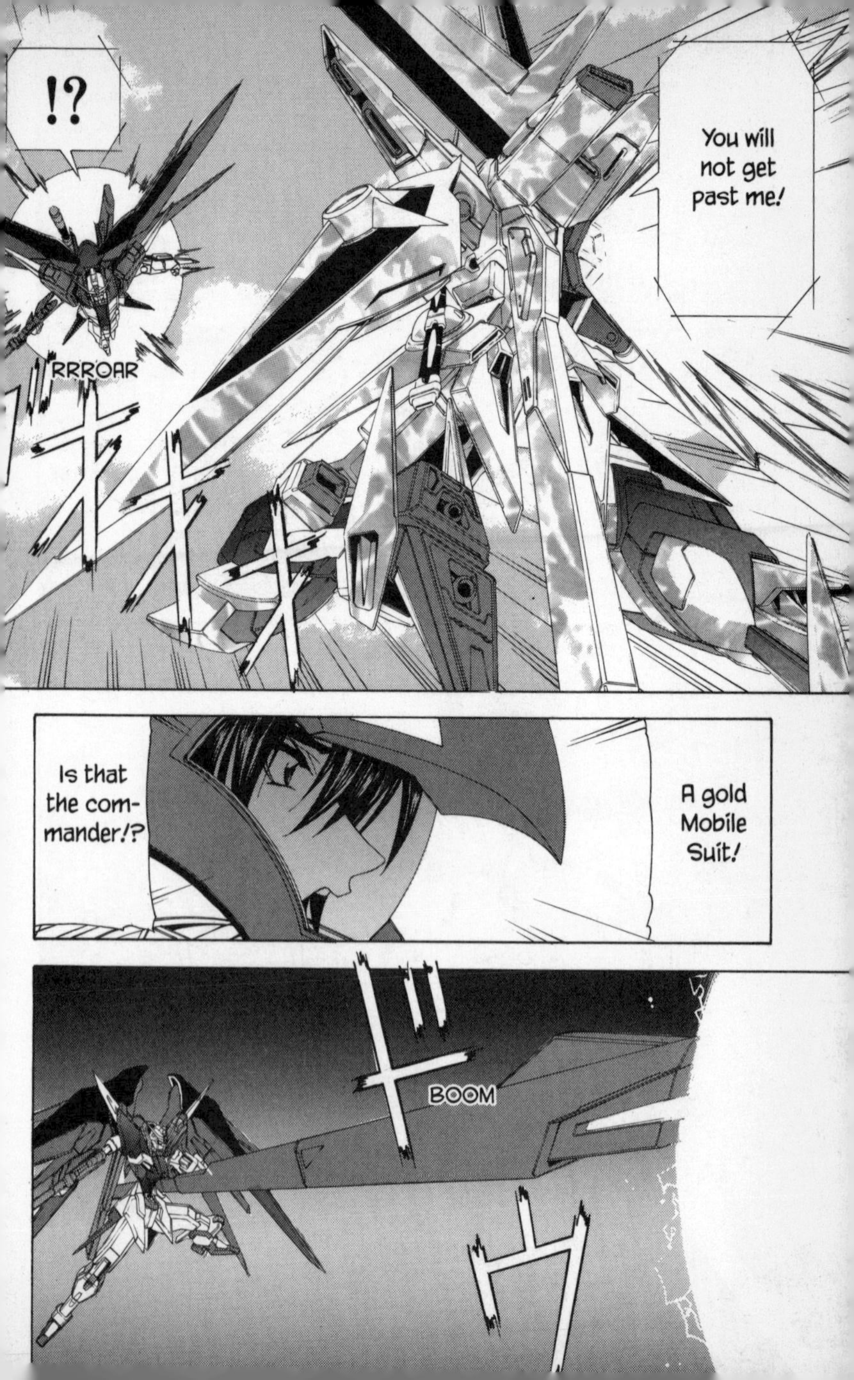
You will not get past me!
!?
RRROAR
A gold Mobile Suit!
Is that the commander!?
BOOM

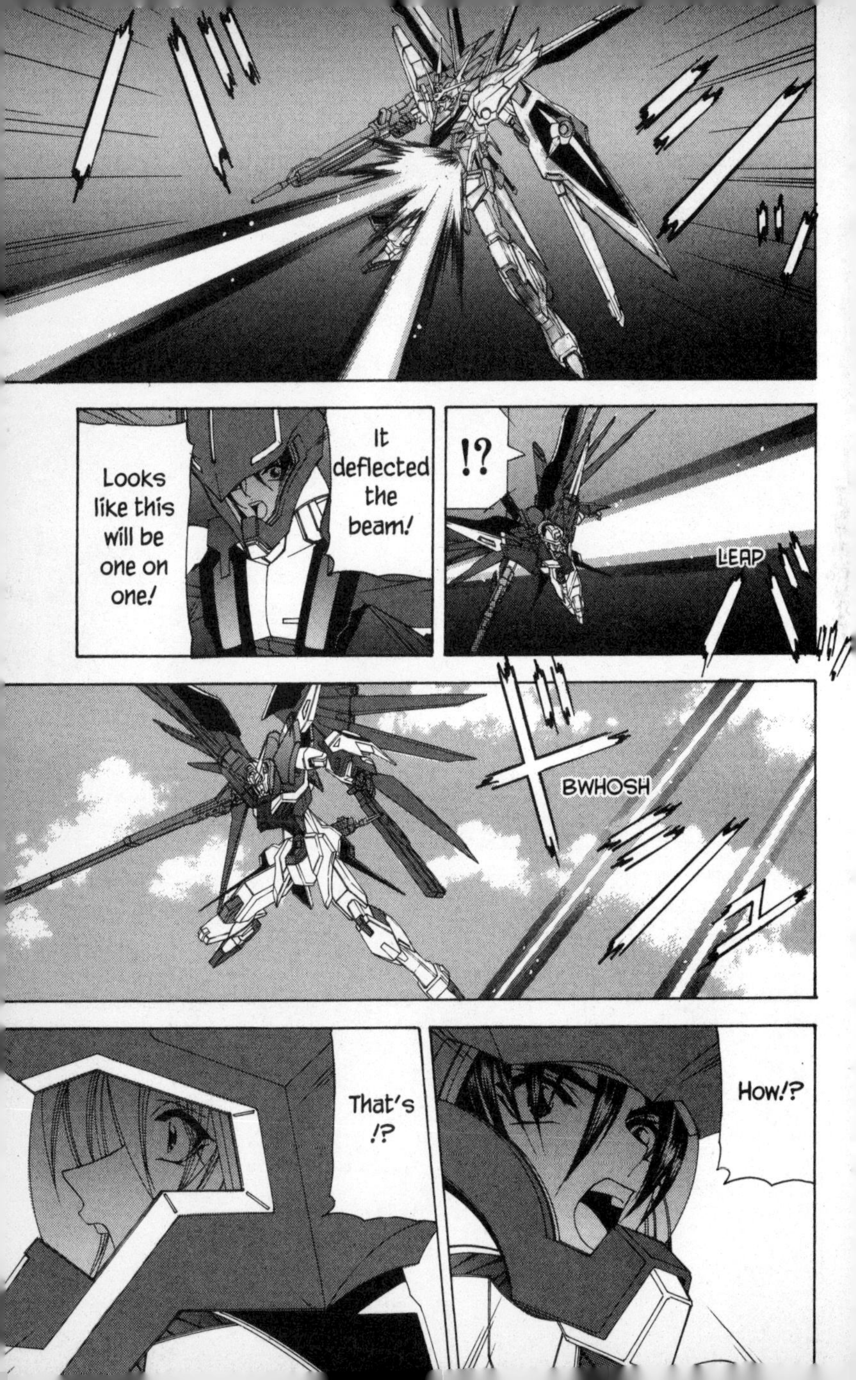
!?
LEAP
It deflected the beam!
Looks like this will be one on one!
BWHOSH
How!?
That's !?

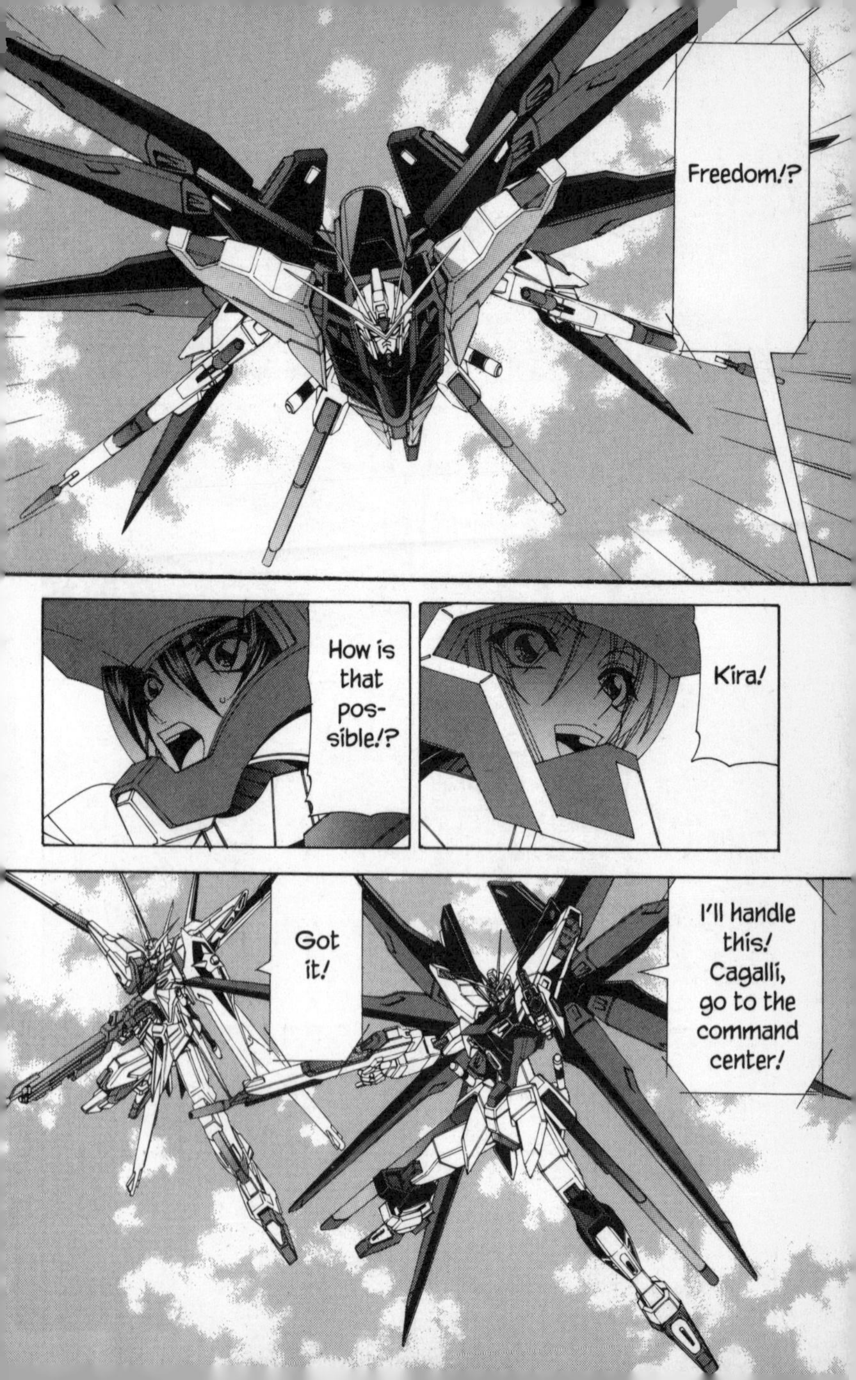
Freedom!?
Kira!
How is that pos-sible!?
I'll handle this! Cagalli, go to the command center!
Got it!

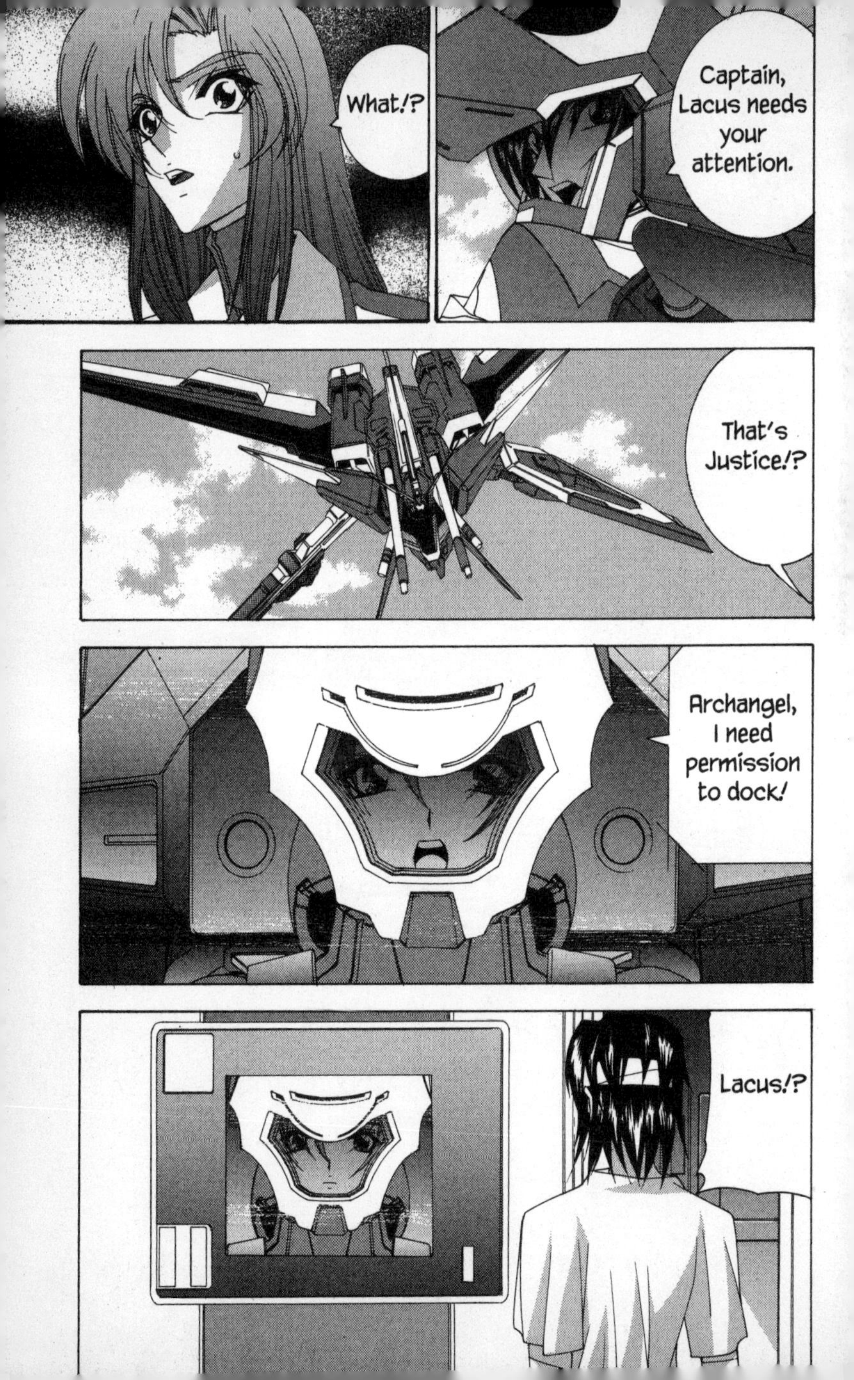
Captain, Lacus needs your attention.
What!?
That's Justice!?
Archangel, I need permission to dock!
Lacus!?

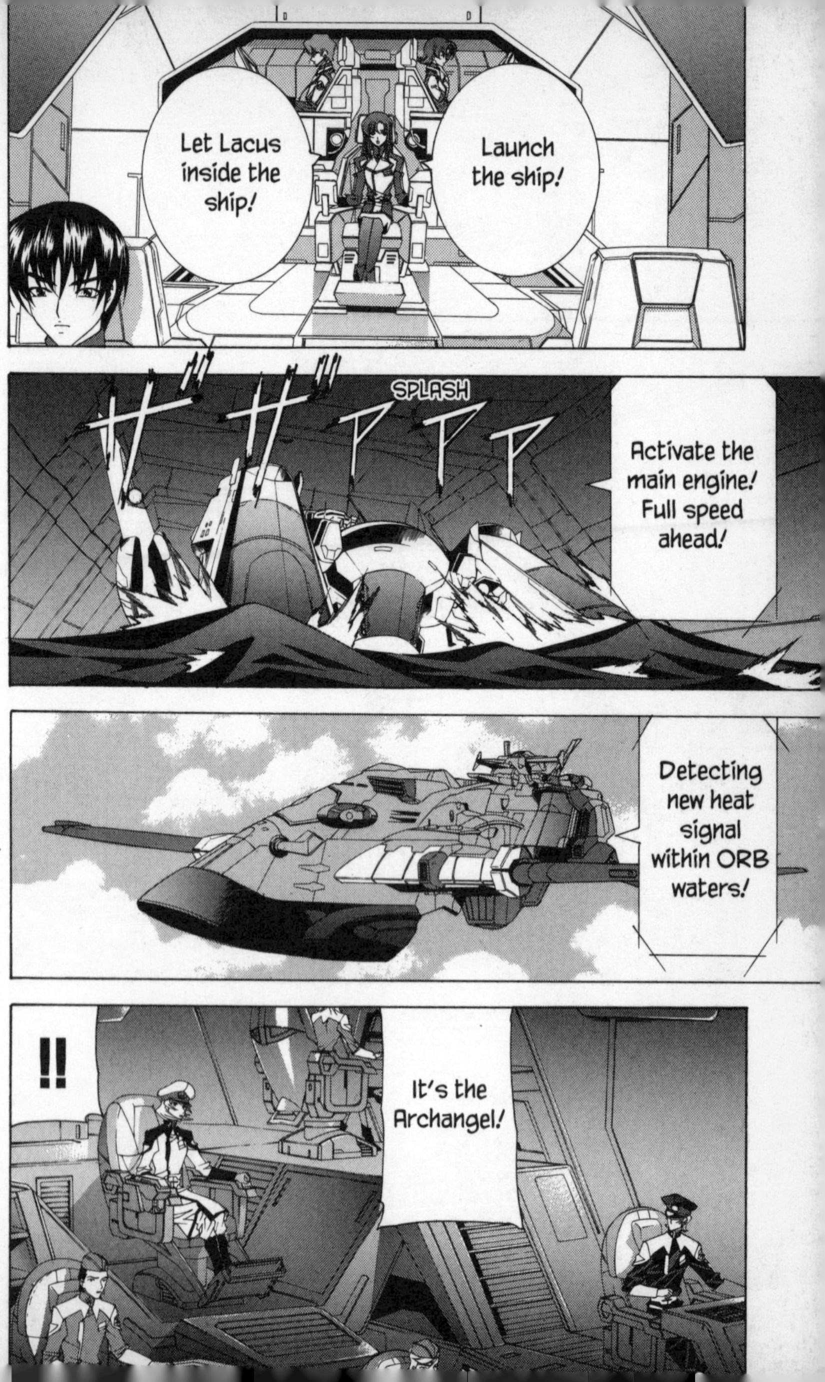
Launch the ship!
Let Lacus inside the ship!
Activate the main engine! Full speed ahead!
SPLASH
Detecting new heat signal within ORB waters!
It's the Archangel!
!!

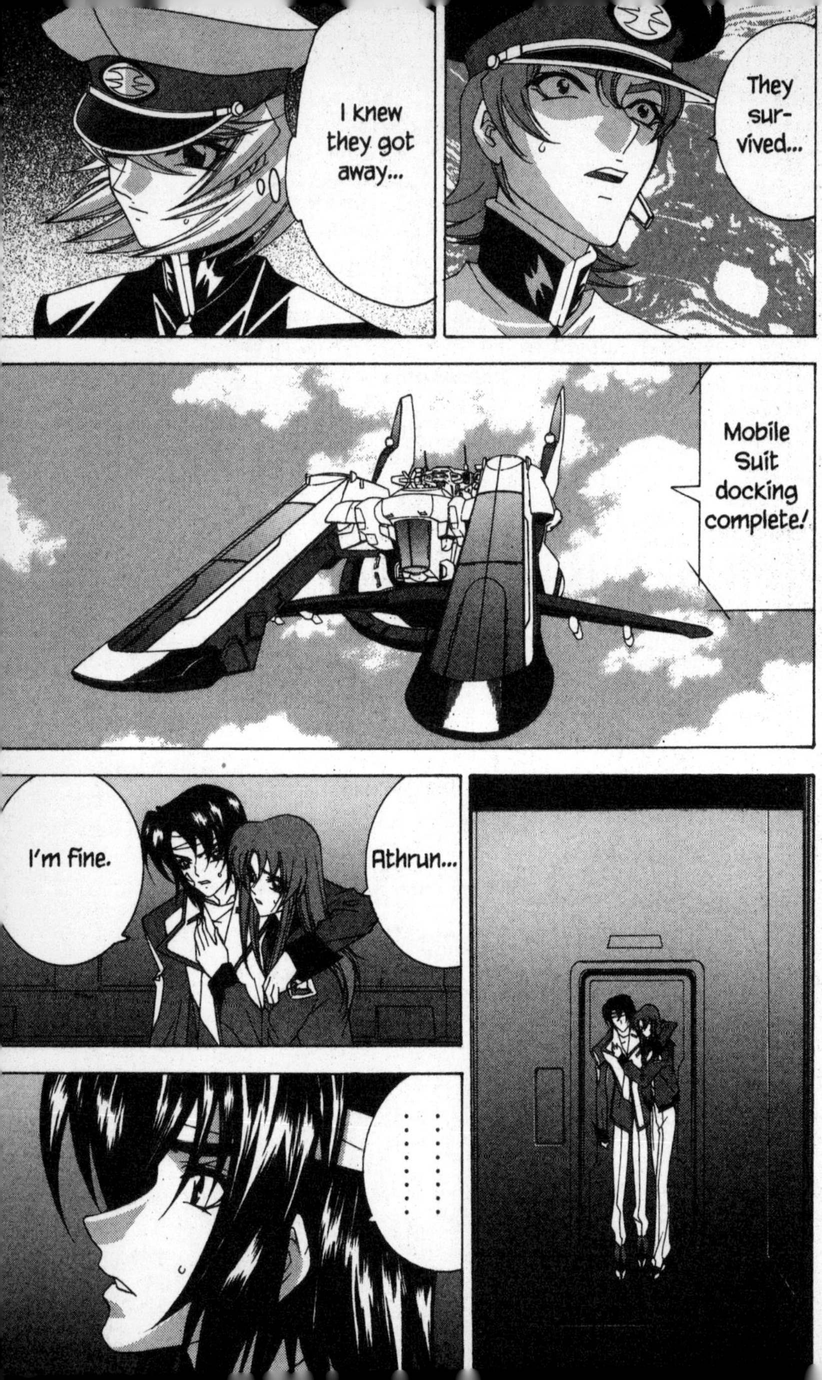
They survived...
I knew they got away...
Mobile Suit docking complete!
Athrun...
I'm fine.
......

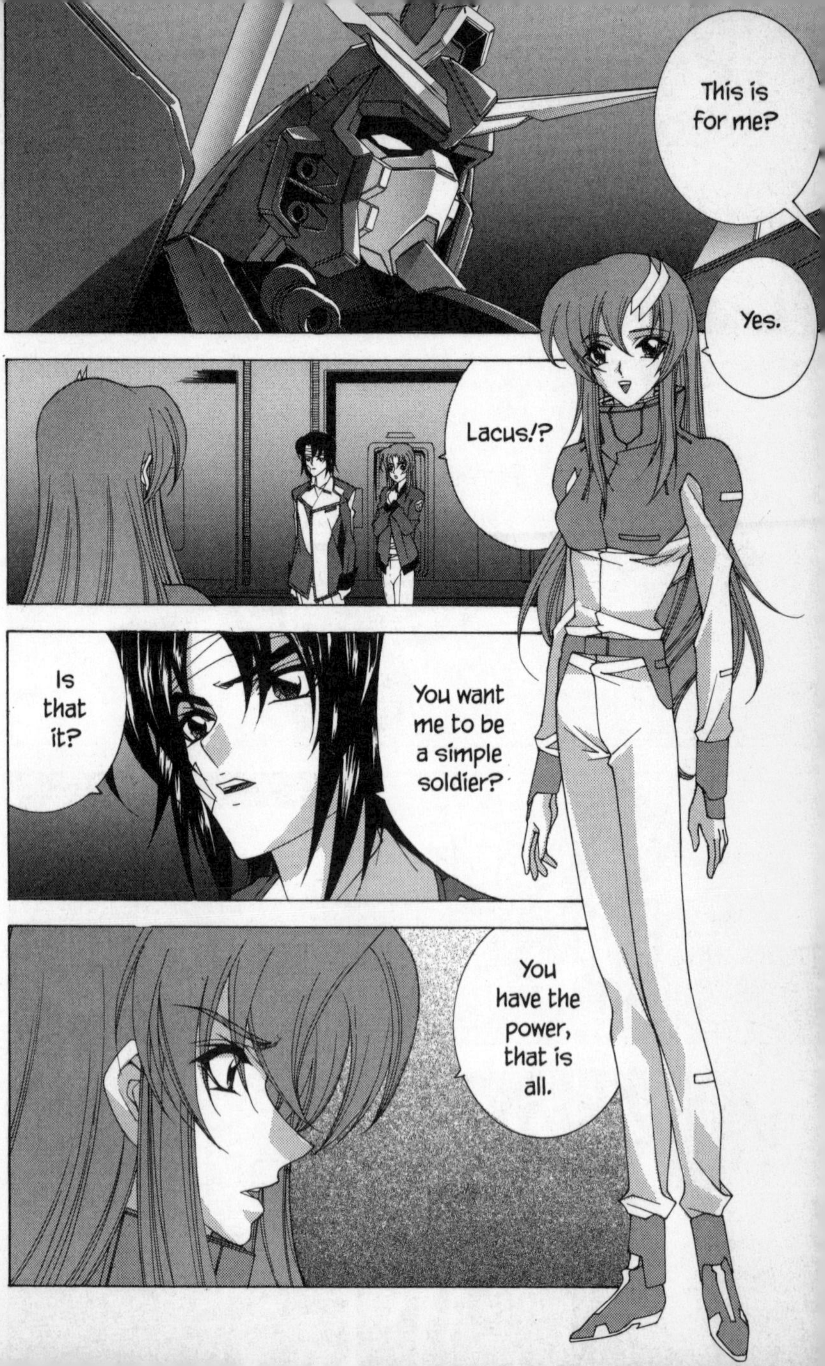
This is for me?
Yes.
Lacus!?
You want me to be a simple soldier?
Is that it?
You have the power, that is all.

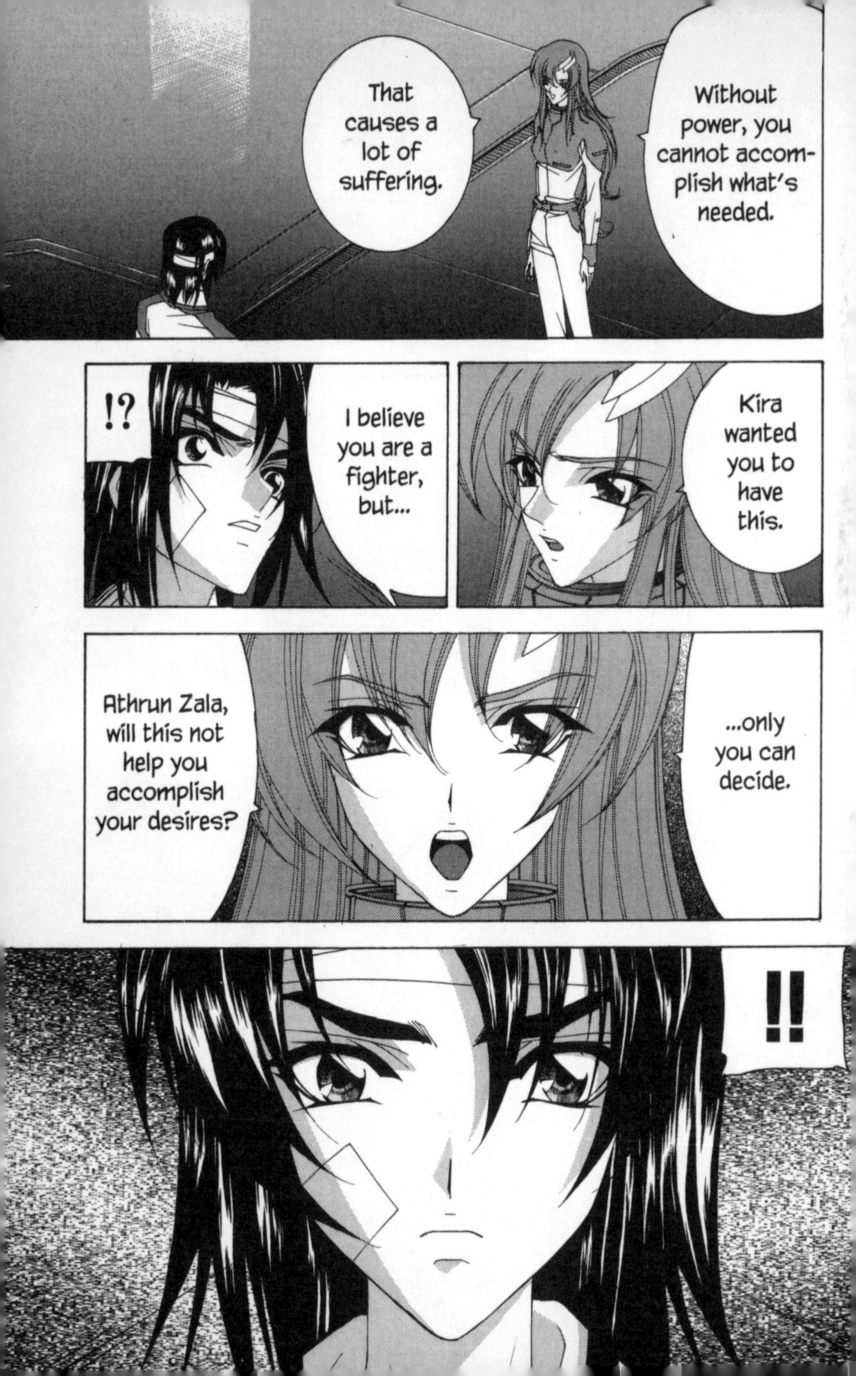
Without power, you cannot accomplish what's needed.
That causes a lot of suffering.
Kira wanted you to have this.
I believe you are a fighter, but...
!?
...only you can decide.
Athrun Zala, will this not help you accomplish your desires?
!!

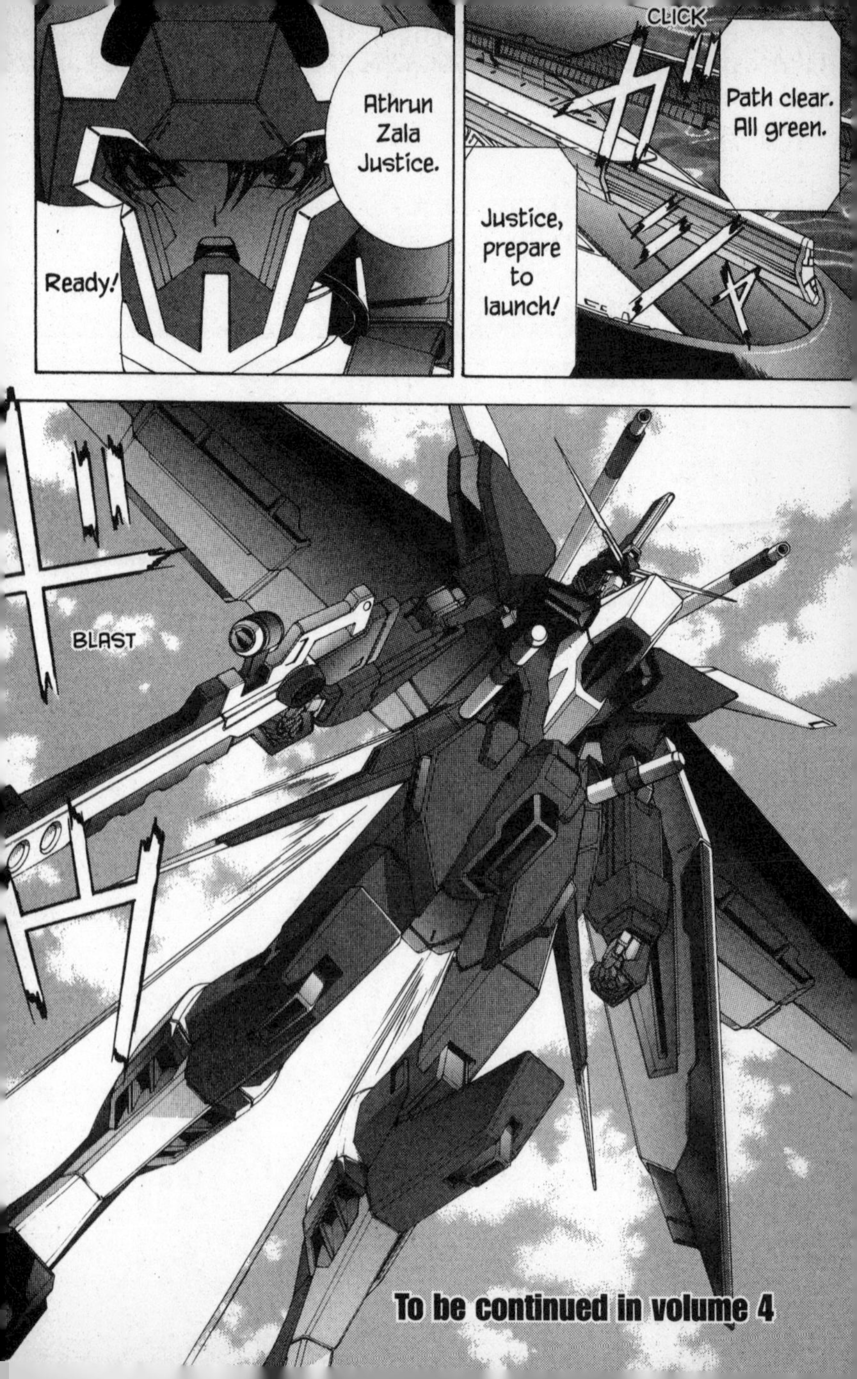
CLICK
Path clear. All green.
Justice, prepare to launch!
Athrun Zala Justice.
Ready!
BLAST
To be continued in volume 4

BONUS PAGE MECHA PARTS DESCRIPTION

ZCMF-X20A STRIKE FREEDOM GUNDAM

A Mobile Suit custom-made for Kira Yamato by supporters of Lacus Clyne using the latest technology. Its special features include a Beam Shield and DRAGOON System.

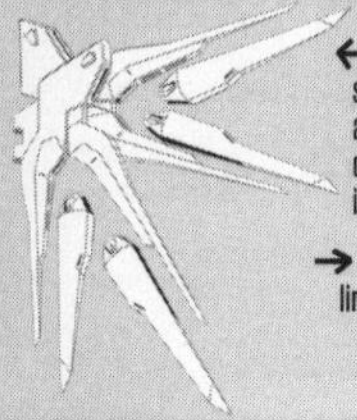

← Each wing can fire 4 beams simultaneously, allowing remote attacks. However, this function is only active while the Mobile Suit is airborne.

→ The rifles on both sides can be linked to increase the firepower.

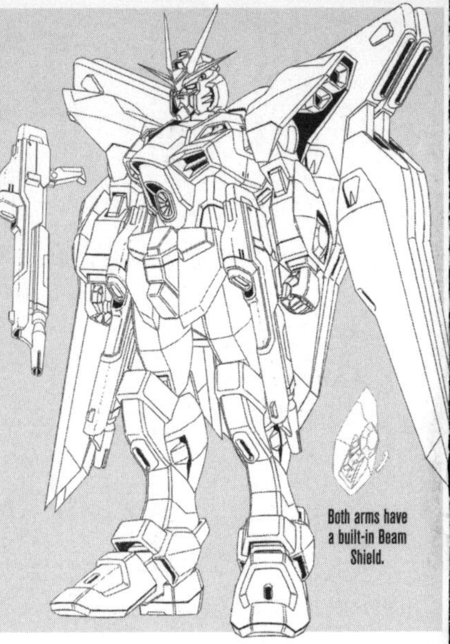

Both arms have a built-in Beam Shield.

Height: 18.88m	Weight: 80.09t
Fixed Weapons	
MA-M21KF high-energy Beam Rifle x2	
MA-M02G "Super Lacerta" Beam Saber x2	
MGX-2235 "Callidus" multi-phase Beam Cannon	
MMI-M15E "Xiphias 3" Rail Cannon x2	

ZGMF-X19A JUSTICE GUNDAM

Similar to Freedom, this was also built by Lacus supporters. The weapons system is upgraded from the original Justice. The upgrades include the Fatum 01 Lifter. The shield also stores additional weapons like the Beam Boomerang.

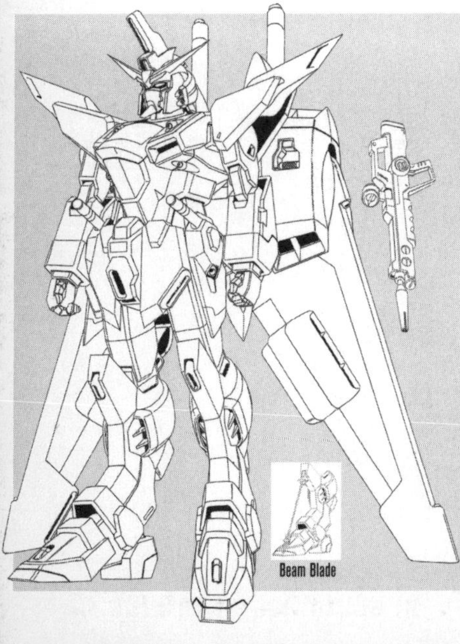

Beam Blade

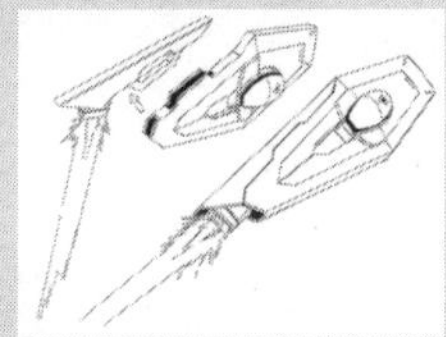

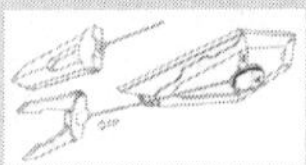

Height: 18.9m	Weight: 79.67t
Fixed Weapons	
MA-M1911 high-energy Beam Rifle	
MA-6J "Hyper Fortis" Beam Cannon x2	
MA-M02S "Super Lacerta" Beam Saber x2	
MR-Q15A "Griffon" Beam Blade x2	
RQM55 "Shining Edge" Beam Boomerang	

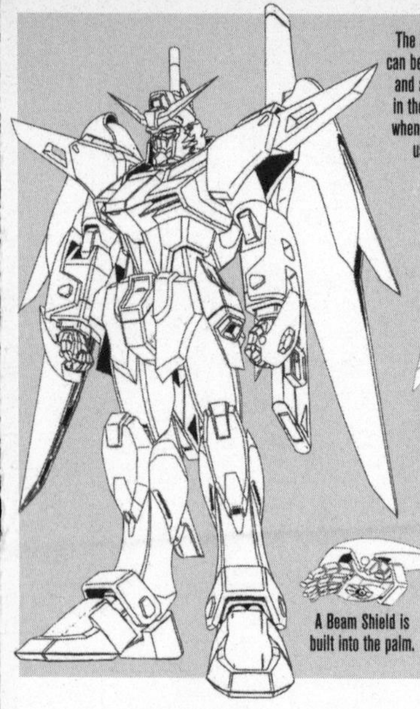

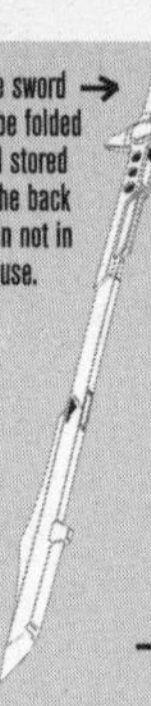

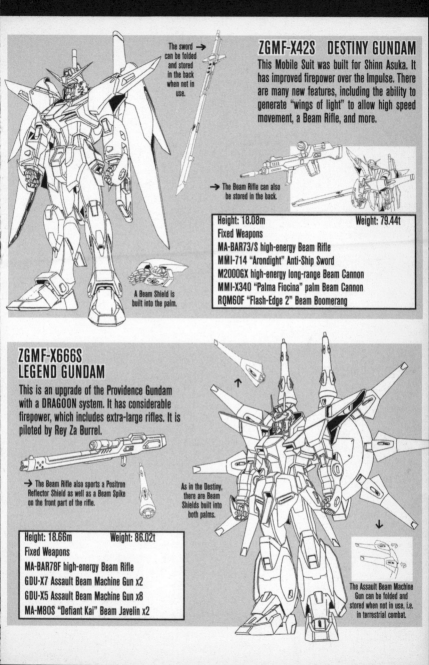

The sword can be folded and stored in the back when not in use.

ZGMF-X42S DESTINY GUNDAM

This Mobile Suit was built for Shinn Asuka. It has improved firepower over the Impulse. There are many new features, including the ability to generate "wings of light" to allow high speed movement, a Beam Rifle, and more.

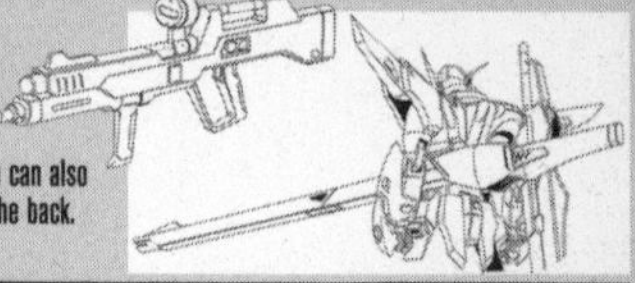

→ The Beam Rifle can also be stored in the back.

A Beam Shield is built into the palm.

Height: 18.08m	Weight: 79.44t
Fixed Weapons	
MA-BAR73/S high-energy Beam Rifle	
MMI-714 "Arondight" Anti-Ship Sword	
M2000GX high-energy long-range Beam Cannon	
MMI-X340 "Palma Fiocina" palm Beam Cannon	
RQM60F "Flash-Edge 2" Beam Boomerang	

ZGMF-X666S LEGEND GUNDAM

This is an upgrade of the Providence Gundam with a DRAGOON system. It has considerable firepower, which includes extra-large rifles. It is piloted by Rey Za Burrel.

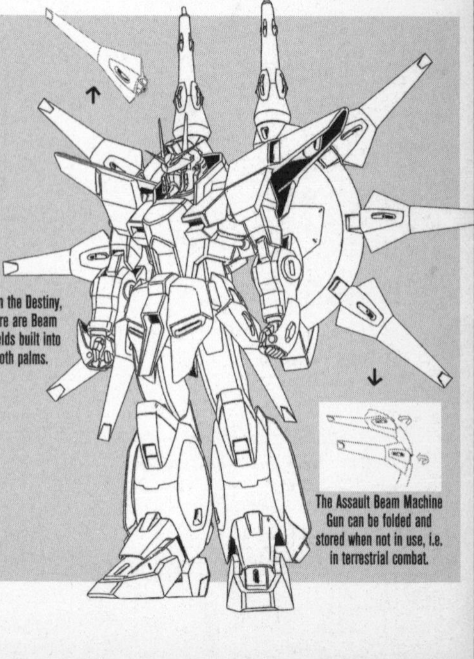

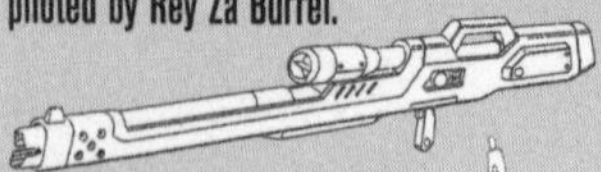

→ The Beam Rifle also sports a Positron Reflector Shield as well as a Beam Spike on the front part of the rifle.

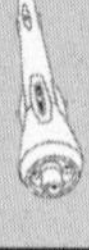

As in the Destiny, there are Beam Shields built into both palms.

The Assault Beam Machine Gun can be folded and stored when not in use, i.e. in terrestrial combat.

Height: 18.66m	Weight: 86.02t
Fixed Weapons	
MA-BAR78F high-energy Beam Rifle	
GDU-X7 Assault Beam Machine Gun x2	
GDU-X5 Assault Beam Machine Gun x8	
MA-M80S "Defiant Kai" Beam Javelin x2	

ORB-01 AKATSUKI (OWASHI SKY PACK)

Uzumi, the former leader of the ORB, commissioned the construction of the Akatsuki for his daughter, Cagalli. It has an Anti-Beam Reflection Defensive System built into the armor. The "Owashi" pack is capable of functioning as a separate fighter. For use in space, the "Shiranui" pack can create a defensive shield in addition to its function as a beam cannon.

Height: 18.74m	Weight: 69.6t

Fixed Weapons
72D5 "Hyakurai" Beam Rifle
"Yata-no-Kagami" Anti-Beam Defensive Reflection System
73F Mobile Beam Turret System (mounts on "Owashi" pack)
M531R Beam Cannon; 2 FX Beam Gun; Beam Shield Emitter (mounts on "Shiranui" pack)
73J2 prototype Twin Beam Saber

GFAS-X1 DESTROY GUNDAM

↑ Both arms are detachable.

It is an EA Mobile Suit created specifically for Extended pilots. It can function as a Mobile Armor as well as a Mobile Suit. The pilot serves as the machine's CPU unit. It contains many weapons of mass destruction, giving it the capacity to destroy cities in a matter of minutes. It includes an enormous Positron Reflector.

Mobile Armor Mode

Height: 38.07m	Weight: 404.93t

Fixed Weapons
2 FX "Aufprall Dreizehn" High-Energy Beam Cannon x2
"Nefertem 503" Thermal Plasma Composite Cannon
1580-mm Multi-Phase Energy Cannon "Super Scylla" x3
200mm "Zorn Mk2" Energy Cannon
"Sturm Faust" detachable arm x2
Mark 62 6-tube multipurpose Missile Launcher x4

Mobile Suit Mode

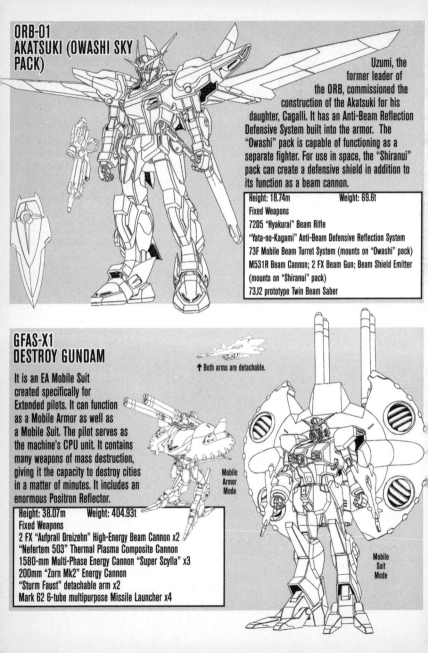

About the Creators

Yoshiyuki Tomino

Gundam was created by Yoshiyuki Tomino. Prior to Gundam, Tomino had worked on the original *Astro Boy* anime, as well as *Princess Knight* and *Brave Raideen*, among others. In 1979, he created and directed *Mobile Suit Gundam*, the very first in a long line of Gundam series. The show was not immediately popular and was forced to cut its number of episodes before going off the air, but as with the American show *Star Trek*, the fans still had something to say on this matter. By 1981, the demand for Gundam was so high that Tomino oversaw the re-release of the animation as three theatrical movies (a practice still common in Japan, and rarely, if ever, seen in the United States). It was now official: Gundam was a blockbuster.

Tomino would go on to direct many Gundam series, including *Gundam ZZ, Char's Counterattack, Gundam F91,* and *Victory Gundam*, all of which contributed to the rich history of the vast Gundam universe. In addition to Gundam, Tomino created *Xabungle, L. Gaim, Dunbine,* and *Garzey's Wing*. His most recent anime is *Brain Powered*, which was released by Geneon in the United States.

Masatsugu Iwase

Masatsugu Iwase writes and draws the manga adaptation of *Gundam SEED* and *Gundam SEED Destiny. Gundam SEED* was his first work published in the United States. This manga creator is better known in Japan, however, for his work on *Calm Breaker*, a hilarious parody of anime, manga, and Japanese pop culture.

Preview of *Gundam SEED Destiny* volume 4

We're pleased to present you with a preview from *Gundam Seed Destiny*, volume 4. This volume is available in English now!

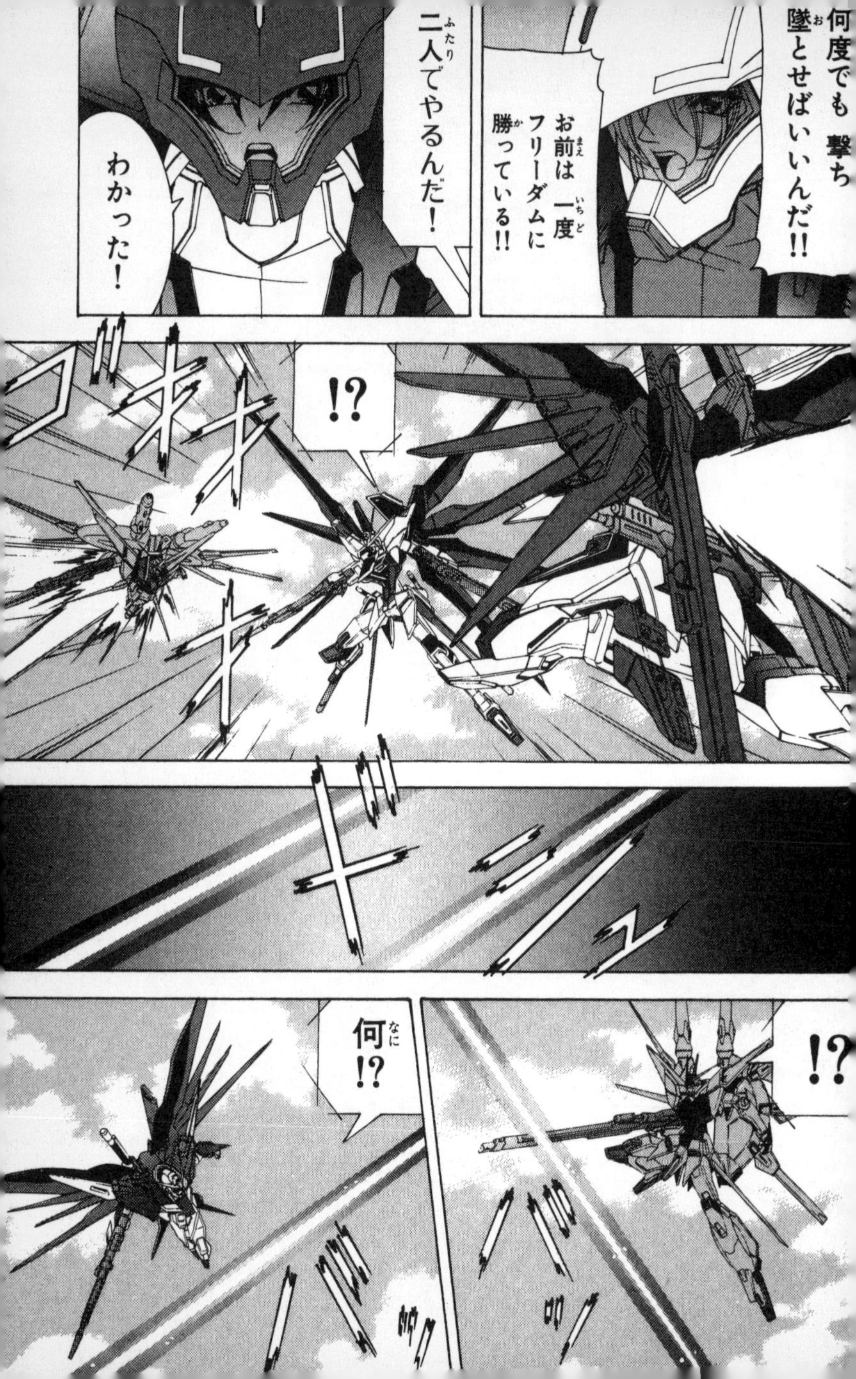
何度でも 撃ち墜とせばいいんだ!!
お前は一度フリーダムに勝っている!!
二人でやるんだ!
わかった!
!?
!?
何!?

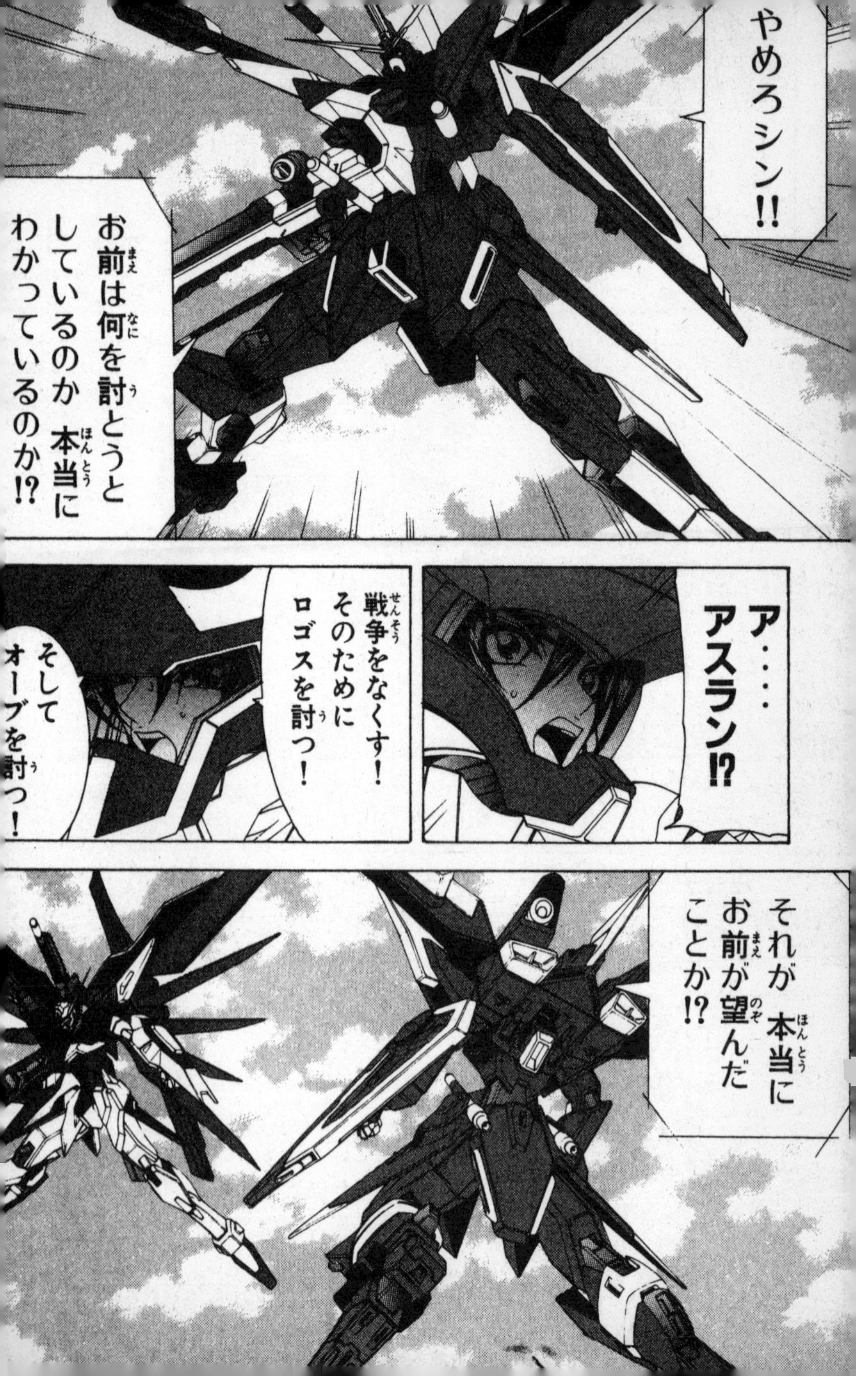
やめろシン!!
お前は何を討とうとしているのか 本当にわかっているのか!?
ア…アスラン!?
戦争をなくす! そのためにロゴスを討つ!
そしてオーブを討つ!
それが 本当にお前が望んだことか!?

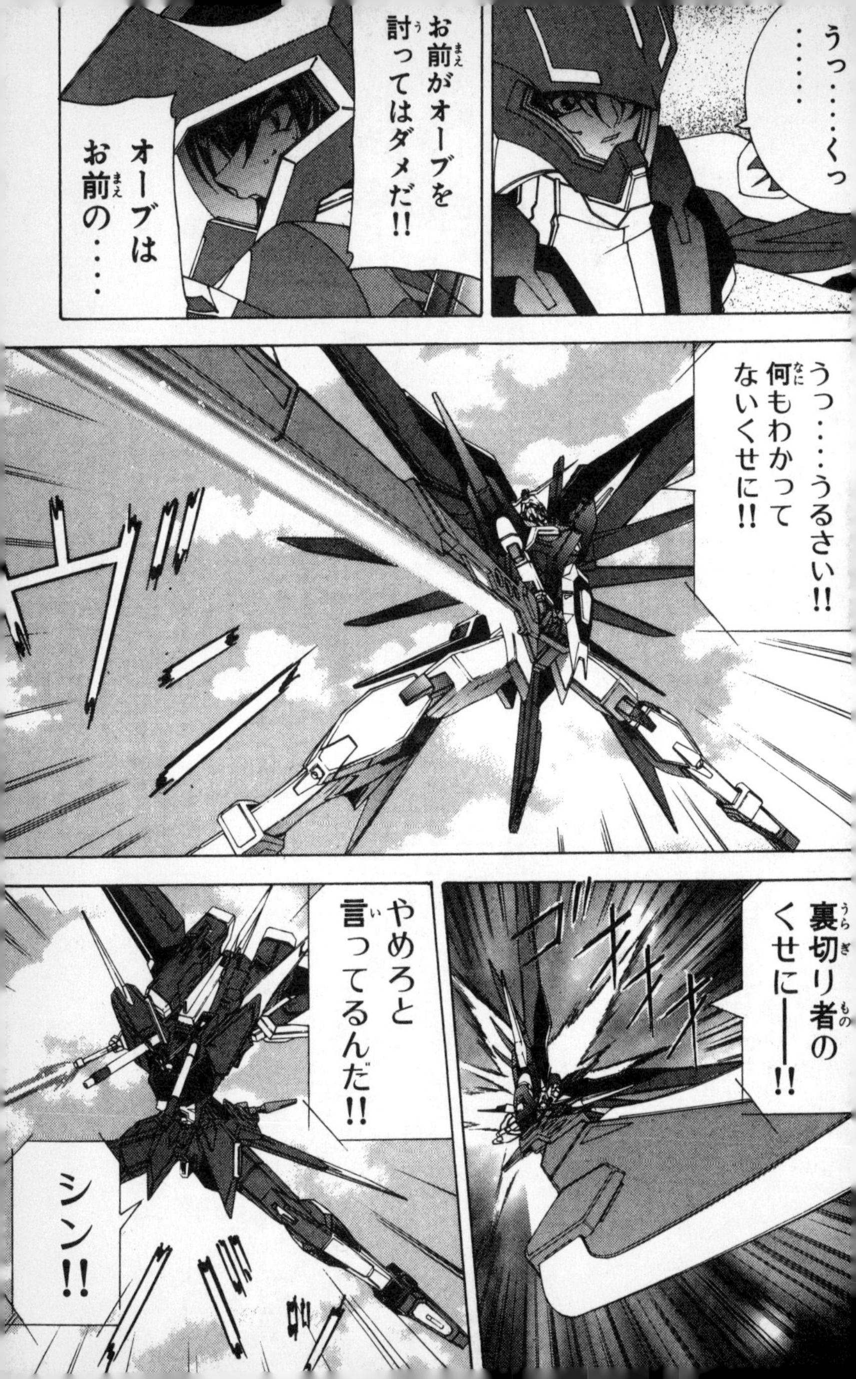
うっ……くっ……
お前がオーブを討ってはダメだ!!
オーブはお前の……
うっ……うるさい!!
何もわかってないくせに!!
裏切り者のくせに──!!
やめろと言ってるんだ!!
シン!!

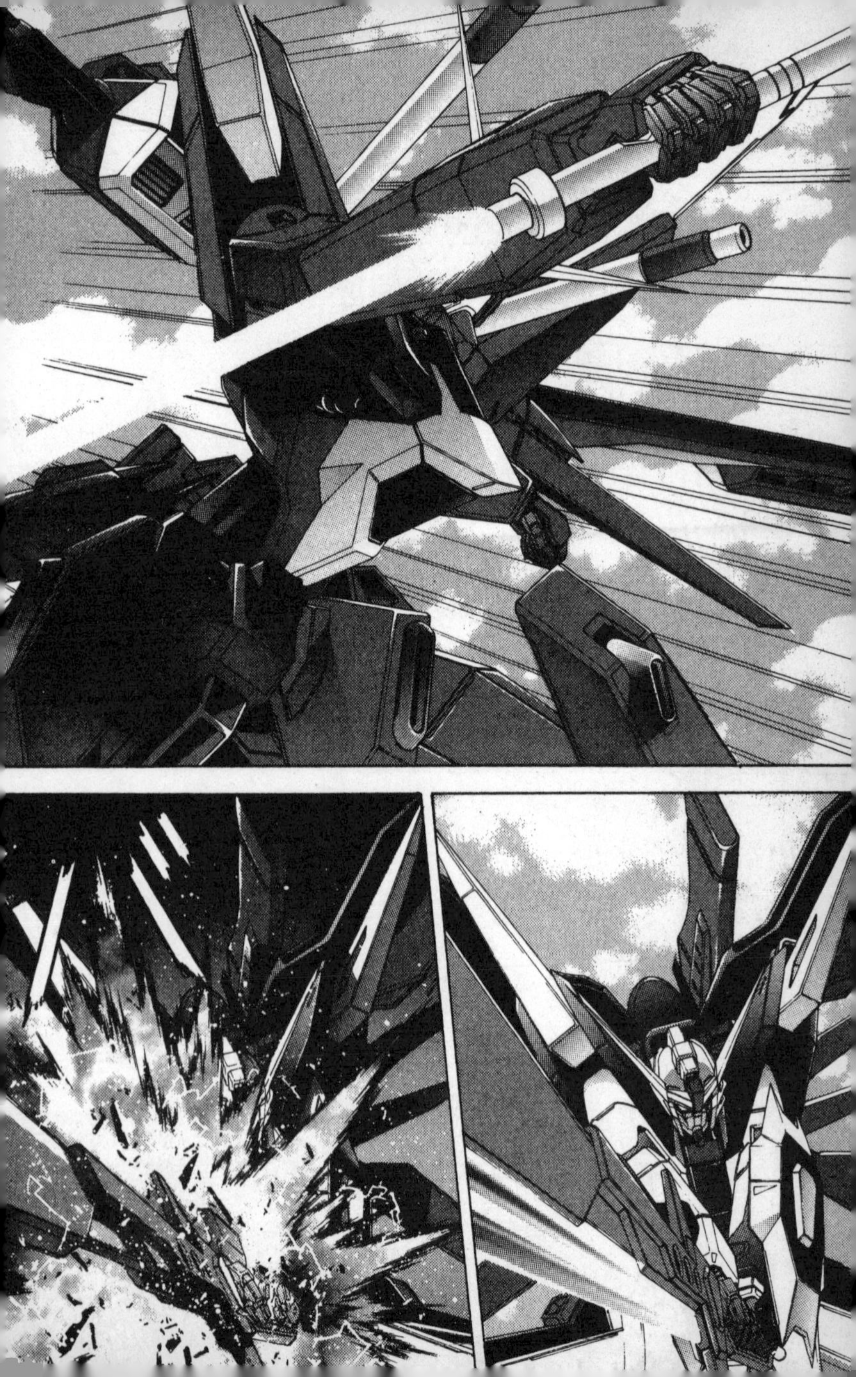

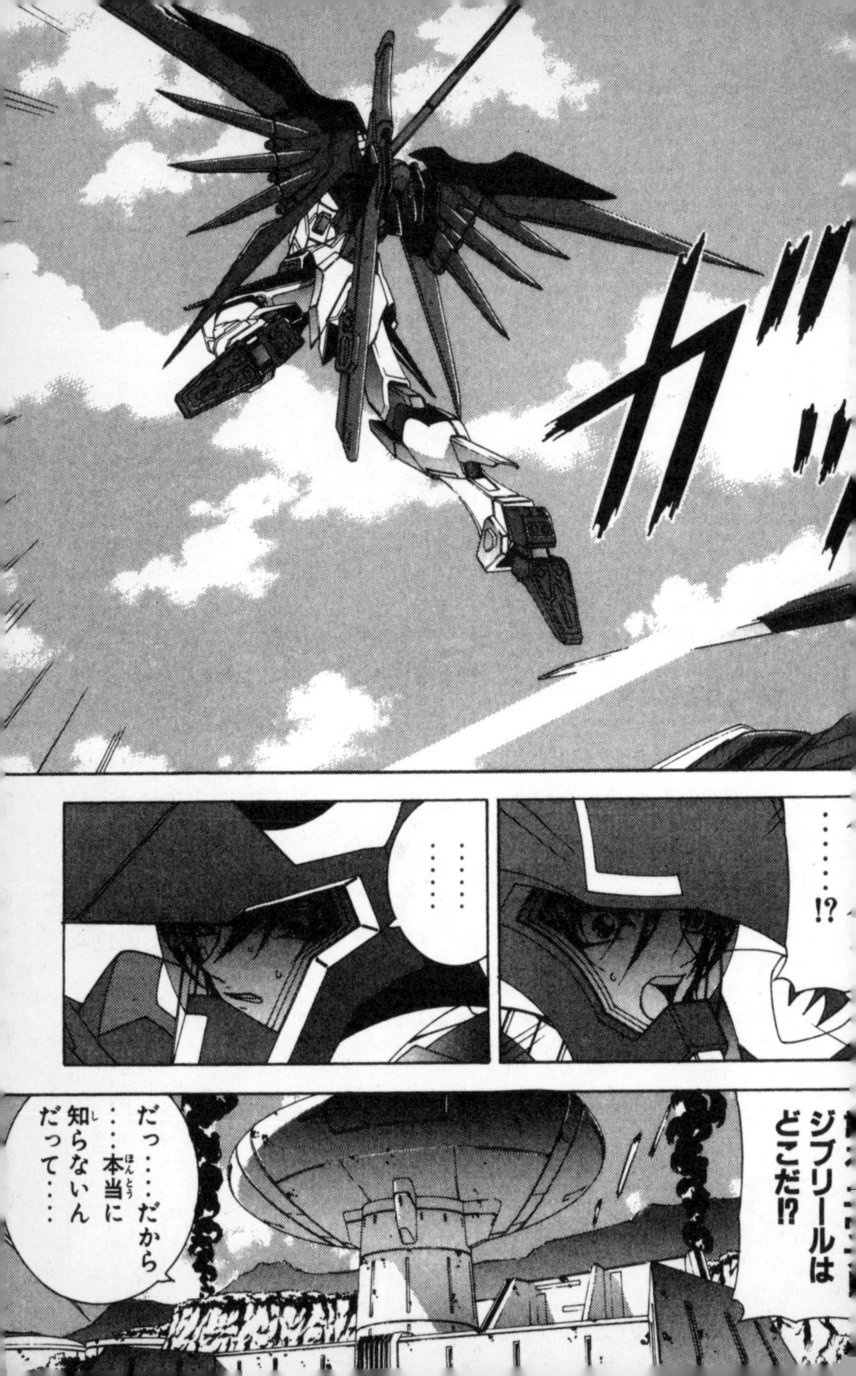
ガッ
……!?
……
ジブリールはどこだ!?
だっ…だから…本当に知らないんだって…

RESERVoir CHRoNiCLE

TSUBASA

BY CLAMP

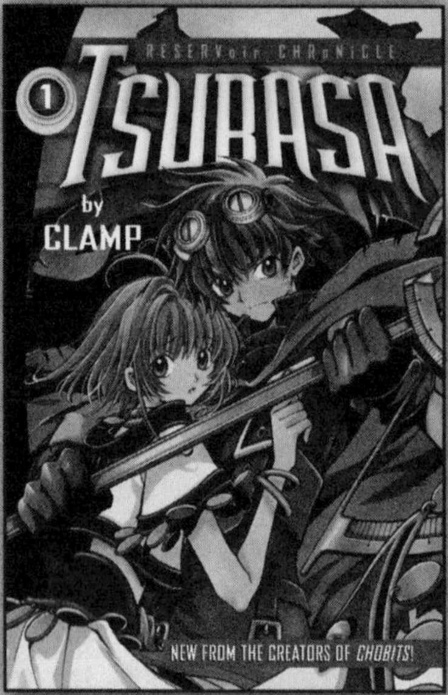
RESERVoir CHRoNiCLE
1
TSUBASA
by
CLAMP
NEW FROM THE CREATORS OF CHOBITS!

Ages: 13+

Sakura is the princess of Clow. Syaoran is her childhood friend, and leader of the archaeological dig that cost him his father. Fans of Cardcaptor Sakura will recognize the names and the faces, but these aren't the people you know. This is an alternate reality where everything is familiar and strange at the same time.

Sakura has a mysterious power, a power that no one understands, a power that can change the world. On the day she goes to the dig to declare her love for Syaoran, a mysterious symbol is uncovered that will have vast repercussions for Sakura and Syaoran. It marks the beginning of a quest that will take Syaoran and his friends through worlds that will be familiar to any CLAMP fan, as our heroes encounter places and characters from X, Chobits, Magic Knight Rayearth, xxxHOLiC, and many more! But all that matters to Syaoran is his goal: saving Sakura.

Special extras in each volume! Read them all!

DEL REY

VISIT WWW.DELREYMANGA.COM TO:
- **View release date calendars for upcoming volumes**
- **Sign up for Del Rey's free manga e-newsletter**
- **Find out the latest about new Del Rey Manga series**

KURO GANE

BY KEI TOUME

AN EERIE, HAUNTING SAMURAI ADVENTURE

Avenging his father's murder is a matter of honor for the young samurai Jintetsu. But it turns out that the killer is a corrupt government official—and now the powers that be are determined to hunt Jintetsu down. There's only one problem: Jintetsu is already dead.

Torn to pieces by a pack of dogs, Jintetsu's ravaged body has been found by Genkichi, outcast and master inventor. Genkichi gives the dead boy a new, indestructible steel body and a talking sword—just what he'll need to face down the gang that's terrorizing his hometown and the mobster who ordered his father's hit. But what about Otsuki, the beautiful girl he left behind? Steel armor is defense against any sword, but it can't save Jintetsu from the pain in his heart.

Teen: Ages 13 +

Special extras in each volume! Read them all!

VISIT WWW.DELREYMANGA.COM TO:
- Read sample pages
- View release date calendars for upcoming volumes
- Sign up for Del Rey's free manga e-newsletter
- Find out the latest about new Del Rey Manga series

Kurogane © 1996 Kei Toume / KODANSHA LTD. All rights reserved.

ANN ARBOR DISTRICT LIBRARY

31621017126950

D-
TEEN

TOMARE!

[STOP!]

You are going the wrong way!

Manga is a completely different type of reading experience.

To start at the beginning, go to the end!

That's right! Authentic manga is read the traditional Japanese way—from right to left. Exactly the opposite of how American books are read. It's easy to follow: Just go to the other end of the book, and read each page—and each panel—from right side to left side, starting at the top right. Now you're experiencing manga as it was meant to be.